Dreaming in the
World's Religions

D1605803

Dreaming in the World's Religions

A Comparative History

Kelly Bulkeley

NEW YORK UNIVERSITY PRESS

New York and London

NEW YORK UNIVERSITY PRESS
New York and London
www.nyupress.org

Library of Congress Cataloging-in-Publication Data
Bulkeley, Kelly, 1962–
Dreaming in the world's religions : a comparative history / Kelly
Bulkeley.
p. cm.
Includes bibliographical references (p.   ) and index.
ISBN-13: 978-0-8147-9956-7 (cl : alk. paper)
ISBN-10: 0-8147-9956-6 (cl : alk. paper)
ISBN-13: 978-0-8147-9957-4 (pb : alk. paper)
ISBN-10: 0-8147-9957-4 (pb : alk. paper)
1. Dreams—Religious aspects—History. 2. Religions—History.
I. Title.
BL65.D67B83 2008
204'.2—dc22   2008004107

New York University Press books are printed on acid-free paper,
and their binding materials are chosen for strength and durability.

Manufactured in the United States of America

c 10 9 8 7 6 5 4 3 2 1
p 10 9 8 7 6 5 4 3 2 1

For Hilary

Contents

Acknowledgments

I suppose I've been working on this book as long as I've been interested in dreams. So I really have to thank *everybody*—all the teachers, colleagues, and students who helped and guided me along the way. Several people have contributed directly to this project in quite valuable ways, so I wish to express special gratitude to Serinity Young, Madhu Tandan, Lewis Rambo, Bill Domhoff, Kimberley Patton, Bart Koet, Lee Irwin, Dimitris Xygalatas, Roger Knudson, Ernest Hartmann, Jeremy Taylor, Tracey Kahan, Justina Lasley, Ryan Hurd, Nina Azari, David Kahn, Kasia Szpakowska, Patricia Davis, Kate Adams, Malek Yamani, Jeff Kripal, Eleanor Rosch, Mark Fagiano, Lily Wu, Lana Nasser, Celeste Newbrough, and the anonymous reader who reviewed earlier drafts. I'm also grateful for the patient encouragement of my editor, Jennifer Hammer, and for the professional work of the production staff of New York University Press.

Note on Translations

A comparative study like this one relies on the efforts of many different translators, who sometimes use different systems of rendering the original language into English. I have used the best translations I could find for each quoted text, and altered the spellings of certain names and titles to conform to my understanding of current transliteration standards.

Introduction

Let us start with what I hope is an uncontroversial assumption: you are a human being. If that is true, then the course of your life follows, and has always followed, a cyclical pattern of waking and sleeping. Like other mammals, you are deeply programmed in your brain and body to alternate between two dramatically different states of being. The survival benefits of being awake are obvious—that's when you're alert, focused, and active in the world, able to provide for your basic physical needs. Less apparent are the survival benefits of totally withdrawing from the world and going to sleep, but they are no less vital. You *need* to sleep. Sleeping is just as essential to your healthy existence as food or water. When you become tired it feels good to sleep, just as it feels good to eat when you're hungry and drink when you're thirsty. Conversely, it feels painful when you don't get enough sleep. Just as you can die from lack of food or water, you would not last long if you were completely prevented from sleeping. When laboratory animals are deprived of all sleep they perish in a matter of days.

As it is, you probably sleep between six and nine hours a night. Plenty of people get by on less and others can't function without more, but your average ratio of time spent awake and asleep is likely to be about 2:1, sixteen or so hours awake vs. eight or so hours asleep. In unusual circumstances (e.g., a natural disaster, a military battle, a family health crisis, a work or school deadline, a really good party) you may be able to stay awake for thirty-six or more hours, but you'll be in sad shape at the end of it. No one can fight the sleeping/waking cycle for long without suffering a big decrease in physical and emotional well-being.

Every time you fall asleep your body passes through a series of complex alterations in breathing, heart beat, and muscular tonality. Your brain remains active during sleep, but not because of any external sensory stimulation or deliberate intention on your part—rather, your brain is being stimulated by internal sources that function independently of your waking self-awareness. The brain's dynamic functioning in sleep is quite different from its activity patterns while awake, and this is why your waking mind rarely recalls what happens to you while you slumber each night. The exception is when you remember a dream.

Dreaming

A dream is an imagined world of sights, sounds, thoughts, feelings, and activities that you (either as a character in the dream or a disembodied observer of it) experience during sleep. Most people spontaneously remember one or two dreams a week, though the memories may be fleeting and the images forgotten within a few minutes after waking. A few people recall several dreams each night, while others say they never remember any dreams at all. Many of the dreams that people do remember are described as "bad" dreams, with frightening images and negative emotions that carry over from sleep into the waking state. Such nightmarish dreams occur especially often in childhood and adolescence, and perhaps two or three times a year for most adults. If you were asked "What is the most frightening dream you've ever had?" I suspect you would have little difficulty bringing to mind the memory of a nightmare that made an especially strong and disturbing impression on you when you woke up.

What strikes most people about their dreams is how weird and bizarre they sometimes appear. A dream can put you any place, with anyone, doing anything—the ordinary limitations of waking life are suspended, allowing for a seemingly infinite range of possible scenarios and interactions. Sometimes the experience is positive (a joyful ability to fly), sometimes negative (being chased by a psycho killer), and sometimes it has no emotional content one way or the other. Most dreams include the basic narrative elements of a story (setting, characters, dialogue, action, plot), though often in strangely fragmented and distorted forms. Oddities abound in dreams—sudden shifts of time and location, strange mixtures of people and personalities, inexplicable behavior and feelings, extraordinary abilities and powers. Nothing is impossible in dreams. Everything seems to be permissible.

The weirdness of dreaming is only half the story, however. The other half is the normality of dreaming, its predictable continuity with the mundane reality of waking life. If you look at a person's dreams over time you will find that the basic patterns of dream content offer a remarkably accurate and consistent portrait of that person's major waking life activities, relationships, and emotional concerns. It is a commonsense idea, really—your dreams reflect who you are and what is most important in your daily existence. If you are a college student, you probably dream about classes, teachers, and dorm life; if a doctor or therapist, you probably dream about patients, colleagues, and offices; if you love playing or watching baseball or both, you will likely dream about that sport; and if you have three sisters and your relationship with the middle one is the closest and most intense, you probably dream about her more often than about the other two. Whatever the circumstances, your dreams are rooted in the particular conditions of your waking world. Whereas some dreams may be bizarre and outlandish, most seem rather ordinary, normal, and reality-based. You tend to be in places you know, with people you recognize, doing the kinds of things you do in daily life.

Dreams are thus a complex weaving together of the strange and the familiar, and this is true for everyone whose dream life has been systematically studied. This leads to the first idea I want to emphasize. *The basic patterns of your sleeping and dreaming are shared by all humans.* Such patterns are a deeply instinctual characteristic of our species. The study of dreams is therefore a necessary source of insight for our knowledge of what it means to be human. The theories of philosophers, theologians, and psychologists will never do justice to the fullness of our existence if they only focus on the qualities of waking life.

We now have available, thanks to the effort of many excellent historical and anthropological studies, a wealth of information showing that people in many different places and times have expressed their dreams by means of talking about them, recording them, interpreting them, acting them out in rituals, and drawing creative inspiration from their meanings. This leads to a second idea I want to highlight. *Dreaming has always been regarded as a religious phenomenon.* Throughout history, in cultures worldwide, people have seen their dreams first and foremost as religiously meaningful experiences. In this widely shared view, dreams are a powerful medium of transpersonal guidance offering the opportunity to communicate with sacred beings, gain valuable wisdom and power, heal suffering, and explore new realms of existence. The historical and cross-cultural evidence is overwhelming on this point: religion is the primary arena in which humans have traditionally expressed their dreams. Whether dreaming is the *origin* of religion is a separate question, to which we'll return in a moment. As a matter of historical fact, however, this book will show that dreams have played a powerful, complex, and dynamic role in the world's religious and spiritual traditions.

Putting the same point in research-oriented terms, the world's religious and spiritual traditions provide the best source of historical information about the broad phenomenological patterns of human dream life. Long before modern psychology arose in mid-nineteenth-century Europe, religiously minded people all over the globe were studying, experimenting with, and theorizing about the workings of the dreaming mind. *This is where the study of dreams begins.* The relevance of religious history for contemporary dream research is enormous, and the time has come for a fundamental reorientation of the field to acknowledge this. We should accept no general theory of dreams (and certainly no theory calling itself scientific) that ignores such a vast source of evidence. To understand human nature, we must study dreams. To understand dreams, we must study religion.

This book provides an integrated overview of the multiple roles that dreams have played through history in the world's religious traditions. It explores the lively interaction between dreaming and religion, tracing the influences in both directions—how individual dreams have shaped religious traditions and how religious traditions have fed back into personal dream experience. The book also, I suspect, will reveal new ways in which *your* dreams are threads in a much larger tapestry continuously created by the dreaming instincts of humankind. Indeed, you may find as you read along that you begin remembering more of your dreams than usual. That happens, at any rate, to many people when they read a book on dreams, and it is one small indication of the continuous interaction of waking and dreaming experience. Dreams have often been compared to a mirror that reflects the true character of the dreamer. What happens when the individual face in the mirror sees itself reflected in the collective dream mirror of all humanity?

Religions

If dreaming is a complex phenomenon that eludes simple definition, then surely the same must be said of religion. The exact meaning of "religion" has been notoriously difficult to pin down in a satisfying way, and it is tempting to think we should abandon the word altogether.[1] The main problem is the Christian bias built into the term. Rooted in the Latin verb *religare* ("tie back" or "tie tight"), *religion* was originally used in the fifth century C.E. to describe Christian monasticism and the practice of binding oneself to the rule of a church order. As an etymological and ideological consequence, Christianity has been regarded by Western academics as the prototypical religion by which all other traditions are measured (and usually found lacking). Even worse, the emphasis on the singular noun "religion" obscures the dynamic personal qualities of religious life and the colorful pluralism of its expression. This leads to reified academic categories that are then analyzed and compared in a quasi-scientific fashion, producing allegedly universal patterns of human religiosity bearing little relation to the lives of actual people. The dangers of this kind of abstract, totalizing research have been well documented in recent years, and scholars today are (or should be) much more careful in launching comparative investigations.

That said, the term "religion" remains useful if properly employed. In this book it is used as a shorthand word for an awareness of powers that transcend human control or understanding and yet have a formative influence on, and active presence within, human life. In many traditions these trans-human powers are represented in the form of gods, spirits, ancestors, mythic beings, and forces of nature. All religions venerate certain places, objects, and texts because of their capacity to bring people closer to these powers, and special practices (e.g., pilgrimage, sacrifice, dance, music, prayer, meditation) are performed to enhance their benevolent, life-affirming influence on people's lives. Although human existence may be filled with pain and misfortune, religions teach various methods for overcoming that suffering, either in this life or in another one to come, by means of harmonizing one's thoughts, feelings, and behavior with transcendent forces. One way religions achieve this is by creating and sustaining a personal sense of connection to a community. Religious traditions have developed various systems to bind (*religare*) people together over the span of multiple generations, carrying on valuable ancestral wisdom and preparing the group for future challenges and opportunities. Aligned with that community-building function, religions usually promote moral teachings to guide people's behavior in relation to both humans and the trans-human powers.

This does not mean that religion should only be viewed in a positive light. On the contrary, we must avoid idealizing the "goodness" of religion. In a book devoted to a broad view of human history, we will have many opportunities to lament religion's perennial involvement with xenophobia, violence, and war. In the process of creating a life-enhancing community for *some* people, religions have actively worked to fight, conquer, and destroy *other* people who do not belong to their community. Religion has hardly been a purely benevolent influence in human life, as any contemporary observer of world events can attest.

Defined in this way, the term "religion" does not automatically elevate or privilege Christianity, nor does it ignore the personal dynamics and variable expressions of lived human experience. Most important for the purposes of this book, it provides a good framework for the comparative study of dreaming. Recall now the initial definition of a dream: *an imagined world of sights, sounds, thoughts, feelings, and activities that you (either as a character in the dream or a disembodied observer of it) experience during sleep.* We may now add to that definition by saying the imagined worlds in dreaming can be *religious worlds* insofar as they relate to the characteristics just outlined: encounters with trans-human powers, efforts to heal suffering, practices of communal bonding, and violent conflicts with outsiders. In the following chapters, these dimensions of religious dreaming will be explored in many different traditions, with special attention to the personal circumstances of the dreamer and the fluid, dynamic processes by which the dreaming imagination interacts with culture, language, history, and waking cognition. I do not argue that dreaming is the origin of religion as such; rather, my thesis is more focused: *dreaming is a primal wellspring of religious experience.* The natural rootedness of dreaming in the human brain-mind system makes it a universally available source of experiential awareness of precisely those powers that people have historically associated with religion. Whether dreaming came before religion or religion came before dreaming is an impossible question to answer. Either way, the historical relationship between the two is strong and clear and worth exploring in more detail.

Histories

The next step in this scholarly ritual of introductory definitions is to consider issues of history and geography. Short of a Borgesian encyclopedia of all dreams from all people through all time, which would require the addition of several billion new entries every night, decisions must be made about which places and eras can and cannot be represented. The most common path taken by books on world religions is to focus attention on those traditions with the largest contemporary populations and widest geographic distributions. Thus Christianity, Islam, Hinduism, and Buddhism usually head the list of the major world faiths. This approach makes some sense, but it is flawed by an overly narrow perspective and a lack of historical awareness. It devalues smaller, less widespread religious traditions and it completely ignores the dynamics of historical change by which "minor" religions become "major" ones, and vice versa. Also, an approach that starts by measuring traditions according to their contemporary size and power automatically positions Christianity as the prototypical religion, which leads straight back to the distortions of comparative knowledge already mentioned.

A slight improvement would be to start with the oldest enduring religious traditions and work our way to the present. Accordingly, Jainism and Hinduism might come first, then Judaism, Confucianism, Buddhism, Taoism, and onward to Christianity, Islam, and perhaps finally the Church of Latter Day Saints. This is better than the "major faiths" approach, but it still ignores vast realms of human religious life. Left out are smaller contemporary traditions, past traditions that are now extinct, and any religious group whose experiences and teachings are not easily captured in the conceptual framework of an "ism."

An entirely different approach is to begin one's historical investigation with the early ancestral environment of the human species, namely, the African savannah of approximately two hundred thousand years ago, and move forward from there. This is the approach favored by evolutionary scientists.[2] It explains universal human phenomena like religion and dreaming by reference to the forces of natural selection that produced the highly adaptive cognitive abilities of the human mind. These abilities gave our species the power to survive and dominate not just in our primal African homeland but in virtually every region and environment around the world. According to a generally accepted time line, the first anatomically modern humans migrated from Africa around 50,000 BCE and quickly spread throughout Eurasia (driving the Neanderthals to extinction in the process), into Australia by 40,000 BCE (wiping out all native large mammals within a few generations), farther north into the icy cold of Siberia by 20,000 BCE (good-bye to the Wooly Mammoth), and across the Bering Strait and into North America by 12,000 BCE. It took only a thousand years for humans to spread throughout the Americas, and for many native species of large mammals to become extinct. Thus, a study of human history that takes this bloody time line into account would start with the religious cultures of Africa, then move to Eurasia, Australia, Northwest Asia, the Americas, and finally Oceania (the chains of tropical islands stretching westward from Australia that were settled in the early centuries of the common era).

An evolutionary approach like this has many virtues. It relies on solid archeological and biological evidence; it foregrounds the adaptive abilities and adventurous spirit of the human species; and it casts a painful but honest light on the violent instincts that have enabled us to become the most powerful creatures on the planet. It is not, however, a sufficient means of understanding religion or dreaming. Evolutionary science as currently practiced is too quick to reduce the wondrous pluralism of human experience to a few simple, predetermined theoretical categories. What is missing is an appreciation for something we have already insisted on emphasizing: the dynamic, creative, open-ended qualities of human life. The human mind has not simply evolved; *it is evolving.* As evolutionary scientists have shown in great detail, the tremendous cognitive abilities of our species have developed over time in direct response to pressing interests stimulated by environmental forces on people's lives. There is no reason to suppose this process stopped two hundred thousand years ago or fifty thousand ago or at any time whatsoever. Indeed, it is possible and perhaps even likely that religion has evolved, *and is evolving,* in human life as part of an ongoing process of responding to the ever new challenges confronting a species with unique cognitive abilities for language, social interchange, consciousness, memory, and reason.[3] Likewise for dreaming: it may have evolved, and still be evolving, in a continuous process of interaction with the relentlessly changing natural and social environments in which we live. If we agree that evolution has not finished with us yet but is still an ongoing force in human life, these possibilities should be considered and explored.

Taking all these factors into consideration, I devised the following approach to organizing the book's chapters, which trace three broad historical continuities. I start with Hinduism in chapter 1, move to the religions of China (principally Confucianism and Daoism) in chapter 2 and then Buddhism in chapter 3. These closely related traditions are among the largest and most ancient in the world. They offer an abundance of teachings, myths, and practices for study, and they remain prominent religious forces in the world today. For these reasons (in addition to the virtue of immediately de-centering Western Christian readers), the book starts with them. The second continuity begins in chapter 4 with the religions of the Fertile Crescent (including the traditions of Mesopotamia, Egypt, and Judaism), followed by the religions of Greece and Rome in chapter 5, then Christianity in chapter 6 and Islam in chapter 7. These traditions have deeply influenced one another through history, and many benefits will come from considering them in this sequence. The third continuity focuses on people and regions whose religious traditions have been violently transformed over the past few centuries by the military, economic, and cultural impact of modernization. Although the religions of Africa (chapter 8), Oceania (chapter 9), and the Americas (chapter 10) have rarely interacted with one another, they share the historical experience of being relatively small-scale, oral traditions that were attacked and conquered by colonizing forces. In each of these cases we have imperfect knowledge of the "pre-contact" culture, since most of the earliest written information was provided by the colonizing forces themselves. Nevertheless, all three of these regions provide abundant evidence of the bursts of new religious creativity that are provoked by situations of dire conflict, severe cultural change, and danger to the community. Dreaming, as we shall see, has played a prominent role in that process.

Ten chapters in total, then—artificial, limited, and exclusive as all historical categorizations must be but at least mindful of the common pitfalls that lie ahead.

Dream Science

Just as religious history is a vital resource for the scientific study of dreams, the reverse is also true—scientific research is a vital resource for the study of religious dreaming. Four areas of contemporary scientific research deserve particular consideration as we prepare to investigate and compare the various roles of dreaming in the world's religions: the neurophysiology of sleep, the frequency of dream recall, the relationship between continuity and bizarreness, and prototypical dreams.

First, let us consider the neurophysiology of sleep. Dreaming, as I have defined it, is a phenomenon that occurs during sleep. This is not to deny the kinship of dreaming with vision, trance, possession, hallucination, and other extraordinary states of consciousness that occur while awake or in other conditions different from both sleeping and waking. Rather, it is to highlight the natural emergence of human dreaming within the mammalian sleep state, and thus to open important avenues for understanding how dreams relate to bodily development, biological functioning, and evolutionary adaptation.[4]

As far as we know, the sleep cycle appeared rather late in animal evolution. Reptiles and fish can be observed in lengthy periods of relative calm and quiescence with reduced responsiveness to the external environment, a basic behavioral pattern that qualifies as sleeping. However, only with the emergence of birds and especially mammals did a rhythmic sleep cycle develop by which periods of quiescence alternate with periods of heightened brain-mind activation. Using the electroencephalograph (EEG) to measure the electrical activity of the brain, researchers have found that sleep onset regularly leads to a slowing of cerebral activity, with simpler, lower-energy brain waves than those found in the waking state. In mammals and birds, this slow wave sleep (SWS) is followed by a shift to a faster and more complex phase of brain activity. In humans, several other somatic changes occur in coordination with this shift: a relaxation of major muscle groups (known as atonia), loss of body temperature regulation, twitching of the eyes under the lids, and an increase in respiration and heartbeat (leading to an increased blood flow to the genitals, producing penile erections in men and clitoral swelling in women). These periods of heightened brain arousal also include ponto-geniculo-occipital, or PGO, "spikes," named for the structures in which they appear most predominantly. These are lightning-like bursts of neural firing that shoot from the brain stem into the forebrain. Researchers have not yet connected PGO spikes to any particular kind of dream content, nor do they even understand why we have PGO spikes in the first place. But they represent an essential activity of the sleeping brain, and later in the book we discover possible connections between such flashes of neural excitement and the experience of religiously powerful dreams.

During sleep, the chemistry of the brain changes dramatically, as different combinations of neurotransmitters flow through the body. The brain stem regulates this complex chemical balancing act, indicating that this part of the brain is the anatomical center triggering the sleep cycle, with the region known as the pons having an especially crucial role in generating those PGO spikes. Recent research using brain imaging technologies has revealed that in humans the onset of sleep leads to diminished activity in the dorsolateral prefrontal cortex (DLPFC). This part of the brain is very active in the waking state, when it serves as the "executive" center for such important mental functions as selective attention, purposeful action, decision making, and short-term memory. When the brain goes to sleep and moves from slow wave activities into those phases of heightened arousal, the DLFPC is reduced to its lowest levels of activation. In its place various other brain regions become much more active, and together they form an integrated neural system. These sleep-intensified brain areas include the limbic region (associated with negative emotions, sexual and aggressive instincts, and long-term memory formation), the extrastriate visual cortex (responsible for secondary visual processing and imagery), the medial prefrontal cortex (supporting the capacity for empathy and intuiting the minds of other people), and other cortical areas involved in multimodal sensory association. Research in this area is providing an increasingly well-defined portrait of the cognitive capacities of the dreaming imagination. Throughout the book, we explore the multiple correlations between this research and the most prominent features of religiously charged dream experience.

We should pause to reflect on yet another issue of definition. What should these highly aroused phases of mammalian and avian sleep be called? Two terms have been employed by contemporary sleep scientists: rapid eye movement (REM) sleep, named after the easily observable feature of the eyes twitching under the eyelids, and paradoxical sleep (PS), so designated because of its self-contradictory character of being very far from waking in some ways and yet very close to waking in others. Most research has been conducted using the term "REM," with the quiescent phases of sleep known collectively as non-rapid eye movement (NREM) sleep. The phases of NREM are further subdivided into NREM stages 1, 2, 3, and 4. A typical sleep cycle involves a person going to sleep and entering NREM stage 1, followed by NREM stages 2, 3, and 4, and then entering the first REM phase of the night; after some time in REM, the person would go back to stage 1 NREM, then onward through the other stages and eventually to another REM phase. One complete cycle of all the sleep stages averages about ninety minutes in length, and a person experiences four or five of them each night. Toward the end of the night, NREM stages 3 and 4 tend to drop out, and a person's sleep alternates almost entirely between REM and NREM stage 2.

However, paradoxical sleep refers to the same cluster of neurophysiological processes as REM sleep, and the two terms are used interchangeably in the book. So, too, are the terms "NREM" and "SWS," even though both are excessively general in scope, lumping together many distinct and fascinating sleep phenomena that occur outside of REM or PS (e.g., the brief bursts of imagery at the beginning of NREM stage 1, the very low-frequency brain waves of early night NREM stage 4, and the dream-like qualities of late night NREM stage 2). At some future point, these terms will probably be discarded in favor of more precise conceptualizations of the complex, multifaceted ebb and flow of sleeping experience.

Several facts confirm the basic idea that the sleep cycle is an instinctive behavior necessary for survival. The simplest way to demonstrate this is by means of sleep deprivation experiments. Depriving an animal of sleep leads fairly quickly to a decrease in physical well-being and weakened responsiveness to the environment, ultimately with fatal consequences. In humans, cognitive abilities suffer tremendously after just one missed night's sleep, and after a few days the emotional suffering becomes so acute that no ethically responsible research has pursued the matter further. It is interesting that when the deprivation stops and the person is again allowed a normal night's sleep, there is a major "rebound" effect in which the person sleeps many more hours than usual. Also proving this point are lesion studies showing that major damage to various parts of the brain produces only temporary effects on the sleep cycle—even after severe damage, the brain keeps the wake-sleep cycle going. It seems that mammalian and avian brains are strongly predisposed to maintain this cycle, even if it means rapidly developing new neural connections to make up for sudden, traumatic disruptions.

In all mammals, the beginning of life is when they experience the highest proportion of sleep with intensified brain activation. Fetuses and newborns have much more paradoxical sleep than adults do (up to 80 percent of sleep in human babies is spent in REM), which indicates a close relationship between this stage of sleep and the growth of the brain. Here is another curiosity inherent in the evolutionary nature of paradoxical sleep: it regularly reactivates in adults the primary brain-mind processes of the earliest stages of child development.

So a broad scientific picture of the sleep cycle has become fairly clear, even if several mysteries remain about its variation among different species. For example, subterranean mammals like the mole and the blind mole rat have an abundance of PS, which casts doubt on any necessary connection between PS and primary visual experience (though leaving open a possible connection between PS, mental imagery, and bodily orientation in space). The platypus and the spiny anteater, the only surviving members of the ancient line of monotremes (egg-laying mammals) have very little PS, which makes sense in light of their neurological primitivity and premammalian tendencies. Unusually low amounts of PS are also found among cetacean species like porpoises and bottle-nosed dolphins. For these sea-dwelling creatures, SWS occurs in one cerebral hemisphere at a time—one side of their brain sleeps while the other side remains awake. There is no obvious link between the amount of PS and general mental ability, and humans are somewhere in the middle of the pack on their proportion of PS. However, the human brain is far more densely interconnected than the brain of any other species, so two hours of PS for a human is likely to have exponentially greater neural complexity than, say, two hours of PS for a hamster.

Before going further, yet another basic question needs to be addressed. What, if anything, does the science of sleep tell us about dreaming? Sleep is an instinctive process rooted in basic biological functions, whereas dreams are memories of imagined experiences. Are the two phenomena essentially the same or fundamentally different? Scholars of a humanistic bent may be tempted to emphasize the differences, but any attempt to separate the study of dreams from scientific research on sleep makes it difficult to explain why dreaming displays so many recurrent patterns that directly relate to our bodily growth and cognitive development. For empiricist investigators who favor physical explanations, any effort to explain dreaming exclusively in terms of sleep physiology must contend with the classic mind-body problem of Western philosophy. Neuroscientific reductionism fails to account for mental causation in dreaming (e.g., in dreams with volition and self-awareness) or in waking (e.g., biofeedback, placebo effect), and it cannot convincingly translate the vivid personal experiences of dreaming into an objective language of electrical and chemical activities in the brain.

The approach used here avoids the two extreme responses to this issue. The neurophysiology of sleep does not tell us everything there is to know about dreams, but neither is it completely irrelevant to the subject. Many experiential features of dreaming are directly correlated with particular aspects of brain-mind functioning during sleep. If there needs to be a philosophical name for the approach used in this book, it would be *interactive dualism*—a view that focuses on the dynamic interplay between the sleeping brain and the dreaming mind, leaving open for now the question of their ultimate metaphysical connection.[5]

Continuing forward on that basis, let us turn to a second area of contemporary scientific research: dream recall.[6] Beginning in the mid-twentieth century, almost all researchers assumed that the activated sleep phases of REM/PS are the only time that people dream (hence another, less frequently used term, "D-Sleep"). Initial data from sleep laboratory research showed that people who were awakened right after a phase of REM sleep usually remembered a dream, whereas awakenings from times outside REM produced little or no dream recall. Later research muddied the picture somewhat, with evidence that REM is not always accompanied by the recall of a dream, and dreamlike mental activity may be recalled from many other stages of sleep besides REM, especially from NREM stage 2 toward the end of the sleep cycle. Current estimates put recall from REM awakenings at 80 percent and recall from NREM awakenings at 43 percent. Much controversy remains on this subject, partly because the "REM = dreaming" equation offers such an appealingly simple explanation for dreams, and some researchers are reluctant to adjust past theories to new realities. At present, the best we can say is that REM is a trigger for dreaming. It is apparently the part of the sleep cycle most reliably connected to dream recall, even though the human brain-mind system seems to be dreaming in some way or other throughout the sleep cycle.

An inevitable question arises: Do animals dream? We currently have no means of proving it one way or the other, just as we have no way to determine whether human fetuses and newborns are genuinely dreaming before they develop the ability to speak and relate their experiences. Some researchers have argued that dreaming, as distinct from PS, requires high-level cognitive and linguistic abilities that only arise in humans after the ages of three to five. That seems unlikely to me. In all known species, PS involves a lively interaction between the brain stem and the forebrain. If we accept the evidence from research on humans showing that a PS-activated forebrain is crucial to the formation of dreams, it is reasonable to assume that other species who undergo this same neural process during sleep are indeed dreaming, albeit in a cognitive mode appropriate to their brain-mind systems. The dreams of nonhuman animals are likely to reflect the primary instinctual abilities and desires of each particular species. We certainly see this in research on cats. When their brains are surgically altered so they enter PS without relaxing their muscles, cats apparently act out their dreams by energetic physical activities including running, climbing, attacking imaginary foes, and mating. Additional evidence comes from research on rats showing that the same brain activation patterns generated during a survival-related learning task while awake (e.g., seeking food on a circular track) were repeated during the subsequent sleep cycle. According to the definition of dreaming I have proposed, it is fair to assume that these rats are indeed dreaming of important activities that occurred during the previous waking state. What experiential form their dreams might take, we cannot say. We do not know which of their brain-mind processes are involved, nor do we know what other topics they might be dreaming about besides running around in human experiments. We know enough, however, to recognize and affirm an authentic dreaming potential in animal species other than our own.[7]

Returning to the case of *Homo sapiens,* it turns out that we actually remember only a tiny fraction of all that happens during the sleep cycle. Our brains pass through several cycles of intense activation every time we go to sleep, cycles that are strongly and consistently associated with dreaming. Yet once we awaken, we apparently forget the vast majority of those dream experiences. This is a point worth keeping in mind, because it suggests that the functions of dreaming may not depend on conscious recollection and may in fact operate unconsciously, outside the sphere of ordinary waking awareness.

That said, people do spontaneously remember some of their dreams. The average among contemporary North Americans and Western Europeans (the main populations on whom research has been conducted) is a recall rate of one or two dreams per week, although, as mentioned earlier, some people report much more than that (two or three per night), and other people report never remembering any dreams at all. Most people say their recall rate fluctuates depending on the conditions of awakening (whether abrupt or gradual), the presence or absence of waking life stress, and the intensity or bizarreness of the dreams themselves. The massive neurochemical shift in brain functioning from sleeping to waking may be another factor, particularly in light of the relative deactivation of short-term memory systems in PS, which makes it very difficult for anything experienced in sleep to be remembered later in the waking state. Nevertheless, some dreams do manage to survive the neurochemical transition from sleeping to waking and impress themselves on people's awareness. Dream recall as a general phenomenon seems to be a sturdy feature of normal human psychology, occurring at more or less the same frequency across the demographic board. People with personalities characterized as "open to experience" and "tolerant of ambiguity" have somewhat higher dream recall than people of other personality types, but the difference isn't huge. Young adults remember dreams a bit more frequently than older adults do, and women tend to recall more dreams than men do, but again the differences are not as significant as the baseline similarities. To remember a small but significant number of dreams is a normal feature of life for most human beings.

An intriguing discovery in this area is that the most influential factor distinguishing low and high recallers is their *attitude* toward dreaming.[8] People who have a positive attitude toward dreams generally have a higher rate of recall than people who have a negative attitude about dreaming. At first sight this is not surprising—if you believe that dreams have meaning and value, you are more likely to remember them than if you believe they are totally random and worthless. Simple methods of promoting a more positive attitude about dreams have been found to lead to a dramatic increase in dream recall. Whether one *should* have a positive attitude toward dreams is a separate issue; the key insight of research in this area is that dream recall is responsive to waking stimulation. When people are encouraged to pay more attention to their dreams, their dream recall usually goes up. This connection between waking attitude and recall rates is significant for our project, because, as we shall see, all religious traditions have actively sought to influence people's attitudes toward their dreams.

It should also be noted that dream content is very difficult to influence or control in an absolute fashion. Numerous investigations have tried, and largely failed, to alter dream content by means of stimulation before sleep (e.g., watching an emotionally arousing movie) or during sleep (e.g., ringing a buzzer by the sleeping person's ear).[9] Some of the following dreams do indeed incorporate the external stimulations, but many of them do not, and those that do are often distorted in strange, unpredictable ways. The dream formation process is stubbornly independent of external control; it has its own purposes that usually relate to, yet are autonomous from, the intentions of the waking world. Even in dreams with a lucid or metacognitive quality of self-awareness, the power of conscious volition is generally quite limited, and the unfolding of the dream continues to produce surprising, unconsciously created experience.

Now to the third research topic, the study of continuous and bizarre factors in dreaming. As just mentioned, some spontaneously remembered dreams attract waking attention precisely because of their intensity and strange deviation from ordinary life. But systematic investigation of dream content has shown that most dreams are fairly mundane and realistic, involving roughly accurate portrayals of the day-to-day realities of the dreamer's life.[10] The continuity between waking and dreaming is strongest regarding personal relationships. The people with whom you are closest

—your husband or wife, boyfriend or girlfriend, parents, siblings, friends, workmates—are very likely to be the people who appear most frequently in your dreams. Indeed, frequency of dream appearance can be taken as a reliable indicator of personal intimacy, so much so that if you read a person's dreams "blindly," without knowing anything about his or her waking life, you can accurately predict the most important relationships in that person's life, along with the emotional tenor of those relationships.[11]

This points to another dimension of dreaming-waking continuity, involving a person's emotional concerns and attitudes. The clearest evidence comes from waking life situations that produce negative emotions, such as an abuse victim's fear of a cruel spouse, an employee's anger at a disrespectful boss, or a child's sadness at the death of a parent. In all such cases, people's dreams consistently portray the exact same emotions that predominate in their waking lives. The same thing happens in positive circumstances (e.g., an athlete's joy in victory, a lover's desire for his or her beloved), when the happy emotions in waking life are reflected in dreams with positive affect. In recognition of this feature, dreaming has been compared to an emotional thermostat, and the analogy is apt.[12] Dreams accurately represent whatever is most emotionally urgent and engaging in a person's waking life, with particular sensitivity toward the negative end of the affective spectrum.

At the same time, many dream elements are *dis*continuous with waking life. Some dreams—not all, but some—display a seemingly infinite capacity for creative fantasy. Researchers have distinguished several different kinds of dream bizarreness, including character metamorphoses, physical distortions, sudden shifts of setting, unrealistic juxtapositions of places and activities, improbable or impossible occurrences, supernatural abilities, and inexplicable behavior. A general neuroscientific theory has been developed by contemporary researchers to account for such oddities.[13] According to this line of thinking, the diminished activity in the brain's executive center during PS makes it difficult for the sleeping mind to pay attention, think rationally, or make intentional decisions while dreaming, leaving the individual cognitively defenseless against random neural firings from the brain stem. This precipitous decline in executive center functioning, combined with the jarring effects of PGO spikes and the hallucinatory effects of changes in brain chemistry, produces the characteristic cognitive deficits we see in bizarre dreams.

Such a theory has some merit and should be taken seriously, but it leaves much of actual dream experience unaccounted for. What about all the accurate continuities with waking life we've just been discussing? Whatever may or may not be happening in the brain during sleep, the processes of dream formation are certainly capable of portraying stable, coherent, realistic scenarios throughout the sleep cycle. What about dreams in which the dreamer regains (or develops new forms of) "higher" cognitive abilities for selective attention, reflective thought, intentional action, and self-awareness?[14] This alone suggests that humans experience a far greater range of complex and sophisticated brain-mind activity in dreaming than is recognized by mainstream neuroscience. What about recurrent, pan-human patterns in dream content? We know of several distinctive types of dream that are consistently reported from a wide variety of demographic sources. Such recurrent dream patterns, virtually universal in our species, are poorly explained by theories emphasizing the random, disorderly, and nonsensical aspects of dreaming.

The bottom line is this: bizarreness in dreaming should not be conceptualized solely in terms of its failures compared to the cognitive attributes of an alert waking state. The bizarre and discontinuous elements in dreams may also be understood as the natural expression of *alternative* modes of brain-mind functioning, modes that are different from, but not necessarily inferior to, waking consciousness. Dreaming characters, places, and activities are connected not by reference to objective waking reality but by far-reaching networks of emotional, conceptual, and imagistic associations. A frightening storm in a dream may not refer to meteorological events in waking life but rather to a person's inner sense of emotional upheaval. An attractive red sports car may not relate to any actual vehicle but to an otherwise inchoate desire for speed, vigor, and youth. The meaningful continuities between dream content and waking life are still there but are expressed in metaphorical rather than literal terms. Ironically, interpretive research on dream symbols and metaphors receives unwitting support from neuroscience, particularly its findings that paradoxical sleep is a time of heightened activation of the association cortex and the secondary visual system responsible for generating internal imagery. This makes good sense in light of interpretive approaches that see in dreams a dramatic expansion of a person's associational creativity, with a special emphasis on visual symbolism and embodied experience. From this perspective, at least some of the bizarre elements of dreaming can be understood as expressions of a *different kind of intelligence* whose natural language consists primarily of image, metaphor, and allegory.

The last area of sleep and dream research to consider before moving ahead regards prototypical patterns of dream content. As just mentioned, certain types of dreams have been found to recur with great regularity in human sleeping experience (e.g., dreams of flying, falling, being chased or attacked, meeting a dead relative, having sex, etc.). Scientific researchers have long recognized such dreams, but to date no consensus has been reached on how best to map their phenomenology. Several different classification schemes have been developed, using terms like "type dreams," "big dreams," "culture pattern dreams," "intensified dreams," "impactful dreams," "highly significant dreams," "extraordinary dreams," and "apex dreaming."[15] The main obstacle for all these theories is that dreams, being dreams, are endlessly variable in their form and content. Any proposed classification system inevitably stumbles over examples that have mixed features from several categories or that do not fit in any category at all. It must be admitted, then, that research in this area is very much a work in progress. Nevertheless, the findings so far give us a decent picture of several distinct forms of dreaming experience, and this is extremely useful information for the puposes of this book. The general term I use, *prototypical dreaming,* is intended to refer to vivid, highly memorable patterns of dream content that recur in the sleep experiences of people from many different backgrounds. Prototypical dreams are not universal in the sense that every single person experiences them all. Rather, they are latent forms of dreaming potential. They reflect innate predispositions to dream in certain ways that, when actualized, make unusually strong impressions on waking awareness. In contrast to the vast majority of sleep experiences that fade into oblivion, prototypical dreams are actually quite easy to remember. Some of them are literally impossible to forget, remaining a vivid presence in people's memories for the rest of their lives.

In the following ten chapters, I argue that prototypical dreams have played a creative role in virtually all the world's religious and spiritual traditions. The consciousness-provoking impact of dreaming has not been sufficiently recognized by scientists or religious studies scholars, and my hope is that this book will present a compelling case for taking dream experiences more fully into account in the comparative study of religion.

1

Hinduism

Have you ever had a dream so realistic that when you woke up you weren't sure for a moment if you were actually awake or still dreaming? Have you ever woken up from a dream only to discover (after you've awakened for "real") that you were still asleep and dreaming? Vivid yet confusing experiences like these grab our attention because they disrupt ordinary assumptions about the line that separates dreams from the waking world. Many people think of waking and dreaming as polar opposites, as synonymous with real and unreal, objective truth versus subjective fantasy. But this kind of sharp distinction is not a psychological given. Humans are not born with a predetermined concept of what happens when we dream. Our ideas about dreaming emerge over time as we grow older, gain experience of the world, and develop new cognitive abilities. Western psychologists have postulated a regular, universal series of conceptual stages in children's understanding of the nature of dreams.[1] This research indicates that very young children tend to believe that dreams are real material events occurring outside their bodies and are perceptible by other people. As they become older and develop greater cognitive maturity, children and their beliefs usually change so that dreams are understood as internal, nonmaterial images that only the dreamer can witness. Depending on the cultural and religious traditions in which the children are raised, a *further* developmental stage may be reached whereby they come to believe that most dreams are immaterial and internal to the individual but that at least some dreams are caused by external sources (God, ancestral spirits, demons, etc.), possessed of an authentic reality, and meaningful to both self and others. Whether this third stage should be considered an advance or a regression depends on your metaphysical point of view.

Whatever views you hold, you are likely to find them reflected somewhere in the multifaceted religious traditions of Hinduism. From its earliest sacred texts and rituals to its modern teachings and practices, Hinduism has much to say about the relationship between waking, dreaming, and reality. What kind(s) of reality do we experience in dreaming? How do those realities relate to waking life? Do experiences in dreams enable us to gain any kind of legitimate knowledge? How can we know if our waking reality right now is indeed real, and not a deceptive dream? I'm going to refer to these issues collectively as *the ontological question of dreaming*. For those of us influenced by the Western philosophical assumption that waking reality *is* reality and no other condition merits that term, the Hindu tradition offers an especially good introduction to the possibility that other authentic dimensions of reality may be disclosed in the natural cycles of sleeping and dreaming.

The Vedas

The Indus River flows for nearly two thousand miles from north to south through the South Asian subcontinent, drawing its original waters from the snowmelt of the Himalaya Mountains. As the Indus makes its way to the Arabian Sea, it is further swollen by the abundant rainfall of the area's tropical climate, leading to fairly predictable patterns of seasonal storming and flooding. The earliest human settlements found along the Indus date back to the seventh millennium BCE. The rich soil of the Indus flood plain proved very hospitable to agricultural food production and thus to the development of increasingly populous and complex urban societies. Over time, several hundred towns and a few large cities arose, with common systems of language, measurement, and trading practice. By the third millennium BCE these people (known as the Dravidians, after their major language group) were at the height of their prosperity. Archeological evidence indicates that their civilization included various collective and private religious ceremonies. Most of the worship was directed at goddess figures responsible for fertility, crop growth, and the cycles of nature. Numerous terra-cotta statues and temple sculptures portray images of voluptuous divine females, along with a variety of other animals and mythical creatures.

Sometime after 2000 BCE a new group of people moved into the Indus River region. They were nomads from Central Asia who herded cattle and horses, and who brought their own complex social, cultural, and religious practices into contact with the agricultural traditions of the Dravidians. The newcomers (known as the Indo-Aryans) quickly established, by means both peaceful and violent, a vibrant new religious orientation for the people of the Indus River region. This new faith centered on ancient collections of knowledge (*Vedas*) that were orally transmitted through the generations, recited in poetic verses (*mantras*) whose spiritual potency emanated from the sacred sound (*brahman*) of the words themselves. Many of the *Vedas* revolved around a dramatic myth in which the world was created from the dismembered body of a cosmic man. An act of supreme self-sacrifice brought humans into being, and it is thus the responsibility of humans to sustain the created world by continuously repeating that primordial sacrifice. This emphasis on proper ritual practice as the essential safeguard for collective well-being naturally gave the Vedic priests (*Brahmans*, those who recite the verses) a great deal of power in society, and, over time, the *Vedas* came to include teachings governing all aspects of human life.

Between 1200 and 900 BCE, major compilations of the *Vedas* were written down, the foremost of which was the *Rig Veda*.[2] With more than one thousand hymns devoted to a colorful multitude of gods and goddesses, the *Rig Veda* is more of a religious encyclopedia than a doctrinal statement, filled with multiple and sometimes conflicting perspectives on a vast array of topics. Many of its verses provide spells and incantations to help people with the practical concerns of their daily lives. Avoiding physical danger, protecting loved ones, gaining wealth and status, satisfying romantic desires, defeating enemies, insuring good weather and harvests —these are the immediate goals of ritual practice. The mundane, this-worldly focus of so much of the *Rig Veda* highlights the close connection in early Hindu tradition between transcendent religious power and the earthly challenges of human survival.

Only a handful of verses in the *Rig Veda* mention sleep or dreams, usually in a negative tone. This suggests that the Vedic priests did not take much interest in these phenomena. One of the few exceptions is the following prayer to Agni, the god of fire, to protect pregnant women and their fetuses:

Let Agni the killer of demons unite with this prayer and expel from here the one whose name is evil, who lies with disease upon your embryo, your womb.

The one whose name is evil, who lies with disease upon your embryo, your womb, the flesh-eater—Agni has driven him away with prayer.

The one who kills the embryo as it settles, as it rests, as it stirs, who wishes to kill it when it is born—we will drive him away from here.

The one who spreads apart your two thighs, who lies between the married pair, who licks the inside of your womb—we will drive him away from here. The one who by changing into your brother, or your husband, or your lover lies with you, who wishes to kill your offspring—we will drive him away from here.

The one who bewitches you with sleep or darkness and lies with you—we will drive him away from here.

The hymn addressed a very real source of danger to the Hindu people of that time, and indeed to all people at all times. Human pregnancy has always been filled with potentially fatal threats for the unborn fetus and gravid mother. Even in the era of modern Western medicine, pregnancy remains a perilous, unpredictable process. This Vedic verse is aimed at protecting the fetus from those perennial dangers that may occur during any of the three stages of pregnancy (settling, resting, stirring). Agni is an appropriate god to ask for such help, as the element of fire brings light to the darkness, banishing demons and foiling their malevolent plans.

A notable shift of subject occurs in the second half of the hymn, when the focus of concern moves from the fetus to the mother. The demons threaten the fetus with death, but they are threatening the woman with something rather different: sexual desire. The demons are said to have the power of deceptively changing their appearance in order to ravish the unsuspecting woman, and they may take forms that are socially legitimate (one's husband), or incestuous and immoral (one's brother), or stimulating and pleasurable (one's lover). In all cases, the demons take sexual advantage of the woman's helplessness while "bewitched" with sleep and darkness. Taken together, these qualities—sexual arousal, shape-shifting characters, loss of self-awareness and control, occurrence during sleep— lead to the conclusion that the demonic attacks described in this ancient Vedic verse are a kind of dreaming experience. It is not clear in the hymn whether the seduction is the *cause* of the fetus's death, that is, whether the demons kill the fetus by having dream sex with the mother. More likely is that the two parts of the hymn are not connected in such a literal fashion but are both expressing a common concern about threats to orderly

human reproduction. From the perspective of social and religious authorities like the Brahmans, promoting healthy pregnancies and controlling
female sexuality were crucial factors in the cause of establishing a stable,
caste-based community with clear lines of familial descent. Such a community could not thrive if fetuses died before birth or if female sexuality
was overly stimulated (opening the door to the socially disruptive problems of illegitimate births and questionable paternity). The possibility that
sexual dreams might actually be pleasurable for the woman, for example,
in dreams of one's husband or lover, was irrelevant. What mattered to the
Brahmans was maintaining the proper order of human-divine relations.
Discouraging women's sexual dreaming was a small but necessary part of
that process.

Such a hymn was recited as a means of fending off bad dreams. Another hymn from the *Rig Veda* was intended to cast a spell of sleep over
others. It was first used, according to some sources, by the sage Vasistha
when he traveled in a dream to the house of the sky god, Varuna. As
Vasistha entered Varuna's house a watchdog attacked him, and the sage
spoke these verses to make him stop his frantic barking:

> White and tawny son of Sarama [the ancestor of dogs], when you bare your
> teeth they gleam like spears in your snapping jaws. Fall fast asleep! . . .

> Let the mother sleep; let the father sleep; let the dog sleep; let the master
> of the house sleep. Let all the kinsmen sleep; let our people all around
> sleep.

Later generations of Hindus have used these verses as bedtime lulla-
bies for their children. Related to this hymn is another one describing
Varuna's anger when he discovers Vasistha in his home. The sage prays
for the god's forgiveness and offers this explanation of his actions: "The
mischief was not done by own free will, Varuna; wine, anger, dice, or
carelessness led me astray. The older shares in the mistake of the younger.
Even sleep does not avert evil." This last line is intriguing, as it expresses
one of the Vedic responses to the ontological question of dreaming. If
dreams can be said to have any kind of reality, it is a *moral* reality, a reality as a fearful arena of darkness, deceit, and temptation. The same evil
forces that threaten people in waking life also threaten them in dreams.
Indeed, the loss of vigilance in sleep makes people even more vulnerable
to those malevolent powers. Vasistha is quick to emphasize the external

nature of the evils that haunt our sleep (which conveniently absolves him of personal blame for his dreaming misbehavior). The earlier hymn about pregnancy also portrayed bad dreams as external assaults during sleep, and this seems to reflect a broader Vedic understanding. In the following verses, a prayer to a god known as the "Master of Thought," the *Rig Veda* takes the notion of the externality of bad dreams to a logical, and vengeful, conclusion.

> If we have done something bad on purpose or not on purpose, or with the wrong purpose, awake or asleep, let Agni place far away from us all these misdeeds that are displeasing.

> We have conquered today, and we have won; we have become free of sin. The waking dream, the evil intent—let it fall upon the one we hate; let it fall upon the one who hates us.

The proper prayers and rituals not only protect us from bad dreams, but they can also redirect those dreams against our enemies. With this view of dreams as external missiles of evil, there is no reason to pay any attention to the *content* of dreams. No interpretation is necessary because no meanings are being conveyed. Dreams have no value as sources of information or knowledge; they may have moral reality, but they lack epistemological reality. Another prayer to Varuna for protection from various threats includes the following verse: "If someone I have met, O king, or a friend has spoken of danger to me in a dream to frighten me, or if a thief should waylay us, or a wolf—protect us from that, Varuna." Nightmares are grouped with thieves and wolves as frightening threats to which humans are perennially vulnerable. What is striking is that even if a dream involves a friend who is warning you of danger, the content is still insignificant. It is not taken seriously as a *real* warning. According to this text, the frightening emotion of the dream trumps all content, proving the dream's demonic origin and epistemological emptiness.

A different set of early Vedic collections, the *Atharva Veda*, includes several spells to ward off bad dreams and manipulate the sleep of others. One of these spells offers insight into the mythic origin of sleep itself:

> You who are neither alive nor dead, you are the immortal child of the gods, O Sleep! Varunani is your mother, Yama [god of the dead] is your father, Araru is your name.

We know, O Sleep, of your birth, that you are the son of the divine women-folk, the instrument of Yama! You are the ender, you are death! Thus do we know you, O Sleep; Please, O Sleep, protect us from evil dreams!

As one pays off a sixteenth, an eighth, or an entire debt, thus do we transfer every evil dream upon our enemy.

The final verse repeats the idea found in the *Rig Veda* that bad dreams can be aimed with almost mathematical precision at our waking-life foes. The prior verses offer praise to sleep as a true god, born of death and the "divine women-folk." The close connection between sleep and death is a recurrent theme in the *Vedas,* as it is in many other religious traditions. Dwelling between and beyond the opposition of life and death, the deity Sleep is believed to have the power of fending off nightmares and protecting people during the vulnerable hours of their slumber.

Unlike the *Rig Veda,* the *Atharva Veda* gives a more detailed view of what early Hindus actually did dream, beyond what they were trying *not* to dream.[3] Even though the *Rig Veda* discourages people from paying attention to the content of their dreams, the *Atharva Veda* recognizes that people still do have dreams and are naturally curious to know what they mean. Thus the *Atharva Veda* includes a chapter on the interpretation of particular types of dreaming, with a lengthy catalog of images and their significance. The interpretations are framed by a Vedic teaching that human character can take three different temperamental forms (bilious/fiery, phlegmatic/watery, and sanguine/windy) which generate corresponding types of dreaming. Thus a fiery person will tend to have dreams of arid land and burning objects, a watery person will dream of cool rivers and flourishing life, and a windy person will dream of moving clouds and running animals. A strong continuity between waking and dreaming is implied in this text, with two practical implications for would-be interpreters. First, pay close attention to the waking life circumstances of the dream (e.g., what time of night it occurred). Second, look for symbols in dreams that may relate to physical disturbances within the individual's body. Dreams may serve as a kind of early warning system for medical practitioners, providing an accurate diagnostic reflection of internal psychosomatic processes.

This medical interest in dream interpretation reveals an important strand of early Hinduism that was more favorably inclined toward the value of dreaming, particularly its prophetic power to anticipate the future. The dreams listed in the *Atharva Veda* are divided into two categories—auspicious (*subha*) and inauspicious (*asubha*)—that foretell either prosperity or misfortune. Many of the interpretive connections seem relatively clear and direct (for example, a dream of teeth falling out means one is going to die), whereas others are much less so (a dream of one's head being cut off means one is going to have a long life). Although the gods are mentioned as a source of some auspicious dreams, dreaming is generally presented in this text as a natural human experience, with multiple dimensions of relevance to the individual's personality and life circumstances. Dreams provide accurate expressions of people's fears and desires, and, if properly interpreted, may be used as a valid source of knowledge and waking action. Remembering one's dreams is crucial to benefiting from them (it is said a forgotten dream will not bear fruit), and authoritative guides like the *Atharva Veda* are aimed at helping people discern the potential significance of their dreams for their future health and well-being.

This kind of dream symbol compendium is a classic instance of the "dream book" genre of writing found in cultures all over the world. As long as humans have been writing, they have been writing about dreams —recording them, categorizing them, and trying to identify general principles by which to interpret them. Many other examples are discussed in the chapters to come.

Fiction and Reality

We should pause to consider once again a methodological question raised in the prologue. Taking the *Vedas* as our first example, how do we know if any of this relates to what Hindu people were actually dreaming during these periods of time? We cannot be sure if the Vedic writers were describing what people truly dreamed or, rather, what they *believed* other people dreamed. What, then, can we learn about dreams from the partly or entirely fictionalized accounts of ancient religious texts?

One of the many inconvenient facts of dream research is that the only direct source of information we have about the subject is our own personal experience. Everything else we know about dreaming comes from indirect observation and other people's self-reports. That means we are *always* dealing with varying degrees of uncertainty when studying the phenomenology of dreams. Indeed, even the seemingly direct insights we gain from our own dream experiences are questionable, as a century of psychoanalysis has taught us. Faced with so many ambiguities, the temptation is to abandon any serious effort to study dreaming. In my view, that would be intellectual cowardice. Failure to achieve 100 percent certainty does not preclude an ability to develop a high degree of confidence about important features of dreaming, based on the widest range of available evidence. Our primary research question should be this: Do religious dream reports *plausibly reflect* actual dimensions of human dreaming experience? Rather than asking whether any particular woman in ancient India dreamed of a demon licking the inside of her womb, we ask whether it is plausible for women in that personal, cultural, physiological, and spiritual context to experience the kinds of troubling sexual dreams attributed to them in the *Vedas.*

The goal here is not to establish the historical factuality of particular dreams but rather to illuminate the full range of human dreaming potential. Such an approach is strengthened by the comparison of dream reports across religious traditions, enabling us to highlight the most prominent themes, motifs, and patterns that recur in the greatest variety of contexts (thereby reducing the likelihood of being misled by single cases). The ultimate aim, I propose, is to build up a broad empirical understanding of the most robust patterns of dreaming form and content, reported by the widest variety of people, throughout history and across different cultures.

That said, a final word should be added in favor of open-minded attention to ostensibly "fictional" dreams. Recall the discussions in the prologue about the continuity of dreaming and waking, and the positive influence of external encouragement on dream recall. It is reasonable, according to the findings of Western dream science, to suppose that people who live in a culture where religious dream texts are widely known and venerated will be more likely to have actual dreams that include the stories, characters, symbols, and themes portrayed in those prominent religious texts. Thus may "fictional" dreams beget "real" dreams. The lively two-way interaction between dreaming and culture must always be kept in mind as we move forward.

Birth Dreams

Continuing with the theme of dreams in relation to pregnancy and birth, the Jain Dharma traditions of ancient India attributed the conception of their greatest sage to a heaven-sent dream experienced by his mother. The Jains of present-day India do not consider themselves "Hindu," and they trace their lineage to pre-Vedic times. In contrast to the Vedic focus on rituals of sacrifice, the Jains have always emphasized nonviolence and compassion toward all life (though with a rigorously ascetic, warlike approach to the control of one's own bodily desires). The *Kalpa Sutra,* a popular Jainist text compiled sometime in the early sixth century CE, tells of the birth of Mahavira (599–527 BCE), a sage who reached the enlightened stage of becoming a *Tirthankar,* a "bridge builder" across the river of human suffering.[4] On the night when the embryo of Mahavira took form in his mother Devananda's womb, she entered "a state between sleeping and waking" and saw "fourteen illustrious, beautiful, lucky, blessed, auspicious, fortunate great dreams." The fourteen dreams were, in order, an enormous elephant, a white bull, a handsome lion, the anointing of the goddess *Sri,* a garland of fresh flowers, a full white moon, a radiant red sun, a colorful flag, a vase full of gold, a lotus lake with water lilies, an ocean with a great vortex of water, a celestial abode with glorious gardens and decorations, an enormous pile of jewels, and a blazing, crackling fire. When Devananda awoke, she felt "glad, pleased, and joyful" at what she had seen. She told her husband, the King Siddhartha, who "firmly fixed the dreams in his mind, and entered upon considering them; he grasped the meaning of those dreams with his own native intelligence and intuition, which were preceded by reflection." Following this process of private exegesis, the king told his wife that the dreams were a prophetic message that she was going to bear a son who would one day become a great king. According to the *Kalpa Sutra,* Devananda happily returned to her bedroom, saying to herself, "These my excellent and pre-eminent dreams shall not be counteracted by other bad dreams." She resolved to "remain awake to save [my] dreams by means of [hearing] good, auspicious, pious, agreeable stories about gods and religious men."

King Siddhartha, meanwhile, desired additional interpretive help, and he sent his servants into town to "call the interpreters of dreams who well know the science of prognostics with its eight branches, and are well versed in many sciences besides!" The interpreters arrived, dream books in hand, and when they heard the king recite Devananda's dreams they replied that their books contained detailed descriptions of two broad classes of dreams, common and great. All Devananda's dreams were identified as great dreams, and the interpreters said that these particular fourteen great dreams were a collective sign that the embryo of a being known as a universal monarch (*Arhat*) had entered the mother's womb. The interpreters went on to explain that a woman who has any seven of these fourteen great dreams will bear a *Vasudeva,* a lesser deity; with any four of the great dreams, the woman will bear a *Baladeva* (still lesser), and a single great dream of these fourteen will signal the conception of a *Mandalika* (least divine of all). Delighted by all this, the king "honored the interpreters of dreams with praise and plenty of food, flowers, perfumes, garlands, and ornaments" and then sent them on their way.

This magical story of Mahavira's birth takes the traditional dreaming-pregnancy connection in a supremely favorable direction. Although bad dreams may signal danger to a pregnant woman, good dreams hold the promise of indicating the very moment of conception, along with a prediction of the child's glorious future. This notion of dreaming as a source of prophetic knowledge is a remarkably widespread religious belief, and we will have many chances to explore it in other contexts. In the *Kalpa Sutra,* the prophetic meaning of Devananda's dreams is confirmed by multiple sources. The dreams themselves are uniformly positive in their images of beauty, vitality, harmony, and power. Devananda's emotional reaction upon awakening is happy, as is her reaction to her husband's carefully considered interpretation. His reading is further supported by the collective wisdom of the professional interpreters and their time-honored dream books. All in all, the *Kalpa Sutra* provides many reasons to believe that dreams have the potential to reveal future developments in waking life. The reference to a class of interpretive specialists with their own technical literature is worth remembering, as is the typological distinction between common dreams and great dreams. Experiencing dreams, remembering them, thinking about their content, sharing them with family members, classifying them, seeking the help of professional interpreters, all with an eye toward their potentially prophetic meanings—the world of the *Kalpa Sutra* presents these as normal, recognizable features of human life. The stylized extravagance and lavish hyperbole of Devananda's dreams may make us question whether they really occurred in exactly this way, but her story nevertheless provides us with a valuable window onto the interplay of dreaming belief, practice, and experience among the Jain audiences of the *Kalpa Sutra.*

The Upanishads

A different strand of Hindu religious reflection led away from the *Vedas* to a mystical quest for altered consciousness. In contrast to the Vedic focus on this-worldly fears and desires, a group of poet-philosophers radically reinterpreted the rituals of Hindu tradition, shifting the focus inward toward a sacrifice of the self in search of progressively deeper realizations of one's identity with ultimate reality. Starting around 700 BCE and continuing for the next several centuries, new religious texts were written that explored these mystical connections (*upanishads*) between ritual practice and spiritual discovery, prompting new interest in self-exploration by means of breathing, meditation, yoga, and dreaming. Several *Upanishadic* texts devoted careful attention to the spiritual qualities of sleep and dreaming, and on the whole these writings mark a dramatic reversal of the earlier *Vedic* antipathy toward dreams.

The *Chandogya Upanishad* included a special ritual for those cases in which "a man is striving to achieve greatness."[5] *Dream incubation* is the general term used for pre-sleep practices aimed at eliciting a favorable dream, and the following passage offers a good illustration of its essential elements. The greatness-seeking man is instructed to prepare a special mixture of herbs, honey, and curd on the night of the full moon, to pour offerings of *ghee* into a fire while praising various gods, to drink the whole of the mixture, and finally to lie down behind the fire, "remaining silent and unresisting." Although no guarantees are made that the ritual will necessarily work, the text goes on to say that:

If he sees a woman, he should know that his rite has been successful. In this connection, there is this verse:

When a man sees a woman in his dreams
During a rite to obtain a wish;
He should recognize its success
In that dream vision.

Nothing more is said about why a dream of a woman should herald a man's future greatness; the symbolic connection is simply assumed. Dream incubation rituals in other religions are usually practiced in locations far removed from the ordinary social world (e.g., a cave or graveyard), but here the fire itself represents a sacred location, a spatial center around which the ritual proceeds. The timing with the full moon insures a harmony with celestial patterns, and the potion is clearly intended as a kind of spiritual agent, though the exact ingredients and effects remain obscure. The pre-sleep prayers chanted before the fire echo the hymn to Agni discussed earlier, suggesting at least one thread of continuity between the *Vedas* and the *Upanishads*. For classical Hinduism, fire is the patron element of sleepers and dreamers.

The efficacy of rituals involving sleep and dreams led many of the *Upanishadic* poets to experiment with various alterations of consciousness across the sleep-wake cycle. For example, the *Kausitaki Upanishad* encourages people to perform the internal fire sacrifice and breath meditation "without interruption, whether one is awake or asleep."[6] While not directly disputing the *Vedic* notion of sleep as a condition of danger, this *Upanishad* suggests that sleep may also be a time for virtuous religious practice. Once that positive potential is affirmed, the whole realm of sleep and dreaming becomes the subject of tremendous spiritual interest, as will be seen in the discussion of modern Hindu teachers at the end of this chapter.

Several *Upanishads* explore the existential dimensions of sleep experience in ways that certainly strive to be empirically grounded in actual human life. In the *Brhadaranyaka Upanishad,* a dialogue between the sage Gargya and the king Ajatashatru turns to the figure of a sleeping man.[7] Ajatashatru calls to the man, but he remains asleep. The king then touches the man, and he awakens. Ajatashatru asks Gargya, "When this man was asleep here, where was the person consisting of perception? And from where did he return?" In a reversal of the normal *Upanishadic* direction of knowledge transmission, it is the king and not the sage who provides the answer:

When this man was asleep here, the person consisting of perception, having gathered the cognitive power of these vital functions [*prana*] into his own cognitive power, was resting in the space within the heart. When that person takes hold of them, then the man is said to be asleep. During that time the breath remains in the grasp of that person, as do speech, sight, hearing, and mind. Wherever he may travel in his dream, those regions become his worlds. He may appear to become a great king or an eminent Brahmin, or to visit the highest and the lowest regions. Just as a great king, taking his people with him, may move around his domain at will, so he, taking the vital functions here with him, moves around his body at will.

This remarkable passage represents one of the earliest psychophysiological analyses of sleep and dreaming. According to Ajatashatru, falling asleep involves the in-gathering of vital functions from their waking engagement with the external world, allowing the liberation of the self within the dreaming imagination. The nearly infinite potential of dream experience is emphasized, with its wishful impulses, grandiose fantasies, and extremities of vision. There is rather more attribution of agency and volition within the dream state than is usually recognized by Western psychologists, but this is consistent with the broader *Upanishadic* theme of cultivating new modes of self-awareness extending *beyond* the simple opposition of waking and dreaming. The *Brhadaranyaka Upanishad* passage continues with Ajatasutra describing the further condition of "deep dreamless sleep" in which the individual "rests there oblivious to everything, just as a young man, a great king, or an eminent Brahmin remains oblivious to everything at the height of sexual bliss." An intriguing analogy, and one that links the *Upanishadic* discussion back to the *Vedic* interest in conception and dreaming.

The most detailed and provocative *Upanishadic* passage comes a little later in this same text, when the sage Yajnavalkya grants the king Janaka the freedom to ask any question he wishes. The grateful king uses this wonderful boon to pose a profound existential question: "What is the source of light for a person here?" Yajnavalkya replies that the self (*atman*) is a person's true source of light, and in explaining the nature of *atman* the sage quickly delves into the phenomenology of sleep and dreaming:

Now, this person has just two places—this world and the other world. And there is a third, the place of dream [*svapna*] where the two meet. Standing there in the place where the two meet, he sees both those places —this world and the other world. Now, that place serves as an entryway to the other world, and as he moves through that entryway he sees both the bad things and the joys.

This is how he dreams. He takes materials from the entire world and, taking them apart on his own and then on his own putting them back together, he dreams with his own radiance, with his own light. In that

place this person becomes his own light. In that place there are no carriages, tandems, or roads; but he creates for himself carriages, tandems,
and roads. In that place there are no joys, pleasures, or delights; but he
creates for himself joys, pleasures, and delights. In that place there are no
pools, ponds, or rivers; but he creates for himself pools, ponds, and rivers
—for he is a creator. On this subject, there are these verses: "Subduing by
sleep the bodily realm, / Remaining awake, he contemplates the sleeping
senses."

Although the *Brhadaranyaka Upanishad* is a religious text, it provides
a surprisingly secular and naturalistic explanation for dream formation.
True, the sage Yajnavalkya locates dreaming between the human and divine realms, in which position it serves as a medium for the transmission of knowledge from one dimension to the other. But dreaming itself
is characterized as a natural, constructive, self-directed mental process.
When a person goes to sleep his or her *atman* comes to life in the pure,
free play of the imagination (the same verb, *srj,* is used in the *Upanishads*
to refer to dreaming, creating, speaking, imagining, and seminal emission).[8] Bits and pieces of the waking world are used to build a whole new
world of experience. The examples of dream content mentioned (horse
travel, positive emotions, bodies of water) reflected common physical
conditions and personal experiences of ordinary human life, and the emphasis on the creative power of the dream-liberated *atman* highlighted
the "mystical connection" between each person and the ultimate creative
power of the universe. Far from the externally aimed blasts of malevo-
lence portrayed in the *Vedas,* dreams in this text are entirely internal, self-
generating phenomena. This does not detract from their reality, however.
On the contrary, dreams vividly display the true creative power of *atman,*
and they even have the potential to disclose one's vital relationship to the
supreme reality of the cosmos. This is why Yajnavalkya responded to the
king's question about *atman* by encouraging him to reflect on the nature
of sleep and dreaming. Whether or not dreams have prophetic significance—this text is silent on the question—their value as a means of spiritual education and enlightenment is profound.

Yajnavalkya went on to consider the folk belief that people who are
sound asleep should not be awakened abruptly because their spirits are
traveling and need time to return safely to their bodies. Yajnavalkya
compared that to another, contrary folk belief that "this place of his [the
dreamer's] is the same as the place he is in when he is awake, because

one sees in a dream the same things one sees when one is awake." The earlier discussion of *atman* and self-creativity in dreams would suggest Yajnavalkya favored the latter belief in dreaming-waking continuity, but his initial response expanded on the travel/journey metaphor of the former: "It is like this. As a large fish moves between both banks, the nearer and the farther, so this person moves between both realms, the realm of dream and the realm where one is awake." This simple image highlighted the cyclical relationship between dreaming and waking, a relationship rooted in the ever-shifting ebb and flow of natural life. The sense of vital movement between waking and dreaming was not, however, intended to mislead people into thinking their dreams constitute a "second reality." Like other *Upanishadic* sages, Yajnavalkya's ultimate interest was guiding people to a transcendent perspective on the whole of reality. Self-reflection on dream experience was offered as one means to achieve that:

> Now when people appear [in dreams] to kill or vanquish him, when an elephant appears to chase him, or when he appears to fall into a pit, he is only ignorantly imagining dangers that he had seen while he was awake. But when he, appearing to be a god or a king, thinks "I alone am this world! I am all!"—that is his highest world. Now, this is the aspect of his that is beyond what appears to be good, freed from what is bad, and without fear. It is like this. As a man embraced by a woman he loves is oblivious to everything within or without, so this person embraced by the self [*atman*] consisting of knowledge is oblivious to everything within and without. Clearly, this is the aspect of his where all desires are fulfilled, where the self is the only desire, and which is free from desires and free from sorrows. Here a father is not a father, a mother is not a mother, worlds are not worlds, gods are not gods, and *Vedas* are not *Vedas*. Here a thief is not a thief, an abortionist is not an abortionist, an outcaste is not an outcaste, a pariah is not a pariah, a recluse is not a recluse, and an ascetic is not an ascetic. Neither the good nor the bad follow him, for he has now passed beyond all sorrows of the heart.

The examples of frightening, deceptively "real" dreams Yajnavalkya mentioned—falling, being chased by an animal, being attacked by other people—are also cited by Western psychologists as especially common types of nightmarish dreaming.[9] Such dreams may be intensely vivid and emotionally arousing, but Yajnavalkya warned against taking them too seriously. Most important was to strive for the realization *within the dream state* of the self-created nature of all reality. The sage urged his listeners to reflect on the radical freedom of social identity, religious authority, and moral behavior they experience in their dreams, as a means of recognizing each person's potential for spiritual growth and self-transcendence. No matter how vibrant things appear in the waking world or in dreams, the truth of *atman* leads beyond all creative illusions to the original creative source of the cosmos itself. This was the basis for an *Upanishadic* categorization of four fundamental states of being, expressed rather cryptically in the *Mandukya Upanishad* as waking, dreaming, deep dreamless sleep, and self-realization [*turiya*, literally "the fourth"].[10] The last of the four was described as "unseen, ungraspable, unthinkable, indescribable, beyond the reach of ordinary transaction," all of which befits a state in which the *atman* is finally released from all worldly attachments and perceives its own pure, authentic nature.

Hinduism has no official, canonical text comparable to the *Qur'an* of Islam, the *Novum Testamentum* of Christianity, or the *Torah* of Judaism. Nevertheless, the *Vedas* and *Upanishads* have provided the primary foundation for Hindu beliefs, practices, and experiences throughout the following centuries. As we have now seen, these age-old texts present a complex and thoughtful understanding of the kaleidoscopic nature of human dream experience. Indeed, many of their observations compare favorably with Western psychological research on dreaming. To summarize the main ideas discussed so far, the classic writings of Hinduism recognize that cycles of sleep and dreaming are natural, healthy, pan-human phenomena. They acknowledge the frightening, disturbing quality of frequent nightmares, and highlight the connections between dreaming, sex, and conception, as well as between dreaming, illness, and death. They describe at length the ways in which some dreams involve bizarre metamorphoses of character, others the flagrant violation of moral law, and still others the surprising awareness that one is dreaming. The specific details of dream content are attributed to the personal characteristics of the dreamer, and interpretation focuses on the discernment of symbolic connections between dream imagery and important waking life concerns.

All this is consistent with the theories and practices of mainstream Western dream science. To be sure, modern researchers would likely disagree with the idea of external dream causation in the *Vedas*, along with any suggestion that dreams can predict the future. But setting those notions aside for the moment, the remaining areas of agreement are large indeed, and they provide encouragement for the general project here of developing a phenomenology of dreaming that integrates historical, cross-cultural, and contemporary research findings.

The remainder of this chapter traces the Hindu engagement with dreaming in mythic literature and in nineteenth- and early-twentieth-century spiritual movements.

Mythic Literature

The *Vedas* and *Upanishads* have enjoyed a high degree of philosophical authority, but the texts that have most deeply aroused the love and enthusiasm of the Hindu people are mythic narratives like *The Mahabharata* and *The Ramayana*. These popular tales were composed over a period of many centuries and recited orally in ceremonial contexts. Both stories essentially revolve around an epic battle of good versus evil. An old king leaves the throne, a new king rises up, evil forces resist him, a climactic battle is fought, the villains lose, and the throne is restored to its rightful heir. In this regard, *The Mahabharata* and *The Ramayana* continue the traditional Hindu concern with the relationship between human action and cosmic power, illustrating the idea of religious duty with colorful stories about heroic efforts to overcome violent physical challenges. The two epics dramatize the existential opposition of chaos and order with vividly rendered characters whose feelings and actions movingly reflect people's actual experiences with the fragility of life. Consistent with *Vedic* and *Upanishadic* teachings, the dreams of these characters accurately reflect their personalities and truthfully anticipate their future prospects.

For example, in *The Mahabharata* the Kuru leader Karna tells his divine friend Krishna about the dreams that he and other Kuru warriors are dreaming about their enemies, the Pandavas, on the eve of the grand battle:

> Many horrible dreams are being seen by the Kurus, and many terrible signs and gruesome omens, predicting victory for the Pandavas. Meteors are falling from the sky, and there are hurricanes and earthquakes. The elephants are trumpeting, and horses are shedding tears and refusing food and water. Horses, elephants, and men are eating little, yet they are shitting prodigiously. . . . I had a dream in which I saw all the Pandavas climb to a palace with a thousand pillars. All of them wore white turbans and white robes. And in my dream I saw you, Krishna, drape entrails

around the earth, which was awash with blood, and I saw the Pandava [leader] Yudhisthira climb a pile of bones and joyously eat rice and butter from a golden bowl. And I saw him swallow the earth that you had given to him; clearly he will take over the earth.[11]

These pre-battle dreams provide horribly clear prophecies of defeat for the rebellious Kurus in their coming battle against the divinely favored Pandavas. More than a simple prediction, the dreams illustrate the terrible suffering that is destined to fall upon those evil people and demonic beings who violate the laws of human society and threaten the foundations of cosmic order. It is both poetic and religious justice that those who try to overthrow the moral order should themselves be violently attacked in their dreams. The "bad guy" Kurus are, appropriately, plagued by bad dreams. The prophetic accuracy of these nightmares does not help Karna and his comrades escape their imminent deaths, but the message would be clear enough to the audiences of *The Mahabharata.* The moral reality of dreaming is inescapable, and woe to those who, by choice or by fate, revolt against the sacred laws of the universe.

In *The Ramayana,* the prophetic moral potency of dreaming is presented in a more ambivalent light, with an intriguing awareness of the difficulty of interpreting dreams that relate to strong but unconscious desires. When the aged King Dasaratha of Ayodhya decides to step down from the throne, he is coerced by Kaikeyi, mother of his third son Bharata, into naming Bharata as his successor rather than Rama, Dasaratha's eldest son and the rightful heir. Bharata has, up to this point in the story, behaved in a perfectly faithful and virtuous fashion, with no indication of any desire to overleap Rama's preeminence in the royal line of succession. Just before he receives the shocking news about Dasaratha's unexpected abdication and his own elevation to the throne, Bharata awakens from this strange nightmare:

Hear the reason for my present sadness! In a dream, my father appeared to me in faded apparel, his hair disheveled, falling from a mountain peak into a pit of dung! It seemed to me he was wallowing in that sea of dung, drinking oil from the hollow of his hands, bursting into laughter again and again. . . . And in my dream I saw the ocean dry up and the moon fall on the earth, the world being plunged into darkness. . . . Finally I beheld a woman dressed in red, a female demon of hideous aspect, who, as if in play, was bearing the king away. This is what I beheld during this terrible night! Assuredly, either I or Rama or the King or Laksmana [another of Bharata's brothers] are about to die. . . . My throat is dry; and my mind is uneasy. I see no reason for my apprehension and yet I am full of fear; my voice shakes, my features are wan, I am ashamed of myself and yet I do not know the reason.[12]

Bharata does not immediately understand the prophetic meaning of his nightmare. It means something bad and inauspicious, he knows that much; it involves the death of someone in the family, and it seems to threaten the overthrow of order and cause worldwide chaos. The impact of the dream is unmistakable—physical suffering, emotional upheaval, mental confusion—but the precise meaning remains obscure. Why might that be? Without forgetting that Bharata is a character in a myth, we can still appreciate the way his dream highlights the potentially sharp conflict between a person's waking ideals and dreaming desires. In waking life, Bharata is a properly behaved and deferential younger son. His dream, however, foresees a radical change to his world, a change that will be extremely beneficial for him, even though it will violate the basic laws of gods and men. The grandiose idea that he, Bharata, could ever become king before Rama is literally unthinkable for his waking mind. What the audience already knows to be true, Bharata is psychologically incapable of seeing. If there is any truth to the idea that dreaming expresses a person's strongest feelings and desires, then the story of Bharata's dream bears witness to the possibility of a painful clash between what we think in waking we *should* do and what we wish in dreaming we *could* do.

Another popular mythic text, the *Yogavasistha,* added new philosophical depth to Hinduism's ontological engagement with dreaming.[13] Written sometime during the eleventh or twelfth century BCE, the *Yogavasistha* gathered dozens of familiar myths and folk tales and wove them together with metaphysical commentary inspired by *Upanishadic* visions of illusion and reality. Dreaming played a central role in several of the stories in which characters experienced a continually recursive process of waking, sleeping, dreaming, and then waking into a new identity (e.g., a Brahmin priest who dreams of being an "Untouchable" peasant who dreams of being a powerful king). The bizarre narrative complexity of the *Yogavasistha* had the effect of decentering its audience, intentionally frustrating people's ordinary assumptions about the ontological boundaries between waking and dreaming in order to provoke a more enlightened spiritual perspective. What the tales described, the people in the audience were led to feel, and what they were led to feel was something akin to the *Upanishadic* insight into the transcendent power of the dreaming *atman*.

Modern Spiritual Movements

New waves of immigrants rolled across India beginning in the eighth century CE as Muslims from Arabia spread farther and farther eastward, extending their formidable military power and novel religious teachings. By the thirteenth century CE, the Delhi Sultanate came to power and established a Muslim political reign over India that lasted for the next three hundred years. Relations between the Hindu and Muslim peoples were difficult from the start, not only because the newcomers repeatedly looted the local Hindu shrines, temples, and palaces. More fundamentally, their religious traditions seemed like mirror opposites of each other. Hinduism presents a polytheistic worldview steeped in ancient myth, symbol, and ritual with no official doctrine, whereas Islam proclaims a monotheistic faith based on the relatively recent revelations of a single man, recorded in a fixed written text. Two more different religious traditions could hardly be imagined. However, the one area where they found common ground was in the realm of mystical experience and the various techniques used for its cultivation. Hindu yogins seeking the development of transcendent modes of consciousness recognized a similar goal in the mystical practices of Muslim Sufis, who also used meditation, prayer, breathing, sound, bodily exercise, and dreaming as modes of spiritual knowledge and insight. Both traditions employed a similar method of master-disciple relationship for the transmission of religious teachings, with the *guru* of Hinduism roughly equivalent to the *pir* or *sheikh* of Sufism as a guide for the disciple's systematic experimentation with different states of consciousness. Here, at least, was something the two traditions could agree on, regardless of their other areas of conflict. In chapter 7, we return to this intriguing connection between the mystical dream practices of Hinduism and Islam.

Commerce between India, England, and other European nations expanded rapidly in the seventeenth century, inaugurating another immigration-driven transformation of the Hindus River region. In 1757, England used the full force of its industrialized navy and army to defeat the last Muslim rulers and establish the British Raj as the official colonial government. Along with British military control came a sudden infusion of new Western technologies, medical practices, scientific theories, and Christian missionary teachings. In a relatively short period, an English-speaking Indian elite with a modernist, pro-Western outlook emerged at the upper echelons of government, business, and education. These people sought to integrate the new Western influences with classical Hinduism, purging their tradition of outdated ideas and highlighting its universal truths. However, many other Indians bitterly resented the oppressive colonial rule of the British. They rejected the cultural supremacy of the West, denounced the decadence of Anglicized Indians, and insisted on the need for a purified Hindu faith grounded in ancestral teachings and practices.

These turbulent religious cross-currents created the conditions for an upsurge of visionary Hindu leadership in the nineteenth and early twentieth centuries. One of the most ardently venerated of these charismatic teachers was Sri Ramakrishna, a Bengali mystic who still commands a large following in present-day India.[14] Ramakrishna was born in 1836, and in classic Hindu fashion his birth was heralded by a divinely sanctioned dream. His sixty-year-old father made a pilgrimage to the city of Gaya, where generations of Hindus have made offerings to their ancestors at a temple of the divine Lord Vishnu. While at the temple the elderly man had a dream in which Lord Vishnu appeared and promised that the man would have a son who would be an incarnation of Vishnu himself. When the divine child was born, he was given the name Gadadhar (meaning the "Bearer of the Mace," a favorite epithet of Vishnu) in honor of his father's auspicious dream. As he grew up, the boy took little interest in school or work, and from an early age was prone to spontaneous visions, trances, and ecstasies involving a host of Hindu deities. In time, his precocious spirituality led him to become a devotee of the destructive mother goddess Kali. His systematic efforts toward spiritual self-transformation included a radical shift in his approach to sleep, as described by one of his disciples:

A deep jungle, thick with underbrush and prickly plants, lay to the north of the temples. Used at one time as a burial ground, it was shunned by people even in the daytime for fear of ghosts. There Sri Ramakrishna began to spend the whole night in meditation, returning to his room only in the morning with eyes swollen as though from much weeping.

By the accounts of his followers, Ramakrishna virtually abandoned sleep in his later life. His contemplative practices flowed across the ordinary boundaries of waking and sleeping, making it difficult to say whether Ramakrishna stopped dreaming or stopped doing anything *but* dream. He did show an interest in hearing other people's dreams, as evidenced by this story from *The Gospel of Sri Ramakrishna*:

> When the song was over, the Master walked up and down the northeast verandah, where Hazra was seated with M. The Master sat down there. He asked a devotee, "Do you ever have dreams?"
>
> *Devotee*: Yes, sir. The other day I dreamed a strange dream. I saw the whole world enveloped in water. There was water on all sides. A few boats were visible, but suddenly huge waves appeared and sank them. I was about to board a ship with a few others, when we saw a Brahmin walking over that expanse of water. I asked him, "How can you walk over the deep?" The Brahmin said with a smile: "Oh, there is no difficulty about that. There is a bridge under the water." I said to him, "Where are you going?" "To Bhawanipur, the city of the Divine Mother," he replied. "Wait a little," I cried, "I shall accompany you."
>
> *Master*: Oh, I am thrilled to hear the story!
>
> *Devotee*: The Brahmin said: "I am in a hurry. It will take you some time to get out of the boat. Good-bye. Remember this path and come after me."
>
> *Master*: Oh, my hair is standing on end! Please be initiated by a guru as soon as possible.

Ramakrishna responds to the devotee's dream not by intellectual interpretation or studied reference to written texts. Instead, he gives an immediate somatic response. The dream evokes vivid physical reactions in Ramakrishna—he's "thrilled," his hair stands on end—and those auspicious bodily sensations convince him that the dream itself is auspicious, that is, meaningful in content and favorable in predictive outcome. He understands the dream to be a call to spiritual initiation, and he urges the devotee to take immediate action in the waking world to carry out its message. Although Ramakrishna does not dwell on the images or narrative details of the dream, we should note the theme of water as it relates to spiritually charged dreaming. The dark, unknown depths of the ocean, the destructive power of waves, the threat of a cataclysmic flood —when these elemental images appear in a dream, they often convey a special intensity of sensory and emotional realism, propelling the dream into waking awareness with an unforgettable impact.

In Ramakrishna's teachings, the common human experience of dreaming illustrates the stubbornly illusory nature of all existence. He said, "It is not easy to get rid of illusion. It lingers even after the attainment of knowledge. A man dreamed of a tiger. Then he woke up and his dream vanished. But his heart continued to palpitate." Ramakrishna recognized that emotions are the most enduring features of a dream, carrying over from sleeping into waking, and for the most part he regarded such dream emotions as reflections of worldly attachments that must be abandoned. However, he also taught his disciples that the Divine manifests itself in waking *and* sleeping, even though waking and sleeping are themselves nothing but illusions, and the Divine is beyond them both. Ramakrishna once told the following parable (which has interesting echoes from his own childhood):

There was a farmer to whom an only son was born when he was rather advanced in age. As the child grew up, the parents became very fond of him. One day the farmer was working in the fields when a neighbor told him that his son was dangerously ill—indeed, at the point of death. Returning home, he found the boy dead. His wife wept bitterly, but his own eyes remained dry. Sadly the wife said to her neighbors, "Such a son has passed away, and he hasn't even one tear to shed!" After a long while the farmer said to his wife: "Do you know why I am not crying? Last night I dreamed I had become a king, and the father of seven princes. These princes were beautiful as well as virtuous. They grew in stature and acquired wisdom and knowledge in the various arts. Suddenly I woke up. Now I have been wondering whether I should weep for those seven children or this one boy."

Nothing could make plainer the extremity of Ramakrishna's otherworldly asceticism. In dreaming as in waking, the emotional bonds of human relationships must ultimately yield to the sole reality of God. Even the death of one's own child should not arouse any special feelings of loss because all attachments are illusory anyway. Life is no more or less real than a dream. The path of enlightenment leads us out of this dreaming world to an ecstatic awakening of pure, complete consciousness of the Divine.

A very different Hindu reaction to Western religious and philosophical beliefs came from Debendranath Tagore (1817–1905), a leader of the modernist *Brahmo Samaj* (Society for Worshipping God).[15] *Brahmo Samaj* was founded in the early nineteenth century as a reform movement aimed at reconciling Christian and Hindu spiritual teachings about God. Polytheism was rejected as mere idolatry, and rituals of sacrifice were abandoned as irrational superstition. The *Upanishads* were upheld as the true essence of Hindu spirituality, teaching a rationalist Brahmanic monotheism that was claimed to be fully compatible with Enlightenment-era Western Christianity. Tagore (whose son, Rabindranath, became a Nobel prize–winning poet) did not come to this faith easily; he had painful personal experience of the tension between the forces of modernization and traditional Hinduism, and it took a dream to help him find the path of moderation that distinguished his later teachings. He tells of this dream in his autobiography:

Which would triumph, the world or religion?—one could not tell—this was what worried me. . . . All these anxieties and troubles would not let me sleep at night, my head felt dazed on the pillow. I would now doze off and again wake up. It was as if I was sleeping on the borderland between waking and sleeping. At such a time someone came to me in the dark and he said, "follow me," and I followed. . . . He seemed to be a shadow-like form. I could not see him clearly, but felt myself constrained to do immediately whatever he bade me. From thence he mounted upwards to the sky. I also followed him. Clusters of stars and planets were shedding a bright luster, right and left and in front of me, and I was passing through them. . . . In the course of my journey I entered one of its cities. All the houses and all the streets were of white marble, not a single soul was to be seen in the clean and bright and polished streets. . . . I found myself in a spacious room, in which there was a table and some chairs of white marble. . . . The phantom had vanished. Nobody else was there. I sat silent in that silent room; shortly afterwards the curtain of one of the doors in front of the room was drawn aside and my mother appeared. Her hair was down, just as I had seen it on the day of her death. When she died, I never thought that she was dead. Even when I came back from the burning ground after performing her funeral ceremonies. I could not believe that she was dead. I felt sure that she was still alive. Now I saw that living mother of mine before me. She said, "I wanted to see you, so I sent for you. Have you really become one who has known Brahma? Sanctified is the family, fulfilled is the mother's desire." On seeing her, and hearing these sweet words of hers, my slumber gave way before a flood of joy. I found myself still tossing on my bed.

The conflict between the "world" of Western modernism and the "religion" of traditional Hinduism was an all-consuming concern of Tagore's, as it was for many people in India at the time, and his dream offered a personal vision of how to overcome this culture-wide crisis. Driven by the intensity of his anxieties and the purity of his desire for divine guidance, he entered a state of consciousness between waking and sleeping, somewhat like the transcendent awareness described by the *Upanishads* and experienced by Ramakrishna. No further details were mentioned regarding Tagore's strange guide, nothing that might identify him as a Hindu deity. He was male, supernaturally powerful, difficult to see clearly, and able to compel Tagore's complete obedience; that is all we hear. Similarly, the misty celestial abode to which he brought Tagore had no apparent precedent in Hindu sacred geography. If anything, this pristine, well-ordered city of cool white marble was reminiscent of an idealized Greek *polis,* which Tagore would recognize as a classical expression of Western philosophical and political values.

The Hermes-like messenger guide disappeared, and Tagore found himself face to face with his deceased mother. It was a climactic moment of dream reality fused with waking unreality. He knew she was dead, and yet she appeared alive. She looked exactly as she had looked when he last saw her, which was right before the cremation of her dead body. In waking life, he could not believe she was really gone, and now in a dream she was right there in front of him, "that living mother of mine."

Profound sadness at the loss of a parent is a perennial human experience, and we shall see many more examples of highly intensified, ontologically ambiguous dreams in which the dead return to the living. What is remarkable about Tagore's experience was that it reflected not only his personal mourning for his own mother but also the collective mourning of the Indian people for their ancestral culture, the primal mother who originally gave birth to human civilization in the Indus River region, worshiped as a fertility goddess by the Dravidians, as Kali by Ramakrishna. Dead and yet not dead, a dream yet more than a dream, lost in the historical past yet still alive in the visionary present—Tagore's "living mother" gave voice to the ongoing vitality of Hindu beliefs that had only apparently been defeated by the rationalistic faith of Western colonizers. His

mother, and Hindu traditions, still had the power to enliven and inspire him. Her question—"Have you really become one who has known
Brahma?"—spoke directly to his conflicted spiritual condition, articulat-
ing for him the possibility of an ancestrally blessed reconciliation of Western culture ("world") and traditional Hinduism ("religion"). Brahma is
an authentic Hindu deity, worshiped in India for centuries; he is also a
male creator God, and thus potentially compatible with Christian monotheism. Tagore's mother did not wait for him to answer her question but
simply left him with the reassurance that, to the extent he *did* become
one who knew Brahma, she and all Tagore's ancestors would be pleased.
At this point he awakened in his bed, with a "flood of joy" carrying over
from one state of consciousness into the other. The subsequent course of
Tagore's life as an activist and philosopher embodied his dream mother's
vision of a Brahmanic spiritual revival that could guide and inspire the
modernization of India.

The last of these modern visionaries we have space to consider is Sri
Aurobindo (1872–1950), whose system of Integral Yoga merged the language of Tantric Hinduism with that of Western evolutionary science.[16]
Aurobindo was born in Calcutta but spent his entire youth in England,
where he attended and excelled at the best schools in the country. Returning to India at the age of twenty-one, he took a position in the colonial
government, but then he secretly began meeting with other anticolonial
Hindus to plan an armed rebellion against the British Raj. Eventually he
quit the government and became a leading voice in the movement for Indian independence, in the course of which he endured constant harass-
ment and physical threats from colonial officials. Then, just a few years
later, his life took a dramatic spiritual turn. He traveled in 1910 to the
south Indian city of Pondicherry with the desire to spend a year in meditation. Pondicherry was a small colony still under French control, and it
provided Aurobindo with a British-free zone where he could live for a
time in relative safety. He ended up staying there for the rest of his life,
breaking his ties with the nationalist movement which he helped to found
and devoting himself entirely to yogic practice. With the inspired help
of a French woman named Mirra Richards, later known as the Mother,
Aurobindo's residence at Pondicherry became an *ashram* at which his increasingly numerous followers gathered to practice his teachings. He remained within his bedroom for the final twenty-four years of his life, giving the whole of his being to a quest for spiritual perfection: "The one aim
of [my] Yoga is an inner self-development by which each one who follows

it can in time discover the One Self in all and evolve a higher consciousness than the mental, a spiritual and supramental consciousness which will transform and divinize human nature."

More than Ramakrishna or Tagore, Aurobindo worked out a highly sophisticated philosophical system to understand, explain, and ultimately transform people's dream experiences. He started by emphasizing the important physical need for sleep: "If you do not sleep enough the body and the nervous envelope will be weakened and the body and the nervous envelope are the basis of the *sadhana* [practice of Integral Yoga]." Seven hours was the minimum he recommended, although he said the truly restful and recuperative phase of sleep lasts only a few moments: "A long unbroken sleep is necessary because there are just ten minutes of the whole into which one enters into a true rest—a sort of *Sachchidananda* [Ultimate Mind] immobility of consciousness—and that is what really restores the system." Sleep generally lowers the spiritual quality of consciousness, dragging it down by "the pull of the subconscient inertia." In Integral Yoga, however, the goal is to maintain consciousness and cultivate spiritual awareness by the continuous practice of *sadhana* during sleep, transforming sleep into an opportunity for mystical experience.

Aurobindo divided dreams into two broad categories. The first and most common type he called "dream formations from the subconscient." These are relatively trivial creations of the waking mind, concerned with thoughts and impressions of daily existence, "much mixed and distorted" by the diminished mental functioning of sleep. Such ordinary dreams may nevertheless be useful as pragmatic diagnoses of one's current life. Indeed, the Mother spoke at length with the disciples at Pondicherry about the meanings of their dreams.[17] "All dreams," she said, "can show you what your present state of consciousness is and how things are combined in the subconscious, what the terrestrial influences are, what traces they leave and how they are combined."

Much more significant, however, are the dreams in the second of Aurobindo's categories, "dream experiences of the subliminal." While ordinary dream formations are the products of degraded, psychologically shallow functioning, other dreams take us beyond the "veil" of the subconscient to the vast subliminal realms of spiritual experience. Aurobindo says that dream experiences leading into the supraphysical are likely to increase with the practice of *sadhana,* just as ordinary dreams will probably diminish in frequency. At the furthest stage of development, *sadhana* leads to a total transformation of sleep: "Even we can by training become

so conscious as to follow our own passage, usually veiled to our awareness and memory, through many realms and the process of the return to
the waking state. At a certain pitch of this inner wakefulness this kind of
sleep, a sleep of experiences, can replace ordinary subconscious slumber."

Aurobindo's teachings carried into modern times the sleep-transform-
ing goals of the *Upanishads*. In this ancient Hindu tradition, sleep and
dreams are valued not simply as sources of revelation but, more important, as opportunities for cultivating new modes of being, acting, and
knowing. The individual aspirant is taught to move through the sensory
distractions of the waking world, past the self-created fears and delights
of dreaming, and finally beyond even the calm emptiness of dreamless
sleep to reach *turiya*, a transcendent awareness that fills the individual at
every moment and in all modes of consciousness with a feeling of ultimate absorption in the cosmos. The ontological question mentioned at
the beginning of the chapter is not so much answered by Hinduism as it
is turned inside out. Waking and dreaming are both real *and* unreal, and
the spiritual seeker is encouraged to discover and embrace the ultimate
divine reality that pervades his or her existence in all states of being.

Summary

In only this first chapter, we have had to contend with a wide variety of
approaches to dreams and their religious significance. The nine chapters
to come will add many new levels of cultural, historical, and linguistic
complexity to our investigation of the dreaming-religion connection. To
help remember and compare all this information, I conclude each chapter with a brief summary of what the traditions in that chapter say about
three basic questions that arise in virtually all theories of dreaming.[18] The
first is a question of origins: How are dreams formed? The second regards
purpose and intentionality: What functions, if any, do dreams serve? And
the third is a question of meaning: How can dreams be interpreted? These,
of course, are not the only important questions to ask about dreaming,
but I hope they provide readers with a shorthand means of evaluating the
various teachings presented in this book.

In the traditions of Hinduism, certain dreams are believed to originate from the gods, but most are believed to be natural products of the
human mind. Hindus attribute several valuable functions to dreaming,
among them the powers of prophetic warning, medical diagnosis, divine

guidance, mystical enlightenment, and the heralding of new birth. Hindus also see dangerous or negative functions in dreaming—sleep is a time of vulnerability to attack by malevolent spiritual forces. The interpretation of dreams in Hinduism generally leads in one of two different directions. In the first, dreams are analyzed symbolically to identify auspicious or inauspicious messages about the future. In the second, dreams are interpreted as illusory creations with no ultimate meaning; in this view, to interpret a dream is to see through it and move beyond it. Hinduism has maintained a generally favorable attitude toward the spiritual potency of dreaming through most of its history and right into the present day. However, the mystical teachings of the *Upanishads* encourage Hindus to look past the illusions of their dreams to achieve a higher state of awareness that transcends both sleeping and waking.

2

Religions of China

Have you ever been a student? Worried about classes? Been forced to study for difficult, competitive examinations? Many readers are probably students right now, and others are almost certainly graduates of some kind of educational system, so you know from personal experience the stressful ordeal of taking tests. You probably also know what it is like to have *dreams* of those tests—vivid, realistic, painfully memorable dreams of arriving to class unprepared for an exam or getting lost on the way or misplacing your backpack or not being able to read the test or receiving a failing grade and suffering public humiliation, and on and on. Strangely enough, these nightmarish dreams often persist well after a person has finished school, with haunting echoes of anxieties the person thought were long gone. The test-taking experience clearly makes a deep impact on the dreaming imagination, and this seems to be true wherever and whenever a society has established a system of rigorous educational testing.

Here is a good example of an exam dream from a young Chinese woman in the senior class at a Beijing teachers' college, interviewed in 1985:

> After I took the post-graduate exams, I had a dream like this: I was asked to take a series of exams, I failed in all of them. I was very depressed and disappointed in myself. When I went back to school, lots of students sneered at me and teased me. When I got home, my father said I was useless and stupid, and all the money he had spent on me was in vain. I cried and cried and asked myself what to do. My mother came and soothed me. She told me that it did not matter and there were many chances. She asked me to go to another exam the next day. But I don't know why I had the dream just like the previous one again.[1]

The ancient Chinese may be the first people ever to experience this distinctive genre of dreaming.[2] An open system of civil service examinations was instituted by the Han dynasty in 196 BCE, and for the next two thousand years these highly competitive tests stood as the all-important gateway into the elite strata of imperial government service. Get a good grade on the exams and you were welcomed into a lifetime of power and prestige. Fail the exams and you were shut out of that world, left to dwell among the poor peasant masses. As we shall see in the coming pages, dreams about the civil service exams have been reported throughout Chinese history, and even today anxiety about tests remains a prominent theme in the dreams of Chinese students. At one level this makes good sense, given our discussion in the prologue about the continuities of waking and dreaming. People tend to dream about whatever is most emotionally urgent and engaging in their waking lives, with particular sensitivity toward threatening situations and painful possibilities. For students and would-be government officials, passing the exam is clearly a paramount emotional concern, and so we would expect to find this reflected with special frequency in their dreaming.

The common occurrence of exam dreams also accords well with the fundamental principles of Chinese culture, particularly the supreme virtue of venerating one's ancestors. This was the core teaching of the philosopher-sage Confucius (551–479 BCE), and the content of the civil service exams always focused on his writings, along with a set of earlier texts (the "Confucian Classics") which he considered central to the traditional worldview of China. The civil service examinations required students to demonstrate a detailed knowledge of all these texts, which effectively meant that the students were required to show a kind of intellectual veneration to ancestral teachings, subjecting their minds to the rule of their forefathers. The exams were not just *about* moral virtue, they were morally virtuous *in themselves* insofar as they compelled the students to think, speak, and behave with fidelity to the finest traditions of China's past.

This connection between the civil service exams and Confucian morality allows us to recognize that, in China at least, exam dreams are related to the broader phenomenon of ancestor dreams. Indeed, many of the Confucian Classics contain favorable stories of dream visitations from the dead, making it all the more natural for students who are poring over those texts to experience such dreams themselves. What we saw in Hinduism emerges in even greater abundance in the religions of China. Dreams of deceased loved ones—parents, spouses, teachers, emperors, heroes—play a profound role in shaping people's spiritual beliefs and practices, illuminating the ongoing influence of ancient cultural wisdom on people's present-day lives.

Shamanic Origins

More than a million years ago, members of the *Homo erectus* species spread out from Africa, moving ever farther north and east, exploring the vast reaches of the Asian continent. They discovered on the far side of the Himalayan Mountains a temperate region of fertile valleys filled with animals, vegetation, and broad rivers leading to the shores of an enormous ocean. Some of the *Homo erectus* people settled in these valleys, where they enjoyed a prosperous hunting-and-gathering lifestyle for the next several hundred thousand years. Around fifty thousand years ago a new wave of African immigrants spread into Asia, this time members of the *Homo sapiens* species. They, too, were hunters and gatherers who stood upright, used stone tools, and cooked with fire. But the larger craniums of *Homo sapiens* allowed for the growth of additional brain matter (the cerebral cortex), giving them expanded cognitive powers—better memory, more precise language, improved forethought, enhanced creativity —with dramatic consequences for their abilities to survive and reproduce. The extinction of *Homo erectus* roughly corresponded to the time when nomadic bands of *Homo sapiens* established themselves as the dominant creatures in all northeastern Asia.

Although archeological evidence regarding these early human communities is fragmentary, one central feature seems fairly clear. Many (and perhaps all) of these groups included at least one person who served as collective dreamer, healer, ritual specialist, and mediator between the living and the dead. The Tungus people of Siberia (their name comes from the Tatar word for "sleeping land") called this person a *shaman,* meaning "one who knows."[3] Much debate currently surrounds the meaning of this term and its applicability outside the Siberian context. For our purposes, the word remains a useful way to refer to the earliest surviving cultural manifestation of dreaming consciousness in our species' history. The general noun *shamanism* is more dubious, as it implies a fixed doctrine or perennial essence that does not seem to exist in the archeological record. The singular noun *shaman,* however, puts the focus on specific individuals, both women and men, whose ritual practices and ecstatic experiences shared several vital features. We will reconsider this topic in many of the coming chapters, but for now we can concentrate on the Neolithic shamans of northeast Asia and their efforts to develop an intensified ability to interact with nonhuman powers and realities. Apparently they used various methods to shift themselves out of ordinary consciousness, including

wilderness sojourns, descents into caves, drumming, dancing, the inges-
tion of psychoactive plants, and dream incubation. In these altered modes
of consciousness, the shamans sought contact with everything from the
spirits of ancestors and local animals to the weather, the earth, and the
stars. If the shamans survived these encounters (many fell prey to illness
and death), they returned to their communities bearing valuable information to aid people in their practical, this-worldly concerns with healing,
hunting, social conflict, and warfare. A person did not choose to become
a shaman but rather was chosen by the spirits via a transformative dream,
vision, or illness. Forever after marked by this initiatory experience, the
shaman became a person able to journey *beyond* this world, and able to
channel energies from those transcendent realms back into his or her
community.

An awareness of shamanic practices is useful in contextualizing the
study of dreaming in Chinese history. Shamans were active throughout
Asia for tens of thousands of years before the rise of China proper, and
many of their practices eventually found their way into the center of the
emerging Chinese dream tradition.

Founding Empires

The end of the last ice age ten thousand years ago brought a new era of
warmer, rainier weather and better growing conditions for the lands east
of the Himalayas. The human groups living there took advantage of the
improved climate to invent a sophisticated system of agriculture with extensive cultivation of rice, millet, and other staple crops. The food sur-
pluses provided by increasingly successful methods of agriculture and animal domestication enabled the human population to grow quickly, with
towns, cities, and professionalized warfare soon to follow.

A key source of information about the religious life of these people
comes from their burial practices, which not coincidentally share many
features with earlier shamanic activities surrounding death, the afterlife,
and spiritual communications between the dead and the living. Numerous grave sites have been found that include, in addition to the dead body,
various tools, weapons, ceramic containers commonly used for food and
water, and, in some cases, specially crafted metal and jade ornaments with
beautifully intricate designs. The presence of these objects in the grave
suggests that the person was prepared for a long journey to a land beyond

death. This is especially true at the spectacular tombs of the kings of the Shang era (1600 BCE on), who were buried with chariots, horses, armies of statue soldiers, and the bodies of numerous human sacrificial victims.

At about this time, that is, the beginning of the second millennium BCE, several cultural achievements enabled the formation of new political dynasties with an unprecedented range of unified territorial control. Improved metal working, domestication of the horse, economic specialization, and the development of writing all combined to create the conditions for a stratified, highly efficient social system capable of imposing peace and stability on increasingly wide swaths of land. The king or emperor who ruled the dynasty was directly responsible for maintaining this prosperous state of affairs, and to do so successfully required careful attention to all possible sources of information, including any guidance from ancestral spirits and other trans-human powers. The extensive political use of dream divination suggests that the earliest kings of China were essentially warrior shamans who combined military prowess with the ritualized function of mediating between human and trans-human realms.

The first definite indications of these shaman-like practices appear in the oracle bone inscriptions of the early Shang period. These brief writings accompanied the divination technique of pyro-scapulamancy, which involved holding a turtle shell or cattle shinbone against a source of extreme heat (e.g., a red-hot metal poker) until cracks appeared. The patterns in the cracks were then interpreted as auspicious, inauspicious, or neutral responses from the spirits to a question posed by the king. The king's questions were usually driven by worries over proper sacrificial offerings to the ancestors. Failure to show due respect to the ancestors could disrupt the harmonious relationship between human society and the cosmos, courting chaos and disaster for the empire. Other questions asked of the oracle bones related to the king's personal experiences, such as a toothache, a consort's pregnancy, or a strange dream. We have precious little information about the actual content of such dreams, but we see in the oracle bone inscriptions the linkage of dreaming, ancestors, and divination that will become a strong element in later Chinese history.

The interpretation of dreams soon became an officially sanctioned practice of the royal court. By the time of the Zhou dynasty (starting around 1100 BCE), a position called *Tai Pu* was filled by an expert skilled in dream interpretation and other methods of divination.[4] Also present in many early imperial courts were individuals known as *wu*, shamanic specialists in healing and spirit communication whose predecessors were primarily peasant women from the outlying, less civilized regions to the south and northeast.[5] The *wu* shamans were eventually banished from Chinese courts because of their emotional instability and association with foreign enemies. But they continued to have a very active presence among the general population, and their "wilder," more spontaneous approach to dreaming remained a shadowy counterpoint to the later writings of the political-philosophical elite.

The earliest surviving text from ancient China is the *Shu-jing* (*Book of Documents*), from the early Zhou period. It described the Zhou overthrow of the corrupt and oppressive Shang dynasty, portraying the Zhou takeover as a righteous victory for the core Chinese value of harmony between human society and the cosmos, with a special emphasis on the idea that such harmony depends on the virtuous behavior of the king, both in his dutiful reverence to the ancestors and in his careful attention to omens of possible danger in the future. The combination of dream interpretation and pyro-scapulamancy was mentioned in a *Shu-jing* story of King Wu, the future founder of the Zhou dynasty, when he addressed his troops just before a great battle against the last Shang ruler.[6] King Wu said, "My dreams are in accord with the oracle-bone crackings; thus the omen is doubly auspicious. We shall triumph for sure in attacking the Shang." And, in fact, he led his army in a successful campaign to capture the imperial capital. King Wu certainly had plenty of incentive to fabricate such a reassuring alignment of portents in order to rouse his soldiers. It is also plausible that King Wu would have experienced unusually significant dreams in the time leading up to an event as momentous, frightening, and uncertain as a rebellion against the emperor. As we saw in chapter 1 with the ominous nightmares of the Kurus and their leader Karna, prebattle dreams are another recurrent type of dreaming mentioned in different cultures and periods of history, including our own era of war and terror.

Another brief story from the *Shu-jing* may or may not reflect a king's actual experience, but it beautifully illustrates the value placed upon dreams by the highest levels of Chinese society. King Wu Ting, a ruler from Shang times, needed a replacement for his longtime teacher and adviser, who had just passed away. The king prayed to Shang-di, the supreme god, for a dream to guide him in making this crucial choice. One night he dreamed of a specific man—no one he recognized from the court but someone with a clearly memorable face. The king awoke and immediately instructed a court artist to make a painting of the face in his dream. This picture was circulated throughout the empire, and after much searching a reclusive commoner named Fu Yue was found in a cave and identified as the man from the king's dream. He was brought back to the imperial court and appointed to the post of prime minister.

Here we have an example of a dream incubation motivated by a pressing political concern, with a dream response that is both direct and surprising. The dream does indeed reveal the right individual for the job —but it is not a person the king currently knows. The artist's portrait enables other people to see what the man looks like, transforming the king's private dream into a collective imaginal experience. When the man is finally found, he turns out to be an entirely ordinary and unassuming person with no qualification for the second-highest post in the government. No qualification, that is, other than appearing in the king's memorable dream. The moral of the tale is simple: do what the dream tells you. A king's dream is an authoritative message from the ancestors and must be obeyed, no matter how strange it may appear to people's ordinary expectations.

This story highlights the strong faith in dreams and other methods of divination on the part of early Chinese rulers, and dramatizes the virtue of the ruler's submission to the mandates of heaven. The best exemplar of this virtue in the *Shu-jing* is the Duke of Zhou, who plays a prominent role in later Chinese dream history.[7] When King Wu died only six years after defeating the Shang, he left his young son in the care of his brother, the Duke of Zhou. The duke protected the boy against possible assassination, and at the same time took charge of successful reforms in agriculture, urban planning, and territorial control. When Wu's son finally came of age, the duke voluntarily yielded his imperial powers and became a faithful subject of the new king. For this selfless act of political and familial devotion, the Duke of Zhou became a revered political figure in Chinese history, the shining model of a good ruler. As we soon shall see, he also became an authoritative guide in the dreams of future generations of Chinese people, including Confucius himself.

Other early Zhou-era texts that became part of the Confucian Classics, such as the *Shi-jing* (*Book of Odes*), reflected the official practice of dream divination:

Your herdsman dreams of multitudes [locusts] and fish, of turtle and serpent and falcon banners.

The chief diviner elucidates their meaning:

The multitudes and fish mean plentiful years.
The turtle and serpent and falcon banners signify an increasing
    population.

Divine my dreams for me; what dreams are auspicious?
They have been of bears;
They have been of serpents.
The chief diviner elucidates their meaning;
The bears are auspicious intimations of sons;
The serpents are auspicious intimations of daughters.[8]

No explanation was offered for these symbolic equivalencies, though it could be significant that all the animals mentioned are "wild," that is, undomesticated, thus representing some degree of autonomy from human control. All the dream animals were interpreted in favorable terms, even the serpent, though the association with daughters (traditionally much less desired than sons) raises doubts. Apparent in these verses is the involvement of the *Tai Pu* in interpreting the dreams not only of kings but of anyone else (like herdsmen) whose dreams might be relevant for community welfare. In ancient China, the king's dreams were definitely the most important, but *anyone* could have a dream that revealed something important for the empire. Signs of new births were especially interesting to both government officials and ordinary people, as everyone felt deeply concerned about the prospects for the next generation. We are already familiar from Hinduism with significant dreams of conception, pregnancy, and childbirth, and we find this same theme throughout the popular dream traditions of Chinese history.

The *Zuo-zhuan* (*Zuo Commentary Tradition*) is another classic historical text from the Zhou era. Dozens of dream stories fill the *Zuo-zhuan*, with images and interpretations that emphasized the danger of disobeying the ancestors.[9] Some stories involved shared dreaming (*tong meng*) in which two people (e.g., a king and a shaman) had the same dream at the same time, a phenomenon taken as additional proof of the dream's importance and veracity. Another *Zuo-zhuan* story described a pair of dreams that were not shared so much as complementary, in a pre-battle context. In 632 BCE, the armies of the Qin and Chu peoples met in a decisive contest, and on the eve of battle their two kings both had dreams that augured their respective fates. Duke Wen of Qin dreamed he was being held down on his back by the Chu leader, who was sucking out his brain matter. When he awoke, Duke Wen was highly alarmed by this bizarre and disgusting dream, but his top minister gave him a surprisingly positive reading of its meaning: "Auspicious! Our side received heaven, while Chu bent face down as if accepting punishment. We have, in addition, softened him!" From an ordinary human perspective, it might have looked like the Chu leader was winning the dream fight, but from a heavenly perspective it was the Jin leader who was facing in the most virtuous direction, that is, toward the sky, which boded well for the Qin in the waking battle to come. The "softening" seemed to be the result of the Qin brain matter (symbolizing intelligence, cunning, guile) passing through the hard teeth (symbolizing weapons and defenses) of the Chu, which again pointed to future military success.

Here we have what I call a *paradoxical interpretation*, in which a dream's true meaning is said to be the opposite of its apparent meaning. The minister, confronted with a frightened and confused leader on the morning of a decisive battle, may have felt a special urgency to discover a paradoxical level of meaning, if only to get the king's mind off the disturbing imagery of the dream's surface content. As it happened, the Qin won the fight, and the minister's paradoxical interpretation was vindicated.

The *Zuo-zhuan* also reported that the Chu leader, Zi Yu, had a prebattle dream that contributed to his side's defeat. In Zi Yu's dream, he was asked by the god of the river to give him a set of beautiful jade ornaments that Zi Yu had specially designed for his horses. In exchange for this sacrifice, the god promised future military success for the Chu. But when Zi Yu woke up, he stubbornly refused to give up the ornaments as requested by the god, even though his advisers and clansmen begged him to do so. His subsequent failure on the battlefield is explained in the *Zuo-zhuan* as the result of disobeying his divine dream. Zi Yu's dream does not directly predict his side's loss, but his unwillingness to heed the dream showed how distant he was from the gods' favor. In the Chinese conception of history, the consequence of such divine alienation is inevitable defeat.

A marvelous story from the *Zuo-zhuan* told of another Qin leader, Duke Jing, who was haunted by a vengeful ancestor from another clan, the Zhao, whose entire population he annihilated in battle:

The Duke of Qin dreamed of a vengeful spirit of immense proportions, with its hair hanging to the ground, beating its chest and leaping. It said,

"For you to murder my progeny was not righteous. I have already gained permission for revenge from the high gods!" Destroying the great door and the bedroom door, it made its entry. The duke was terrified and entered the inner chamber, and the spirit destroyed its door also. The duke woke up and summoned the shaman of Mulberry Fields. What the shaman described corresponded exactly to the dream. The duke said, "What will happen?" He replied, "You will not [live to] eat the grain of the new harvest!" The duke fell ill and sought doctors from Qin. The Qin ruler sent a doctor named Huan to treat the duke. Before he arrived, the duke dreamed of his illness assuming the form of two boys and saying to each other, "He is a skilled doctor, I fear he will harm us, where can we escape?" One of them said, "We will reside above the area between the heart and the diaphragm, and beneath the fat at the tip of the heart —what can he do to us?" The doctor arrived and said, "There is nothing to be done about the illness. It is above the area between the heart and the diaphragm, and beneath the fat at the tip of the heart—where it can neither be attacked [with heat treatment] nor reached [through acupuncture]. Medicine will not get to it. There is nothing to be done." The duke said, "[He is] a good doctor." He gave him handsome gifts and sent him back. In the sixth month, on the *Bing-wu* day, the Duke of Qin wanted to taste the new grain. He had the official in charge present it and the cook prepare it. He summoned the shaman of Mulberry Fields, showed him [the new grain] and had him killed. When he was about to eat, he felt swollen, went to the toilet, fell in, and died. A eunuch had dreamed in the morning of carrying the duke and ascending to heaven. At midday, he carried the Duke of Qin out of the privy; thereupon he was killed to attend the duke in death.

Virtually the whole of early Chinese dream theory is encapsulated in this story. The dream reveals the will of heaven to a ruler who has violated a fundamental tenet of ancestral piety. By slaughtering every member of the Zhao clan, the Duke of Qin left no one alive to continue performing the necessary rites to their ancestors (victorious Chinese kings usually spared at least one member of an opponents' royal family for exactly this reason). The implacable anger of the vengeful spirit is vividly rendered in the duke's dream, with a sense of inescapable pursuit and terrifying vulnerability familiar to anyone who has had a chasing nightmare (or seen a horror movie). Upon awakening, the duke immediately called on a shaman, who was apparently able to describe what happened in the dream before the duke had even told him—a remarkable feat, though one that would be consistent with the powers of spiritual knowledge that shamans were reputed to possess. Unfortunately for the duke, the shaman had no paradoxical interpretation to offer. Instead, he gave a specific and symbolically appropriate prediction of when the duke would die. Unlike Duke Wen's dream, which offered him a chance to alter fate by sacrificing his jade ornaments to the river god, the Duke of Qin's dream left no room for hope. His second dream (which illustrated a traditional belief in the medical significance of dreaming) confirmed his fatal condition. The doctor essentially repeated the shaman's diagnostic practice, telling the duke what he had dreamed and interpreting its meaning. The shaman and the doctor were both correct in their diagnoses, though the duke treated them rather differently. Killing the shaman after showing him the new grain was a spiteful, vainglorious attempt to repudiate the dream prophecy, but death seized the duke all the same, and in a most disgusting and humiliating fashion. Rulers who defy the gods, beware.

Confucian Dreams

Political unity in harmony with the heavens was the supposed ideal of the Zhou dynasty, but in practice every military leader had a different belief about who should be at the top of the dynastic social pyramid. Improved weaponry meant that armed clashes were becoming increasingly bloody and ruthless, with harsh consequences for the already tenuous lives of ordinary farmers and townspeople. At a certain point it no longer mattered who reigned in the Zhou court, because the land had fragmented into so many competing factions that no one ruled over very much for very long. For people who equated social tranquility with heavenly favor, the relentless bloodshed was interpreted as a sign that something was badly amiss in human relations with the ancestors. This prompted an unprecedented burst of philosophical reflection on fundamental questions of nature and society, with a special focus on practical methods of restoring the kind of social peace and prosperity their forefathers had once enjoyed. Later known as the time when "a hundred schools of thought contended," the dynamic debates of this new generation of political philosophers were sponsored by military leaders eager to find any possible source of advantage over their rivals.

Confucius (551–479 BCE) was born into this turbulent time, and he grew up to become the leader of one of those hundred schools of thought. His family name was *Kong,* and he became known as *Kong FuZi,* or Master Kong ("Confucius" is the Latinized version). Coming from a family of modest means in Lu, a small state once governed by the Duke of Zhou, Confucius was three years old when his father died. Most of his early life was devoted to farm labor and clerical work to support his mother and family. After marrying a young girl and fathering a child, he opened a small private school where he taught an increasing number of students his simple, reason-based beliefs about virtue, justice, piety, and political order. Confucius put tremendous emphasis on education. Learning to read and write, to understand important texts from the past, to analyze current political problems in rational, dispassionate terms—these intellectual skills were open to everyone, no matter how humble their background. Confucius held a deep faith in the Chinese people's potential to become civilized, and this faith echoes the egalitarian ideals implicit in some of the dream stories we considered earlier, particularly Wu-Ding's dream that led to the appointment of a commoner, Fu Yue, as prime minister. But whereas Fu Yue was the passive recipient of divine favor, Confucius advocated an active striving for a life of rational clarity and moral virtue. He discouraged speculation about life after death, and he questioned spiritual explanations of natural phenomena. His primary goal was to concentrate his students' minds on the practical application of moral reasoning to the problems of this world.

In the *Analects,* the core collection of his teachings, Confucius praised the Duke of Zhou as the supreme example of a good ruler—humble, intelligent, and respectful of tradition. Despite his generally skeptical attitude toward divination of any kind, Confucius did mention in the *Analects* an interest in his own dreams, specifically his dreams of the Duke of Zhou.[10] In a conversation he had with a student toward the end of his life, Confucius said, "I must be growing weak; I have not dreamed of the Duke of Zhou for a long time now." Confucius evidently dreamed of the Duke of Zhou earlier in his life, and he associated those dreams with a feeling of personal vitality. That would be consistent with his reverence for the Duke in waking life, and with his general philosophical belief in following the guidance of one's ancestors. Confucius's dreams thus expressed a harmony of personal and collective virtue, an internal unity of purpose that inspired his life and philosophy. When the dreams stopped coming, no elaborate divinatory technique was needed to recognize what it foretold.

A later Confucian text, the *Li-ji* (first century BCE), described the last dream the Master was said to have experienced before he died. A disciple came to the aged philosopher one morning and found him singing a mournful song. In response to the student's question about the cause of his sadness, Confucius spoke of different funeral practices and the significance of their ritual details. The Zhou custom was to perform the funeral ceremony at the top of the royal hall's western steps, placing the deceased person in the symbolic position of an honored guest. However, Confucius's family traditionally performed the rites between the two entrance pillars of the hall, in a middle space between the usual positions of host and guest. Confucius then said, "Some nights ago I dreamed that I was sitting between the two pillars, with the sacrificial offerings in full view. Since sage-kings do not arise, who on earth will honor me? I am dying, I suppose." He fell ill soon after, and he died seven days later.

Confucius's melancholy was the result of his recognition that, for all his success in spreading his teachings, he had failed to improve the behavior of the late Zhou rulers. Indeed, the years following his death, a time known as the "Warring States" period (475–221 BCE), brought a complete collapse of Zhou authority and a fragmentation of political power into small, intensely rivalrous regional kingdoms. According to this story in the *Li-ji,* the dying philosopher knew that his political and moral ideals were further from realization than ever, and he knew that no genuine sage-kings had arisen who could rule wisely or perform the necessary and proper rites welcoming him into death. This was the unvarnished reality of his situation at that moment—he was about to die, alone and unheeded. The message of his last dream was as straightforward as he tried to be in his waking life teachings.

Butterflies

In contrast to the reform-minded Confucius, other teachers from the "Hundred Schools of Thought" period rejected the idea of actively working to improve society through moral and political change. As Confucius's career proved, such meddling only made things worse. Other philosophers emphasized the natural way (*Dao*) of the cosmos, in which humans find the greatest harmony and contentment by living a life of passive noninterference (*wu-wei*). The spiritual tradition that grew from their teachings (reified in English as *Daoism*) offered its followers a mysterious, otherworldly process of discovering their own personal connection with the primal energies of creation. The earliest Daoist sages, Lao Zi (third century BCE?) and Zhuang Zi (369–286 BCE) took a decisive turn away from Confucian political activism and toward mystical dimensions of awareness and insight very similar to the *Upanishads* of Hinduism. Particularly in Zhuang Zi's playful, multilayered poetic text known as the "Inner Chapters," the experience of dreaming is mentioned as a direct means of realizing one's innate spiritual freedom:

> When we sleep, our spirits roam. When we wake, we open to the world again. Day after day, all that we touch entangles us, and the mind struggles in that net: vast and calm, deep and subtle.[11]

In the Daoist view the continuity of waking and dreaming was a pathological sign of our existential imprisonment. "Entangling" experiences in the waking world of human society accumulate through life, binding us in ever tighter knots of futile action, despite (and because of) our increasingly desperate attempts to escape. We fail to realize that our true home lies within the ultimate reality of the cosmos, the *Dao*, which is always and everywhere, "vast and calm, deep and subtle." Sleep and dreaming are, at least potentially, a natural opportunity for people to experience that kind of ultimate freedom, where "spirits roam" beyond the limits of mortal bodies, beyond the artificial boundaries created by social authorities.

In a particularly significant departure from Chinese tradition, the Daoists offered an alternative way of understanding the relationship between the living and the dead. They minimized ancestor worship and concentrated instead on each person's existential fear of death, trying to transform that fear into a heightened state of philosophical self-awareness and spiritual tranquility. Key to that process of transformation was a realization that life, death, and all other categories of existence are not real—everything in life is unstable, impermanent, and unpredictable. The natural interplay of waking and dreaming provides the means of illustrating this philosophical insight.

> You might dream that you're drinking fine wine, then the next morning you're weeping and sobbing. You might dream that you're weeping and sobbing, then the next morning you're out on a rollicking hunt. In the midst of a dream, we can't know it's a dream. In the midst of a dream, we might even interpret the dream. After we're awake, we know it was

a dream—but only after a great awakening can we understand that all of this is a great dream. Meanwhile, fools everywhere think they're wide awake. They steal around as if they understood things, calling this a king and that a cowherd. It's incredible! Confucius is a dream, and you are a dream. And when I say you're both dreams, I too am a dream.

Here is the first direct Chinese effort to answer the ontological question of dreaming. Up to this point, the working assumption of Chinese divinatory practice was a direct connection between the ancestral spirits and dreaming, with little speculation about what this connection meant in a grander understanding of reality. Foretelling the future was the only concern. But Daoists like Zhuang Zi took little interest in that kind of divination. Instead, they wanted to question the underlying idea that waking and dreaming are stable, meaningfully related categories of existence (with a not-so-subtle critical jab at social hierarchies and Confucian piety). A good dream might be followed by bad feelings in waking, a bad dream might be followed by a good waking experience—what, Zhuang Zi asks, is the connection? We may think we are awake right now, but while we are asleep we usually don't know we're dreaming, so who knows for sure if they are not dreaming this very moment? The impermanence of this world is revealed in the spontaneous, unpredictable interplay of dreaming and waking, and Zhuang Zi's startling confession that he himself is a dream compels a deeper philosophical question of what it means to be human. The most dramatic expression of that comes in the famous "Butterfly Dream" passage.

Long ago, a certain Zhuang Zi dreamed he was a butterfly—a butterfly fluttering here and there on a whim, happy and carefree, knowing nothing of Zhuang Zi. Then all of a sudden he woke up to find that he was, beyond all doubt, Zhuang Zi. Who knows if it was Zhuang Zi dreaming a butterfly, or a butterfly dreaming Zhuang Zi? Zhuang Zi and butterfly: clearly there's a difference. This is called *the transformation of things.*

The poetic elegance of this story is unique in the history of human dream traditions. To dream of a butterfly is to imagine a life of flying, freedom, and blissful ignorance of all human sorrows. Zhuang Zi's evocation of such a happy dream feeling grew out of his intuitive recognition of the experiential power of people's actual dreams of flying. To this widely experienced and deeply felt dream theme Zhuang Zi added the specific figure of the butterfly, a creature whose life cycle involves a radical transformation of physical structure, from larva to chrysalis to butterfly. Dreaming of this particular creature not only means the power to fly; it also means the experience of transformation itself, life moving effortlessly from one mode of being to another, the *Dao* made manifest. The ultimate awakening leads beyond the question "human or butterfly" to a joyful surrender to the eternal flow of dreaming and waking, reality and unreality, being and becoming, living and dying.

A later Daoist text, the *Lie-zi* (fourth CE?) took this theme of dreaming-waking interaction in a more socially and economically subversive direction:

> Mr. Yin of Zhou managed a large estate. Those who worked for him scuttled about from dawn to dark without respite. There was an old servant whose muscular strength was all spent, yet he was put to work all the harder. By day, whining and groaning, he went about his job. At night, giddy and tired, he fell sound asleep. Then his spirit was set afield, and every night he dreamed that he was a ruler, lording it over the people and in control of all affairs of state. He roamed about and gave banquets in his mansions and palaces, doing as he pleased. His joy was beyond compare.

> Upon awakening, however, he was on the treadmill again. When someone expressed sympathy for his hard lot, the servant said, "A man's life may last a hundred years, which are divided into days and nights. In the daytime I slave it out and, speaking of wretchedness, this is wretched indeed. But at night I become a ruler, and my joy knows no bounds. What is there to care about?"

> Mr. Yin's mind was preoccupied with mundane affairs. His concern revolved around the family inheritance. Thus he wore himself out body and mind. Now, every night he dreamed that he was a bondsman. He scurried about, doing all kinds of menial work. Abused, reviled, caned and whipped, he sustained all manner of ill-treatment. He muttered, mumbled, whined and groaned in his sleep, and found peace only at daybreak.

> Sick of it all, Mr. Yin went to see a friend, who told him, "With a social position high enough to make you distinguished, and with enough assets

and to spare, you are far better than others. If at night you dream that you are a slave, this reversion from ease to suffering proves the constancy of fate. How can you justifiably crave the best of both dream and waking worlds?"

Having listened to his friend, Mr. Yin reduced his servants' workload and his own worries as well. Consequently, his ailment was somewhat relieved.[12]

As in the pre-battle dreams of the leaders of the Chu and Qin armies, Mr. Yin and his old servant experienced complementary dreams that mirrored each other's waking life situations. The lowly servant had good dreams, the powerful master had bad dreams; their social positions while dreaming were the opposite of their social positions while awake. The servant dreamed of being a ruler with infinite power and control over others, and the master dreamed of being a slave with no power or control whatsoever, subject to the wanton abuse of his masters. The two dreams suggested a deeper force of existential balancing at work in human life. The social inequalities of the waking world may be evened out by compensating experiences in the dreaming world.

The parallels were not exact, however. Mr. Yin may have enjoyed wealth and social prominence, but the emotional tenor of his waking life was decidedly negative. Bad feelings plagued him in waking *and* dreaming. Like a dutiful, traditionally virtuous son he worked hard to preserve the family inheritance, but it was (in the Daoist view) precisely these energetic activities that were causing his failing health and restless sleep. Mr. Yin just wanted to make the dreams stop; he wanted to control them just like he controlled his servants in the waking world. His friend was wiser, however, and asked Mr. Yin to reflect instead on the larger existential question of his striving desires. To realize the "constancy of fate" meant surrendering those desires and accepting whatever came in life, whether good or bad, in dreaming or while awake, because whatever happened in one moment would be balanced by something else in another moment. Although his friend offered no specific practical advice, Mr. Yin seemed to have learned something from his words. He lightened the working conditions of his servant and himself, a change that moderated, though did not totally eliminate, the dark clouds of feeling that hung over his days and nights. The implication is that a more humane society is possible in this world, even if active striving always leads to entanglements and suffering.

The text does not say whether the old servant experienced fewer pleasurable dreams after this change; perhaps he would not have cared one way or another.

A final dream story to share from the Daoist tradition is known as *Huang-liang meng*, or "The Yellow Millet Dream."[13] The earliest version is found in the *Zhen Zhongyi* (An Account of What Happened Inside a Pillow) by Shen Yi (eighth century CE). A young man met a Daoist priest at a roadside inn. As they talked about the young man's dissolute life, the innkeeper was steaming a pot of millet (something that would usually take no more than half an hour). The young man grew tired, and the Daoist gave him a strange green porcelain pillow to lay his head upon. The pillow somehow enabled the sleepy young man to suddenly appear back at his home, just like he'd never left. The young man was surprised at this abrupt change in location, but after a while he thought nothing more of it. For the next fifty years he went on with his life, getting married, accumulating wealth, passing the civil service exams, rising in government service, fighting against political enemies, suffering betrayal and defeat, but ultimately succeeding in gaining universal honor and respect. Then one night he became ill and died—and suddenly woke up in the roadside inn. The Daoist priest was still there sitting next to him, and the innkeeper was still cooking the millet. The startled young man was moved to exclaim:

> I know now at last the way of honor and disgrace and the meaning of poverty and fortune, reciprocity of gain and loss and the mystery of life and death, and I owe all this knowledge to you. Since you have thus deigned to instruct me in the vanity of ambition, dare I refuse to profit therefrom?

Even a dream that would seem, according to traditional Chinese divination, to be a clearly auspicious sign of future happiness is portrayed in the Daoist story as a warning against "the vanity of ambition." Even if you lead a good and virtuous life and gain all the wealth and status and family honor you may desire, none of it is any more real than a dream that comes in a few moments of slumber. There is no point in trying to distinguish waking from dreaming, no purpose in worrying about what is real or unreal. Such oppositions are mere fabrications of the human mind, and the *Dao* embraces them all.

The Golden Age

If this were a book devoted entirely to China, now would be the time to talk about Buddhism and its spectacular growth from the arrival of a few Indian monks in the first century CE to thousands of temples and monasteries thriving throughout China by the seventh and eighth centuries CE. In this case, however, we consider Buddhism separately in the next chapter and for now merely note that Buddhism did, in fact, enter China at this time, becoming part of the country's increasingly fertile (and highly contentious) religious landscape. The other spiritual traditions we have discussed—the Confucians, Daoists, and *wu* shamans—continued to prosper as well, remaining highly active in their respective spheres as the centuries unfolded. In actual practice, most Chinese people lived their lives by blending different elements from several traditions. For example, a person might hold Confucian political ideals, practice Buddhist meditation, participate in Daoist rituals, and seek the healing skills of shamans. All the Chinese traditions valued the spiritual potentials of dreaming, and popular interest in dreams expanded dramatically through the next several periods of dynastic rule. By the time of the late Ming (1368–1644) and early Qing (1644–1911) dynasties, the dynamic multiplicity of dream beliefs and practice reached a peak of cultural creativity, inaugurating what I would call a "golden age" of Chinese dreaming. This can be seen in three interrelated areas: popular dream books, incubation practices, and artistic creativity.

The difficulty of learning China's logographic script meant that reading and writing started as elite skills, restricted to those with social and political power. Over time, however, the egalitarian opportunities offered by the civil service exams promoted somewhat greater literacy among the general population, and this had the cumulative effect of strengthening China's cultural cohesiveness by imprinting traditional ideas and values on an increasingly broad range of people. This process was greatly accelerated by the invention of the printing press in the eleventh century CE, which in turn led to the rising production of books aimed at popular audiences. When the Catholic missionary Matteo Ricci first visited China in the early seventeenth century CE, he wrote to his superiors in Rome about "the exceedingly large numbers of books in circulation around here and the ridiculously low prices at which they are sold."[14] Thousands of volumes circulated on such topics as bookkeeping, funeral rituals, moral improvement, language education, and test-preparation materials on the

Confucian Classics. Numerous books were also being printed on the practice of dream interpretation, and these texts both consolidated past traditions and added new refinements.

Two of these dream books are worth considering.[15] The *Meng-zhan-lei-kao* (A Categorical Study of Dream Interpretation), written in the late sixteenth century CE by Zhang Fengyi, presented itself as a systematic survey of all Chinese knowledge relating to dreams. Zhang Fengyi said that he decided to write the book because of a beneficial dream of his own:

> Some years ago I had an illness so serious that both physicians and quacks could do nothing about it. I recovered, however, thanks to a dream. Then I thought: Although the secret art of the ancient sages had got lost in translation, the proven cases on record could still be verified. Thus, I traced the source to the Six Classics and searched through the histories, relating my findings to various other texts, tangentially touching on writings of a fictive nature as well. No matter how remote or recent it might be, or whether the people involved were Chinese or outlandish, so long as the material provided some evidence for dreams, I would pick and include it in this work, which I have entitled *Meng-zhan-lei-kao*.

Zhang Fengyi applied the same diligent scholarly approach to the study of dreams that Confucian scholars had long been applying to other phenomena of the natural world. His dream of healing inspired him to work toward the recovery of this "secret art" of dream interpretation; what better evidence of the power of dreams than one's own dreaming experience? He said past generations had their own famous experts in this art, but in more recent times it had fallen into neglect and disrepute to the point where "people had lost so much interest in it [dream interpretation] that some crafty ones in the book market appropriated the name 'Duke of Zhou.'" In fact, many dream books circulating at this time did claim to be written by the legendary duke, and at least some people took his authorship seriously. Zhang Fengyi argued that the Duke of Zhou never wrote any of these books, and readers should use their common sense in evaluating the fantastic claims made in their pages. His approach, by contrast, was grounded in actual texts and references not only from the Confucian Classics but also from the widest possible gathering of relevant information about dreams. A strong empirical spirit permeated the analysis of dreams in the *Meng-zhan-lei-kao*.

Similarly, the *Meng-zhan-yi-zhi* (An Easy Guide to Dream Divination) by the late Ming writer Chen Shiyuan based its claims on extensive observations of people's actual dreams. These observations led to the development of a few basic methods for discerning the meaning(s) of a dream. Many cases could be interpreted as fairly straightforward messages of advice and warning from ancestral spirits. Others could be understood in relation to classic dream images or cultural themes from Chinese history or both. Still others were analyzed according to word structure and linguistic usage. A well-known example of this type concerned the Yellow Emperor of ancient times, who had a dream in which he saw a mighty wind blowing away the dust and dirt, and then a man with an enormously heavy cross-bow leading a herd of sheep. The emperor interpreted the dream to mean that he had to find a new prime minister named *Feng* (wind) *Hou* (dirt/leader) who would sweep the royal palace of corruption, and a man named Li (strength) *Mu* (shepherd) to serve as a general in his army. Several other dreams in the *Meng-zhan-yi-zhi,* and in other contemporary dream books, included similar interpretations where reference was made to puns, word play, and logographic similarities (e.g., a dream of a turtle [*gui*] means that something good and honorable [*gui*] will happen).

Caution was urged in the *Meng-zhan-yi-zhi* and other dream books regarding the use of fixed interpretive categories. The same dream could have different meanings for different people, depending on their particular life circumstances. Chen Shiyuan was clear on this point, stating that good dreams will not necessarily come true for unlucky people, whereas bad dreams may not harm lucky people. A frequently cited story in the dream books referred to the dream specialist Zhou Xuan from the Three Kingdoms period (220–265 CE), who interpreted three dreams a man experienced of the same image (straw dogs) as foretelling three different outcomes (eating good food, a painful fall from a carriage, and a house fire). All three predictions came true, and Xuan explained his reasoning thus:

> Straw dogs are sacrificial offerings to the gods. Hence, your first dream meant you would get food and drink. When the sacrifice is over, the straw dogs are crushed under a wheel, thus your second dream prefigured your fall from a carriage, ending in broken legs. When the straw dogs have been crushed, they are bound to be carted away as firewood. And so the last dream warned you of fire.[16]

Zhou Xuan's seemingly arbitrary interpretation was, in fact, based on the parallel between a series of dreams and a series of ritual and post-ritual actions. In a culture where sacrificial ceremonies are part of everyone's life, making a symbolic connection between inner dream and external ritual has a fair degree of plausibility. The final twist to the story is that the dreams were not "real"—the man admitted he made them up to test Xuan's skill. Xuan replied, in good Daoist fashion, "It was the spirits that moved you and made you say those things; that's why they were no different from real dreams." Made-up dreams and real dreams, there's no ultimate distinction; they all come from the same place, caused by the same spiritual powers, leading along the same path.

Most dream books included at least a few theoretical comments explaining the formation and functions of dreaming. The consensus view, which drew upon philosophical teachings reaching back to the Han dynasty, spoke of *Hun* and *Po* as two vital aspects of the self or soul, with the *Hun* liberated during sleep to journey in spirit realms while the *Po* remained with the slumbering body (echoing earlier shamanic dream practices).[17] The dream books of the Ming and Qing era also referred to ancient classifications of dream phenomenology, categorizing the different types of *Hun* soul experience.[18] The earliest of these systems came from Confucian writers in the Zhou and Han dynasties. The *Zhouli* (The Rites of Zhou) presented a six-dream typology:

1. *Zheng-meng*, regular or positive dreams; usually forgotten, inconsequential.
2. *E-meng*, nightmares, with groaning and screaming during sleep; caused by evil actions from the previous day.
3. *Si-meng*, yearning dreams; caused by excessive thinking, worry, preoccupation with some problem.
4. *Wu-meng*, transient-state dreams; occurring just as a person falls asleep or wakes up.
5. *Xi-meng*, happy dreams; related to happy events in a person's past or future.
6. *Qu-meng*, fearful dreams; continuing fears a person experienced when awake.

A later text, the *Qian-fu-lun* (Essays by a Hermit) by Wang Fu, revised and expanded this system. The result was a ten-dream typology:

1. *Zhi-meng*, straightforward or literal dreams, with a direct connection between dream content and future events.

2. *Xiang-meng* (a), symbolic dreams of future events; examples are given from the *Shi-jing*, such as dreams of bears portend sons, dreams of serpents foretell daughters.

3. *Jing-meng*, earnest thinking dreams, a continuation of focused concentration from waking through sleeping and dreaming; an example is Confucius's dreams of the Duke of Zhou.

4. *Xiang-meng* (b), pensive or longing dreams, resulting from a person's worried preoccupation with a waking life problem.

5. *Ren-meng*, personal dreams whose meanings are relative to the dreamer's life circumstances (e.g., wealth, social status, age, gender); a dream that is good for a rich person might mean something bad for a poor person.

6. *Gan-meng*, dreams reflecting the influence of the climate, with dark, cold weather prompting gloomy dreams.

7. *Shi-meng*, time dreams, reflecting the changes of the seasons; hence growing dreams in the spring, hot dreams in the summer, harvest dreams in autumn, storage dreams in the winter.

8. *Fan-meng*, paradoxical or oppositional dreams; the pre-battle dream of the Jin ruler is offered as the prime example.

9. *Bing-meng*, pathological dreams reflecting and in some cases anticipating illness; useful as a tool of medical diagnosis.

10. *Xing-meng*, affective dreams reflecting the character or personality of the dreamer; virtuous people usually have good dreams and evil people usually have bad dreams, although caution is advised about interpreting anyone's dreams without taking their individual circumstances into account.

Without having space to analyze these typologies in the detail they deserve, we can note the following. First, these two classifications (and the many others that proliferated in Chinese history) recognized the multiplicity of dreaming—the variations of cause, function, and significance that made it challenging, but not impossible, to interpret their meanings. Second, they understood the continuity between waking life concerns and dream content, with particular emphasis on the frequency of anxious dreams and nightmares. People tend to worry about their problems in waking life, and those feelings show up in their dreams. Third, the Chinese typologies allowed for the possibility that some dreams are influenced by physiological or environmental conditions or both (very much in keeping with traditional cosmology). And, fourth, along with these naturalistic and fairly commonsensical observations, the Chinese dream classifiers also identified a small portion of dreams as spiritual in origin, positive in feeling, and truthful in predictive significance.

It should be noted that a thread of rationalist skepticism runs through the history of Chinese dreaming. From early times, some people rejected the whole superstitious business of popular dream interpretation. Foremost among these skeptics was Wang Chong (27–97 CE) of the Han dynasty, who sharply questioned the common belief that each human has an immortal soul apart from his or her material body. Why, he asked, do spirits always appear wearing clothes? Do clothes have spirits, too, that accompany their wearers to Heaven? Or are there heavenly clothes makers awaiting us once we get there? Wang Chong took the same dim view of popular beliefs in the reality of dreams:

> The meaning of dreams is dubious. Some say that dreams are [caused by] the subtle spirit which lingers by itself in the body, thus producing good and evil signs. Others say that the subtle spirit acts and intermingles with people and things. . . . Some say that people may also have literal dreams. One saw A [in a dream] and the next day one indeed saw A. One saw Mr. X [in a dream] and the next day one indeed saw Mr. X. Yes, people may also have literal dreams. But such dreams consist in images. It is their imageries that are literal. How do we demonstrate this? When a literal dreamer saw A or Mr. X in a dream, and the next day he indeed saw A or Mr. X, this [type of dream] is literal. If we asked A or Mr. X, however, neither of them would [say they had] seen [the dream]. If neither of them saw the dreamer, then the A and the Mr. X seen in the dream were nothing but images that looked like them.[19]

Wang Chong remained a minority voice in the broader sweep of the Chinese dream tradition. But his key insight about imagery in dreams was prescient in its anticipation of cognitive scientific approaches to dreaming in the contemporary West.

The strong Chinese interest in classifying dreams went hand in hand with practical efforts to cultivate and influence them. Rituals to fend off bad dreams were called *rang-meng,* and praying for good dreams was called *qi-meng.* Dream incubation flourished during the late Ming and Qing dynasties, with people sleeping in temples, caves, graveyards, and wilderness sanctuaries in the hope of securing an auspicious message from the spirits relating to an urgent worry or desire. A text by Zhou Lianggong

(1612–1672 CE) described a beautiful incubation site in the mountains of Fujian province called *Xian-men-dong* (Cave of the Immortals' Gate), surrounded by trees, high cliffs, and waterfalls, where people had dreams that were "marvelously efficacious."[20] As might be expected, many of the dream supplicants were students seeking divine guidance in preparing for their exams, and numerous incubation sites catered specifically to these anxious young scholars. Dream incubation was also regularly practiced at the temple to the *Cheng-huang-ye* (God of Walls and Moats) found in most Chinese cities. Particularly during Ming times, any official entering a city was obligated to spend a night in the temple in order to receive dream instructions on proper behavior, and judges sometimes slept in the temple if they needed help deciding a difficult case.

Even skeptical Confucian philosophers saw some benefit in trying to influence their dreams. The Qing scholar Wei Xiang-shu (1617–1687 CE) equated good dreams with a virtuous personality and bad dreams with an unsettled mind: "If our mind is at ease, so will be our speech and action. If our speech and action are at ease, so will be our *Hun* [dream soul]."[21] The practice of dream incubation naturally followed from such a view: "To be able to hold one's own while dreaming is a sign of consummate scholarship. Such an ability ensures orderliness in the management of important affairs. My own experience has attested to this." Here is another appeal to personal experience as valid evidence in the study of dreams. Wei himself apparently developed the ability to control his dreaming in such a way that his waking mind's orderliness carried over into sleep, allowing him to "hold his own" during the emotional chaos of dreaming. Seeking such an ability would make good sense for a Confucian philosopher (perhaps even for a skeptic like Wang Chong), though the majority of people practicing dream incubation were much more interested in the classic questions of Chinese divination: What do the ancestors want of me? Will I pass the exams? What will the future bring for my family and my community?

Another area of "golden age" dreaming to consider involves the literary arts. The Ming and Qing dynasties were times of great theatrical creativity, and the scripts of popular plays were printed and widely available for new performances. The Daoist story of *Huang-liang-meng* (The Dream of Yellow Millet) was a popular drama, and the Ming playwright Tang Xianzu wrote a version of it titled *The Dream of Han Tan*.[22] Xianzu also wrote *Peony Pavilion*, a romantic comedy in which a girl dreams continuously of a young scholar whom she is forbidden to see. She eventually dies of sadness, and then she begins appearing in the young man's dreams, beckoning him to visit her grave and open her coffin. He does so, and miraculously the girl comes back to life, revived by his love. The play ends with the scholar finishing first in his exams, after which he marries the girl, and the whole family embraces in happiness. Whatever you think of magical tales like this, the fictional dreams portrayed in these plays were entirely consistent with the long, rich Chinese dream tradition, vividly displaying centuries-old beliefs about dreaming, death, and desire.

By all accounts, the greatest literary creation of this era was the *Hong-lou-meng* (Dream of the Red Chambers).[23] Written by Cao Xueqin (1715–1764), the 120-chapter novel follows the lives of the Jia family, a moderately wealthy and socially prominent clan living in imperial Beijing. The story is framed by a mythic encounter between a Buddhist monk, a Daoist priest, and a divine piece of jade, which was witnessed in a dream by the man (Zhen Shiyin) whose subsequent actions, both good and bad, set the narrative in motion. Several dream episodes are recounted that illuminate additional dimensions of plot, character, and mood. One of these episodes is a straightforward spirit visitation from a character who was about to die (Chin-shih), warning her friend (Shen-shen) to be careful of future threats:

> It was not until after midnight that she began to feel sleepy. Suddenly through her drowsy eyes, she saw Chin-shih standing before her. "What a time to be sleeping," Chin-shih said with a smile. "I am going away, and you do not even get up to see me off. But I cannot go without saying good-bye to you. Besides, there is something I can confide to no one but you. . . . Our family has prospered for over a hundred years. If one day misfortune should overtake us, would it not be laughable if we were as unprepared for it as the proverbial monkeys when their tree home falls from under them?"

Chin-shih went on to provide a detailed and quite sensible economic plan to insure that Shen-shen and her family would always have enough money to worship their ancestors properly.

Another dramatic dream episode from the *Hong-lo-meng* involved the novel's protagonist Bao Yu, a moody adolescent boy who essentially lost his virginity to the "Goddess of Disillusionment" in a dream. Bao Yu fell asleep in Chin-shih's bedroom one afternoon, and in a dream the beautiful Chin-shih gave way to the figure of the Goddess, who invited him to listen to a series of twelve songs she created, called "Dream of the Red Chamber." She then guided him on a strange journey of spiritual vision and poetic mystery, leading ultimately to a chamber "where to his astonishment he found a girl who reminded him of Precious Virtue [a major character in the novel] in graciousness of manner and of Black Jade [another major character] in beauty of features." Unsure of what to do, Bao Yu heard the Goddess speaking to him:

> It is necessary for you to experience what most men experience, so that you may know its nature and limitations. I have therefore arranged that you should marry my sister Jian-mei [lit. "combining the best features of both"]. This is the night for you to consummate your union. After you have seen for yourself that the pleasures of fairyland are but thus and so, you may perhaps realize their vanity and turn your mind to the teachings of Confucius and Mencius and devote your efforts to the welfare of mankind.

The Goddess's plan did not turn out quite like she expected. Bao Yu proceeded to "disport himself with his bride in ways that may well be imagined but may not be detailed here." He then awakened in a cold sweat, crying out with fear. The maids came rushing into the room to see if he was all right. One of the maids noticed something "cold and clammy" on his bedclothes, and she brought him a change of clothing. Bau Yu told her of his dream, blushing when he got to the part about the bridal chamber. When she blushed in return, he offered to "demonstrate what the Goddess had taught him." The maid found this an appealing prospect, and she thereafter became his secret consort.

Dreaming in Modern China

The wealth of dream teachings from China's ancestral past provided its people with a valuable source of cultural continuity through the dark times that began in the nineteenth century in the final years of the Qing dynasty. This was, by any reckoning, a terrible and humiliating era for the Chinese. From the outside they suffered relentless military defeats by Britain, Japan, and various European colonial powers. From the inside, the government's authority was battered by marauding groups of rebels and bandits. Physically weakened and emotionally dispirited, many Chinese naturally interpreted their plight in terms of a failure of proper ancestral reverence. A late Qing writer, Chen Shiyuan, described a dream incident that encapsulated the tragic condition of his time (1856):

> The *Zhou Li* speaks of an officer for dream divination, who interprets good and bad dreams in many ways. It is a pity that this art is now lost. . . . My late wife Madame Wen became ill during the epidemic. Then my father unaccountably dreamed of my late mother. He took the occasion to tell her, "Do you know that our daughter-in-law is dying?" "She's lucky," said my mother. On waking, my father said to me, "Your wife is dying and your mother says it is her luck. I am afraid the ravages of war will soon reach our province." And, indeed, in the following year, Jin-hua [his province] was attacked by the bandits, and two years later the whole of Chekiang fell. Our family had to evacuate and disperse, resulting in nine deaths. They were all cursorily interred, without ceremony. It was indeed good fortune that my wife had died beforehand.[24]

A dream of a beloved ancestor would usually be a cause for relief and reassurance, but in these times her words convey a paradoxical meaning: To be lucky is to die now, before things get even worse. Shiyuan and his family maintained a degree of connection with the ancestors, just as Chinese people traditionally had done since the earliest dynasties. Yet that traditional world was falling apart all around them, unable to survive except, perhaps, in their dreams.

Summary

The history of religiously significant dreaming in China includes the shamanistic practices of the early imperial dynasties, the rationalist philosophy of Confucius, the mystical musings of the Daoists, and the artistic and literary creativity of the Ming and Qing dynasties.[25] Most of these traditions recognize a divine origin for dreaming, although some Chinese teachings either downplay the importance of dreams (the Confucians) or dismiss them as illusions (the Daoists). In terms of sleep physiology, the Chinese have generally accepted the idea that dreaming occurs when the *Hun* soul is liberated from the body during sleep. The primary function of dreaming has always been to communicate with the ancestors, that is, with deceased family members who provide their living relatives with helpful messages or frightening warnings or both. To interpret their dreams, the Chinese have used various divinatory methods: comparing dream images to common symbols from waking life, linguistically analyzing them for puns and word play, and religiously associating them to classic texts and beloved teachers. Some Chinese people have reported dreams so vivid and realistic that the dreams seem to need no interpretation at all, and the Daoists have claimed that the ultimate interpretation is to let go of the grasping, entangling desire to know what any dream means.

3

Buddhism

A good case can be made that Buddhism is not so much a religion as a psychology. Its focus on the systematic analysis of mental processes, along with its experimental methods of changing and redirecting those processes, give Buddhism much in common with cognitive science in the contemporary West. The similarities should not be pushed too far, because the Buddha's teachings encompass much more than psychology, but it is helpful to keep these cognitive dimensions in mind as we begin to consider the dream traditions of Buddhism. Many of the topics of greatest interest to Western psychology—vision, memory, language, emotion, attention, dreaming—have a long history of discussion among Buddhist monks and laypeople. It is fair to say that in terms of understanding the nature and potential of the human mind, Buddhism anticipated by many centuries the research of modern-day Western scientists.

A term useful in this discussion is *metacognition,* the hallmark of which is self-reflection: thinking about thinking, awareness of awareness, knowing that one is knowing.[1] In other words, metacognition involves the mind considering itself, stretching out the time between perception and action, taking its own processes as objects of thought. It also includes pondering one's options ("should I do this or that?"), making plans for future action, monitoring one's inner feelings, and regulating the expression of desires and wishes. Metacognition has long been assumed by many Western psychologists to be essentially absent in dreaming. In this commonly held view, dreams are primarily characterized by deficiencies of mental functioning, particularly a lack of metacognition. When people fall asleep and dream, they lose their awareness of where they really are (asleep in bed) and hallucinate about being in other places (a foreign country, outer space, a strange house). People accept all sorts of bizarre, incongruous occurrences in dreams without critical thought or questioning. A football can morph into a sheep, a bedroom may suddenly transform into a jungle, a character's face changes from one person to another

—none of this strikes the dreamer as odd. It is all accepted as normal by the sleep-diminished mind. In sum, dreams are a hodge-podge of illogical ideas, inexplicable behavior, and failures of memory, all indicating a severe deficit of metacognitive abilities found in a normal waking state.

That, at any rate, is the general version of the "deficit theory" endorsed by many leading researchers.[2] A conceptual problem for most versions of this theory is the occurrence of authentically metacognitive phenomena in dreaming—often referred to as "lucid dreaming," the experience of being aware within the dream state that you are dreaming. The simple fact that people have this experience means that metacognitive abilities are not entirely absent in dreaming but are *variable* in their activation. A simple opposition of clear waking thought and garbled dreaming nonsense must yield to a more complex picture in which the human brain-mind system possesses many abilities that operate in various combinations across the waking-sleeping cycle. You do not have to delve into ancient religious history to realize this is true—a moment's reflection on your own dreaming will probably suffice. Most people have had at least one dream in which they had some degree of awareness that they were dreaming. Many others have had the experience of watching a dream from a floating, disembodied perspective, or simultaneously watching a dream and participating in it, or going into a dream *within* a dream. Ordinary dreams also include much of the same mental activity that characterizes the waking state: thinking over ideas, formulating plans, making decisions, wondering about strange events, controlling your physical needs, and so on. All these phenomena indicate the activity in dreaming of a remarkable variety of high-order metacognitive processes.

The metacognitive potentials of dreaming have been recognized in the Buddhist tradition from its very inception, and the story of that tradition revolves largely around people's efforts to cultivate those innate psychological potentials for specifically religious purposes.

Queen Maya's Conception Dream

In contrast to Hinduism and Chinese religions, whose origins are difficult if not impossible to identify, Buddhism's founding can be specified with a fair degree of certainty. Siddhartha Gautama was born in 563 BCE, a prince in a royal family that ruled in northeast India. At the age of twenty-nine he sat down to meditate under a bodhi tree in a forest near present-day Benares, where he experienced Enlightenment and became the Buddha ("The Awakened One"). His life and teachings formed the core of the Buddhist tradition, which spread from its Indian roots to become the faith of hundreds of millions of people throughout Asia, and now millions of people in North America and Europe as well. Buddhism has changed, adapted, and transformed itself wherever it has been practiced, and yet all the different branches remain connected by a shared veneration for Siddhartha's life story and the path he followed to achieve Enlightenment. More interesting from our point of view, is that all the earliest biographies of the Buddha begin his story with a dream that his mother, Queen Maya, experienced.[3] Here is a version from the *Nidana-Katha,* an ancient text from the Therevada school of Buddhism:

> At that time the Midsummer festival was proclaimed in the city of Kapilasvatthu. . . . During the seven days before the full moon Maya had taken part in the festivities. . . . On the seventh day she rose early, bathed in scented water, and distributed alms. . . . Wearing splendid clothes and eating pure food, she performed the vows of the holy day. Then she entered her bed chamber, fell asleep, and saw the following dream:

> The four guardians of the world lifted her on her couch and carried her to the Himalaya Mountains and placed her under a great *sala* tree. . . . Then their queens bathed her . . . dressed her in heavenly garments anointed with perfumes and put garlands of heavenly flowers on her. . . . They laid her on a heavenly couch, with its head toward the East. The future Buddha, wandering as a superb white elephant . . . approached her from the North. Holding a white lotus flower in his trunk, he circumambulated her three times. Then he gently struck her right side, and entered her womb.

Recall the discussion in chapter 1 regarding Vedic teachings about dreaming in relation to sexuality, conception, and pregnancy, and recall, too, the similar conception dream of Devananda, the mother of Mahavira, the founder of the Jainist tradition. Mahavira was Siddhartha's contemporary, and both were part of a broader cultural reaction at that time against what they perceived as an overly restrictive Brahmanic religious authority and social order. Their mothers each had an auspicious dream of bearing a son, which in traditional Vedic terms would be the highest good one could ever ask. Yet, in these two cases, the dreams heralded the birth of sons who would grow up to renounce Brahmanic ideals and create a radically different spiritual path. In Buddha's case, when the Brahmans heard of Queen Maya's dream, they said it predicted two possibilities: one, that she would bear a son who would become a universal ruler; or, two, that her son would one day choose to become a celibate renunciant who would save all humankind. This meant that Queen Maya did not directly give birth to the Buddha; rather, she gave birth to the *potential* of Buddhahood.

Looking at the story in relation to the other dreams we have considered thus far, we can see clear elements of an incubation ritual in Maya's dream. It came at the climax of a religious festival, after she had purified herself and performed the proper ritual duties. Though she evidently did not intend or expect such a divine dream, everything she did in her eminently virtuous life was, in effect, preparing her for it. The dream began in her customary place of sleeping, from which it transported her (and her bed) through the air to the highest mountains in the world, the place where earth and the heavens meet. The experience of flying was joined with the beautiful aesthetic qualities of the dream and the majestic white elephant to create a positive, enjoyably stimulating atmosphere. Elephants were traditionally associated with Hindu royalty, both human and divine. Earthly kings used them as formidable weapons in war, and the supreme god Indra rode an elephant as his mount. Perhaps Maya might have preferred a human consort in her dream—that we do not know—but if she had to receive the attentions of any animal, an elephant would be the most powerful and prestigious of all. The phallic movement and magical potency of his trunk suggests an awareness of sexual symbolism in dreaming, though without any particular feelings of shame or repression. Indeed, the story makes it clear that the Buddha impregnated his own mother, creating himself through an act of divine incest. A forceful rejection of Brahmanic moral authority is expressed in this mythic rejection of a human father for the Buddha—his birth, his life, his self-directed creation involved an entirely different generative process from that of ordinary human reproduction.

The story of Queen Maya's dream has been frequently and reverently portrayed in paintings, sculptures, and stories throughout Buddhist history. Whether it actually happened is another question. The similarities between the dreams of Maya and Devananda indicate a kind of sub-genre of sacred biography in which the legitimacy of a new religious leader was demonstrated by post-hoc stories of divine conception within a dream. That was surely true to some extent in Buddhism and Jainism, and it accounts for the stylized, well-polished quality of the stories. It is also true that, whether or not the dreams actually occurred, we learn something important about the *beliefs* of Buddhists and Jainists by examining their conception dream stories. And, as already discussed, we should not forget that people's beliefs about dreams have a tangible impact on their actual experiences in dreaming. The story of Maya's conception dream both reflected and stimulated a propensity of the dreaming imagination (particularly in women) to envision a blissful process of bringing new life into being.

Dreams of the Awakening One

The early life of Queen Maya's son, Siddhartha, followed the conventional, highly privileged course of events for a young prince of his time and place. He grew up in a safe and prosperous kingdom, became skilled at martial combat, married a princess, and fathered a child. Considered in light of traditional Hindu values, he was enjoying an ideal existence. Everything changed, however, when at the age of twenty-nine he ventured outside the palace walls and found himself confronted by shocking sights of aging, sickness, and death. The discovery that his pleasurable life within the palace was hiding him from the real pain and misery of human existence led Siddhartha to decide that he must renounce the world and seek truth, wisdom, and tranquility as a wandering ascetic. The night before he was planning to make his secret departure from the palace, his wife, Gopa, awoke with the following nightmare (described in the ca. third-century-CE Sanskrit text the *Lalitavistara*):

> She sees the whole earth, including oceans and mountain peaks, shaken, and trees broken by wind. The sun, moon, and stars fall from the sky. She sees her hair cut off by her left hand and her crown fallen. Then her hands and feet cut off, and she is naked, her pearl necklaces and jewels broken and strewn about. She sees her bed broken, lying on the floor, the king's parasol broken and fallen ornaments carried away in a river. Her husband's ornaments, clothing, and crown are scattered in disorder on their bed. She sees light coming from the city, which is plunged in darkness. The beautiful nets made of precious materials are broken, and the pearl garlands have fallen. The great ocean is in turmoil, and Mount Meru is shaken to its foundations.[4]

By any traditional Hindu reckoning, this was *not* an auspicious dream. More than anything else, it sounded like one of the pre-battle nightmares that plagued the villains in the mythological warfare of the *Mahabharata* and the *Ramayana*. The destruction of Gopa's body and personal identity is accompanied by social decay, global upheaval, and cosmic chaos. If Mount Meru, the very center of the universe, is shaken to its foundations, clearly something horrendous is about to happen. The details of Gopa's dream strongly suggested that it would be the death of her husband, since Hindu widows were compelled to cut off their hair and stop wearing jewelry. But when Gopa described the dream to Siddhartha, he gave a paradoxical interpretation:

> Be joyful, these dreams are not evil. Beings who have previously practiced good works have such dreams. Miserable people have no such dreams. Seeing the earth shaken and the mountain peaks fallen to earth means that the gods, *nagas, raksasas,* and *bhutas* will render you the greatest homage. Seeing trees uprooted, and your hair cut off with your left hand means that soon you will cut the nets of passion and remove the veil of false views that obscures the conditions of the world. Seeing the sun, moon, stars, and planets fall means that soon, having conquered the passions, you will be praised and honored. . . . Be joyful, not sad; be content and satisfied. Soon you will be delighted and content. Be patient, Gopa; the omens are auspicious.

Siddhartha's interpretation was paradoxical because it claimed that the true meaning of the dream was the exact opposite of its apparent meaning. He denied the customary, common-sense belief in a direct continuity of dream content and waking reality, and he offered instead a reevaluation of the dream according to a spiritually transcendent perspective. Siddhartha's situation is similar in some ways to that of the Chinese minister who interprets Duke Wen's pre-battle dream, the one about his opponent pinning him to the ground and sucking out his brains. Like the Chinese minister, Siddhartha's interpretation turned a bad dream into a good one, a cause of alarm into an occasion for joy. And like the minister, Siddhartha had a personal stake in successfully persuading the dreamer not to dwell on coming dangers but to trust in the ultimate goodness of a higher religious vision. The minister needed to keep his military leader focused and self-confident, and Siddhartha needed to keep his wife ignorant of his impending flight. The difference between the two cases is that the minister's interpretation came true (Duke Wen defeated his enemies and won the next day's battle), whereas Siddhartha's did not (Gopa lost her husband the next day and effectively became a widow). Or, rather, Siddhartha's interpretation both did and did not come true: Gopa's dream accurately foretold her imminent estrangement from her husband, *and* it prophetically revealed a new spiritual wisdom that sought true reality beyond the expectations, values, and attachments of this world. Gopa's dream predicted the death of her husband at the same time that it anticipated the birth of the new religious path of Buddhism. Progress along that path depended on the abandonment of earthly desires, meaning that a dream of the world falling apart would now be interpreted as an auspicious sign of spiritual development. As Siddhartha himself said, such nightmarish dreams only come to those who have attained a certain level of religious merit. The continuity of dreaming and waking was thus broken at one level, only to be reestablished at a loftier spiritual level.

Siddhartha went on to tell Gopa about the dreams that holy men experience just before they leave their homes and families.[5] Presumably he was including himself in that company, and so the following represented the Buddha's own dream experiences of spiritual awakening:

He saw his hands and feet stir the water of the four great oceans, and the whole earth became a well-adorned bed with Mount Meru as a pillow.

He saw a light spread throughout the world, dispelling darkness, and a parasol came out of the earth, spreading light in the three worlds and extinguishing suffering.

Four black and white animals licked his feet.

Birds of four colors became a single color.

He climbed a mountain of repulsive dung, and was not soiled by it.

To be sure, these were marvelous and symbolically rich dreams. Interpreted in traditional continuity terms (i.e., not paradoxically), they augured a future of harmony, power, and salvation. The whole cosmos would become a personal bed for Siddhartha to sleep upon, and when he awakened from that slumber he would heal and enlighten all who live in the three worlds. He would be shown reverence by all creatures, he would magically unite all that appears different, and his teachings would remain pure despite his struggles with the disgusting morass of human society. Once awakened, he would bring spiritual illumination to a dark and ignorant world. And this, we are told in the biographies, was exactly what happened. Siddhartha slipped out of the palace at night while everyone else was asleep (some texts emphasize his feeling of revulsion at the sight of the sprawled, drooling, half-naked bodies of the palace's sleeping servants and dancing girls), and he set out wandering in quest of a new truth. Setting aside both Brahmanic worldliness and Jainist asceticism, Siddhartha sought a middle way, pursuing a spiritual purification of the mind through meditation. The precise moment of his Enlightenment came in what sounds very much like a dream incubation ritual. Siddhartha sat under a sacred bodhi tree at nightfall on the anniversary of his birth, with a full moon in the sky, and vowed not to move until he discovered the ultimate truth of reality. The demon Mara appeared and tried to stop Siddhartha by attacking him all night long with vicious armies, sensual temptations, elemental storms, and cruel taunts. But the purity of Siddhartha's intention was strong enough to defeat everything Mara threw at him, and as dawn broke he arose enlightened, the Awakened One at last.

It is interesting to note that some of the biographies describe a long, harrowing nightmare suffered by the evil Mara just before Siddhartha's Enlightenment. Once again, the Buddhist approach to dreaming takes a well-known genre (i.e., the pre-battle nightmare) and transforms it into a spiritual allegory, elevating it from a worldly to an otherworldly context. The dream content may be the same but our perspective on it has changed, and that in turn helps to change our perspective in *all* states of awareness.

The prominence of dreams in the life story of the Buddha signaled an extremely high veneration for dreaming as an agent of spiritual insight. Through his dreams Siddhartha became the Awakened One—his dreaming prepared his awakening. And once awakened, he evidently never dreamed again. The Buddha's Enlightenment seemed to have created in him a state of mind beyond dreaming (implying that a person who still dreamed was definitely *not* enlightened). As a result, Buddhism taught a fundamental depreciation of dreaming, a belief that it is no better than the waking state in its ultimate inferiority to enlightened consciousness. Still, dreams were valued by Buddhists as meaningful guides in spiritual development, and Siddhartha himself said that dreams accurately reflect the religious character of the dreamer, with the potential to reveal important developments in one's future. Hence, the dual view that has characterized Buddhist dream theory from the beginning: dreams are ultimately illusory, the product of a pre-Enlightenment mind, but they can also beneficially influence a person's progress along the path toward final awakening.

Questions of King Milinda

The spread of the Buddha's teachings was energetically promoted by a loyal community of monks (the *sangha*) who, like Siddhartha, renounced their families and became devoted seekers of Enlightenment. Over the coming centuries they traveled throughout Asia, converting people everywhere they went. A few of the converts became monks, but most became lay Buddhists, ordinary people who gave alms to support the *sangha* and followed the basic moral teachings of the Buddha (while maintaining a multitude of pre-Buddhist religious beliefs and traditions). Large populations of people were at least nominally converted to Buddhism by virtue of royal decree, as some of the early Buddhist monks were especially successful at converting the political rulers of large and important Asian kingdoms. From a missionary perspective it was an excellent strategy—convert the king, and the rest of the country will follow.

A long and fascinating text describing one such missionary encounter is the *Milinda-panha* (*Questions of King Milinda*), from the second century BCE. King Milinda (probably synonymous with King Menander, the Indo-Greek ruler of northern India at that time) engaged in a long conversation with a monk named Nagasena, who endeavored to teach the king the basic principles of Buddhism.[6] After lengthy discursions into various complex existential questions, the discussion turned to dreaming, and Milinda asked Nagasena to explain some of the natural, easily observable features of human dream experience.

> Venerable Nagasena, men and women in this world see dreams pleasant and evil, things they have seen before and things they have not, things they have done before and things they have not, dreams peaceful and terrible, dreams of matters near to them and distant from them, full of many shapes and innumerable colors. What is this that men call a dream, and who is it who dreams it?

In just a few short sentences the king does a wonderful job of evoking the multidimensional range and diversity of dreaming. In so doing he placed a heavy explanatory burden on the Buddhist monk, asking him to account for the infinite pluralism of dreaming experience. And if that wasn't enough of a challenge, the king also asked Nagasena to explain the nature of self-identity in dreaming. These questions came after several days of conversation, and by this point Nagasena and Milinda had developed their own kind of interpersonal philosophical discourse: the king described the world as it appeared to traditional human understanding, the monk reinterpreted that world by explaining its processes in light of Buddhism, and then the king asked a new question and the monk gave a new answer, and so on. The universal human experience of dreaming was one more test case in this back-and-forth discussion, and Nagasena had a ready answer for Milinda. A dream, the monk stated, is a *nimittam,* a portent or suggestion, that "comes across the path of the mind." He then identified "six kinds of people who see dreams—the man who is of a windy humor or of a bilious one or of a phlegmatic one, the man who dreams by the influence of a god, the man who does so by the influence of his own habits, and the man who does so in the way of prognostication." Only the last kind has true dreams, and the other five are false.

This answer did not satisfy the king, and we can readily imagine why. Simply defining a dream as a "portent" was not much of an explanation, and the dream's relationship to the mind still remained unclear. Nagasena's six-person typology was an odd mixture of traditional Hindu medical theory, common religious belief, and folk psychology. The surprising designation of nearly all dreams as false, even those influenced by a god, was peculiar and begged for further comment. All in all, the monk's response failed to answer the king's question, though it did hint at some interesting ideas. The king's next question focused on the issue of true, that is, predictive, dreams, and he asked by what means the mind could acquire accurate knowledge of the future. Here Nagasena went into more detail about the nature of sleep and dreaming:

His own mind does not itself seek the omen, neither does anyone else come and tell him of it. It is like the case of a looking-glass, which does not go anywhere to seek for the reflection; neither does anyone else come and put the reflection on the looking-glass. But the object reflected comes from somewhere or other across the sphere over which the reflecting power of the looking-glass extends.

The simile of a mirror allowed Nagasena to present a psychological portrait of the Buddhist mind in dreaming. That mind is neither grasping outward nor inwardly influenced by others; it merely reflects whatever crosses within range of its "reflecting power." Nagasena deliberately declined to say where the omens came from or how they could be true, and he left their interpretation to professional fortune-tellers, whose skill in such matters he seemed to accept. Nagasena's primary interest was in teaching the king about the nature and potential of the mind, and this also was exactly what Milinda wanted to discuss: "Venerable Nagasena, when a man dreams a dream, is he awake or asleep?" This seems to have been the right question at the right time, because the monk responded with his fullest, most psychologically detailed answer yet:

> Neither the one, O king, nor yet the other. But when his sleep has become light (*okkante middhe*, "like a monkey's sleep") and he is not yet fully conscious, in that interval it is that dreams are dreamed. When a man is in deep sleep, O king, his mind has returned home (has entered again into the *Bhavanga*), and a mind thus shut in does not act, and a mind hindered in its action knows not the evil and the good, and he who knows not has no dreams. It is when the mind is active that dreams are dreamed. Just, O king, as in the darkness and gloom, where no light is, no shadow will fall even on the most burnished mirror, so when a man is in deep sleep his mind has returned to itself, and a mind shut in does not act, and a mind inactive knows not the evil and the good, and he who knows not does not dream.

The categories of "monkey's sleep" and "deep sleep" would be fairly compatible with traditional *Upanishadic* notions about the different stages of sleep and dreaming, and they would also be consistent with people's common experience of variations in sleep depth—sometimes sleep feels light, restless, and scattered, and at other times it is entirely absorbing and unconscious. Nagasena's categories would be easily understood by the king and his subjects, and the monk used them to advocate a distinctly Buddhist view of the dreaming process. Dreams occur in monkey's sleep, an active state of mind not so far removed from waking. This would account for the bizarre diversity of dream content mentioned in the king's original question, as monkey sleep could take any crazy form imaginable. By contrast, Nagasena said that deep sleep was *beyond* dreaming. It was the cessation of mental activity, the suspension of moral evaluation, the total withdrawal from all engagement with the world. Described in these terms, deep sleep became a proxy for Enlightenment, another metaphor helping Nagasena convey to Milinda an understanding of the deeper truths of Buddhism.

The king asked for more information regarding the sleep cycle—"Venerable Nagasena, is there a beginning, a middle, and an end in sleep?" —and the monk replied:

> The feeling of oppression and inability in the body, O king, of weakness, slackness, inertness—that is the beginning of sleep. The light monkey's sleep in which a man still guards his scattered thoughts—that is the middle of sleep. And it is in the middle stage, O king, in the monkey's sleep that dreams are dreamed. Just, O king, as when a man self-restrained with collected thoughts, steadfast in the faith, unshaken in wisdom, plunges deep into the woods far from the sound of strife, and thinks over some subtle matter, he there, tranquil and at peace, will master the meaning of it—just so a man still watchful, not fallen into sleep, but dozing in a monkey's sleep, will dream a dream.

This answer elicited an enthusiastic response from the king—"Very good, Nagasena! That is so, and I accept it as you say." The conversation on dreams ended here, and talk turned to other topics.

What made this response so conclusively persuasive for Milinda? I would say it was the monk's clever portrayal of the dual paradox of Buddhist dream theory. After explaining the illusory, spiritually inferior characteristics of dreams, Nagasena acknowledged that a virtuous man could remain "watchful" and "dozing" in monkey's sleep in such a way as to enhance his mind's powers of reflection and understanding. Thus Nagasena helped the king realize that dreams are both to be valued *and* transcended, both useful *and* dispensable. It probably did not hurt Nagasena's cause that, according to his theory, Buddhist monks would be the most capable practitioners of this kind of "watchful" dreaming, when the mysterious omens of the future mentioned in the first question would be most easily perceived as they passed through one's sphere of awareness. Kings have always made use of advisers with advanced dreaming skills, and Buddhist monks like Nagasena presented themselves as the latest and best generation of dream-interpreting spiritual/political counselors. Whereas ordinary dreaming in monkey sleep involved a rudimentary level of cognitive activity, the dreams of spiritually advanced Buddhist monks included the tremendous powers of metacognition cultivated by long practice of mental discipline.

Crucial to an understanding of Buddhist dream theory is to recognize that no gods or supernatural beings were being invoked here. Nagasena's explanation of sleep and dreaming remained entirely on the natural plane, referring to nothing more than the innate potentials of the human mind. His one mention of the gods, in the fifth category of his six-person typology of dreamers, was incidental and dismissive. In Nagasena's view, the only dreams worth any attention were those of virtuous people who could maintain a high degree of "watchful" metacognition during monkey sleep —and even those dreams were insignificant in the larger Buddhist vision of release from suffering.

Buddhism Becomes Chinese

As Buddhism spread through Asia over the next several centuries, two branches developed that offered differing perspectives on the path to Enlightenment. The *Therevada* ("The Way of the Elders") claimed to follow the original teachings of the Buddha, with an emphasis on monastic discipline as the necessary means of becoming an *arhat,* that is, one who has reached *nirvana,* eliminated all desire and suffering, and become liberated at last from the cycle of rebirth. By contrast, the *Mahayana* ("The Great Vehicle") drew inspiration from the emergence of new texts (*sutras*) allegedly written by Buddha to hide his deepest wisdom until the time was right to reveal it. These *sutras* criticized the exclusive Therevada focus on monks becoming *arhats,* and they taught instead that anyone, whether a monk or layperson, could become a *bodhisattva,* a "being striving for Enlightenment" whose overflowing compassion led to a total devotion to helping release other people from their suffering while abandoning any personal interest in achieving *nirvana* for oneself.

The Therevada and Mahayana traditions also shared many fundamental beliefs, and the doctrinal disagreements between them never reached the level of bloody rancor found, for example, between Christian Catholics and Protestants or Muslim Sunnis and Shi'ites. Over time, the Therevada came to its greatest power and prominence in Sri Lanka and southeast Asia (present-day Thailand, Cambodia, and Laos), and the Mahayana thrived in China, Tibet, Japan, Korea, and Vietnam. It is one of the great ironies of religious history that Buddhism, despite its successful spread to so many other countries, was virtually extinguished in India, the land of its origin, first by traditionalist Hindu kings who reinstated Brahmanic teachings in the fourth century CE and then by Muslim armies who pillaged and destroyed every Buddhist temple and monastery they could find in the twelfth century CE.

Buddhism came to China from India in the first century CE, and, according to legend, the original encounter was prompted by a dream of the Chinese emperor Ming (58–75 CE) in which he saw a huge golden Buddha. When Ming woke up he sent a mission to India to learn more about this image, and in response the first Buddhist monks entered China bearing scrolls of *sutras*. By now this pattern should be familiar enough—new beginnings in Buddhist history are heralded by remarkable dreams. Within a few hundred years Buddhism became a major force in Chinese religious life, competing with Confucians and Daoists for spiritual primacy and political authority. Mahayana Buddhism in China gradually branched out in many different directions, with the "Pure Land" school becoming an especially popular and influential approach. The "Pure Land" referred to *Sukhavati,* a utopian realm in the far, far West representing the best possible rebirth in which perfect virtue is enjoyed by all under the benevolent rule of a Buddha named *Amithaba* ("Boundless Light"). Pure Land Buddhism is especially interesting from a dream perspective because of its emphasis on devotion to imagery (in both external artistic representations and inner visualization practices) as the most powerful means of progress toward *Sukhavati.* As Emperor Ming's dream demonstrated, the Buddha's image had a tremendous power to inspire, awaken, and guide people in their spiritual development. Pure Land teachings made concentrated use of the human mind's capacity for visual imagination as a way of opening people to Buddhist truth and insight. A good example of this practice as related to dreaming comes in a text from Yuan times (1264–1368 CE), the *Lang-huan-ji* (An Account of Lang-uan) by Yi ShiZhen:

> Recently my friend Wang Chiu-lien, a lay believer, was engaged in cultivating the Pure Land, on which he meditated single-mindedly. At night he dreamed that he saw the Buddha, but always as a sculpted image, not as the living Buddha. He could do nothing about it.
>
> One day he met Master Chi the monk and told him the matter.
>
> "This is easy to deal with," said the monk. "When you think of your late father, can you hold [in your mind] his usual comportment?"

"Yes."

"Can you see him in your dreams in such a way that he is no different from when he was living?"

"There is no difference."

"The Buddha in himself has no appearance," said the monk; "the appearance is manifested only in conformity with the way of things. From now on, you should think of your late father as Amitabha. Little by little, imagine that there are white streaks of light in between his brows, that his face is as of real gold, and that he sits on a lotus flower. You can even imagine that his body grows larger and larger. Then your late father *is* himself the living Buddha."

Mr. Wang applied the method as prescribed. From then on, whenever he dreamed of his father, he mentally said to himself, "This is the Buddha." Then, sometime later, his father led him to sit on the lotus, and explained to him the essence of the teaching. He learned something, and became even more devout in his special exercise.[7]

To the list of dream types that Buddhism has recognized and transformed, we may now add ancestor visitation dreams. Dreams of this kind are, as we have seen, among the most intense and memorable in human experience. This Pure Land text showed how such dreams could be utilized in the service of a different kind of spiritual understanding. In this approach, the content of the dream was less significant than the process of cultivating certain mental abilities within the dream state, particularly the power of visual imagination. A vivid dream of one's deceased father, which in a traditional context would be interpreted as a positive reconnection with the soul or spirit of a loved one, was reframed as an opportunity to overcome all such emotional attachments. The goal was literally to look beyond one's human father to see, and be seen by, the eternal living Buddha.

This connection between vision and dreaming also emerged in a tradition of Chinese Buddhist art known as *arhat* paintings. A painter known as Kwan Hiu (832–912 CE) reportedly developed a method of combining meditation, visualization, and dreaming to create the images of his art.[8] He used pre-sleep prayers to petition the Buddhist saints for a vision of an *arhat,* and when such a vision was granted him he fixed the dream picture in his mind and painted it as accurately as he could. This spiritual-artistic process of dream incubation enabled him to create images that were strange by conventional painting standards yet marvelous and inspiring nevertheless. "I paint what I see in my dreams," he said to those who asked him where the images came from.

As much as they valued amazing dream creations like these, Chinese Mahayana Buddhists also taught (consistent with the earliest traditions) that dreams were ultimately nothing but the illusory fabrications of an unenlightened mind. Indeed, simply recognizing the true emptiness of dreams could itself be a realization of considerable spiritual progress. Such was the moral of this story from the early Mahayana text *Mahaprajnaparamita sastra* ("The Sutra of the Great Transcendent Wisdom"), attributed to Nagarjuna (ca. 150–250 CE) and translated into Chinese in the fifth century CE:

> When the Buddha was still in the world, there were three brothers. They heard that in the region of Vaisali there was a lovely woman by the name of Amrapali, that in the city of Sravasti there was another woman named Sumana, and that in the city of Rajagrha there was yet another woman called Utpala-vendana. These three men had each heard people extol the matchless integrity of the three women. They thought of them with such absorption and intensity that liaisons happened in their dreams. Upon awakening, they pondered, "The ladies didn't come to us, neither did we go to them, and yet this illicit affair took place!" Thence it occurred to them that all *dharma* [worldly phenomena] might well be just like that. To resolve this problem, they went to see the Bodhisattva Bhadrapala, who said, "Such is indeed the case with all *dharma*. It all arises, in all its variety, from our thoughts." Then he took the opportunity to explain, with tact, the vacuity of all *dharma*. And so the men achieved *Avivartin* [the state of no retrogression].[9]

This is the first mention we have heard in Buddhism of sexual desire in dreaming, something we know from present-day research to be neurally hard-wired into the human dreaming process. Consistent with his renunciation of all craving, the Buddha advocated a life of total celibacy, a practice adopted by nearly all monks and nuns of the *sangha*. Many Buddhist texts grapple with the question of how humans should think about (i.e., metacognitively reflect upon) the natural sexual impulses all of us feel. Sexually stimulating dreams posed a special challenge because they seemed to be caused by factors outside ordinary human control. Hence the surprise and shame the three brothers felt upon awakening—the "liaison" could not possibly have happened in the real world, yet it clearly *felt* as real as a waking experience, and perhaps it even left some evidence of its physical reality in the form of a seminal emission. These things happen in dreams, and the Buddhist response was to use perplexing experiences like this as a lesson about the emptiness of all realities, in waking *and* dreaming. If we form strong personal attachments in the waking world, they will carry into our dreaming world (an early recognition of dreaming-waking continuity), and this may be truest about our sexual attachments. But in no case do the attachments amount to anything more than vain illusion. If an unusually vivid dream can trigger this realization, that is as legitimate a means of religious insight as any other.

Japanese Dream Diaries

Buddhism reached Japan around the sixth century CE and merged with the island's indigenous religious traditions (now known as *Shinto*), spreading the Buddha's teachings in new geographic and philosophical directions. Dreams were a fertile source of religious innovation, as the Japanese had a long history of dream belief, practice, and experience that colored their interactions with the Buddhist monks.[10] Much like early Chinese traditions, dreams were widely recognized in pre-Buddhist Japan as an authentic means of communicating with the gods and as a source of prospective knowledge about personally or collectively significant events in the future. Rituals of dream incubation were used in official state contexts (e.g., royal successions, legal disputes) and in personal situations of illness and suffering. Dream incubation among the general public was most frequently practiced at the temples of fertility goddesses and female deities of caves and rocks, all of whom were credited with healing powers in dreams. The Japanese word for dream, *yume,* referred to "the eyes in sleep," and could be used both for dreams and for visions experienced while awake (another instance showing the importance of visual perception in dreaming).

Buddhism did not supplant these deeply rooted Japanese dream traditions but rather added a new layer of psychological meaning to what people had long believed about their dreaming experiences, stimulating their metacognitive potentials in ways that enhanced their spiritual development. To mention one example, a lay Buddhist woman from the eleventh century CE, now referred to as Lady Sarashina (her real name is not known), recorded a number of dreams in a personal diary that has been preserved to this day.[11] Toward the end of her life, after her husband had died and her hopes of working in the romantic world of the Imperial palace had been dashed, she saw an especially powerful and reassuring *yume*:

> Yet we continue to live despite all our suffering. I was greatly worried that my expectations for the future world would also be disappointed, and my only hope was the dream I remembered from the thirteenth night of the Tenth Month of the third year of Tenki. Then I had dreamed that Amida Buddha was standing in the far end of our garden. I could not see him clearly, for a layer of mist seemed to separate us, but when I peered through the mist I saw that he was about six foot tall and that the lotus pedestal on which he stood was about four feet off the ground. He glowed with a golden light, and one of his hands was stretched out, while the other formed a magical sign. He was invisible to everyone but me. I had been greatly impressed but at the same time frightened and did not dare move near my blinds to get a clearer view of him. He had said, "I shall leave now, but later I shall return to fetch you." And it was only I who could hear his voice. Thereafter it was on this dream alone that I set my hopes for salvation.

The sacred imagery of Sarashina's dream was entirely consistent with the portrayals in Mahayana Buddhism of a brilliant, magically empowered Buddha who was eternally devoted to each individual's care, healing, and enlightenment. Her dream replicated this traditional image, bringing it into a personal connection with her own troubled situation. More powerful than just looking at a painting of the Buddha or intentionally forming a mental image of him in a waking state, Sarashina's dream gave her a vibrant, deeply felt *experience* of the Buddha's real and abiding presence in her life. The mixed emotions that arose in her—amazement mingled with fear—propelled her into a mystical state of knowing that transcended ordinary human categories and perceptions, as further indicated by the fact that only she could see and hear the Buddha. Her dream revealed a special truth that extended beyond the sphere of usual human cognition, beyond the sorry, dead-end circumstances of her life. Whatever other people could or could not see and hear, she now knew, because of her dream, that Amida Buddha was as devoted to her as she was to him.

An even more detailed dream diary was kept by Myoe Shonin (1173–

1232 CE), a widely venerated monk and leader of the Kegon sect of Japanese Buddhism, which centered its approach on the Buddha's teachings in his first sermon at Benares. Myoe was an active meditator and accomplished visionary, and he took his dreaming as seriously as any other realm of spiritual practice. For about forty years, from the ages of nineteen to fifty-eight, Myoe wrote out his dreams in an ongoing autobiography of religious experience he titled *Yume no ki* ("Records of Dreams").[12] This extraordinary document deserves much more attention than is possible in this limited space, but several features can be mentioned. To begin, many of the dreams appear entirely *un*spiritual and are recorded without any further comment or interpretation. Myoe evidently accepted that not all dreams are explicitly religious in their significance, though he still found it worthwhile to write them down. Several of his dreams were, of course, spiritually meaningful to him, and to these he applied a symbolic interpretation according to traditional Buddhist iconography. He looked to his dreams for practical guidance and encouraging insight, commenting after one, "I should know this." The full range of human emotion was represented in Myoe's dreams, from joy and wonder to anger, fear, and sadness. Notwithstanding his fidelity to a celibate lifestyle, he reported a few dreams of intimate relations with women, though without mentioning any particular anxiety about them. Myoe saw his dreams as real experiences in another dimension of human reality, no different from waking reality in holding out both endless temptations of emotional attachment *and* excellent opportunities for cultivating greater spiritual knowledge and metacognitive power. As an example of the latter, Myoe recorded this dream when he was forty-seven years old:

> On the night of the 20th day of the 9th month of [1220 CE], I had a dream about a large object which resembled a sheep in the sky. It went through unending transformations. Sometimes it was like a light, sometimes it resembled a human figure. When it was like an aristocrat wearing a cap, it suddenly changed into a commoner who descended to the ground. The priest Girin was there. He looked at it, was disgusted, and detested it. It turned to me and seemed to want to say something. I thought to myself that this was a constellation that had transformed and manifested itself. I thought highly of it. I wanted to resolve my uncertainty. Then it turned to me and said, "Many [priests] should not accept the faith and offerings of other people." Then I understood it. I asked it, "Where will I be reborn next?" It replied, "In the *Trayastrimsas* Heaven." I asked, "When

I am reborn there, will I already be unattached to the five desires and be practicing the Buddha's way?" It replied, "Yes." The heavenly being said, "Shouldn't you keep from burning your head?" I replied, "Yes." I thought, My next life will be good. Why do I try to anticipate it? I think it was telling me that I need only do what I must before people in this world. Again I said, "Will you always protect me like this?" It said, "Yes." Then I awoke.

Myoe added nothing more about the dream, which essentially interpreted itself. He found himself witnessing the paradoxical movement of an endlessly transforming object or constellation of energy, shifting from pure light to human form, then from a person of high status to a person of low social rank. The priest's reaction of disgust to the object's manifestation as a commoner was symptomatic of a broader misunderstanding of the key Buddhist insight that all such appearances are illusory and should not elicit any emotional reaction, positive or negative. It should be noted that sudden transformations of form and character are a rare but widely reported dream phenomenon in all populations, reflecting the natural dissolution in dreaming of ordinary cognitive boundaries. Whereas the priest turned away from the socially insignificant figure, Myoe approached the being with a sense of curiosity, purpose, and respect. His metacognitive reflections did not turn to analyzing the dream state itself; he was looking for insight beyond the simple recognition "I am dreaming." Myoe wanted to learn as much as he could from this extraordinary spiritual entity. His first questions regarded the fate of his next rebirth (a natural source of preoccupation for a monk) and the favorable answer from the heavenly being pleased him. But then the cryptic advice to "keep from burning your head" prompted an even higher level of self-reflection in Myoe, as he questioned his own anxious anticipation of a good rebirth. At this point he was able to understand (whether in waking or dreaming is unclear) that, in practical terms, the being's advice could be crystallized as one of Buddhism's basic truths: forego attachments to all worlds and follow the middle path of doing what one must do, neither more nor less. Like Lady Sarashina, Myoe asked for and received a final reassurance that this compassionate heavenly being would continue caring for him in waking life as much as in dreaming.

The *Yume no ki* was widely admired in Japan as the chronicle of a wise and spiritually conscious life, a life worth every effort to emulate in one's own personal circumstances. Myoe's dreaming autobiography very likely provoked new dreams in other people who, after reading about his experiences, opened themselves to similar potentials in their own visionary imaginations.

Tantric Buddhism in Tibet

For tens of thousands of years the Tibetan plateau was the home of resilient groups of humans who survived as nomadic herders and hunters in the cold, arid environment, surrounded by the tallest mountains in the world. These people developed a tradition of shamanic-style religious practices (*Bon*) involving nature spirits, elemental forces, and specialized healing techniques. In the seventh century CE the first Buddhist monks arrived from India, bringing with them texts to be translated into the Tibetan people's own language. These teachings promoted a new offshoot of the Mahayana school, known as *Tantrayana* (also referred to as *Vajrayana*). Indeed, the approach of Tantrayana was so distinctive that some people regarded it as a third vehicle of the Buddha's truth. It focused on the personal, secret transmission of wisdom from a master (*siddhi*, "perfected one") to a disciple. These esoteric teachings included various pre-Buddhist rituals and yogic practices such as chanting mantras, visualizing deities, and controlling multiple aspects of one's physical functioning. Some Tantric practices involved ritualized iconoclasm and transgressions of monastic morality (e.g., eating meat, drinking wine, having sex). The unifying theme in all this was the notion that the human body is a spiritual microcosm that can be deliberately used and cultivated as a conduit for divine energy.

The teachings of Tantrayana found their way into both Buddhist and Hindu traditions throughout South Asia, but nowhere did they take deeper root or grow to greater cultural power than in Tibet. The numerous analogies with traditional *Bon* spirituality must have helped, and so did a visit in 774 CE by the famous Indian Tantric monk Padmasambhava which led to the founding of several schools that are still primary forces in Tibetan Buddhism today. One of these lineages, the *Kagya*, put special emphasis on the teachings of the eleventh-century Indian sage Naropa, and here is where dreaming emerged as a special theme in the Tantrayana of Tibet. Naropa wrote a lengthy text (*Na Ro Chos Drug*, "The Six Yogas of Naropa") in which he gathered and systematized a wide range of ancient Tantric rituals. The six yogas were Inner Heat (*Tummo*), Illusory Body

(*Gyulus*), Dream (*Milam*), Light (*Odsal*), Transference of Consciousness (*Phowa*), and the Intermediate State (between death and rebirth) (*Bardo*). These were secret teachings designed to help disciples develop greater control of body and consciousness across all states of being, from waking to dreaming, from living to dying.

The third yoga of dreams was predicated on the disciple already having mastered the first two yogas under the supervision of an experienced instructor, and its practice was specifically motivated by the same desire for Buddhist Enlightenment that animated all Tantric teachings.[13] Thus, it is difficult to discuss the yoga of dreams in isolation from that broader religious framework. A full account would require more attention to linguistic and philosophical details than is possible here. Still, we have been gathering enough comparative information from other religious traditions (with much more to come) to justify a few comments about significant features in Naropa's text that directly relate to religiously meaningful dream phenomena that we have identified in other places and times.

The third yoga of Naropa presents what we can recognize as a detailed program of dream incubation. Disciples were carefully instructed on various means of controlling their sleep and dream patterns, including the use of visualizations, prayers, chanting, breathing exercises, and bodily postures. These are classic methods used in many religious traditions for the purpose of eliciting a spiritually meaningful dream. The distinctive feature of Naropa's yoga was that the disciple's only goal should be achieving consciousness within the dream—in other words, cultivating powers of dreaming metacognition. Naropa saw sleep and dreaming as further opportunities to develop the same self-reflective insights that came from waking meditation. To realize that one's dreams are self-created illusions is to move one step closer to the final realization that all realities are self-created illusions. In this regard, Naropa's yogic teachings have much in common with dream themes from the Upanishads, Daoism, early Buddhism, and latter-day Hinduism. Taking little interest in the content of dreams, all these traditions seek to transcend the experience of dreaming in quest of a higher state of dreamless sleep, leading ultimately to the pure consciousness of Enlightenment.

Naropa's teachings were given vividly colorful expression in the mystical autobiography of Milarepa, the twelfth-century-CE sage who was something of a spiritual grandson to Naropa. The Six Yogas were brought to Tibet by Naropa's disciple Marpa, who in turn passed them on to Milarepa. The story of Milarepa's path toward spiritual perfection was widely known and venerated among the Tibetan people, and most remarkable from our perspective is how crucially important dreams were at every step of his development.[14] To begin (of course), the night before Milarepa first met Marpa the latter had a dream of Naropa in which the Great Master blessed Marpa and guided him through a ritual practice within the dream itself:

> Naropa gave Marpa a slightly tarnished, five-pronged *vajra* [scepter] made of lapis lazuli. At the same time he gave him a golden vase filled with nectar and told him, "With the water in this vase wash the dirt from the vajra, then mount it on top of the banner-of-victory. This will please the Buddhas of the past and make all sentient beings happy, thus fulfilling both your aim and that of others." Then Naropa vanished. Following the instructions of his Master, Marpa washed the *vajra* with water from the vase, and mounted it on top of the banner-of-victory. Then the brilliance of this *vajra* lit up the whole universe. Immediately the six classes of being, struck with wonder by its light, were freed from sorrow and filled with happiness. They prostrated themselves and paid reverence to the Venerable Marpa and his banner-of-victory, which had been consecrated by the Buddhas of the past.

At this moment, "somewhat surprised by this dream," Marpa awoke. His initial reaction was "joy and love," but just then he was approached by his wife, who said she had just awakened from a dream, too. In her dream,

> Two women who said they came from Ugyen in the north were carrying a crystal *stupa* [Buddhist monument/reliquary]. This *stupa* had some impurities on its surface. And the woman said, "Naropa commands the lama to consecrate this *stupa* and to place it on the summit of a mountain." And you yourself cried out, "Although the consecration of this *stupa* has already been accomplished by Master Naropa, I must obey his command." And you washed the *stupa* with the lustral water in the vase and performed the consecration. Afterward you placed it on the mountaintop, where it radiated a multitude of lights as dazzling as the sun and moon and where it projected numerous replicas of itself upon the mountaintops. And the two women watched over these *stupas*.

These shared dreams provided a strange, dual-focused perspective on the imminent arrival of Milarepa. Both dreams involved Marpa receiving ritual instructions from Naropa and then performing the ritual while still in the dream, and in both he enjoyed brilliant success for his efforts. In Marpa's own dream the instructions came directly from Naropa, and the ritual culminated in a rather grandiose scene of the whole universe bowing down and worshiping Marpa. In his wife's dream the instructions came indirectly, via the two mysterious women, and Marpa did not understand the ritual's purpose, though of course he faithfully performed it. The result was a dazzling but more earthly spectacle of light reflected against the familiar mountaintops encircling the Tibetan plateau. The differences between the two dreams may be attributed in part to the gender dynamics between Marpa and his wife, with his dream accurately reflecting his masculine authority and religious centrality and her dream accurately reflecting her feminine subservience and religious marginality.

Either way, the two dreams augured well. Naropa was calling on Marpa to perform a spiritual service that would be to his and the whole world's benefit. And that service would be to initiate Milarepa into the Six Yogas. As in so many other Buddhist stories, a moment of spiritual "birth" is marked by anticipatory dreaming. The phenomenon of shared dreams at the beginning of Milarepa's story indicated that this would be an especially momentous birth. It also suggested that Milarepa's story would be unusually rich in dream experience. There was no question, however, of forgetting the fundamental Buddhist tenet that dreaming has no ultimate meaning or value, as the text made clear in a scene of unapologetic marital deception. Marpa's wife finished her narrative and said to her husband, "Such was my dream. What is its meaning?" Marpa instantly recognized her dream's favorable import and its connection to his own dream, and he felt secretly happy. But he told none of this to his wife. Rather, he used the Buddhist depreciation of dreams to shut her up: "To his own wife he only said, 'I do not know the meaning since dreams have no source. Now I am going to plow the field near the road. Prepare what I need.'" No explanation was given for Marpa's behavior, and perhaps none was needed given the enormous differences of status between men and women in Buddhism. Still, the incident is noteworthy in that it shows the potential of the "dreams are illusory" idea to be used as a means of stifling other people's dreaming imaginations. Nothing more was heard from Marpa's wife. She acceded to his odd decision (plowing fields was usually the work of much younger men) and packed him provisions for the day. Thus prepared by his silent wife, Marpa set out for the fields where later that day he would first meet Milarepa.

Dreaming became a surprisingly precise force of guidance in Milarepa's spiritual growth. In one instance, Milarepa dreamed of a *dakini,* one of the powerful and unpredictable feminine deities of Hindu-Buddhist mythology. She appeared as a gloriously beautiful figure of blue light and told him he must ask to be taught the fifth yoga of Naropa, on the Transference of Consciousness to Dead Bodies. Milarepa awoke and immediately felt unsure of the dream's legitimacy as a religious teaching. He thought to himself, the woman was only *dressed* in the costume of a *dakini*—so maybe she wasn't a real messenger from heaven at all, maybe the whole thing was just a demon's trick. Troubled and confused, Milarepa went to ask for Marpa's interpretive help. The irascible teacher berated Milarepa for breaking his meditative practice, and then declared that the dream was a warning from the *dakinis* requiring Marpa to make an arduous journey to Naropa's hermitage in India to ask the Master for this very teaching. When Marpa finally reached Naropa and told him of Milarepa's dream, the Master praised the disciple as a marvel: "In the dark land of Tibet, this disciple is like the sun rising over the snows."

Later, the unexpected death of Marpa's son prompted a succession crisis in the lineage, with his disciples anxiously questioning the future leadership of the Kagyu doctrine. Marpa responded by declaring that he, Naropa, and all of the Master's spiritual descendents had the power to prophesize through dreams. Marpa thus instructed his disciples to focus their attention on their own dreams, and to be on the lookout for guidance from Naropa. The next morning the disciples gathered to discuss their dreams. All the dreams were happy and positive, but none provided the sought-for prophetic guidance. Then Milarepa told of his dream:

> I dreamed that in the vast North of the world
> A majestic snow-clad mountain arose,
> Its white peak touching the sky.
> Around it turned the sun and moon,
> Its light filled the whole of space,
> And its base covered the entire Earth.
> Rivers descended in the four cardinal directions,
> Quenching the thirst of all sentient beings,
> And all these waters rushed into the sea.
> A myriad of flowers sparkled.
> Such in general was the dream I had.

Milarepa went on to describe in poetic detail the further visions of his dream, including the four pillars of the world in the East, West, South, and North. The latter he associated with himself, as the pillar of the North corresponding to the mountain of the North. Milarepa finished by interpreting his own experience: "The dream of the North is not ill-fated. It is favorable, O monks and disciples assembled in this place." Taken as a whole, Milarepa's dream prophesized a future of strength and prosperity for the Kagyu lineage and its "perfect teaching." Marpa and the others responded joyfully to Milarepa's dream, and Marpa (who may have noticed similarities with his own lofty dreams) instructed him to remain there in meditative seclusion for the next several years until his initiation was completed. Milarepa obediently withdrew to a cave. However, a short time later Marpa's plan for him was disrupted when Milarepa experienced a vivid and deeply disturbing dream:

> While in seclusion I did not normally fall asleep but early one morning I dozed off and had this dream: I had come to my village of Kya Ngatsa. My house, Four Columns and Eight Beams, was cracked like the ears of an old donkey. The rain had leaked throughout the house and had damaged the sacred books, Castle of Jewels. My field, Fertile Triangle, was overrun with weeds. My mother and my relatives were dead. My sister had left to wander and beg. Because our relatives had risen up as enemies against my mother and son, I had, from my youth, been separated from my mother and had not seen her again. This thought caused me immense pain. I called to my mother and sister by name and wept. I awoke and my pillow was wet with tears.

This dream had an immediate and decisive impact on Milarepa's waking life. His mind was filled with memories of his mother. He continued to cry in sadness, and with no further thought he "resolved to do everything necessary to see her again." The contrast between this dream and his "mountain/pillar of the North" dream could not be sharper. The former was pure heavenly order and serene contemplation, and the latter overflowed with raw emotion, human frailty, and earthly decay. Milarepa had already benefited from the guidance of dreams, and in this case he wasted no time in rising from his cave and informing Marpa of his decision to return home to see his family. Marpa warned Milarepa of what he might find, and added that if Milarepa left he would never see Marpa alive again (because Milarepa had awakened Marpa from sleeping to tell him this news).

Milarepa was not to be deterred, and after a lengthy farewell he took his leave. When he finally arrived in his native land he found to his sorrow that everything was exactly as his dream had foretold. His fields were overgrown with weeds, his house was an abandoned wreck, his sacred books were covered in mud, and there, in the middle of the ruins, was a pile of bleached, crumbled bones—all that was left of his mother. Choking with emotion, Milarepa nearly passed out, but suddenly the teachings of Marpa sprang into his mind, and a change came over him. He sat down amid the bones and began meditating with an absolute purity of concentration that lasted for the next seven days, after which he chanted a song about the futility of *samsara* and the illusory attachments of the human family. In this way Milarepa went beyond a mere intellectual acceptance of Marpa's Tantric Buddhist teachings to a deeply felt, life-transforming experience of them. His dream catalyzed the process, propelling him out of the incubatory space of the cave into the passionate, ultimately vain entanglements of family relations and finally to a new realm of insight and understanding. The dream was accurate in its clairvoyant portrayal of the situation at his home (adding to the notion of Tantric Masters as magical dreamers), and its alarmingly extreme emotions, so contrary to the Buddhist ideal of freedom from emotionality, actually served as a means to the end of a major advance in Milarepa's initiation. What seemed at first to be an impulsive deviation from Marpa's teachings turned out to be exactly what Milarepa needed for his further spiritual development.

A similar process unfolded a while later, while Milarepa was visiting with former relatives and neighbors. He had a dream "foretelling a happy event if I were to remain for a few days." Immediately afterward he re-encountered a woman named Zessay, a villager with whom he had once shared a flirtatious relationship. Milarepa and Zessay reminisced about his mother, and they both shed tears over her death. Then Zessay asked why Milarepa had never married. He tried to explain his choosing a life of celibacy, and Zessay countered with questions about why an authentically religious life could not also include sexual intimacy. He offered to give her his family fields as a kind of consolation for not marrying her, and she angrily refused. The conversation ended awkwardly. Then Milarepa's aunt, who saw profitability for herself in her nephew's celibate ways, persuaded him to give her title to the house and fields. Milarepa said that these upsetting events made it difficult to meditate afterward:

> I was completely unable even to attain the blissful experience of inner warmth and, while I was wondering what to do, I had this dream: I was plowing a strip of my field. The earth was hard and I asked myself if I should give it up. Then the venerable Marpa appeared in the sky and said to me, "My son, strengthen your will, have courage, and work; you will furrow the hard and dry earth." Speaking in this way, Marpa guided me and I plowed my field. Immediately a thick and abundant harvest sprang up.

Milarepa said that he awoke filled with happiness at what was clearly an important message of reassurance and encouragement from his Master. From his first meeting with Marpa, the image of the field was a key emblem of Milarepa's spiritual life, and here it gave him a vision of himself finally letting go of his attachments to earthly life in favor of higher spiritual work. But Milarepa also chided himself for his gullibility in taking any dream seriously, and in this he displayed the characteristic ambivalence of Buddhism toward dreaming: "Since dreams are nothing more than projections of hidden thoughts, not even fools believe they are real, I am more foolish than they are. Even so, I took this dream to mean that if I persevered in my efforts at meditation I would attain a new quality of inner experience." Dreams themselves may be illusions, but the dreams of a Tantric adept may convey valuable teachings nevertheless. The popular belief in prophetic dreams was elevated from an earthly to a spiritual plane, as Milarepa interpreted his dream as a symbolic expression of Buddhist practice—"I cultivate the field of fundamentally nondiscriminatory mind with the manure and water of faith, and sow the seed of a pure heart"—rather than as a literal reference to the actual field of his family, the one he just gave away to his aunt, the one he could have plowed in worldly contentment with Zessay. Milarepa's interpretation harkened back to a different field, the one Marpa was tilling when Milarepa first met him, and in this context the dream served as a revitalization of Milarepa's commitment to Marpa's guidance. It also marked a decisive repudiation of his involvement in the whole process of biological reproduction, from terrestrial agriculture to his family of origins to his future progeny. Now he pledged to follow the guidance of his spiritual father, Marpa, and to focus all his field-plowing energies on the master's teachings.

Milarepa's advances in this psychospiritual training took the tangible form of remarkable powers across all states of consciousness. He later reported that he developed the ability in dreaming to fly at will, to explore the universe "from one end to the other," to change shapes in a multitude of different ways, and to learn profound esoteric religious teachings. "My body could be both in flames and spouting water," he said. Magical powers such as these might seem highly desirable from a worldly point of view, but for a Tantric adept they were simply the by-products of true spiritual devotion, valuable only insofar as they contributed to one's progress along the Buddhist path.

This same perspective is still being taught by the leader of Tibetan Buddhism today, Tenzin Gyatso, the fourteenth Dalai Lama ("Ocean Teacher"). The position of Dalai Lama as political and religious leader of Tibet was instituted by the ruling Mongols in the seventeenth century, and to this day the Tibetan people believe that each successive Dalai Lama is the reincarnation of Avalokitesvara, the bodhisattva of compassion. The present Dalai Lama (b. 1935) has shown great enthusiasm for the research of Western psychologists, and in 1992 he convened a group of researchers for a discussion about sleep, dreaming, and death.[15] He listened to their description of the stages of sleep, the psychoanalytic theory of the unconscious, and the characteristics of lucid dreams. When asked to describe the Tibetan view, the Dalai Lama replied:

> There is said to be a relationship between dreaming, on the one hand, and the gross and subtle levels of the body, on the other. But it is also said that there is such a thing as a "special dream state." In that state, the "special dream body" is created from the mind and from vital energy (known in Sanskrit as *prana*) within the body. This special dream body is able to dissociate entirely from the gross physical body and travel elsewhere. One way of developing this special dream body is, first of all, to recognize the dream as a dream when it occurs. Then, you find that the dream is malleable, and you make efforts to gain control over it. Gradually, you become very skilled in this, increasing your ability to control the contents of the dream so that it accords to your own desires. Eventually it is possible to dissociate your dream body from your gross physical body. In contrast, in the normal dream state, dreaming occurs

within the body. But as a result of specific training, the dream body can go elsewhere.

The Dalai Lama was effectively restating the traditional Tantric Buddhist teachings of Naropa, Marpa, and Milarepa, bringing their ideas into dialogue with contemporary brain-mind science. His account of a "special dream body" created by the subtle manipulation of *prana* went well beyond the conventional boundaries of Western psychology, though it did make sense of the magical dream powers attributed to Milarepa and other Tibetan Buddhist saints. The Dalai Lama made clear his disinclination to value dreams too highly—"if you ask why we dream, what the benefit is, there is no answer in Buddhism"—at the same time as he acknowledged that some dreams (particularly vivid, recurrent ones) could be indicators of one's spiritual status. He advocated the continuation of meditation practice in sleep, "otherwise at least a few hours each night will be just a waste." In this regard, he continued the Buddhist (and Hindu) tradition of intentionally and systematically cultivating metacognition in dreaming. In other settings, the Dalai Lama has found it useful to instruct initiates in dream incubation practices involving special prayers, sleep postures, and *kusha* grass (to be put under one's mattress and pillows as agents of purification).[16] Upon awakening, the initiates are told to focus on those dreams occurring around dawn: a good dream portended a positive ritual outcome, and a bad dream was a negative omen and must be countered by reciting a mantra and scattering water around oneself. Little attention is given in this approach to the emotional or imagistic content of the dreams. The Dalai Lama, like most Buddhists, regarded dreaming as a psychological means to a religious end.

Summary

In each of the three major strands of Buddhism—Therevada, Mahayana, and Tantrayana—dreaming has been dismissed as a meaningless illusion and, at the same time, venerated as a harbinger of new spiritual beginnings. Ambivalence and paradox are the hallmarks of Buddhist dream theory. Little attention is paid in Buddhism to the origins of dreaming, beyond the obvious recognition that human mental processes are active in the formation of particular dreams. In terms of function, Buddhism regards ordinary dreaming as a distracting nuisance, although most Buddhists will grudgingly acknowledge a prophetic power in certain dreams. The highest functions of dreaming are those the Buddhists cultivate for themselves through conscious meditation and incubation rituals. These functions include reflecting on one's current spiritual condition, receiving new sacred teachings, and practicing one's skills at metacognition. In Buddhism, the question of how to interpret dreams is answered not by a waking analysis of the dream's contents but by an enlightened awareness *within* the dream of its illusory nature.

4

Religions of the Fertile Crescent

Sooner or later any discussion of dreams leads to a controversial question. Can dreams really foretell the future? For the large majority of humankind, the answer has always been *yes*. In the first three chapters we have already seen several instances of belief in the predictive power of dreaming: the *Atharva Veda*'s catalog of medically diagnostic dream symbols, the pre-battle dreams of Chinese warriors, and the conception dreams of Queens Devananda and Maya, to name a few. In all these, we found dreaming presented as a means of expanding the range of one's temporal perception, allowing people to see (with varying degrees of clarity) important events and developments coming in the future. As we are about to discover, the dream reports that have survived from the ancient religions of the Fertile Crescent are deeply concerned with predicting the future, even more so than in other traditions we have considered to this point. There are many reasons (political, literary, archeological) why the prophetic aspect of dreaming is so strongly emphasized in this region, and much of this chapter is devoted to sorting through the multiple influences on these enigmatic dreams. But first let us dwell for a moment on the issue of precognitive dreaming and the perennial human belief in its occurrence.

The idea that dreams can foretell the future seems totally alien to the modern scientific worldview. From a strictly skeptical perspective, allegedly prophetic dreams are best explained as post-hoc associations of two anomalous events. When a weird dream occurs just before an unexpected event, many people mistakenly interpret the dream as having predicted the event. But nothing magical is really at work in such cases, just a faulty application of reason. Even if the dream appears to be a direct "hit"—for example, a dream of fire right before an actual fire—countless people are probably dreaming of fire on any given night, and chances are that once in a while someone's fire dream will be followed by an actual fire in waking life. That is the law of averages, not prophecy or precognition. And if this were not enough cause for doubt, we can never rule out the possibility that the individual is simply making up the whole story. Consciously or unconsciously, people are always tempted to embellish or fabricate impressive dreams in order to enhance their social status, self-esteem, and political/religious authority. Many of the reports to be considered in this chapter are likely fabrications of just that kind.

Still, we should be wary of allowing rationalist skepticism to dominate the study of dreams. Such a view has the unfortunate consequence of making the rest of humanity look stupid and naïve, while inflating the intellectual superiority of our own age. The truth is, humans have been skeptically questioning their dreams all through history. We have already seen a high degree of critical awareness in the *Upanishads,* in the Chinese philosopher Wang Chong, and in the teachings of the Buddha and several of his disciples, all of them offering naturalistic explanations of the origins and significance of dreams. Later in this chapter, we hear several additional voices of caution and doubt from ancient peoples. For now, the main point is this: modern scientists are not the first humans ever to apply a skeptical eye toward dreaming. On the contrary, we find in the earliest teachings of several religious traditions an emphasis on examining the legitimacy of dreams very carefully, testing their truthfulness and demanding clear, reasonable explanations for their effects in waking life. The Western academic dichotomy between modern rationality and premodern irrationality does not fit the data from cross-cultural and historical dream research. A different orientation is required, one that does justice to the rationalist thread in the dream teachings of the past while also recognizing that throughout history most humans, including many contemporary Westerners, have believed in the prophetic potential of dreaming.

A better way to approach this aspect of dream phenomenology is to view it in the context of the human mind's tremendous (and entirely natural) ability to think ahead and plan for the future. This ability is rooted in the unusually large and complex development of our brains. We Homo sapiens have a cerebral cortex far bigger and more densely interconnected than any other species, and one of the great advantages of this expanded brain network is that it enables humans to think not only about what is immediately in front of us but also about what might be coming in the future, guided by present observations and past memories. The promethean, forward-gazing orientation of human consciousness is a hallmark of our species and the basis for much of our evolutionary success.[1]

In light of this, the dream research question we are considering should be rephrased in a more precise and empirically testable fashion. Are the anticipatory, forward-looking powers of the human mind operative only during the waking state, or do they continue to be active during sleep and dreaming? The prophetic dreams discussed in this chapter provide some fresh ideas about how to answer that question.

The Rise of Civilization in Mesopotamia

Around ten thousand years ago, the valley lands of the Tigris and Euphrates rivers (*Mesopotamia* = "between rivers" in Greek) provided an idyllic environment for human settlement and growth. With temperate weather, rich soil, highly nutritious wild grasses like wheat and barley, and an abundance of large mammals capable of domestication (e.g., goats, sheep, pigs, and cows), the region had everything necessary for the large-scale development of methods of food production. At about the same time (ca. 8500 BCE) as humans in China were shifting from small hunter-gatherer bands to larger agriculture-based communities, the people of Mesopotamia were likewise developing impressive skills at mass agriculture that enabled a rapid increase in population and dramatically more complex forms of social organization.

As in the earliest years of China's agricultural era, when bloody warfare between rival states never seemed to end, the first Mesopotamian city-states were also prone to constant fighting with one another. More food from crops and domesticated animals meant that larger armies could be raised and deployed. Larger armies meant more power to control greater expanses of land, which meant more food production, spurring the recruitment of even larger armies, and so on. Beginning around 3000 BCE in the southern portion of Mesopotamia (present-day Kuwait and Saudi Arabia), a group of people known as the Sumerians established several large city-states—Ur, Eridu, Lagash, and Uruk among them—covering hundreds of miles of farmland. The unprecedented size and power of these city-states created a need for better record-keeping and quicker ways to communicate information from one part of the government to another. To meet this need, the Sumerians devised a logographic script (generally regarded as the earliest system of writing ever invented) that used simple pictures to convey basic ideas and pieces of data. The oldest Sumerian texts that have survived are primarily concerned with mundane bureaucratic affairs, but some of them record the royal declarations of various kings. Among these is a stone relief called the "Stele of Vultures" that includes what appears to be the first written reference to dreaming.[2] The stele was created by King Eanatum I (2454–2425 BCE) of the city-state of Lagash in order to memorialize his most recent military conquests. Although badly damaged, the text tells how the god Ningirsu personally came to Eanatum and predicted his success in future battles. The setting in which this divine revelation occurred—"for him [Eanatum] who lies there he [Ningirsu] took his stand at his head"—implicitly identifies it as a dream, a plausible reading given that in later Mesopotamian, Egyptian, and Greek texts dreams are regularly described as experiences in which a deity appears at the head of a sleeping person to deliver a prophetic message. Eanatum's dream, though fragmentary and hard to decipher, has clear similarities to the pre-battle visions of Hindu and Chinese warriors insofar as it involved a revelation of coming events on the battlefield and a divine blessing for those warriors who would be victorious.

Another ruler of Lagash, Gudea (ca. 2100 BCE), described his dream-inspired devotion to the god Ningirsu in a remarkably poetic document, written on three clay cylinders that have survived mostly intact.[3] The primary subject of the text was Gudea's efforts, prompted by a striking dream, to construct an elaborately decorated sanctuary in honor of the god.

> In the dream, the first man—like the heaven was his surpassing size, like the earth was his surpassing size, according to his horn-crowned head he was a god, according to his wings he was the bird of the Weather-god, according to his lower parts he was the Storm-flood, lions were lying to his right and left—commanded me to build his house; but I do not know what he had in mind. Daylight rose for me on the horizon. The first woman—whoever she may have been coming out ahead did . . . a . . . stylus she held in her hand, a tablet of heavenly stars she put on her knees, consulting it. The second man was a warrior, he . . . , a tablet of lapis lazuli he held in his hand, set down the plan of the temple. Before me stood a pure carrying pad, a pure brick-mold was lined up, a brick, determined as to its nature, was placed in the mold for me, in a conduit standing before me was a slosher, a bird-man, keeping clear water flowing, a male donkey at the right of my lord kept pawing the ground for me.

It is hard to know if the whole story is being presented as a dream, or if Gudea woke up at the point when daylight appears and then had a waking vision of what followed. Either way, two features are immediately notable

—the dream's complex, vivid imagery, and the king's uncertainty about its meaning. The dream thrust Gudea into a fantastic world filled with a strange mix of common objects, potent beings, and mysterious symbols. The overwhelming nature of the experience confused him at first. Even though a divine figure gave him an explicit command ("build my house"), the king was unable to process the full import of what he was seeing and hearing. He went to the goddess Nanshe (or one of her priestesses) for help, and she readily provided an interpretation. The first man was her brother, the god Ningirsu; the woman and the second man were the deities Nisaba and Nindub; the brick represented the building of a temple to Ningirsu; the flowing water meant "sweet sleep will not enter your eyes because you are busy building the house"; and the donkey indicated that "you are pawing the ground impatiently like a choice foal eager to build the temple."

The text went on to describe the construction process in florid detail, and at the end we cannot help but wonder if Gudea's dream is genuine or a pious fiction. Either way, it is noteworthy that Nanshe's interpretive approach was based on the recognition of symbols, metaphors, and metonymies in dreaming (e.g., the extraordinary size of the first man as a metaphor for the god's transcendent power, the brick as a metonymy for the temple). This indicates that in the earliest periods of recorded history people were already familiar with the idea that dreaming could be meaningfully related to waking life, either directly in clear messages or indirectly through symbolic imagery and creative word play.

Not only could the Sumerian gods interpret dreams, they were also capable of experiencing strange prophetic dreams themselves. A poem known as "Dumuzi's Dream" told the story of Dumuzi, the god of vegetation and fertility, who suffered a perplexing nightmare:

The shepherd [Dumuzi] lay down in the southwind, to dream he lay down. He arose—it was a dream, he arose—he rubbed his eyes, full of daze; "Bring my sister, bring! Bring my Gestinanna, bring my sister! Bring my scribe who understands tablets, bring my sister! Bring my songstress who knows songs, bring my sister! Bring my little-one who knows the heart of matters, bring my sister! I will report [*bur*] my dream to her; in my dream, oh my sister who knows dreams well, rushes were rising for me, rushes grew for me, one reed alone shook its head for me, of two several reeds one was removed."[4]

The dream included several other disturbing images of decline and loss. The strong carryover feelings of surprise, confusion, and alarm prompted Dumuzi to seek immediate assistance in unraveling its meaning. His sister, however, could only give him unfortunate news: "My brother your dream is not favorable, it may not be removed [*bur*]." The same Sumerian word *bur* has the dual connotations of (a) reporting or telling a dream; and (b) taking away or dissolving the dream's evil contents. In this case, the latter was not possible. Gestinanna went on: "Rushes rose for you, this means bandits will rise up against you; a single reed was shaking its head for you, this means your mother who bore you will shake her head for you; two several reeds—one removed for you, this means I and you, one of us will be removed." The dream, in short, was a symbolic prophecy of Dumuzi's impending death. The rest of the poem chronicled the shepherd god's vain attempts to escape his fate.

Another Sumerian mythological text offers a brief but lyrical meditation on the nature of dreaming generally. "Lugulbanda in the Mountain Cave" described the spiritual adventures of the warrior-king Lugulbanda, an early ruler of Uruk (and father of Gilgamesh) who became lost and ill during a battle.[5] He took refuge in a cave, where he desperately prayed to the gods and went to sleep in hopes of a divine dream. The god Anzaqar appeared and gave Lugulbanda a series of ritual instructions which ultimately led to the hero's salvation and transformation into a kind of deity. The preface to Lugulbanda's experience offered a fascinating insight into Sumerian ideas about dreaming as a phenomenon in human life:

> Dream—a door cannot hold it back, nor can a doorpost; to the liar it speaks lies; to the truthful the truth. It can make one happy or make one lament; it is a closed archive basket of the gods. It is the beautiful bedchamber of Ninlil, it is the counselor of Inana. The multiplier of mankind, the voice of one not alive—Zangara, the god of dreams, himself like a bull, bellowed at Lugulbanda.

This passage is reminiscent of King Milinda's eloquent portrayal of the pluralism of dreams in chapter 3. The Sumerian myth spoke of dreams as a subtle, irresistible force, a mysterious oracle whose value and trustworthiness was directly proportional to the individual's moral integrity in waking life. Dreams could have many positive feelings and delightful effects, though the comment about "the closed archive basket of the gods" suggested there were limits to what humans could understand within the dream state. Still, as "the multiplier of mankind" dreaming was recognized as an endlessly fertile source of insight and revelation, especially in relation to the realm of the dead.

Gilgamesh the King

Throughout Mesopotamia a king's power was believed to emanate from the divine order of the cosmos, and this gave heavenly legitimacy to his earthly rule. Kings were uniquely favored by the gods, and at times they were considered to be gods themselves. In the king's multiple roles as army chief, legal judge, social services administrator, and supreme religious official, we find one single individual holding the awesome responsibility of insuring the city-state's favorable treatment by the capricious, unpredictable, yet all-powerful gods. That so many Fertile Crescent dream reports come from kings is surely a reflection of their near-total control of the social processes involved in writing, building monuments, preserving archives, and so on. But it also suggests the possibility that *some kings were having especially powerful dreams,* dreams that reflected their intense waking-life experiences, unprecedented in human history, of standing at the pinnacle of massively complex societies and mediating between them and the forces of the cosmos.

Such was the case, I believe, with Gilgamesh, the hero of a Sumerian poem first recorded in writing around 2000 BCE and later translated into several other Mesopotamian languages.[6] Verses of Gilgamesh's adventures were orally recited and sung for hundreds of years before that, making it one of the oldest known stories of all time. The epic opened with the people of the city of Uruk crying out in distress to the gods, asking them to stop Gilgamesh from abusing his power: "Gilgamesh does not allow the son to go with his father; day and night he oppresses the weak. . . . Gilgamesh does not let the young woman go to her mother, the girl to the warrior, the bride to the young groom." Here was the shadow side of a king's power—the mightier his rule, the greater his potential for tyranny. Upon hearing of Gilgamesh's crimes, the gods created "a second image of Gilgamesh," a half-human, half-animal being called Enkidu whose job was to counteract the excesses of the king and restore peace to Uruk. Following this, Gilgamesh had a dream—not a clear revelation from a kindly deity but rather a nightmarish scenario of helplessness, misfortune, and impotence, very much like sleep paralysis or a night terror as described by modern sleep medicine. When the king awakened he went straight to his mother Ninsun (another Sumerian female with expertise in dream interpretation) for help: "Gilgamesh rises, speaks to Ninsun his mother to untie his dream. 'Last night, Mother, I saw a dream. There was a star in the heavens. Like a shooting star of Anu it fell on me. I tried to lift it; too much for me. I tried to move it; I could not move it.'" Then he told her of a second dream in which a mighty ax fell from the sky, and he goes to it and "hugs him like a wife." Ninsun "untied" the dreams by explaining them as both prophecies and directives for action: "The star of heaven is your companion. . . . Like a shooting star of Anu his strength is awesome. . . . The axe you saw is a man. You loved him and hugged him like a wife. . . . Go, find him, I say; this is a strong companion able to save a friend." Her response to his dream followed the same basic principles used by Nanshe, Gestinanna, and other women dream interpreters of Mesopotamia in focusing on symbols, metaphors, and metonymies that reveal prophetic information about future dangers and opportunities.

Soon thereafter Enkidu arrived at the walls of Uruk and challenged Gilgamesh to single combat. They fought, and after a fearsome battle they suddenly reversed emotional course and became the closest of friends, just as Ninsun had predicted. Flush with feelings of power and confidence, Gilgamesh and Enkidu set out on a quest to Cedar Mountain to fight the legendary monster Humbaba. On the way there, Enkidu prayed to the mountain to bring the king a dream of encouragement before the battle. Gilgamesh did not, however, receive what a Mesopotamian king usually was given in response to an incubation ritual:

Friend, I saw a dream—bad luck troublesome. . . . I took hold of a wild bull of the wilderness. He bellowed and kicked up earth; dust made the sky dark. I ran from him. With terrible strength he seized my flank. He tore out. . . . Besides my first dream I saw a second dream. In my dream, friend, a mountain toppled. It laid me low and took hold of my feet. The glare was overpowering. A man appeared, the handsomest in the land, his grace. . . . From under the mountain he pulled me out, gave me water to drink. . . . Friend, I saw a third dream, and the dream I saw was in every way frightening. The heavens cried out; earth roared. Daylight vanished and darkness issued forth. Lightning flashed, fire broke out, clouds swelled; it rained death. The glow disappeared, the fire went out, and all that had fallen turned to ashes.

Before the dreams, Gilgamesh bragged that he had no fear of death; but after the dreams he was filled with dread and uncertainty. Although the text becomes fragmentary at this point, what remains is Enkidu's attempt to *bur* the dream by means of a paradoxical interpretation: "Friend, your dream is good luck, the dream is valuable. . . . Friend, the mountain you saw . . . we'll seize Humbaba and throw down his shape, and his height will lie prone on the plain." At first, it seemed that Enkidu's reading was correct. They went forth the next day to battle Humbaba, and they succeeded in defeating him. But their victory aroused the anger of the gods, who announced their punishment in two new dreams sent to Enkidu:

> Hear the dream I had last night: Anu, Enlil, Ea, and heavenly Shamash were in council, and Anu said to Enlil: "Because . . . Humbaba they have slain, for that reason the one of them who stripped the mountain of its cedar must die." But Enlil said: "Enkidu must die. Gilgamesh shall not die." . . . Friend, I saw a dream in the night. The heavens groaned; earth resounded. Between them alone I stood. There was a man, his face was dark. . . . he seized me and led me down to the house of darkness . . . the house where one who goes in and never comes out again.

Ironically, Enkidu's nightmares came on the same night that Gilgamesh (who suffered "a restless heart that will not sleep") was able, for the first time in the story, to lie down and sleep peacefully. The dramatic contrast in their sleep experiences signaled a crucial shift in the epic. Now that Enkidu's fate was sealed, Gilgamesh's quest changed from the standard heroic desire for glorious victory to a deeper existential yearning to understand death. The king immediately recognized what the dreams meant, and there was only so far he could go in untying it: "the dream is sound. For the living man it brings sorrow: the dream causes the living to mourn." When Enkidu finally died, Gilgamesh sat by his body and cried out, "What is this sleep that has taken hold of you?" Death was like an eternal nightmare, and the king had no hope of untying or dissolving its effects.

Still, Gilgamesh tried. He set out to find the immortal man Utnapishtim to learn how to escape death. As he began his journey Gilgamesh asked once more for divine guidance by means of an incubated dream: "I lift my head to pray to the moon god Sin: For . . . a dream I go to the gods in prayer. . . . preserve me!" As he did at Cedar Mountain, Gilgamesh invoked the prerogative of Fertile Crescent kings to request heavenly dreams that would provide divine legitimacy for their actions. Here, however, Gilgamesh was not even warned by terrifying nightmares; this time he received no dream at all. "Though he lay down to sleep, the dream did not come." The silence from the gods was extremely upsetting to Gilgamesh, as shown by his violent reaction upon awakening: "Gilgamesh takes up the axe in his hand; he drew the weapon from his belt and like an arrow. . . . he fell among them. He struck . . . smashing them" (the fragmented nature of this part of the text means we do not know the identity of "them"). This failed dream incubation signaled another turning point in the story, as Gilgamesh was now completely cut off from the civilization he used to rule. He was leaving his city, leaving his kingdom, leaving the whole known world in search of the mysterious Utnapishtim and the meaning of death. The refusal of the gods to heed his dream incubation indicated the frightening extent to which Gilgamesh had lost his identity as a king. His journey was taking him beyond all bounds of religiously and socially ordered life.

Ultimately Gilgamesh's journey failed, as we knew it must. But his frightening dreams and mournful experiences transformed him. At the end of the story, Gilgamesh was less powerful but more human. He reentered Uruk not with a triumphant flourish but with a quiet wisdom won at the cost of much suffering. No longer a brash, out-of-control tyrant, he was still the king, and he did finally return to his city, his people, and civilized life. "Go up, onto the walls of Uruk," he said in the epic's closing verses, his words now carrying a much deeper resonance than when he uttered these same lines at the beginning of the poem: "Inspect the base, view the brickwork. Is not the very core made of oven-fired brick? Did not the seven sages lay down its foundation?" Pride in the works of human hands—that was all Gilgamesh had left, and it was good enough.

Royal Divination

The story of Gilgamesh spoke of a golden age lost in history, before the fall of Sumeria to the Akkadians. The dominance of the Akkadians yielded in time to the Babylonians, then to the Hittites, and then to the Assyrians. As these successive empires grew in size, complexity, and power, the status of their kings was elevated to the point where each one became a god himself who deserved constant worship and total obedience from his people. This royal-religious fusion helped the kings hold their societies together by establishing a cosmic communal bond between people that transcended their ties of kinship to smaller family groups. Declaring oneself a god was, in political terms, an effective means of seizing absolute authority over a population, and dreams continued to serve as a convenient source of divine approval for Mesopotamian kings needing to legitimize their powers. At the same time, we find evidence that interest in dreaming gradually spread throughout Mesopotamian society to include the dream experiences not just of kings but of ordinary people as well. This, too, had a religious foundation. If the king became a god, then the people within his dominion became special members of a divinized whole; they were participants in a cosmic drama that gave meaning to every aspect of their lives. In such a grand religious context, each individual's dreaming could become a personal means of discerning divine activities.

The best indication of this development comes from the Sumerian-era city-state of Mari, which flourished in the third and early second millennium BCE along the Euphrates River (in modern-day Syria). The kings of Mari established a network of government officials who kept track of all potentially meaningful signs, including dreams.[7] If anything was observed that seemed politically relevant, it was recorded and forwarded to the royal court. Several letters from these officials to the king have been found and translated, and they reveal a world in which dreams were widely shared, discussed, and interpreted. Conceived as external phenomena separate from the individual's mind, the dreams of Mari's people were systematically examined for indications of the kingdom's future. Dreaming provided something like a free market of divine revelation, giving everyone (at least in theory) a means of contributing to the common good. Addu-duri, a Mari noblewoman with official connections to the court, wrote letters to the king regarding dreams she had gathered from people in her area, and in one letter she described two particularly haunting dreams of her own:

> Tell my lord: Addu-duri, your maidservant, says: since the destruction/ restoration of your father's house, I have never had a dream such as this. Previous portents of mine were as this pair. In my dream, I entered [the goddess] Belet-ekallim's chapel; but Belet-ekallim was not in residence. Moreover, the statues before her were not there. Upon seeing this, I broke into uncontrollable weeping. This dream of mine occurred during the night's first phase [during the evening watch]. I resumed dreaming, and Dada, priest of Istar-pisra, was standing at the door of Belet-ekallim's

chapel, but a hostile voice kept on uttering *tura dagan, tura dagan* ("O Dagan, return here/come back/reconsider"?).

The last part of this translation is especially uncertain, and we cannot know for sure what exactly Addu-duri found so ominous about the dreams. We do know she emphasized their unique impact on her, with the strong emotional carryover of crying. The disappearance of the goddess and her statues from her temple would naturally be very upsetting to a religiously pious person like Addu-duri, and such an image would indicate (following a continuity approach) grave danger and misfortune ahead. There is some evidence that the priest Dada was already dead at the time of the dreams, and hence his appearance might be a sign of heavenly favor to counterbalance the ill tidings of the absent goddess. Whether or not that is the case, an unmistakably negative tone pervaded the dreams, and Addu-duri clearly felt a sense of urgency in reporting them to the king, Zimri-Lim.

We do not know what Zimri-Lim thought of her dreams, nor of the many other omens, signs, and warnings he was hearing from his advisers. All we know is that a few years later the Babylonian ruler Hammurabi defeated Zimri-Lim in battle, and the kingdom of Mari was lost forever.

Later Mesopotamian texts included a number of royal dreams in which kings received clear or symbolic messages from the gods, providing them with divine inspiration, political legitimacy, and pre-battle encouragement. Very much like the early rulers of China, the kings of Mesopotamia recited their dreams (either actual or fabricated) as a means of justifying and strengthening their immense power over society. Another similarity with China is that soon after the invention of writing, a new Mesopotamian literature arose devoted specifically to the divination of dreams. One of the best and earliest examples of the dream book genre came from the Babylonian Empire in the seventh century BCE.[8] The book (actually a series of clay tablets) opened with a prayer of invocation to the God of Dreams, *Zaqiqu* (also referred to as MA.MU). *Zaqiqu* was capable of blessing people with good dreams and protecting them from the harmful effects of bad dreams. The main portion of the book listed various types of dreams and their corresponding meanings. Although only a fifth of the original text has survived, it still covers a wide range of dream themes, including felling trees and plants, seeing astronomical bodies, being given objects, seeing animals, performing a particular occupation, making objects, eating and drinking certain items, turning into various animals, standing or sitting in a specific place, carrying objects, descending to the underworld, ascending to the heavens, seeing the dead and the divine, visiting certain temples and towns, flying, having sex, and urinating. Each dream theme or image was followed by an interpretation referring to the prediction of some future event. Some of the interpretations make no sense to modern readers, but others follow recognizable patterns such as punning (e.g., a dream of a raven [*arbu*] meant getting income [*irbu*]) and paradox (e.g., "If the god utters a curse against the man; his prayers will be accepted").

This dream book, along with many other Mesopotamian texts, referred to the frequent occurrence of evil dreams and nightmares, which were conceived as external entities that attacked people in sleep. Such dreams could not be interpreted; they could only be fought and deflected. Ritual texts known as *namburbu* described various techniques for defending against nightmares and in some cases turning bad dreams into good ones.[9] The texts advised performing the *namburbu* rituals immediately upon awakening, "in the early morning, on the day after the dream was seen. . . . before the dream's evil took ahold of its victim." One of the rituals involved telling the dream to a lump of clay and then dissolving it. Other *namburbu* rites focused on purifying the space around the individual's bed, banishing evil influences, and creating a more hospitable sleep environment.

Unlike the philosopher-mystics of the *Upanishads,* the people of Mesopotamia left no evidence indicating that they felt any great concern over the ontological question of dreaming. They seemed comfortable in their belief that the experiences of sleep are *real* events, real in the sense of being externally generated, strongly felt, and consequential for the future. Sensitive to a wide range of dreaming phenomena, the Mesopotamians used their formidable skills of observation, analysis, and forethought to explore dreaming as a primary (though not always clear or decisive) source of anticipatory knowledge.

The Ancient Egyptians

To the south and west of Mesopotamia another mighty river civilization grew, one whose founding was prompted by the major climate changes that transformed the previously lush forest lands of North Africa into a parched, windswept desert within a few thousand years. The humans who had roamed those forests for untold millennia were forced to seek a more hospitable ecosystem, and some of them migrated north and settled along the fertile banks of the Nile River, the most abundant and consistent source of water in the increasingly arid region. With less and less to gain from nomadic hunting, these people began experimenting with agriculture, and by around 6000 BCE the first evidence of systematic food production appeared. As in Mesopotamia, India, and China, the development of agriculture had an explosive effect on the early Egyptians. Their small villages grew rapidly in size and complexity until 3100 BCE, when the whole Nile region was unified into one all-powerful, densely populated, and widely interconnected empire. The practice of writing appeared at this time (whether by independent invention or Mesopotamian influence is not clear) to serve its primal bureaucratic purposes of record-keeping, communication, and propaganda. Flush with power, the Pharaohs of the Old Kingdom period (2650–2134 BCE) initiated several large-scale public works programs to facilitate crop irrigation, food distribution, and trade practices. The Pharaohs also devoted much of the dynasty's wealth and human labor resources to the construction of immense monuments to themselves and the gods, including the "step pyramid" of the Pharaoh Djozer and the Great Sphinx of Giza.

In all the surviving texts, tablets, and monuments from these early centuries of Egyptian civilization there is not a single mention of dreams. We do not know whether this means that (a) the ancient Egyptians had no interest in dreams; or (b) no writings mentioning dreaming have yet been found. A comparative book like this one inevitably favors the latter possibility. So many *other* early societies venerated their dreams that it must be true here as well, right? Maybe, maybe not. Intellectual honesty, not to mention respect for the individuality of others, requires constant attention to the former possibility, namely, that the Archaic and Old Kingdom Egyptians (at least those with access to writing) might *not* have regarded dreaming as a noteworthy topic. They wrote about many things—gods and crops and battles and journeys—but nothing, it seems, about dreams. Why not? We may never know for certain. I suspect the divine status of the early Pharaohs was so secure, so integrally established in the society, and so thoroughly accepted by the people that they felt little need for any extra validation from god-sent dreams.

Eventually dreams do appear in the surviving records. During the First Intermediate Period (2150–2055 BCE), when drought and poor crop yields led to severe political upheaval and internecine warfare, some of the people who belonged to Egypt's large class of literate officials practiced religious rituals in which they tried to communicate with deceased relatives or friends. The texts used in these rituals are known as "Letters to the Dead," personal missives addressed by the living to the dead in quest of guidance and protection.[10] The letters were probably combined with prayers, offerings, and other ritual practices to enhance their desired effect. The Egyptians had been burying their dead with great care and religious devotion for many thousands of years, and these letters, written with touching emotional intimacy, give us a glimpse of their personal experience of death and the divine. Here is a letter from a man to his deceased wife:

A saying by Merirtifi to Nebetotef: "How are you? Has she, the [goddess of] the West, been taking care of you according to your desire? See, I am your beloved upon earth; fight on my behalf and guard my name! I did not muddle a spell before you, while I was perpetuating your name upon earth. Expel the pain of my body! Please be beneficial to me in my presence, while I see you fighting on my behalf in a dream. I will lay down gifts before you . . . when the sun rises I will set up offerings for you."

Another text alludes to a troubling dream visitation by a dead man with whom the letter-writer had conflicts in waking life. The dreamer addresses the letter to his deceased father, begging him to intervene and prevent any more guilt-provoking dreams from coming—"that which happened against him [the dead man], did not happen by the hand of me. . . . it is not I who first caused wounds against him. . . . Please, may his lord [the dreamer's father] be protective, and do not allow him to do harm." Brief as they are, these passages reflect a common awareness of dreaming in both its positive and negative aspects, especially its close relationship with death. At least as far back as the late third millennium BCE, ancient Egyptians were treating their dreams as a personal and potentially beneficial means of communicating with those who dwell in the realm of the dead.

The Egyptian word *resut* was used in these early texts to refer to dreaming, a term literally meaning "awakening," with the sign of an open eye that was also used for other vision-related words like "see" and "be vigilant." This linguistic usage reflected what other cultures have also noticed about the prominence of visual perception in dreaming. A second Egyptian word, *qed,* was used to refer to "sleep" (accompanied by the sign of a bed) but could also mean "dream" when accompanied by the open eye sign. For the Egyptians, a dream was something one saw in sleep—something objective and external to the individual, appearing as an autonomous force that temporarily suspended the ordinary boundaries of waking life.

The first mention of dreams among the Pharaohs appeared several centuries later, during the New Kingdom era (1570–1069 BCE) that followed a devastating period of foreign invasion and occupation by the armies of Mesopotamia. Once the foreigners were ejected, the new Pharaohs set out to reestablish traditional dynastic authority over Egypt. They were undoubtedly influenced by the religious and political ideas of their former masters, and thus it comes as no surprise to find at this time the first reports of dreams providing divine sanction for the Pharaoh's prowess in warfare. A stela from ca. 1500 BCE Memphis tells of Pharaoh Amenhotep II receiving a dream during battle from the god Amun "in order to give valour to his son [the Pharaoh], his father Amun being the protection of his body, guarding the ruler."[11] A later New Kingdom Pharaoh, Merneptah, recorded a dream (in a fragmented text) that came in the midst of warfare with the Libyans: "His Majesty saw in a dream, as if it were an image of [the god] Ptah standing before the Pharaoh. He was as tall as. . . . He said to him 'Grab hold here!' while he was giving to him the Khepesh sword, 'And drive away the heart-sickness within you.'"[12] These dreams brought divine reassurance at times when the power of the Pharaoh was being put to a military test. Both as political propaganda and as honest portrayals of understandable anxiety ("heart-sickness") before battle, dreaming was now regarded as an acceptable source of guidance and legitimation for Egypt's rulers.

In addition to reinvigorating Egypt's military forces, the New Kingdom Pharaohs also sought to restore the grand civic spirit of the earlier dynasties. One of the best-preserved Egyptian dream texts involved Thutmose IV (ca. 1400 BCE), whose reign was distinguished by a major restoration of the Great Sphinx at Giza.[13] Thutmose commissioned a stela to commemorate his success in this holy task, including an account of the experience that originally inspired him:

> One of these days the King's Son Thutmose was strolling at the time of the midday and he rested in the shadow of this Great God [the Sphinx]. Slumber and sleep overcame him at the moment when the sun was at the zenith, and he found the majesty of this august god speaking with his own

mouth as a father speaks to his son, as follows: "Behold me, look upon me, my son Thutmose. I am your father Harmakhis-Khepri-Re-Atum. I will give to you my kingly office on earth as foremost of the living, and you shall wear the crown of Upper Egypt and the crown of Lower Egypt. . . . To you shall belong the earth in its length and its breadth and all that which the eye of the All-Lord illuminates. You shall possess provisions from within the Two Lands as well as the great products of every foreign country. For the extent of a long period of years my face has been turned to you and my heart devoted to you. You belong to me. Behold, my state is like that of one who is in suffering, and all my members are out of joint, for the sand of the desert, this place on which I am, presses upon me. I have waited to have you do what is in my heart, for I know that you are my son and my champion. Approach! Behold, I am with you. I am your guide." He completed this speech. And this King's Son awoke when he heard this. . . . He recognized the words of this god and he placed silence in his heart.

The dream theophany of Thutmose involved a clear message of divine support and future good fortune. There was no Gilgamesh-like disconnect between the earthly ruler and the gods, no ambiguous symbolism needing to be untied. The Pharaoh understood the significance of the dream at once. The Sphinx had given him a benevolent prophecy and then demanded greater respect in the form of a physical restoration of his statue, protecting it against the encroaching desert sands. The setting of the dream was unique in the region's dream literature—a midday nap, precisely at the sun's zenith, in the very shadow of the Sphinx. The dramatic contrast between lightness and darkness created a spontaneous opening through which the Pharaoh shifted from a sleeping unconsciousness beside the statue of the Sphinx to a dreaming awareness before the living presence of the god himself. Thutmose described the experience as a kind of unintentional incubation, with the god's appearance serving as the creative spark for his monumental labor to renovate the statue. The public narration of his dream was the strongest indication yet that dreaming was entering into the general awareness of Egyptian society.

During the New Kingdom, more and more dreams begin to appear in non-royal texts such as hymns, poems, spells, and medical guides. Some of the hymns involve mystical kinds of experiences related to other practices of religious worship, as in these verses from the *Biography of Ipuy*: "It was on the day that I saw her beauty—my heart was spending the day in celebration thereof—that I saw the Lady of the Two Lands [Hathor] in a dream and she placed joy in my heart."[14] The medical texts, meanwhile, focused on remedies for bad dreams. No interest was taken in the content or potential meaningfulness of such dreams; they were treated as maladies to be cured, nothing more. Only one instance of what we have been calling a "dream book" has survived from ancient Egypt, a papyrus text found in Der el-Medineh from the reign of Ramses II during the thirteenth century BCE (making it the oldest surviving member of this genre).[15] Known as the Ramesside Dream Book, it included the future-oriented interpretations of 227 dream images (all addressed to male dreamers), along with spells to fight off bad dreams and a brief, badly fragmented section describing the dreams of men who were "followers of Seth." The book's interpretations were consistent with the social realities of the literate villagers known to have lived in this region, and it displayed many of the linguistic features we have found in other dream books—word play, punning, metaphor, cultural references, and religious symbolism. A dream of sailing downstream was interpreted as bad because the wind usually blew upstream along the Nile, and thus to sail downstream was heading in the wrong direction. A dream of a large cat (possibly the god Ra) was good and signaled a large harvest; a dream of being on top of a roof was good and meant "something will be found." The paradoxical approach was also represented: "If a man sees himself in a dream seeing himself dead; good, it means a long life is before him." And a few dreams included polymorphous sexual imagery: "If a man sees himself in a dream after his penis has enlarged; good, it means an increase of his possessions"; "If a man sees himself in a dream copulating with his mother who is issuing fluid; good, it means that he will be joined by his clansmen"; "If a man sees himself in a dream copulating with a pig; bad, it means that his possessions will be emptied" (the words for "pig" and "empty" sounded similar in Egyptian).

The interpretations focused on a few basic existential concerns such as health, social status, wealth, mortality, and one's relationship to the gods. Dreams were presented as accurate omens relating to these concerns, capable of being understood in fairly reasonable terms. Once understood, the dreams served as motivations for waking-life actions that were intended to enhance the predicted benefits or avoid the predicted harm. The Ramesside book's spells to protect against bad dreams operated on the same principles used in other Egyptian magical texts to help people in their dealings with demons and hostile dead spirits. Different combinations of prayers, herbs, potions, amulets, and specially designed bedposts were employed in what was apparently a widespread desire for protection in sleep from the dark forces of the netherworld. Fire was an especially useful element in anti-nightmare spells, and the Ramesside book included the following reassurance, cast as a dialogue between the goddess Isis (the healing mother/interpreter) and her son Horus (the nightmare sufferer): "Do not divulge that which you saw, in order that your numbness may be completed, your dreams retire, and fire go forth against that which terrifies you."[16]

All in all, the Ramesside text provided a brief but impressively wide-ranging summary of ancient Egyptian dream knowledge and interpretive practice. We have no way of knowing if there were any other dream books circulating in Egyptian society, or if anyone ever actually used the inter-pretations contained in this one. It may have been the solitary work of a lone genius, or it may have been one of numerous manuals written by a larger community of interpretive specialists. Either way, the Ramesside Dream Book stands as a monument to human curiosity about the pat-terns, functions, and meanings of dreams.

Jewish Interpreters

During the third and second millennia BCE, small bands of people rest-lessly traveled in and out of the Fertile Crescent lands controlled by the larger empires of Mesopotamia and Egypt, seeking a safe place to settle and develop their own agricultural societies. According to the *Tanakh* (i.e., the Hebrew Bible, the primary collection of sacred texts of the Jewish reli-gion), one such group coalesced around a man named Abram, who in ca. 1800 BCE led his kinfolk into Canaan, the fertile lands of the Jordan River valley. Abram (later given the name Abraham) told his followers about the visions and auditory revelations he had received from the god YHWH in which a future of landed prosperity was promised for them.[17] One of Abram's earliest theophanies occurred in reply to his audacious question-ing of YHWH regarding the trustworthiness of the god's promise—"O Lord God, how am I to know that I shall possess it [Canaan]?" Apparently the direct voice of God in the waking state was not sufficiently convincing proof for Abram. In response, YHWH instructed him to sacrifice several animals, cut them in two, and lay the pieces in two opposing rows. Then, "as the sun was going down, a deep sleep fell upon Abram; and lo, a dread and great darkness fell upon him. . . . [B]ehold, a smoking fire pot and a flaming torch passed between these pieces. On that day the Lord made a covenant with Abram, saying, 'To your descendents I give this land, from the river of Egypt to the great river, the river Euphrates." The eerie ritual seemed to generate a kind of dream incubation effect for Abram, with the brilliant element of fire bringing illumination to the frightening darkness. This vivid, otherworldly sleep theophany from YHWH gave Abram the convincing reassurance he was seeking, with a clear message of future territorial independence. Considering Abram's experience in the context of widely shared Fertile Crescent ideas about kings, gods, and dreams, we can easily understand why it would be transformative for him and politically legitimating in the eyes of his people.

The story of Abraham and his immediate descendents contained numerous references to highly significant dreams. Dreaming was, in this sense, a primal source of inspiration and divine guidance during the founding era of the Jewish religion. The dreams narrated in the Hebrew Bible often included unusual twists on the classic Fertile Crescent patterns, and these twists highlighted distinctive features of the emerging Jewish tradition. For example, in Genesis 20, YHWH sent a frightening dream to a king, Abimelech of Girar, warning him to stay away from Abraham's wife. The story demonstrated the omnipotence of the Lord by using the familiar Mesopotamian idea of a warning dream to benefit not just the current king but, more important, the chosen people of YHWH. Abraham and his followers might have appeared weak and powerless, but in dreams God was revealing the truth of their gloriously fertile future.

The dramatic theophany of Abraham's grandson Jacob at Bethel also included dream elements both familiar and unique:

> [Jacob] came to a certain place, and stayed there that night, because the sun had set. Taking one of the stones of the place, he put it under his head and lay down in that place to sleep. And he dreamed that there was a ramp set upon the earth, and the top of it reached to heaven; and behold, the angels of God were ascending and descending on it! And behold, the Lord stood above it and said, "I am the Lord, the God of Abraham your father and the God of Isaac; the land on which you lie I will give to you and your descendents; and your descendents shall be like the dust of the earth, and you shall spread abroad to the west and to the east and to the north and to the south; and by you shall all the families of the earth bless themselves. Behold, I am with you and will keep you wherever

you go, and will bring you back to this land; for I will not leave you until I have done that of which I have spoken to you." Then Jacob awoke from his sleep and said, "Surely the Lord is in this place; and I did not know it." And he was afraid and said, "How awesome is this place! This is none other than the house of God, and this is the gate of heaven."[18]

This story reflected a widespread Mesopotamian belief in dreams as a source of divine comfort in periods of difficulty and distress (Jacob was being pursued at the time by his murderously-minded brother Esau), with a clear auditory message of future prosperity, both geographic and genetic. Yet unlike most other Mesopotamian royal dreams, Jacob's experience also included intensified visual and emotional elements—the dramatic image of the heavenly ramp or stairway (like the Mesopotamian sacred towers called *ziggurats*) and the carryover feelings of shock, fear, and wonder he described upon awakening. In gratitude for the dream, Jacob built a ceremonial stone pillar and pledged his lifelong faith to YHWH. What is unusual in the Mesopotamian context is not the dream revelation itself, nor the waking ritual to honor the dream. Rather, it is that such a dream experience could come to someone *other* than a king. Jacob was, as he rested his head on the stone pillow, as remote from royal authority as a person could be. Yet God spoke to him in a dream, gave him a glimpse of divine reality, and promised to guide and protect him in the future. Alone and powerless in the waking world, Jacob was treated like a king by YHWH in dreaming.

A large portion of Genesis is devoted to the story of Jacob's son, Joseph, who displayed a personal receptivity to predictive dream visions and an uncanny skill at interpreting the dreams of others.[19] The next-to-youngest of twelve boys, Joseph's dreams marked him for greatness in the future. In one dream he held a tall sheaf of grain that stood upright; "and behold, your [his brothers'] sheaves gathered round it, and bowed down to my sheaf." In a second dream, "the sun, the moon, and eleven stars were bowing down to me." Not surprisingly, Joseph's older brothers were angry at the shameless grandiosity of his dreams, and they cast him into a pit and abandoned him to the elements. Their fratricidal actions were aimed at destroying all predictive potential in Joseph's night visions—"we shall say that a wild beast has devoured him, and we shall see what will become of his dreams."

But Joseph survived, rescued by passing traders who promptly sold him into slavery in Egypt. Falsely accused by his master's wife, Joseph was then sentenced to the Pharaoh's prison. In this bleak situation, Joseph had the opportunity to hear the dreams of two other inmates, the Pharaoh's chief butler and chief baker.[20] Both of them awoke one morning with "faces downcast," troubled by dreams they could not interpret. When Joseph heard this, he said, "Do interpretations not belong to God? Tell them to me, I pray you." This was quite a radical claim on Joseph's part, as he explicitly linked the power to interpret dreams with one's faithfulness to YHWH. For the butler's dream of three grape vines pressed into the Pharaoh's cup, Joseph said it meant that in three days the butler would be restored to his former position. For the baker's dream of birds eating three cake baskets on top of his head, Joseph said it meant that in three days he would be hanged by the Pharaoh, "and the birds will eat your flesh." The interpretations hinged on a fairly simple metaphorical connection (number of objects = duration of time), and they foretold dramatically different fates for the two dreamers. As the story unfolded, Joseph's interpretations were proven correct: three days later, the butler returned to the Pharaoh's court, and the baker was executed.

This set the stage for Joseph's greatest feat of dream interpretation, involving the Pharaoh himself and his two disturbing dreams ("in the morning his spirit was troubled"). In the first dream the Pharaoh saw seven thin cows coming out of the Nile and eating seven fat cows, and in the second he saw seven thin and blighted ears of grain swallowing seven plump and full ears of grain. None of Egypt's magicians and wise men could interpret these two dreams until Joseph (recommended by the butler) appeared and said, "It is not in me; God will give Pharaoh a favorable answer. . . . The dream of Pharaoh is one. . . . [T]he doubling of Pharaoh's dream means that the thing is fixed by God, and God will shortly bring it to pass." Joseph identified the same object-time metaphor in the Pharaoh's dreams as in the dreams of the butler and baker. Thus the seven cows and seven ears of grain corresponded to seven years of time. The fat vs. thin contrast in both dreams served as a metonymy for agricultural plenty vs. famine, and the swallowing of one animal or crop by the other was a vivid, disturbing image of violent transition. Putting these elements together, Joseph concluded that the dreams portended seven years of bountiful crops in Egypt followed by seven years of terrible famine. Now that Pharaoh knew this, Joseph urged him to set aside extra grain in the next seven years in order to prepare for the seven lean years to come. Pharaoh did as Joseph recommended, and future events proved this to be a wise course of action. When the famine years came, Joseph's older brothers journeyed to Egypt in desperate search for grain, and without recognizing him (Joseph had been appointed Pharaoh's chief aide) the brothers bowed down to him, just as his dreams had predicted they would.

One of the morals of Joseph's story was that faith in YHWH brings a person the power not just to experience dream revelations oneself but also to know how to interpret the meaning of *other* people's dreams. Dream interpretation as a religious art, as a political tool, as a community sentinel, as a means of survival—all this emerged in the story of the dreamer Joseph, whose heroic adventures echoed throughout the later Abrahamic traditions.

After several hundred years of increasingly harsh slavery in Egypt, the Jewish people escaped Pharaoh's control and fled back to Canaan ca. 1600 BCE, led by the charismatic visionary Moses, who was believed to have the most intimate relationship with God of all: "If there is a prophet among you, I the Lord make myself know to him in a vision, I speak with him in a dream. Not so with my servant Moses; he is entrusted with all my house. With him I speak mouth to mouth, clearly, and not in dark speech; and he beholds the form of the Lord."[21] Dreams and visions remained valuable in this perspective, though sometimes "dark" and hard to understand. Greater emphasis was placed on a higher and purer mode of human-divine relationship, one that was apparently exclusive to Moses alone. In later teachings, Moses took an even more skeptical view of dreams:

> If a prophet arises among you, or a dreamer of dreams, and gives you a sign or a wonder, and the sign or wonder which he tells you comes to pass, and if he says, "Let us go after other gods," which you have not known, "and let us serve them," you shall not listen to the words of that prophet or to that dreamer of dreams; for the Lord your God is testing you, to know whether you love the Lord your God with all your heart and with all your soul. . . . [T]hat prophet or that dreamer of dreams shall be put to death, because he has taught rebellion against the Lord your God.

This was a markedly more hostile attitude toward dreams than was found in the Genesis stories. Indeed, it sounded like what Joseph's brothers might have said to justify themselves as they tossed their "dreamer" sibling into the pit. The passage reflected the broader struggle of Moses against idolatry and polytheism, and in a stroke he completely subsumed dreaming to the authority of God and his chosen leaders. Thus a fundamental polarity was established in the *Pentateuch,* the first five books of the Hebrew Bible and the holiest of Jewish scriptures, a polarity between dreaming as divine revelation and dreaming as tempting, misleading delusion. This tension played out in the rest of the *Tanakh,* with revelatory dreams described in Judges 7 (Gideon overhearing an ominous pre-battle dream from his opponents, the Midianites), 1 Samuel 3 (the young Samuel experiencing unintentional incubation dreams in the Temple), 1 Kings 3 (the great king Solomon intentionally incubating a dream at a "high place" at Gibeon), and Daniel 2 and 4 (the Babylonian ruler Nebuchadnezzar's two horrifyingly true nightmares).

The latter story is especially notable because Daniel, very much like Joseph, demonstrated a distinctive skill at dream interpretation, a skill that directly aided in the Jewish people's survival.[22] Nebuchadnezzar called all the kingdom's magicians and enchanters to help him with his bad dream; "his spirit was troubled, and his sleep left him." Incredibly, the king insisted they describe his dream *before* he told them anything about it. The magicians and enchanters replied that he asked the impossible; no one could satisfy such a demand. Nebuchadnezzar angrily ordered the execution of all Babylon's wise men. This would mean the death of Daniel and the other Jewish leaders, so Daniel led his kinsmen in prayer to God for help. "Then the mystery was revealed to Daniel in a vision of the night"; he went to Nebuchadnezzar and told him the dream:

> You saw, O king, and behold, a great image. This image, mighty and of exceeding brightness, stood before you, and its appearance was frightening. The head of the image was of fine gold, its breast and arms of silver, its belly and thighs of bronze, its legs of iron, its feet partly of iron and partly of clay. As you looked, a stone was cut out by no human hand, and it smote the image on its feet of iron and clay, and broke them in pieces; then the iron, the clay, the bronze, the silver, and the gold, all together were broken in pieces, and became like the chaff of the summer threshing floors; and the wind carried them away, so that not a trace of them could be found. But the stone that struck the image became a great mountain and filled the whole earth.

Daniel interpreted the dream as a future prediction sent to Nebuchadnezzar by God showing that his reign (symbolized by the golden head) was destined to fall and disappear, to be replaced by the eternal kingdom of God. Ironically, Nebuchadnezzar responded to this interpretation not with greater humility and piety but rather by ordering the construction of a huge "image of gold" in front of which he forced all his people to bow down and worship. Then a second nightmare came to him—"I had a dream which made me afraid; as I lay in bed the fancies and the visions of my head alarmed me." This dream centered on a massive, beautiful tree which was cut down by "a watcher, a holy one" who came down from heaven to punish Nebuchadnezzar with madness ("let a beast's mind be given to him") for his faithlessness. Daniel came again to interpret the dream, telling the king it was a warning to change his ways, but unlike the Pharaoh, Nebuchadnezzar could not escape his fate. He lost his mind and his kingdom and turned into a virtual animal (he "ate grass like an ox . . . his nails were like birds' claws") before finally recognizing God as supreme ruler of heaven and earth.

Several biblical stories testified to the revelatory power of dreaming, and more of this power was hoped for in the future, as when God promised in the Book of Joel, "It shall come to pass afterward, that I will pour out my spirit on all flesh; your sons and your daughters shall prophesy, your old men shall dream dreams, and your young men shall see visions. Even upon the menservants and maidservants in those days, I will pour out my spirit."[23] This was a remarkably democratic appeal to the spiritual potential of all humans. But a contrary theme ran through the *Tanakh* as well, one that cannot be ignored if the Jewish dream tradition is to be understood in its full complexity. The skepticism of Moses was repeated in several places, from Ecclesiastes 5 ("For a dream comes with much business, and a fool's voice with many words") and Zecheriah 10 ("The dreamers tell false dreams, and give empty consolation") to Psalms 73 ("They [wicked wealthy people] are like a dream when one awakes, on awaking you despise their phantoms") and 90 ("Thou dost sweep men away; they are like a dream, like grass which is renewed in the morning"). The prophet Jeremiah gave the most full-throated articulation of this dismissive attitude, speaking on behalf of God:

> I have heard what the prophets have said who prophesy lies in my name, saying, "I have dreamed, I have dreamed!" How long shall there be lies in the heart of the prophets who prophesy lies, and who prophesy the deceit of their own heart, who think to make my people forget my name by their dreams which they tell one another, even as their fathers forgot

my name for Ba'al? Let the prophet who has a dream tell the dream, but let him who has my word speak my word faithfully. What has the straw in common with the wheat?[24]

Jeremiah was speaking at a time when the Jewish people were suffering as an exiled community held captive in Babylon. Just like Moses, Jeremiah warned them not to follow misleading and deceptive dreams but to obey the true faith, which was far more valuable than any dream, just as nutritious wheat was better than empty straw. One senses that Jeremiah attacked dreaming so harshly precisely because a significant number of his Jewish contemporaries were in fact talking passionately about one another's dreams as alternative visions of creative action in desperate times.[25]

Over the next several centuries Jewish rabbis engaged in lengthy discussions of the stories in the *Tanakh*, trying to understand their meanings more clearly and applying their teachings more effectively to present circumstances. From 200 to 500 BCE these discussions were written down, edited, and compiled in the *Talmud*, a kaleidoscopic compendium of ancient perspectives on the Jewish tradition. Dreams were the focus of a particular section of the *Talmud* known as *Berachot*, chapters 55–57.[26] There is an incredible wealth of material here, but we must content ourselves with a few general observations.

Revelation and nonsense. The rabbis directly debated the fundamental meaningfulness of dreaming, with some of them reporting heaven-sent dreams and others questioning the epistemological reliability of dreams ("the truth is, that just as wheat cannot be without straw, so there cannot be a dream without some nonsense"). In this way, the polarity from the *Pentateuch* was carried forward into the rabbinic discourse of later Judaism, with one significant addition—true dreams were now attributed to angels, and false dreams to demons.

Prototypical dreams. Berachot included reports not only of precognitive dreams but dreams of visitations from the dead, nightmares, healing dreams, and intense sexual experiences. The *Talmud* is not a perfect historical record, but these passages suggest that at least some Jewish people were actually experiencing highly impactful dreams (whether independently or under Mesopotamian influence, it is impossible to say) and openly wondering about their meanings. Regarding sexual dreams (particularly the troublingly erotic dreams of the demoness Lilith), Rabbi Huna stated, "Even if the [seminal] emission is connected with feelings of gratification, the dreamer is not responsible, because it was not real sexual intercourse."

Incubation. Several rabbis warned people against the practice of dream incubation in sacred temples (such as those of the Greek healing god Asclepius, discussed in the next chapter), and other rabbis described rituals to use in praying for good dreams and dispelling the negative effects of bad ones. Once again, the *Talmud* presented different perspectives on a religious practice, cautioning against its misuse while encouraging responsible attempts to benefit from it.

Interpretation. The most famous line from *Berachot*, "A dream which is not interpreted is like a letter which is not read," suggested a religious obligation to heed the divine messages conveyed by dreams. Interpretation served as an effective remedy for unpleasant dreams, and the recommended methods of deciphering a dream included the familiar ones of metaphor, puns, word play, and scriptural references. The *Talmud* also acknowledged the multiple possibilities in dreaming, as in the story of Rabbi Bana'ah, who told a dream to twenty-four interpreters in Jerusalem and received twenty-four interpretations in return, and each of them came true. "All dreams follow the mouth" was the rabbi's enigmatic conclusion.

Many other Jewish teachers participated in this dream conversation beyond those represented in the *Tanakh* and *Talmud,* and much more could be said about dreams in Flavius Josephus's writings about the Jewish-Roman wars (first century CE), in the allegorical commentaries on Genesis of Philo (first century CE), in the rationalistic philosophical texts of Maimonides (twelfth century CE), in the mystical and ethical texts of the *Zohar* and *Sefer Hasidim* (thirteenth century CE), in the popular interpretation manual of Solomon Almoli (sixteenth century CE), and in the folk and fairy-tales told among ordinary Jews up to this day.[27] Throughout these many centuries, and despite frequent and violent persecutions, a common thread of belief and practice continued to shape the Jewish community's attitudes toward dreaming. Like their Mesopotamian and Egyptian neighbors, the Jews believed that at least some dreams were divine messages about the future—the people of the Fertile Crescent were essentially in agreement on that. Where the Jews differed was in their early and repeated questioning of the authenticity of particular kinds of dream knowledge. They fully understood the numinous power of dreaming, and for that very reason were extremely wary of its potential for abuse. The skeptical voices of early Judaism were not questioning dreams in order to question all reality, as in the *Upanishads* or in Buddhism. Rather, they were anxiously trying to control a potentially valuable but dangerous and unpredictable force that could threaten their already tenuous survival as a people.

Summary

"The Fertile Crescent" refers to a kindred group of ancient civilizations whose creative interactions and constant warfare helped establish many of the basic religious principles that still govern the Western world. The Sumerians, Akkadians, Babylonians, Assyrians, Egyptians, and Jews shared a deep faith in dreaming as a means of communicating with the divine. Although we must be especially cautious here since the surviving texts are so fragmentary, the available evidence indicates that most of these cultures taught that dreams originate outside the individual, sent either by the gods or evil spirits. Very few people in the Fertile Crescent seem to have thought about the ontological question of waking vs. dreaming realities, and for the most part they accepted the idea that dreams are external entities which humans passively receive during sleep. For these traditions, prophecy was by far the most important function of dreaming. Dreams served as a key source of information about the will of the gods, foretelling the fates of both individuals and whole kingdoms. Many of the dreams reported from these cultures involved messages so clear and un-ambiguous that no interpretation was necessary. But many other dreams included strange images and odd feelings, and a professional class of interpreters arose to help people (especially the rulers) decipher the prophetic meanings of their night visions. Similar to what we found among the Chinese, the dream diviners of the Fertile Crescent used numerous methods to interpret people's dreams, including a search for puns, word play, metaphors, metonymies, cultural symbols, and religious associations. In this broad historical context, the Jews were unusual in at least two ways: first, their patriarchs Abraham, Jacob, and Joseph benefited from the divine power of dreaming even though they were not kings; and, second, their prophets Moses, Jeremiah, and others gave voice to skeptical warnings against dreams as deceptive fancies that can lead people away from God.

5

Religions of Ancient
Greece and Rome

Several times now we have heard stories of people performing rituals of dream incubation, and readers may be wondering if these practices actually work. Can the right combination of prayer, sacrifice, and sleep posture really produce a revelatory dream? Is there some kind of naturalistic explanation for the effectiveness of dream incubation, or is it just a superstitious fantasy with no basis in fact?

If we assume that incubation is an automatic process by which humans mechanically force a divine dream to appear, then we would have to say no, there is very little evidence to support that (if nothing else, recall Gilgamesh's miserably failed incubation in the previous chapter). But if incubation is regarded as a conscious attempt to influence the likelihood of experiencing a powerful dream, then yes, we can find good reasons for taking it seriously. As discussed in the prologue, modern research has shown that dream recall is responsive to waking attention. If you simply formulate the conscious intention to remember more dreams, you will be surprised at how easily your recall rate increases. It is no great leap from that to a more focused kind of intention relating to a specific, emotionally salient topic. This, too, is well grounded in research showing that dream content accurately reflects the most important emotional concerns in a person's life. For example, if you are in the midst of a painful and messy divorce, you will be highly primed each night to dream about that waking life situation. In that setting, any *extra* effort you make to remember dreams relating to the divorce will very likely succeed.

So far, it sounds like dream incubation is an extended exercise in self-suggestion. But the rituals we are discussing push the boundaries of the "self" well beyond its ordinary usage, to the point where psychological language seems inadequate to the descriptive task. The power of these rituals derives not simply from their conscious intentionality but, more important, from the ways in which they create a space during sleep for heightened receptivity to extraordinary energies emanating from outside the usual sphere of waking awareness. This is why dream incubation requires more than just an emotional concern; it also requires a change in a person's physical sleeping conditions, a reorientation of body and soul within the broader meaning-structures of the cosmos. Whether practiced in a cave, a temple, a mountain, a desert, or a graveyard, the underlying logic of dream incubation always involves a dramatic shift *away* from one's normal sleep patterns and *toward* an unusual place where the powers of whatever the individual holds sacred are gathered in especially concentrated form. *To see an extraordinary dream, you should sleep in an extraordinary place.* When combined with additional activities like fasting, sacrifice, purification, chanting, and so on, the mind-altering, dream-stimulating effects of these rituals become all the stronger, and we can begin to appreciate why people have practiced them in so many different cultures and historical eras. Dream incubation is a species-wide spiritual practice, a naturally appealing and easily accomplished extension of the insights that emerge in spontaneous dream experience.[1]

One of history's most striking traditions of dream incubation was the cult of the Greek healing god Asclepius. For many centuries, thousands upon thousands of Greek and Roman people made sacred pilgrimages to the temples of Asclepius and slept there in hopes of a divine dream. These time-honored practices brought together dreaming, healing, prophecy, and wisdom and wove them into a seamless, spiritually rejuvenating whole. The widespread popularity of the Asclepian cult testifies to the high public regard of dreams in Graeco-Roman civilization, even though many philosophers and poets of this era expressed a deep skepticism toward dreaming and contrasted it with the superior power of reason as a guide to truth and knowledge. By now we are familiar with this tension between revelation and doubt in dreaming, having seen it in every culture considered so far. In the case of the Greeks and Romans, we find it articulated with a vivid intelligence and stirring clarity that has rarely been surpassed.

Myth and History

One hundred thousand years ago, bands of Homo sapiens from Africa were migrating along the Mediterranean coast and into Europe, and by

40,000 BCE they were leaving unmistakable evidence of symbolic expression and death-related rituals performed in caves (e.g., in Lascaux, France).[2] We do not know if dream incubation occurred in the caves, or if any of the spectacular wall paintings of animals, hands, geometric patterns, half-human creatures, and so forth, were directly inspired by dreams. Archeology is, and will probably forever be, mute on those questions. But everything we know from dream research, both historical and contemporary, strongly suggests that yes, the experience of seeing the paintings or sleeping in the caves very likely stimulated actual dreams of extraordinary power and memorability, and these dreams may well have served in turn as a visionary resource for new cave paintings. Some scholars have called what happened in these caves a "creative explosion," a revolutionary leap in human cognitive and cultural development. From our perspective, it looks like the natural outgrowth of a species that has learned how to intensify its psychospiritual capacity to dream big dreams.

The caves of mainland Greece were occupied by humans as far back as thirty thousand years ago. Over time these people built larger settlements, learned how to use metal, developed seafaring skills, and interacted both commercially and militarily with the great civilizations of the Fertile Crescent. The origins of their language are uncertain, but we know that by the second millennium BCE the people of Greece had built a powerful and sophisticated network of fortified cities (the first was discovered at Mycenae, hence the whole era is known as the Mycenaean period). The surviving evidence of their culture indicates that it revolved around hunting, war, and seafaring. At its height, the Mycenaean network spread across the islands of the Aegean and as far east as the Turkish coast. When this civilization collapsed around 1100 BCE (for reasons still unknown) several centuries of social fragmentation ensued, and the written form of the Greek language was effectively abandoned. During these "dark ages," stories began to circulate about the mighty exploits of heroic warriors who braved fantastic dangers and fought glorious battles. Two particular cycles of these stories (originally sung at public festivals and much later recorded in writing) became associated with a poet named Homer, traditionally believed to be a blind man who lived early in the first millennium BCE. The *Iliad* and the *Odyssey* recounted the adventures of an army from Greece who attacked the distant city of Troy (the *Iliad*) and then embarked upon a perilous journey home (the *Odyssey*). Whether or not the Trojan War actually occurred, the stories sung by bards like Homer were immensely popular, testifying to a growing sense of historical and cosmic self-awareness among the Greeks of this era. A close reading of the dreams in these two epics provides us with the best foundation for understanding later Greek and Roman dream discussions.[3]

The *Iliad* opened with a bitter argument between Agamemnon (the leader of the Greek armies fighting against Troy) and Achilles (the greatest warrior in the Greek ranks) because Agamemnon had just seized from Achilles a girl whom Achilles had won as a prize in an earlier battle.[4] Furious at this disrespectful treatment, Achilles withdrew from the Greek army and prayed to the gods for justice. In response Zeus, the mightiest of the Olympian deities, decided to help Achilles by sending down an "evil dream" to deceive and mislead Agamemnon. The dream took the shape of Agamemnon's most trustworthy counselor, the aged Nestor, who stood at Agamemnon's head to deliver a rousing message of heavenly encouragement for the next day's battle. In the morning, "Agamemnon awoke from sleep, the divine voice drifting around him," and immediately launched his troops in a new assault on the Trojans—a battle that Zeus had already decided the Greeks would lose, to prove how badly they needed Achilles back on their side.

The deception worked so well because of the expectation (familiar to anyone influenced by Fertile Crescent cultures) that kings and military leaders were regularly blessed with pre-battle dreams of divine reassurance. Agamemnon was an easy mark for this kind of deceptive dream, though it is hard to imagine that anyone could resist such a compellingly presented message. These early verses of the *Iliad* boldly expressed the Greek perception of a deeply troubling existential vulnerability in dreams. What if the gods really do come to us in our dreams, but to harm us rather than help us? What if both the doubters *and* the believers are wrong?

That might seem like more significance than should be drawn from a dream fabricated by a god and sent to a fictional character in a myth. We cannot forget that the *Iliad* was a literary creation meant to entertain an audience, and not necessarily a historical record providing objective information about actual people. Yet, we must also grant that Homer frequently described scenes using remarkably accurate details about the activities in question (e.g., combat techniques, sailing skills, religious rituals, and domestic customs). His fictional narrative was firmly grounded in the experiential life-world of the ancient Greeks, and this was true of dreaming as well. In Book 22, Achilles returned at last to the battlefield (after the death of his best friend Patroklos) and chased the Trojan champion Hektor around the city's mighty walls. In describing the scene Homer said, "As in a dream a man is not able to follow one who runs from him, nor can the runner escape, nor the other pursue him, so he [Achilles] could not run him [Hektor] down in his speed, nor the other get clear." This was a direct and, in the context, quite appropriate simile based on the pervasive human experience of chasing nightmares. Similarly, in Book 23, Homer presented a type of dream (a visitation from the dead) that we know is widely reported by people in virtually all places and times. "The ghost of unhappy Patroklos," looking exactly as he did in waking, came to Achilles in a dream to chide him for failing to attend to his burial rites:

> The ghost came and stood over his head and spoke a word to him: 'You sleep, Achilles, you have forgotten me; but you were not careless of me when I lived, but only in death. Bury me as quickly as may be, let me pass through the gates of Hades.

In the dream Achilles promised he would do so, and he asked Patroklos to stay:

> "But stand closer to me, and let us, if only for a little, embrace, and take full satisfaction from the dirge of sorrow." So he [Achilles] spoke, and with his own arms reached for him [Patroklos], but could not take him, but the spirit went underground, like vapour, with a thin cry, and Achilles started awake, staring, and drove his hands together, and spoke, and his words were sorrowful: "Oh, wonder! Even in the house of Hades there is left something, a soul and an image, but there is no real heart of life in it."

This is a classic visitation dream in terms of its perceptual intensity, emotional arousal, and carryover impact on waking consciousness. The pattern we have identified in other cultural and historical contexts is displayed here in full flower, indicating that at least by the time of Homer (and probably much earlier than that) the ancient Greeks were familiar with the experience of dream visitations from the dead. The message Achilles received was more reliable than Agamemnon's, although it revealed a much bleaker vision of reality that only intensified his sadness and despair. Yet, it was not an evil dream. On the contrary, it became a turning point in Achilles' mourning process, honestly expressing the awful depth of his feelings of loss, feelings that a fame-seeking, honor-conscious warrior might not otherwise want to acknowledge.

The dreams presented in the *Odyssey* were also notable for some interesting features of psychological verisimilitude that enhanced their effectiveness as literary devices.[5] Early in the story Telemachus, Odysseus's son, secretly left home to seek news of his father. Penelope, his mother and Odysseus's wife, was terrified when she discovered that Telemachus had left. But in her sleep that night her divine patron, the goddess Athena, sent a dream in the trustworthy form (*eidolon*) of Penelope's sister, who stood at her head and told her that Telemachus was protected by the gods and would return home safely. " 'Courage!' the shadowy phantom reassured her. 'Don't be overwhelmed by all your direst fears.' " In its hopeful and uplifting prophetic message Penelope's dream could fairly, and without embarrassment, be called a wish-fulfillment—"Icarios's daughter [Penelope] started up from sleep, her spirit warmed now that a dream so clear had come to her in darkest night." More than any other character in either epic, Penelope drew deeply from the well of dreaming, where she found the emotional strength and intellectual resourcefulness to face the challenges of her exceedingly dire waking-life situation. Odysseus had been gone for twenty years, she was the captive of a horde of men (the "suitors") who were demanding she choose one of them as her new husband, and she had discovered they were secretly plotting to murder her son. When Odysseus returned in the disguise of a beggar, Penelope requested a private audience with the old wanderer to see if he had any news of her husband. The ensuing dialogue between the long-suffering queen and the beggar-in-disguise was in many ways the most dramatic scene of the whole story, and at its heart was a dream. Before parting for the evening, Penelope said,

My friend, I have only one more question for you . . .
[P]lease, read this dream for me, won't you? Listen closely . . .
I kept twenty geese in the house, from the water trough
They come and peck their wheat—I love to watch them all.
But down from a mountain swooped this great hook-beaked eagle,
Yes, and he snapped their necks and killed them one and all
And they lay in heaps throughout the hall while he,
Back to the clear blue sky he soared at once.
But I wept and wailed—only a dream, of course—
And our well-groomed ladies came and clustered round me,
Sobbing, stricken: the eagle killed my geese. But down
He swooped again and settling onto a jutting rafter

Called out in a human voice that dried my tears,
"Courage, daughter of famous King Icarius!
This is no dream but a happy waking vision,
Real as day, that will come true for you.
The geese were your suitors—I was once the eagle
But now I am your husband, back again at last,
About to launch a terrible fate against them all!"
So he vowed, and the soothing sleep released me.
[Odysseus replied] "Dear woman, . . . twist it however you like,
Your dream can mean only one thing. Odysseus
Told you himself—he'll make it come to pass,
Destruction is clear for each and every suitor;
Not a soul escapes his death and doom . . ."
[Penelope responded] "Ah my friend, . . .
Dreams are hard to unravel, wayward, drifting things—
Not all we glimpse in them will come to pass . . .
Two gates there are for our evanescent dreams,
One is made of ivory, the other made of horn.
Those that pass through the ivory cleanly carved
Are will-o'-the-wisps, their message bears no fruit.
The dreams that pass through the gates of polished horn
Are fraught with truth, for the dreamer who can see them.
But I can't believe my strange dream has come that way,
Much as my son and I would love to have it so.

Here as elsewhere in the story, Odysseus displayed a remarkable ability to create his own destiny, bending fate to his purposes. His confident
interpretation of the positive prophetic symbolism of Penelope's dream
(the mountain eagle killing the geese meaning that Odysseus will kill the
suitors) came true because he *made* it come true. A short time later he
did indeed destroy the suitors, thereby reclaiming his throne, his honor,
and his wife. Modern scholars have traditionally regarded this scene as
another example of Odysseus's cunning intelligence, in contrast to the
queen's hapless confusion. I prefer a different reading, however, one that
credits Penelope with an equally cunning awareness of the beggar's true
identity. In my view, Penelope knew perfectly well that it was Odysseus
standing before her, refusing to reveal himself to her. She fabricated the
dream of the twenty geese in order to test her husband's understanding of
what she had endured on his behalf, and he failed the test (there were not

20 suitors, but 108; the number 20 more likely referred to the number of years of their marital separation). Odysseus may have gone on to defeat the suitors, but only by placing his desire for vengeance higher than his love and regard for Penelope.

Either way, Penelope's speech about the "two gates" of dreams stands as a brilliant sentinel in the history of Greek dream speculation. Although we still do not fully understand the significance of horn and ivory as contrasting dream substances (perhaps ivory is more opaque than horn, so horn is easier to see through), the mysterious image of the two gates illuminated a fundamental duality of oneiric experience: some dreams are nonsense and have no consequence in our lives, whereas others have the potential to reveal meaningful truths, but only "for the dreamer who can see them." As a theory of dreaming, this reflected a cautious, well-considered balance between skepticism and hope, vain fantasy and genuine insight. The haunting spirit of Penelope's words echoed throughout classical Greek philosophy and literature, where the revelation vs. deception dichotomy branched out in several creative directions.

The final chapter of the *Odyssey* made a brief reference to a different vision of the geography of dreaming, when the ghosts of the suitors slaughtered by Odysseus were led by the god Hermes on their final journey:

And Hermes the Healer led them on, and down the dank
moldering paths and past the Ocean's streams they went
and past the White Rock and the Sun's Western Gates and past
the Land of Dreams (*demos oneiron*), and they soon reached the fields of
asphodel
where the dead, the burnt-out wraiths of mortals, make their home.

Also translated as "Village of Dreams" or even "People of Dreams," this was the last stop on the way to the final residence of the dead. Physically speaking, dreams were located far, far beyond this world. They came from a place as distant from ordinary life as one could go without actually dying.

From Homer we learn where dreams dwell. From Hesiod we are told when they were born. In the *Theogony*, Hesiod, an eighth-century-BCE poet and possible contemporary of Homer, gave dreams a parentage and mythological family of origin.[6] Hesiod's poem was the earliest Greek creation story, telling "how the gods and earth arose at first," and dreams appeared fairly early in the process. Chaos was alone at the beginning, and then there appeared Gaia the Earth, Tartarus the misty underworld, and beautiful Love. "From Chaos came black Night [*Nyx*]," followed by a whole host of incestuous, violent, and quarrelsome gods and goddesses. After the "most terrible of sons," Kronos, castrated Ouranos (his father and the god of heaven) while making love to Gaia, we learn that "*Nyx* bore frightful Doom and the black *Ker* [an evil female spirit], and Death, and Sleep, and the whole tribe of Dreams [*Oneiroi*]." Somewhat like the Homer's *demos oneiron*, Hesiod's *Oneiroi* suggested a vague personification of dreaming, a tendency to take humanly recognizable form, perhaps even to the extent of generating a sense of community among the dreams themselves. But Hesiod, even more than Homer, emphasized the primal darkness of dreaming, the frightening kinship with the most destructive and hostile forces of the cosmos. Long before humans were created, prior even to the appearance of Zeus and the Olympian gods, dreams were spontaneously conceived in a primordial era of seething aggression, polymorphous sexuality, and reality-bending elemental conflicts.

Classical Philosophy

After Hesiod and Homer's time, the city-states of the Greek mainland and surrounding islands grew rapidly in power and prosperity, spreading their influence once again as far east as the shores of Asia Minor. Over the next several centuries, the writings of these people became increasingly sophisticated, self-reflective, and philosophically minded. Everything in nature and human experience became subject to a probing rational analysis that sought knowledge of the fundamental laws of the cosmos. Dreams were brought into this process both as an object of analysis and, more controversially, as a guide in the reasoning process itself. An early version of physiological dream theory appeared in a fragment from the works of Heraclitus of Ephesus (sixth century BCE) in which he said that, "for those who are awake there is a single, common universe, whereas in sleep each person turns away into his own, private universe."[7] By sharply distinguishing the reality of waking and the reality of dreaming, Heraclitus removed the latter from the realm of mythological power and relocated it within a naturalistic, purely subjective framework. A different approach was taken by Parmenides of Elea (fifth century BCE) who wrote treatises on logic that were directly inspired by his experiences as an *Iatromantis,* a healer and prophet who slept on animal skins inside of caves.[8] In

Parmenides we find a philosophical elevation of dreaming as a kind of oracle of inspiration, in contrast to Heraclitus's philosophical domestication of it as a private sphere detached from social reality.

A similar dynamic can be seen in the philosophical lineage of Socrates (470–399 BCE), Plato (427–347 BCE), and Aristotle (384–322 BCE). They were all denizens of Athens, a city-state that for several centuries enjoyed a spectacular flowering of intellectual, literary, and artistic creativity. Socrates was the most renowned philosopher of his day, a skilled public debater and tricksterish critic of conventional thinking. He left no writings of his own, and our best knowledge of his teachings comes through the dialogues written by his student, Plato. We know of at least two dreams Socrates reportedly experienced, both of which were told in the final days of his life as he awaited execution by the Athenian authorities, convicted of the crimes of corrupting the city's youth and disrespecting the gods. The dialogue known as the *Crito* opened with Socrates sleeping in his prison cell, while the Athenian authorities awaited the arrival of a religiously ceremonial boat that would signal the time for his execution.[9] His friend, Crito, was sitting there when Socrates awoke just before dawn, and Socrates immediately declared that the boat in question would not arrive that day:

> *Crito*: What makes you think that?
> *Socrates*: I will try to explain. I think I am right in saying that I have to die on the day after the boat arrives?
> *Crito*: That's what the authorities say, at any rate.
> *Socrates*: Then I don't think it will arrive on this day that is just beginning, but on the day after. I am going by a dream that I had in the night, only a little while ago. It looks as though you were right not to wake me up.
> *Crito*: What was the dream about?
> *Socrates*: I thought I saw a gloriously beautiful woman dressed in white robes, who came up to me and addressed me in these words: "Socrates, 'To the pleasant land of Phthia on the third day thou shalt come.'"
> *Crito*: Your dream makes no sense, Socrates.
> *Socrates*: To my mind, Crito, it is perfectly clear.

At one level this was the most common (and dubious) of dream types, the symbolic omen of death. Crito's confusion may be owing to his surprise that so eminent a philosopher as Socrates would give credence to a common folk belief, but Socrates was content with his own comprehension of the dream and felt no need to explain it further. Strangely, the words spoken by the beautiful woman (no other information is known about her) were quoted from the *Iliad* (9.363), from a passionate speech given by Achilles when he was planning to abandon the Trojan War and return to his home in Phthia. As it turned out in the *Iliad*, Achilles never made it back home. He returned to the battle, fought heroically, and died. Socrates was about to die for a very different cause, that of truth and spiritual freedom. His dream seemed to suggest that death would bring him to an ultimate spiritual paradise, a kind of transcendental homecoming. The philosopher would achieve what the warrior could not.

Throughout his life Socrates used the powers of rational analysis and critical questioning to guide people to the very edge of their intellectual and psychospiritual development. Crito's confusion was a common experience among his students, and in another dialogue Socrates referred to such epistemological uncertainty as the birthplace of philosophical inquiry itself.[10] A bright young man named Theaetetus, for whom this dialogue was named, was brought to Socrates for inspection. The master asked Theaetetus one perplexing question after another, and the young man quickly found himself thoroughly befuddled and amazed at how little he really knew. Socrates said that was a good thing: "This sense of wonder is the mark of the philosopher. Philosophy indeed has no other origin." Socrates then went on to ask Theaetetus a version of what we are calling the ontological question of dreaming:

> *Socrates*: Have you not taken note of another doubt that is raised in these cases, especially about sleeping and waking?
> *Theaetetus*: What is that?
> *Socrates*: The question I imagine you have often heard asked—what evidence could be appealed to, supposing we were asked at this very moment whether we are asleep or awake, dreaming all that passes through our minds or talking to one another in the waking state?

The wonder-struck youth admitted that he could not find a way to sharply distinguish the two. You might think you are awake, but it is always possible that you are in fact experiencing a highly realistic dream. Socrates left this vertiginous question without further comment, as he was interested less in answers than in opening people's minds to free inquiry. Socrates' playful, mischevious practice of questioning people regarding the underlying principles of their beliefs (his students enjoyed the process, most of the Athenian elite did not) had a profoundly wonder-working effect, decentering his conversation partners from their customary perspectives and recentering them within a broader perspective of conceptual possibility. Socrates spoke of himself as a "midwife" whose concern was "not with the body but with the soul that is in travail of birth." He helped people open themselves to the pursuit of wisdom, though he did not claim to provide them with wisdom itself.

Eventually the ship arrived, and the day of Socrates' execution was set. In the dialogue *Phaedo,* he received one last prison visit from his distraught friends, who were startled to discover that their teacher has been spending his final hours of life writing poems based on Aesop's fables for children.[11] Why, his friends asked, was he engaged in such a frivolous activity? He answered as follows:

> I did it in the attempt to discover the meaning of certain dreams, and to clear my conscience, in case this was the art which I had been told to practice. It is like this, you see. In the course of my life I have often had the same dream, appearing in different forms at different times, but always saying the same thing, "Socrates, practice and cultivate the arts." In the past, I used to think that it was impelling me and exhorting me to do what I was actually doing; I mean that the dream, like a spectator encouraging a runner in a race, was urging me on to do what I was doing already, that is, practicing the arts, because philosophy is the greatest of the arts, and I was practicing it. But ever since my trial, while the festival of the god has been delaying my execution, I have felt that perhaps it might be this popular form of art that the dream intended me to practice, in which case I ought to practice it and not disobey. I thought it would be safer not to take my departure before I had cleared my conscience by writing poetry and so obeying the dream.

As in the *Crito,* Socrates' friends were so baffled by this dream-talk that they could not even comment, and the conversation moved to other topics. But, from our perspective, perhaps we can better appreciate what Socrates was trying to say. As he prepared to die (the *Phaedo* ended with his suicide) he wanted to leave his friends with one last moment of philosophical wonder, one final spark of encouragement to remain open to the new, the unexpected, the surprising. He revealed to them his experience of a lifelong recurrent dream which he had always interpreted, quite agreeably, as an affirmation of his vocation as a philosopher. But now, facing the imminence of death, Socrates felt the need to question that interpretation, raising the possibility that his whole life had been a mistake. Socrates took this on as his final challenge, and he approached it with characteristic playfulness and good cheer. By reinterpreting his recurrent dream and responding to it with this simple, childlike practice, Socrates illustrated a kind of transcendent philosophical spirit that could freely question its own self-understanding without anxiety or despair. His final words, after draining a cup of poison hemlock, were these: "Crito, we ought to offer a cock to Asclepius. See to it, and don't forget." The most eminent of philosophers ended his life by humbly offering thanks to the god who heals with dreams.

Plato was twenty-eight years old when Socrates was condemned to death by the citizens of Athens, and the young man's philosophical development was profoundly shaped by what he angrily perceived to be the moral, political, and religious failings of the Athenian state. Uncertainties remain over how many of Socrates' words in the Dialogues came directly from him and how many from Plato. I sense that the passages about dreams we have just discussed are more reflective of Socrates' ideas, and the dream references in Dialogues like the *Republic*, the *Timaeus*, and the *Laws* are more likely the ideas of Plato. That, at any rate, is the basis of the following analysis.[12]

The *Republic*, arguably the central work of Plato's mature thought, presented a sweeping vision of social perfection in which "philosopher-kings" were carefully trained from birth to develop the intelligence, skill, and fortitude they would need as adults to rule the state wisely and justly. In Plato's utopia the prime virtue was rationality, and he stressed the importance of using reason to drive out deluded thinking and superstitious beliefs. He criticized Homer on this score, particularly the *Iliad* passage in which Agamemnon was deceived by the evil dream sent by Zeus: "Though there are many other things that we praise in Homer, this we will not applaud, the sending of the dream by Zeus to Agamemnon."[13] According to Plato, reason teaches that God must be simple and true, not an irascible liar. Thus any stories suggesting otherwise were banned from the Republic.

One section of the dialogue examined the advantages and disadvantages of different forms of government, and most interesting from our perspective was the way Plato developed a psychological analysis in tandem with his political analysis. Each type of political state had its matching type of personality, an analogous form of psychological self-government.

When Plato turned his analysis to the worst type of state and man, that is, the tyrannical, he mentioned sleep and dreaming in order to illustrate the lawless instincts and desires that dominated in this condition. These awful appetites dwell within all humans, as proven by the natural, species-wide phenomenon of dreaming:

> [These desires] are awakened in sleep, when the rest of the soul, the rational, gentle, and dominant part, slumbers, but the beastly and savage part, replete with food and wine, gambols and, repelling sleep, endeavors to sally forth and satisfy its own instincts. You are aware that in such case there is nothing it will not venture to undertake as being released from all sense of shame and all reason. It does not shrink from attempting to lie with a mother in fancy or with anyone else, man, god, or brute. It is ready for any foul deed of blood; it abstains from no food, and, in a word, falls short of no extreme of folly and shamelessness. . . . There exists in every one of us, even in some reputed most respectable, a terrible, fierce, and lawless brood of desires, which it seems are revealed in sleep.[14]

From the vantage of Plato's philosophy, dreaming appeared as a dangerous psychological rebellion, a temporary defeat for the legitimate authorities of reason and a brief but savage reign of terror by the animal instincts. In contrast to Socrates' delight in dreaming, Plato was plainly scared of it. The pluralistic nature of dreams took on a much darker hue in his vision, and he brooded on their socially disruptive and taboo-violating potential, their hideous revelation of our primitive roots, and their total opposition to reason. The worst thing one could do, either politically or psychologically, was to allow these desires any influence over waking life: "The most evil type of man is . . . the man who, in his waking hours, has the qualities we found in his dream state."[15]

Plato did, however, grant the possibility that someone with extraordinary philosophical training could make use of insights gained during the condition of sleep:

> But when, I suppose, a man's condition is healthy and sober, and he goes to sleep after arousing his rational part and entertaining it with fair words and thoughts, and attaining to clear self-consciousness, while he has never starved nor indulged to repletion his appetitive part, so that it may be lulled to sleep and not disturb the better part by its pleasure or pain, but may suffer that in isolated purity to examine and reach out

toward and apprehend some of the things unknown to it, past, present, or future, and when he has in like manner tamed his passionate part, and does not after a quarrel fall asleep with anger still awake within him, but if he has thus quieted the two elements in his soul and quickened the third, in which reason resides, and so goes to his rest, you are aware that in such case he is most likely to apprehend truth, and the visions of his dreams are least likely to be lawless.[16]

This passage indicated that it was not dreaming per se that troubled Plato but rather the beastly passions they unleashed. In words that sound remarkably like a philosopher's ritual of dream incubation (with an almost Buddhist, middle-path approach to the preparation of mind and body), Plato outlined the possibility of *dreaming guided by pure reason,* the divine soul liberated from the sleeping body and capable of gaining true insight and trans-temporal knowledge. His description of a sleep state of "clear self-consciousness" recalls both Hindu and Buddhist teachings that likewise equated a person's psychospiritual purity with heightened clarity and control of dreaming. The difference is that Plato never followed up on his own suggestion. He left it open as a logical possibility within his philosophy, but apparently never tried to apply it in practice. Ultimately, Plato could not find a place in his vision of the world for oneiric experience.[17]

Nor, really, could his student, Aristotle. Like Plato, Aristotle acknowledged certain potentials in dreaming that, if taken seriously, would seem to warrant much more investigation; and, like Plato, he left no evidence that he ever engaged in such investigations. Aristotle wrote two short treatises on the subject, *De Insomniis* (On Dreams) and *De Divinatione per Somnum* (On Prophesying by Dreams), in which he analyzed the basic features of sleep and dreaming, and explained them in terms of the natural laws of physics.[18] In *De Insomniis,* he observed that when humans are sleeping the faculties of sense perception and rational thought cease their normal operation. Therefore, dreams cannot arise from sense perceptions or the intellect, which in Aristotle's philosophy were the only faculties by which humans acquired true knowledge. He argued that dreams were, in fact, merely echoes of sense perceptions from daily life. What appeared to be external objects were really internal representations of past experiences, particularly those of unusual emotional intensity:

We are easily deceived respecting the operations of sense-perception when we are excited by emotions, and different persons according to their different emotions; for example, the coward when excited by fear, the amorous person by amorous desire; so that, with but little resemblance to go upon, the former thinks he sees the object of his desire; and the more deeply one is under the influence of emotion, the less similarity is required to give rise to these illusory impressions.

In Aristotle's rendering of human psychology, the state of sleep allows a passion-driven hyper-connectivity to generate internal images that reflect the distinctive emotional concerns of each individual's waking life. His formulation of this basic idea has itself echoed through the following centuries of Western civilization, eventually shedding its ties to his outdated notions of human anatomy but still preserving the core insight that dreaming is a natural product of the mind's activities during sleep with meaningful connections to the individual's waking life.

In *De Divinatione per Somnum,* Aristotle evaluated claims regarding divine dreams foretelling the future. He was skeptical of such claims because they violated his elitist sense of the Athenian social and intellectual hierarchy: "It is absurd to combine the idea that the sender of such dreams should be God with the fact that those to whom he sends them are not the best and wisest, but merely commonplace persons." Nevertheless, he went on to analyze prophetic dreams in terms of three categories: causes, tokens, and coincidences. Dreams may sometimes be the cause of future actions, when "the movements set up first in sleep . . . prove to be starting-points of actions to be performed in the daytime." Aristotle said that dreams could also be tokens of the future, and here he gave the example of dreams revealing the onset of an illness before the individual has become aware of it. Sounding much like Plato, he explained these dreams by reference to the liberation of reason during sleep. In the sensory withdrawl and quietude of sleep, the mind is capable of perceiving subtle movements, stirrings, and beginnings that are ordinarily lost in the bustle of daily life: "It is manifest that these beginnings must be more evident in sleeping than in waking moments."

Aristotle concluded his analysis by dismissing most so-called prophetic dreams as mere coincidences in which people mistakenly perceive a connection between a dream and an external event. In so doing he returned dreaming to the realm of folk belief, a safely remote location from which it had no further influence on his philosophy. Unfortunately, Aristotle never explored the intriguing possibilities raised by his first two categories. If the internal movements of sleep and dreaming can be the "starting points" and causes of waking actions, what does that imply about the intentionality and autonomous creativity of the nonrational forces within us? If the liberation of reason in sleep enables it to gain such potentially valuable knowledge, what is the full extent of this oneiric ability? These are questions deserving deeper and more sustained attention than Aristotle was able or willing to give them. To his credit, however, he did leave open the possibility that people could find worthwhile insights in their dreams if they learned how to filter out the distorting influences of their emotions in order to perceive the underlying psychological movements and forms. To become a "skillful interpreter," Aristotle said, one should develop the "faculty of observing resemblances," that is, the ability to "rapidly discern, and at a glance comprehend, the scattered and distorted fragments of such forms." In this way one could, with the blessings of Aristotle's rationalist philosophy, practice a naturalistic approach to dream interpretation.

Dreaming in the Polis

The philosophical teachings of Socrates, Plato, and Aristotle were part of a culture-wide conversation about the nature and meaning of dreams. Everywhere we look in classic Greek culture—in drama, poetry, history, and medicine—we find dreaming represented both as a valuable source of heavenly knowledge and as a frightening portal into the nether regions of the psyche and the cosmos.

   Oedipus Rex by Sophocles (fifth century BCE) displayed on stage the tragic fate of a man doomed by the horrors of irrational passion.[19] The play tells the mythological story of Oedipus, the righteous and upstanding king who discovers the shocking truth that he murdered his father and married his mother. At one point in the play, Oedipus's wife/mother Jocasta mentions the frequency of son-mother incest dreams, and she says not to worry about them: "As to your mother's marriage bed—don't fear it. Before this, in dreams too, as well as oracles, many a man has lain with his own mother. But he to whom such things are nothing bears his life most easily." The audience for Sophocles' play knew that Oedipus was, without consciously knowing it, living out this common incestuous dream in waking reality. Jocasta's dismissive attitude thus becomes an ironic reminder that such dreams could be truthful revelations of the awful depths of human desire.

In *Hecuba*, by Sophocles' contemporary Euripides, the play's heroine experienced an intensely frightening nightmare portending the death of her children, moving her to exclaim,

> What apparition rose, what shape of terror stalking the darkness? O goddess Earth [*potnia Chthon*] womb of dreams [*meter oneiron*] whose dusky wings trouble, like bats, the flickering air! Beat back that dream I dreamed, that horror that arose in the night.[20]

This unsettling passage presented a geneology of dreams different from Hesiod's but equally as dark and forbidding. Dreams were born of the primordial female power of the earth, the goddess *Chthon*, whose oracle at Delphi was stolen from her by Apollo. In retaliation, she created dreams: "And so in anger [the goddess] bred a band of dreams which in the night should be oracular to men, foretelling truth. And this impaired the dignity of Phoebus [Apollo] and of his prophecies."[21] The revelatory, truth-telling power of dreams was, in this story, the product of *Chthon's* vengeful effort to spread the power of prophecy beyond the exclusive control of Apollo. Euripides offered a mythic vision of dreaming as a divinely inspired but conflict-ridden gift shared (at least potentially) by all humankind.

Aeschylus, the third great tragedian of classical Greece, included a deeply disturbing nightmare at a pivotal moment in the *Oresteia*, the trilogy of plays telling the story of the bloody downfall of the mythic hero Agamemnon and his family's "House of Atreus." Agamemnon's victory in the Trojan War was purchased at a terrible price: he had to kill his daughter, Iphigenia, as a sacrifice to gain the gods' favor. When Agamemnon returned home after the war his wife Clytemnestra slew him for that crime, and then several years later their son Orestes (with the help of his sister Electra) murdered Clytemnestra for killing his father. In the middle play (*The Libation Bearers*), before Orestes has taken his vengeance, the Chorus reveals to him a bizarre recurrent dream experienced by his mother: Clytemnestra gives birth to a snake, wraps it in blankets like a baby, and puts it to her breast to nurse; but the snake bites her nipple and draws blood.[22] Upon hearing this Orestes cries,

> This is not meaningless! . . . [M]y prayer, by this land, by my father's grave, [is this]: may this dream find fulfillment for me! I judge it will, too; all of it fits. For if the snake came from the same place I did, and wore my swaddling clothes, and sucked the breast that gave me sustenance,

mixed the dear milk with clots of blood, and she was terrified at what had happened—then, it must be so that, as she raised this fearful monster, she must die violently! For I that became that very snake will kill her, even as the dream has said.

The Greek audience of Aeschylus' play would know from their familiarity with Homer that dreams are not always trustworthy oracles and that strong emotions can be confusing factors in their interpretation. But Orestes shows no such misgivings. He instantly accepts the dream as a favorable prophecy that fits with his gathering plan to kill his mother. The perverse sexual imagery of the dream reflects the unholy horror of what Orestes is contemplating. That is why he doesn't pause over the alarming detail of his own identity being symbolized by a monstrous serpent—he knows this is what he must become to fulfill his sacred duty to his father.

The poet Pindar (522–443 BCE) told a story in *The Olympian* about a brave and adventuresome young man named Bellerophon, son of the god Poseidon and his human wife Eurynome, whose most famous feat depended on a magical dream incubation.[23] Bellerophon's greatest desire was to possess the winged horse Pegasus, a marvelous creature born from the blood of the monster Gorgon after being slain by Perseus. An old wise man told Bellerophon that if he wanted to capture Pegasus he should go to the temple of Athena and sleep there in hope of a revelatory dream. The young man did as advised, and while he slept next to the temple's alter the goddess appeared before him holding a golden object. "Asleep?" Athena asked him. "Nay, wake, here is what will charm the steed you covet." Bellerophon awoke in amazement to find a horse's bridle made entirely of gold on the floor beside him. He immediately set out in search of Pegasus. When he finally found him, the horse willingly allowed the young man to strap on the bridle and ride him. From thenceforth Pegasus and Bellerophon became a united heroic team. This was a very popular story among the ancient Greeks, and the transformation of the golden bridle from dreaming to waking object reflected a lively sense of potential interpenetration between the two states of being. As a divine gift that bridged the dreaming and waking worlds, the bridle had the special power to bond Pegasus and Bellerophon in peaceful mutuality, without violence or coercion.

Turning to a mode of discourse more akin to the social sciences of today, numerous dream reports were included in the *Histories* of Herodotus (484–425 BCE).[24] Known both as the "Father of History" and the

"Father of Lies," Herodotus wrote detailed descriptions and analyses of his extensive travels across the Mediterranean and into Mesopotamia, and he provided additional evidence of different cultural beliefs about dreaming. For example, Herodotus mentioned an incestuous dream of the Athenian traitor Hippias that motivated his decision to help the Persians attack his home city: "In the past night he had seen a vision in his sleep, in which he thought that he lay with his own mother. He interpreted this dream to signify that he should return to Athens to recover his power, and so die as an old man in his own mother country." Hippias's dream of violating a sexual taboo foreshadowed his waking violation of a political taboo. Like Jocasta, he missed the deeper truth in this dream and suffered accordingly—the Athenians routed the Persians in the Battle of Marathon (490 BCE). Elsewhere in the *Histories* Herodotus spoke of the political-military leaders Xerxes of Persia and Astyages of Media seeing troubling, ominous dreams with elusive messages that defied the kings' wishful interpretations. These reports are consistent with the kinds of royal dreams we have encountered frequently in Greek and Mesopotamian cultures, strengthening our overall sense of the popular matrix of dream belief, practice, and experience that predominated in this era.

Asclepius, God of Healing

Among the ancient Greek medical specialists, Hippocrates (460–377 BCE) was the most revered. His naturalistic investigations into the workings of the body marked a huge advance in the understanding of the biological systems and physiological processes upon which human life depends. Many centuries later, the Roman physician Galen (129–200 CE) applied Hippocrates' insights in surgical practice and experimental dissections, in the course of which he established the basic anatomical principles that have guided Western medicine right up to the present day.

That much of medical history is fairly well known. Less familiar is that Hippocrates, Galen, and many other Greek and Roman physicians were originally trained as priest-healers at the temples of Asclepius, where they developed a strong and lasting interest in dreams as tools of healing. Hippocrates served at the god's sanctuary in his hometown of Cos, where he later founded his own school of medical education. The Hippocratic text *On Regimen* offered a kind of doctor's manual of dream interpretation, explaining the bodily symbolism of common dream images and seeking diagnostic signs of future illnesses.[25] For his part, Galen was trained as a *therapeutes* at the Asclepian temple of Pergamum (modern-day Turkey). His voluminous medical writings frequently mentioned "our ancestral god Asclepius" and the medically predictive value of dreams.[26] Thus the two most esteemed physicians of antiquity were fully trained initiates of Asclepius, the same deity to whom Socrates dedicated a sacrificial cock with his final breath.

Who was this god who inspired the greatest healers of classical Greece and Rome?[27] Asclepius was born of Apollo, the mighty oracular god of Delphi, and a mortal woman named Coronis. When the pregnant Coronis fell in love with a human man, Apollo in his wrath ordered her immediate death. As Coronis's lifeless body lay on the funeral pyre, Apollo rescued their baby from the flames by performing what amounted to the first caesarean delivery. The child was raised by the centaur Chiron, who taught him the arts of medicine. Soon Asclepius became famous as an amazingly gifted physician whose skill was so great he could bring the dead back to life. Unfortunately Zeus viewed this as a rebellion against the divinely mandated balance between life and death, and he punished Asclepius by striking him dead with a bolt of lightning. Still, even Zeus had to acknowledge that humans had loved Asclepius, and so he placed the healing god in the sky as the constellation *Ophiocus* (which depicts a man holding a snake, the god's sacred animal), where people could see Asclepius every night if they looked up to the heavens.

In practical terms, those who worshiped Asclepius sought his specific guidance in treating the whole spectrum of injuries, illnesses, and psychosomatic maladies that humans suffer in the natural course of life. The central means of eliciting this guidance was, as mentioned, the practice of temple-based dream incubation. Our knowledge of the Asclepian temples comes from several sources covering many centuries, and a number of temples remain intact today, so we have a good idea of the kinds of ritual activities that occurred during the god's long reign in the Greek and Roman imagination. Most of the temples were set in aesthetically beautiful and somewhat remote locations, with a large statue of the god prominently placed to greet the pilgrims who had journeyed there in search of relief from their pains. Nonpoisonous snakes roamed the grounds freely, and people spent their days bathing, praying, and generally cleansing themselves of their ordinary cares and concerns. The temple walls were inscribed with stories of the miraculous cures performed by the god, something that certainly heightened a sense of expectation among new visitors. At night the temple priests guided the supplicants into the *aba-ton,* the inner sanctum of the temple, to lie down upon a *kline* ("clinic," a ritual bed). While serpents slithered on the floor around them, the people went to sleep in hopes of a curative dream visitation from Asclepius. When people awoke in the morning they reported their dreams to the temple priests, who promptly explained their diagnostic significance for the illness at hand. The incubation process would continue for as many nights as it took for the person's suffering to disappear.

Most of the therapeutic techniques used at the Asclepian temples were consistent with Hippocrates' basic regimen of healthy diet, walking, cleanliness, and fresh air. We can never be sure whether these techniques were actually as effective or lasting as their advocates proclaimed. Considering the Asclepian temples in terms of contemporary medical science, they can be seen as centers for generating a dream-mediated placebo effect.[28] The fertile combination of intense personal desire, ritually consecrated space, and repeated external encouragement created a perfect environment for an unusually vivid and memorable dream that would plausibly have the effect of stimulating whatever autonomous healing systems are at work in the human body. The temple priests may not have fully understood the physiology of those self-healing systems (nor, to be honest, do doctors today), but they were experts in practical methods of activating them and putting them to therapeutic use. The cultivation of revelatory dreams was firmly believed to be an integral part of this process.

Dreaming and Empire

While Athens was busy persecuting its brightest mind, a city-state to the west was beginning its transformation from a regional center of trade and commerce to a vast empire ruling millions of people. Rome was a fortified settlement as far back as the eighth century BCE, in a region of the Italian peninsula highly favorable for agriculture but subject to constant warfare among competing city-states. Defeated and sacked by the Gauls in 387, Rome quickly rebuilt itself and counterattacked its enemies, winning one victory after another until it found itself ruling all of Italy and the overseas kingdom of Carthage. From there the familiar cycle of social-structural development took over. The more slaves and arable land Rome controlled, the more food it could reap from systematic agriculture, and those larger crop yields produced the necessary resources for ever larger professional armies, which enabled the further acquisition of land and slaves, and so on. One consequence of Rome's explosive growth was a dramatic increase in opportunities for travel and communication between different regions of the empire. People were allowed (or violently compelled, depending on one's point of view) to develop novel syntheses of beliefs and practices drawn from more than one cultural tradition. This was certainly true in the realm of dreaming, with creative new integrations of Mediterranean and Mesopotamian dream teachings appearing in literature (Virgil, Ovid, Apuleius, Lucian, Plutarch), ritual (Asclepian Temples, magical dream spells), medicine (Galen and his followers), history (Pausanias), and philosophy (Cicero, Lucretius, Macrobius).[29]

The speed of Rome's military and political ascent far outpaced its native cultural development, and its founding myth had to be commissioned by the emperor Octavian late in the first century BCE. The task was given to his loyal follower, the renowned poet Virgil (70–19 BCE). Over the final ten years of his life Virgil wrote *The Aeneid,* an epic poem that both glorified the empire and confessed its crimes and inhumanities. The story followed the relentlessly dutiful hero Aeneas as he journeyed from the flaming walls of Troy to the distant shores of Italy, where he established Rome as his new home. Borrowing freely from *The Iliad* and *The Odyssey,* Virgil included numerous dream episodes in *The Aeneid,* more than in both of Homer's epics combined (which, I imagine, was exactly the point). Most frequently reported were ancestral visitation dreams. Aeneas and several other characters experienced vivid warning dreams in which deceased family members alerted them to dangers in waking life. The dream figures were described as ghostly wisps, pale in form but wise and trustworthy in spirit. Aeneas also received several dreams of divine reassurance from his father and other deities that roused his courage during a crisis or before a battle, motivating him with magnificent visions of Rome's future destiny. Virgil furthermore described Latinus, the father of Aeneas's eventual wife, as practicing a time-honored form of Greek dream incubation by sleeping on an animal skin and seeking an answer during sleep from the local deity Faunus. Latinus received a divine dream ordering him to save his daughter for marriage to the stranger who would soon arrive on the shores of Italy.

In contrast to these generally positive and helpful divine revelations, Virgil also spoke of the terrible nightmares suffered by Queen Dido of Carthage, who had fallen in love with Aeneas and whose dreams accurately foresaw that he would ultimately abandon her. Dido's dreams had nothing divine about them; they were brutal, painfully honest self-portraits, and when they came true she killed herself. The association between dreaming, death, and women also arose in a false divine dream reported by the mischievous goddess Iris, who disguised herself as a human in order to stir panic among the Trojan women. She told them she saw a dream in which the prophetess Cassandra appeared with burning pieces of wood, and screamed, "Look here for Troy. Here is your home!" This was an obviously fabricated dream, a ruse intended to deceive and mislead the listeners, much like the evil dream sent by Zeus to Agamemnon in *The Iliad*. The irony, of course, is that in this case the false dream came true—its apocalyptic imagery eventually proved prophetic.

Virgil also included passages that envisioned a cosmic genealogy for dreams, with intriguing references to Hesiod and Homer.[30] During Aeneas's visit to the underworld he reached the kingdom of the spectral lord Dis, at whose gates he found a horrible phantasmagoria of evils: Disease, Old Age, Fear, Hunger, Poverty, Death, and "Death's brother, Sleep," and "all the evil Pleasures of the Mind," and the Furies, and War, and Strife. And in the midst of this darkest and most forlorn of places, Aeneas came upon the Tree of Dreams:

> Among them stands a giant shaded elm, a tree with spreading boughs and aged arms; they say that is the home of empty Dreams that cling, below, to every leaf. And more, so many monstrous shapes of savage beasts are stabled there: Centaurs and double-bodied Scyllas; the hundred-handed Briareus; the brute of Lerna, hissing horribly; Chimaera armed with flames; Gorgons and Harpies; and Geryon, the shade that wears three bodies. And here Aeneas, shaken suddenly by terror, grips his sword; he offers naked steel and opposes those who come. Had not his wise companion [his father] warned him they were only thin lives that glide without a body in the hollow semblance of a form, he would in vain have torn the shadows with his blade.

Like his Greek forebearers, Virgil recognized the primal darkness of dreaming, its natural affinity with evil spirits and monsters, its deceptively realistic and emotionally overwhelming qualities, and its external reality as a mysterious force beyond the control of humans. Even the heroic Aeneas with his "naked steel" was powerless before it.

Virgil appropriated Penelope's "two gates" speech from *The Odyssey*, though with a puzzling twist.[31] The verses came at the end of a long dream vision in which Anchises revealed to Aeneas the glorious future destiny of his son in Rome, concluding with this:

> There are two gates of Sleep: the one is said to be of horn, through it an easy exit is given to true Shades; the other is made of polished ivory, perfect, glittering, but through that way the Spirits send false dreams into the world above. And here Anchises, when he is done with words, accompanies the Sibyl and his son together, and he sends them through the gate of ivory.

This kind of direct Homeric reference was Virgil's way of anchoring the story of Rome in the wisest, most authoritative traditions of the Greeks. *The Aeneid* endorsed the basic duality of dreaming expressed by Penelope in *The Odyssey*, acknowledging the possibility of both divine revelation and deceptive nonsense in dreams. What is strange is the departure of Anchises through the gate of ivory—the portal for false dreams. Was this a subversive critique of Rome's inflated perception of its own grandeur, or was it simply a typographical error that Virgil did not live long enough to correct? We do not know, and the uncertainty adds an extra dimension of epistemological instability to any attempt to distinguish sharply between true and false dreams in *The Aeneid*.

Oneirocritica

By far the best source of information about dreams in ancient Rome is the *Oneirocritica* (*Interpretation of Dreams*) by Artemidorus of Daldis, a professional diviner from a Roman province in present-day Turkey.[32] As we shall see in coming chapters, his text, originally written in part as a private training manual for his son, has been copied and translated so often that it could be the single most influential dream book in the world. Artemidorus lived in the second century CE, during a relatively peaceful and prosperous era of Roman history. Few details of his life are known, beyond that he read a great deal and traveled widely throughout the Mediterranean world. He referred to many other dream manuals he had studied, indicating a lively tradition of these kinds of books in Roman culture. He made a point of emphasizing the rationality of his approach and the empirical basis of his interpretations, even when his studies led him into folk practices scorned by the cultural elite. He said he had "consorted for many years with the much-despised diviners of the marketplace" in order to deepen his oneiric knowledge:

> People who assume a holier-than-thou countenance and who arch their eyebrows in a superior way dismiss them as beggars, charlatans, and buf- foons, but I have ignored their disparagement. Rather, in the different cit- ies of Greece and at great religious gatherings in that country, in Asia, in Italy, and in the largest and most populous of the islands, I have patiently listened to old dreams and their consequences. For there was no other possible way in which to get practice in these matters.

Artemidorus was familiar with the skepticism toward dreams expressed by authoritative voices of Roman culture (e.g., Cicero, Lucretius). He wrote the *Oneirocritica* as a response to that skepticism, aiming to prove the legitimacy and practical value of dream interpretation in ordinary people's lives. To that end he developed a rational classification of typical dreams and their common meanings. To begin, he divided dreams into two categories, *enhypnion* and *oneiros*: "*Oneiros* differs from *enhypnion* in that the first indicates a future state of affairs, while the other indicates a present state of affairs." As examples of *enhypnion* Artemidorus described hungry people dreaming of eating, thirsty people dreaming of drinking, and fearful people dreaming of what they fear, all of which were accurate reflections of the present concerns of the dreamer. *Oneiros,* by contrast, went beyond the present to "call to the dreamer's attention a prediction of future events." Artemidorus then made a second distinction, between *theorematic* and *allegorical* dreams. *Theorematic* dreams were said to be direct in their imagery and meaning (a dream of a shipwreck foretell- ing an actual shipwreck), whereas allegorical dreams involved indirect imagery, symbols, and metaphors; in such cases, "the soul is conveying something obscurely by physical means." Here and elsewhere Artemido- rus expressed a broadly spiritual appreciation for the prophetic powers of the human soul and the divine provenance of certain dreams, though he made it clear that his focus was on interpretive practice, not philosophical theory:

> I do not, like Aristotle, inquire as to whether the cause of our dreaming is outside of us and comes from the gods or whether it is motivated by

something within, which disposes the soul in a certain way and causes a natural event to happen to it. Rather, I use the word in the same way that we customarily call all unforeseen things god-sent.

The main body of the *Oneirocritica* consisted of an extensive catalog of dream images and their interpretations. Hundreds of examples were discussed, including dreams of going blind, losing teeth, being beheaded, and many other forms of bodily misfortune; dreams of rivers, mountains, clouds, trees, kings, priests, gods, mythological beasts, family members, and all manner of sexual partners. A lengthy section considered the traditional Greek and Roman theme of a son dreaming of sex with his mother: "The case of one's mother is both complex and manifold and admits of many different interpretations—a thing not all dream interpreters have realized. The fact is that the mere act of intercourse by itself is not enough to show what is portended. Rather, the manner of the embraces and the various positions of the bodies indicate different outcomes."

The interpretations Artemidorus offered were related primarily to the dreamer's personal life (e.g., health, occupation, finances, family), though he granted that political leaders could have dreams with significance for the broader community as well. He emphasized that dream interpretation was not simply a matter of looking up meanings in a dream dictionary, and that a detailed knowledge of the dreamer's life was required to insure the accuracy of any interpretation: "It is profitable—indeed, not only profitable but necessary—for the dreamer as well as for the person who is interpreting that the dream interpreter know the dreamer's identity, occupation, birth, financial status, state of health, and age." Artemidorus described several cases of multivalent interpretation in which the same dream experienced by different people yielded different meanings, and also paradoxical cases in which good contents portended bad results (e.g., a man dreamed of receiving two loaves of bread from Helios the sun-god, and died two days later) and bad contents foretold good results (e.g., a poor man dreaming of being hit by a thunderbolt meant the gaining of wealth). Paradoxical interpretations were always possible, but in practice Artemidorus usually focused on direct similarities between dream content and waking life, guided by what I would call a principle of psychosocial harmony—whatever appeared in accordance with social customs was good, whatever deviated from those customs was bad.

Although the *Oneirocritica* was intended to benefit his readers, Artemidorus insisted that books were not enough: "I maintain that it is necessary

for the interpreter of dreams to have prepared himself from his own resources and to use his native intelligence rather than simply to rely upon
manuals." Throughout the book he emphasized that personal experience
was the only reliable guide.

> I have always called upon experience as the witness and guiding principle
> of my statements. Everything has been the result of personal experience,
> since I have not done anything else, and have always devoted myself, day
> and night, to the study of dream interpretation.

Soon after Artemidorus's time, the Roman Empire collapsed. The city
was finally overrun by Visigoth and Vandal armies in the fifth century
CE, and from thenceforth Graeco-Roman civilization no longer reigned
supreme over the Western world. The Mediterranean culture of dreaming
continued, however, and we can still see living traces of it today, inter-
mixed with local versions of Christianity.[33] The mountain villagers of the
Greek island of Naxos, for example, continue to practice dream incubation in hopes of divine healing and guidance. Greek Orthodox Christians
in Thebes and members of the religious community known as *Anastenaria*
in Bulgaria pay close attention to their dreams, sleeping in churches and
the shrines of saints to elicit heavenly revelations and favorable prophecies. Long before Christianity came on the scene, an ancient and complex network of Greek, Roman, and Mesopotamian dream traditions had
profoundly shaped the sleeping and waking imaginations of the people of
this part of the world. The Christian dream teachings to be discussed in
the next chapter are, in historical terms, a response to (and continuation
of) those deeply rooted traditions.

Summary

Judging by their myths and epic poems, the ancient Greeks and Romans
believed dreams were externally caused encounters with the gods. But a
closer look at these mythic tales reveals a more sophisticated psychological understanding of the dreaming imagination. Once we take into account the writings of the philosophers, poets, and historians of Greece
and Rome, we have to acknowledge a strong kinship between their dream
theories and the theories of modern Western scientists. For the Greeks
and Romans, a few dreams were accepted as genuine conduits of divine

energy and religious experience, but most dream experiences had their origins in the natural processes of the sleeping mind. Many of the greatest philosophers dismissed dreaming as inferior to waking rationality, and they took little interest in exploring any of its possible functions or purposes. Nevertheless, dreams remained very popular over the centuries as a universally accessible source of divine guidance and prophetic knowledge. More important than prophecy, however, was the power of healing in dreams. The dream incubation rituals of Asclepius and the medical practices of Hippocrates and Galen all cultivated the healing resources of dreaming to an unprecedented degree of effectiveness. The interpretation of dreams in Greek and Roman cultures was believed to be a perilous affair, with dangerous consequences for those who misread the will of the gods. Hence the prominence of dream books and professional interpreters who were skilled in the process of translating dream images into waking meanings. Building on the wisdom of the Egyptians, Assyrians, and other Fertile Crescent cultures, the dream interpreters of Greece and Rome (best exemplified by Artemidorus) developed a systematic approach that relied on the interpreter's "native intelligence," common sense, and personal experience of the world. Such a simple and straightforward approach enabled anyone to practice dream interpretation, not just professional experts—planting a democratic seed in a realm of experience that would increasingly become constrained by religious authority.

6

Christianity

Here, midway in the book, we should consider the strong cross-currents developing in our knowledge of the dreaming-religion connection. Along with abundant evidence of the positive value of dreaming in religious history we have also found many voices of caution, mistrust, and doubt regarding the divine meaningfulness of dreams. If nothing else, recognition of these different perspectives should put to rest any attempt to characterize the minds of ancient peoples as somehow irrational, deficient, or primitive in comparison with the scientific mind of today. Debates about the truth vs. nonsense of dreaming are nothing new. They extend as far back in time as recorded history allows us to see. From the Upanishads and the Chinese philosopher Wang Chong to Jeremiah, Penelope, and Aristotle, a degree of rational skepticism has been a recurrent feature of human interaction with dreaming, generating several explanations that disregard heavenly causes and focus instead on the physical, emotional, and environmental conditions of the dreamer. Ancient peoples did not possess the research technologies to study these factors the way modern scientists do, but they were just as aware of the naturalistic influences on dream formation and function.

The story becomes even more complicated when we take into account other historical teachings (e.g., from Buddha and Plato) that treat the bodily basis of dreaming as the beginning, not the end, of critical analysis. From these perspectives, physically arousing dreams were seen as evidence of mental or spiritual weakness, a failure to control the emotions, desires, and impulses that impeded the highest forms of human development. This was especially true regarding sexual dreams, the occurrence of which has been reported in every culture considered so far. The universal prevalence of sexually stimulating dreams has been solidly confirmed by modern sleep laboratory research, with the discovery that each phase of REM sleep is automatically accompanied by an increase in blood flow to the genitals, producing erections in men and clitoral swelling in women, occasionally leading all the way to physical climax.[1] It is obviously difficult to study such phenomena with much precision, but apparently these nocturnal climaxes initially occur before people have had any waking-life sexual activity, and they recur later in life regardless of the individual's waking sexual behavior. All this poses a serious problem for religious and spiritual traditions that emphasize celibacy, asceticism, and strict control of sexual desires. If your tradition begins with a strong emphasis on the dangers of sexuality and bodily instincts generally, then dreaming automatically becomes a threat to religious purity, and sleep becomes a life-long battleground between good and evil. This has been an especially difficult challenge for Christianity, as its historical appreciation for the divine power of revelatory visions has competed with a fearful hostility toward the sensual temptations of oneiric experience.

Novum Testamentum

Christianity originated in the ministry of a Jewish prophet and healer named Jesus, who was born sometime in the last years of the first century BCE in the eastern Mediterranean town of Bethlehem, in an area (present-day Israel) under the control of the Roman Empire. His birth was a miraculous event in many ways, and dreams were said to have played a significant role. The Gospel of Matthew opened with Joseph (named after the greatest dreamer of the *Torah*) receiving a series of four heaven-sent dreams that guided him in the care and protection of Jesus, his newborn foster-son.[2] When Joseph first learned of Mary's pregnancy, which occurred "before they came together," he decided he should quietly divorce her:

> But as he considered this, behold, an angel of the Lord appeared to him in a dream, saying, "Joseph, son of David, do not fear to take Mary your wife, for that which is conceived in her is of the Holy Spirit; she will bear a son, and you shall call his name Jesus, for he will save his people from their sins." . . . When Joseph woke from sleep, he did as the angel of the Lord commanded him; he took his wife, but knew her not until she had borne a son; and he called his name Jesus.

Here, at the very beginning of Jesus's life, a dream was credited with having a remarkably powerful and beneficial impact—protecting his family, establishing his divine identity, prophesizing his future mission, and revealing the name he should be called. This marks another striking instance of religious dreaming at a time of birth, a moment of newly emergent power. The heavenly provenance of Joseph's dream was never questioned; he awakened and immediately obeyed. Likewise, he immediately obeyed the warning he received in another dream regarding the murderous intentions of the Roman governor Herod. Following the birth of Jesus and the departure of the "wise men from the East" (who were themselves warned in a dream to avoid Herod), "an angel of the Lord appeared to Joseph in a dream and said, 'Rise, take the child and his mother, and flee to Egypt, and remain there till I tell you; for Herod is about to search for the child, to destroy him.' And he rose and took the child and his mother by night." In this dream the heavenly message was so urgent and the predicted threat so dire that Joseph could not wait until morning to act. He rose in the night and fled with his family to Egypt, waiting there for further heavenly guidance, which came some years later: "An angel of the Lord appeared in a dream to Joseph in Egypt, saying, 'Rise, take the child and his mother, and go to the land of Israel, for those who sought the child's life are dead.'" Once back in Israel, Joseph realized he still had to reason to fear persecution from Herod's son, "and being warned in a dream he withdrew to the district of Galilee," specifically the town of Nazareth. Thus, by means of a series of clear, direct, and unquestionably trustworthy dreams, Jesus was brought to the safety of his new home, where he would live for the next thirty years in apparent anonymity as an Aramaic-speaking Jewish carpenter.

The rise of Jesus's career as a teacher, healer, exorcist, and prophet was stimulated by several powerful religious experiences, some visual and others auditory, in which he was said to have felt an overwhelming presence of God's spirit. Not all these experiences were pleasant; at one point, "the spirit immediately drove him out into the wilderness. And he was in the wilderness for forty days, tempted by Satan; and he was with the wild beasts."[3] Nor were his visions exclusively private, as when he took some of his followers away to a high mountain, where "he was transfigured before them, and his garments became glistening, intensely white, as no fuller on earth could bleach them. And there appeared to them Elijah with Moses; and they were talking with Jesus."[4] It is significant that none of these mystically charged experiences were described as dreams. The religious status of Jesus was so lofty that his spiritual capacities had evidently developed beyond the need for dreaming. Like his visionary companion, Moses,

Jesus spoke to God face to face, directly and without the interfering medium of dark speech. The absence of dream reports in Jesus's life may also have been because of the editorial interests of the Gospel writers, who were actively trying to strengthen and defend their small countercultural movement. As we have seen in the last two chapters, the pagan civilization surrounding the early Christians was permeated with fantastic stories of gods and goddesses helping humans in their dreams, and thus it would be an effective way of highlighting the divine superiority of Jesus to portray him as beyond dreaming.[5] Why would God need to send a dream to Himself?

One other dream was mentioned during Jesus's life in the Gospel of Matthew, and it came to an unexpected figure at a critical moment in the narrative.[6] Jesus had been captured and brought before Pilate, the Roman governor of Jerusalem, who was contemplating the fate of the self-proclaimed Messiah. Just then, Pilate received a message from his wife: "Have nothing to do with that righteous man, for I have suffered much over him today in a dream." Pilate already suspected that the charges brought by the Pharisaic Jews against Jesus were false, and he was considering whether to pardon the prisoner. But his wife's dream turned him away from making any active decision. In her message she acknowledged the spiritual worthiness of Jesus, but the distressing quality of her dream drove her to plead for Pilate's total withdrawal from the situation. Not knowing the content of her nightmare (if it actually happened), we cannot say whether her interpretation or Pilate's final decision—washing his hands before the crowd and delivering Jesus to be crucified—were justified responses to the dream. The ambiguous meaning of this dream, along with its obscure source (nothing else is said of Pilate's wife) and tragic contribution to Jesus's death, suggest a doubtful Christian attitude toward dreaming generally, effectively saying that the new religion did not rely on the misleading divination practices of the pagans. An alternative possibility is that the story reflected a deeper Christian recognition of emotionally intense, highly memorable dreams as capable of shaping the behavior of pagans and Christians alike (many early converts were Roman women), all according to the ultimate salvation plan of God.

In the rest of the *Novum Testamentum* (the canonical text of Christianity, written in the first and second centuries CE and canonized in the fourth century CE) four other dreams were mentioned, all experienced by Paul, the Roman convert and pioneering missionary.[7] Paul reported many types of religious experiences and communications with God, and it was clear that he (or the biblical editors) felt some degree of familiarity and comfort with dreaming as an authentic source of Christian revelation. However much his teachings pushed for a radical break between Christian and pagan worldviews, Paul accepted the general belief, so widely shared among Mesopotamian, Greek, and Roman people, that dreaming bore a divine potentiality. The four dreams described in the Book of Acts were all related to Paul's missionary activities, and they were described in terms that would be easily understood by the people of his time: "The following night the Lord stood by him and said, 'Take courage, for as you have testified about me at Jerusalem, so you must bear witness also at Rome.'" A deity appears during the night and stands before a sleeping person to deliver a message of reassurance in the face of dire waking challenges—this was the prototypical form of a mystical dream, and in Paul's case it provided a legitimate source of inspiration, encouragement, and guidance for his missionary activities: "And a vision appeared to Paul in the night: a man of Macedonia was standing beseeching him and saying, 'Come over to Macedonia and help us.' And when he had seen the vision, immediately we sought to go on into Macedonia, concluding that God had called us to preach the gospel to them." Nothing was said yet about the question of true vs. deceptive dreams; Paul's spiritual integrity was apparently sufficient to guarantee that whatever messages he received were genuinely sent by God and absolutely trustworthy as guides to future action.

Other than a quotation from the Book of Joel regarding the marvelous powers of spirit that will be given to all people in the Messianic age ("your sons and your daughters shall prophesy, and your young men shall see visions, and your old men shall dream dreams"), these are the only dream references in the *Novum Testamentum*.[8] The final text of Christian scripture, the Revelation to John, could perhaps be considered an epic-length visionary nightmare, comparable in its awful allegorical symbolism to the horrifying dreams of Nebuchadnezzar or the world-destroying nightmares of Buddha's wife Gopa and the Kuru warrior Karna. If nothing else, the spectacular visual imagery of Revelation and its evocation of primal existential fears of annihilation and death combined to create a metaphorical template for later expressions of Christian apocalypticism in dreams and other modes of visionary expression.

Converts and Martyrs

Moving from canonical texts to the actual lives of the early Christians, dreaming appears to have been a lively arena for the interplay of Christian and pagan religious practices. The subject of dreams provided a kind of common spiritual language among all Mediterranean peoples, and Christian missionaries found that speaking to people in that dream language could be a fruitful means of converting them to the new faith. Good evidence of dreaming as an impetus toward Christian conversion comes in a work of the late first century CE known as *The Shepherd,* by the former Roman slave Hermas.[9] *The Shepherd* presented a personal testimony of spiritual struggle and Christian triumph in the form of five elaborate dream visions (*horaseis,* a term related to vision and seeing). In these dreams Hermas spoke at length with an angel who guided him in a painful but cleansing analysis of his moral weaknesses, transforming his personality and attaining the spiritual purity that only the Christian faith could provide. As always, we do not know if anyone named Hermas actually dreamed these dreams. But as a literary document aimed at persuading an audience, *The Shepherd* clearly assumed that first-century Romans would understand, and could be swayed by, references to powerful dream experiences. Hermas's cause may have been further strengthened by his honest acknowledgment of the taboo-violating, morally transgressive tendencies of dreaming, tendencies that Christianity promised to overcome. At one point in his story Hermas reported experiencing a kind of vision-within-the-vision:

> During my prayer I saw the heavens open and that woman of whom I was enamored saluting me with the words: "Greetings, Hermas!" With my eyes fixed on her, I said, "Lady, what are you doing here?" Her answer was: "I have been taken up to convict you of your sins before the Lord." To this I said: "Are you my accuser at this moment?" "No," she said, "but you must listen to what I am about to tell you. God who dwells in heaven, the creator of beings out of nothing, he, who increases and multiplies them for the sake of his holy church, is angry with you for your offenses against me." For answer I said: "Offenses against you! How so? Have I ever made a coarse remark to you? Have I not always regarded you as a goddess? Did I not always show you the respect due to a sister? Lady, why do you make these false charges of wickedness and

uncleanness against me?" With a laugh she said: "In your heart there has arisen the desire of evil."

The figure in the dream vision was a Christian woman named Rhode, whom Hermas had once served during his years as a slave. In describing the dream, Hermas recalled an incident from the past in which Rhode asked for his help while she was bathing, an experience that naturally elicited sexual desires in Hermas. Although he never acted on those desires in waking life, they remained a disturbing presence in his inner world, and the dream-Rhode had come to force Hermas to face the reality of those hidden personal desires. The Christian faith required not just a change of behavior but a change of heart, and in the coming centuries many Christians would turn to their dreams for self-analytical insights into that deeper process of psychospiritual transformation.

The most dramatic narratives of early Christianity involved the deaths of martyrs who were persecuted and gruesomely killed because of their faith. One of the earliest and most influential of these martyr texts consisted of the diary of a young woman named Vibia Perpetua, who was mauled to death by wild lions in a Carthage amphitheater in 203 CE.[10] Perpetua was an educated member of a well-to-do family, but her conversion to Christianity put her into conflict with the Roman imperial government and its requirement that everyone participate in rituals of fidelity to the emperor and the gods. Perpetua refused, and so she was imprisoned and sentenced to public execution. During the weeks leading up to her death, Perpetua recorded a diary in which she described arguing with her distraught father, worrying about her infant child (she was secretly breast-feeding him in prison), and dreaming. Her first dream came in response to an incubation prompted by her brother, who said to her, "My lady, my sister, you are now greatly blessed; so much so that you can ask for a vision, and you will be shown if it is to be suffering unto death or a passing thing." Perpetua did as he suggested, and was shown a remarkable dream that blended Christian imagery with surrealistic details from her own personal condition:

> I saw a bronze ladder, marvelously long, reaching as far as heaven, and narrow too: people could climb it only one at a time. And on the sides of the ladder every kind of iron implement was fixed: there were swords, lances, hooks, cutlasses, javelins, so that if anyone went up carelessly or

not looking upwards, she would be torn and her flesh caught on the sharp iron. And beneath the ladder lurked a serpent of wondrous size, who laid ambushes for those mounting, making them terrified of the ascent.

With the encouragement of a fellow Christian, Perpetua stepped on the head of the serpent and rose up the ladder, praying for safety "in Christ's name." Once she reached the top of the ladder, she found herself in a spiritual utopia of pastoral bliss:

> I saw an immense space of garden, and in the middle of it a white-haired man sitting in shepherd's garb, vast milking sheep, with many thousands of people dressed in shining white standing all around. And he raised his head, looked at me, and said, "You are welcome, child." And he called me, and gave me, it seemed, a mouthful of the *caseo* he was milking; and I accepted it in both my hands together, and ate it, and all those standing around said: "Amen." And at the sound of that word I awoke, still chewing something indefinable and sweet. And at once I told my brother, and we understood that it would be mortal suffering; and we began to have no more hope in the world.

In response to her incubation prayers, Perpetua received a prophetic vision that confirmed her grim bodily fate while reassuring her about the fate of her eternal soul. The dream directly incorporated a great deal of imagery from classic Christian belief and iconography—the malevolent serpent, the ladder to heaven, the benevolent shepherd, the shining white garments. But the climactic moment of the dream came in the experience of eating the *caseo,* variously translated as cheese, milk, or sweet curds. This was the moment when Perpetua awoke, with that vividly pleasant taste sensation carrying over into waking awareness. The personal impact of this experience must have been tremendous, given that Perpetua was a nursing mother who was abandoning her child in obedience to a higher religious cause. In waking life she was worried about failing to provide her child with biological nourishment, but in her dream *she* was blessed to receive the ultimate in spiritual nourishment. A few days later a minor miracle occurred: "And somehow, through God's will, it [the child] no longer needed the breast, nor did my breasts become inflamed—so I was not tormented with worry for the child, or with soreness." Perpetua's Christian transformation was complete.

Her next two dreams reflected her shift of existential interest and orientation from this world to the next. While praying one day in prison, the name of a long-deceased brother, "Dinocrates," suddenly popped out of her mouth. Asking God for another vision, Perpetua received "that very night" a dream of Dinocrates, with cancer marring his face as it did right before he died, pathetically trying to reach his thirsty lips to a pool of water. When Perpetua awoke she resolved to pray for her brother's soul, feeling confident she had the ability to aid his struggles. A few days later she dreamed of Dinocrates healthy and clean, happily drinking from a golden bowl of water that never ran dry. Thus, as her own death approached, Perpetua concentrated her energies not on her own plight but on helping a deceased loved one in his spiritual journey beyond this life. Her final dream came the day before her execution, and it portrayed an epic battle between herself (transformed into a male wrestler) and "an Egyptian, foul of aspect." The wrestler-Perpetua fought ferociously with her/his fists and feet, rising off the ground at one point to land several flying kicks against the Egyptian's head. Finally, she/he was declared the winner, "and triumphantly I began to walk towards the Gate of the Living. And I awoke. And I knew I should have to fight not against wild beasts but against the Fiend; but I knew the victory would be mine."

Her diary ended there. The next day she walked out into the amphitheater and was mauled to death by lions in front of a cheering crowd. A worse fate could hardly be imagined, at least in worldly terms. But in her dream visions Perpetua discovered a deeper reality within herself, the reality of her Christian soul. No longer identifying herself as a daughter or mother, no longer attached to her gender or her physical body, willfully violating the biological instinct for self-preservation, Perpetua gloried in the spiritual power and freedom that came from surrendering herself entirely to God.

Not all Christians were persecuted so viciously, but Perpetua was hardly alone in suffering the wrath of Roman officials who saw the new religion's lofty monotheism as a challenge to their authority and a threat to the empire's social order. Despite (and partly because of) this governmental hostility, Christianity grew rapidly, aided by stories about converts like Hermas and martyrs like Perpetua, and also by the energetic caregiving practices of local church members. Inspired by Jesus's healing miracles, the early Christians concentrated their missionary work on providing aid, comfort, and medical attention to anyone who was sick and suffering. When the people regained their health, they frequently became devoted members of the Christian faithful who could offer personal testimonies of healing power. In just the one hundred or so years between Perpetua's death and the rise of Constantine the Great, Christianity was transformed from an oppressed minority sect to the dominant faith of the empire. According to legend, a dream marked a particularly decisive moment in the process of Constantine's conversion.[11] Before his crowning victory against Maxentius at the Milvian Bridge in 312 CE, Constantine saw a daytime vision followed by a nocturnal dream in which he beheld a brilliant image of the *labarum,* the sign of the Cross and emblem of the Christian God. The next day he ordered his troops to inscribe this image on their shields, and when they won the battle (despite being outnumbered five to one) Constantine gave credit to the God of the Christians. His battlefield conversion decisively shifted Roman sentiment in favor of the new faith, with momentous consequences for its future development. Although persecutions continued in various places, Constantine's "Edict of Milan" in 313 gave Christianity official status as a legal religion, and his personal testimony persuaded many people in the ruling classes to forego their pagan allegiances and submit to the Christian God. Thus Christianity took the fateful step of assuming the powers, and burdens, of ruling an empire.

Fathers of the Church

During the long period of Roman hostility to their faith, many of the early Christians took up residence in the unpopulated wilds and hinterlands of the empire, seeking a life of spiritual simplicity and purity away from the worldly temptations of pagan cities. Even after Constantine's conversion and the subsequent elimination of official repression, many Christians still felt drawn to seek God's presence in the desert, inspired in large part by Jesus's transformational sojourn through the wilderness. And, like Jesus, the so-called desert fathers were besieged in their solitary contemplations by demons. Dreaming took on a decidedly negative character in this context, and strenuous efforts were made to disregard the seductive images and alluring sensations that came during sleep. Evagrius Ponticus (346–399 CE), one of the most literate of the desert fathers, developed an elaborate categorization of the many temptations facing the solitary Christian, and he said that each type of temptation had its corresponding type of nightmare.[12] His system left no place for spiritually positive dreams, and he advocated instead a detachment from all dreaming experience:

> Natural processes which occur in sleep without accompanying images of a stimulating nature are, to a certain measure, indications of a healthy soul. But images that are distinctly formed are a clear indication of sickness. You may be certain that the faces one sees in dreams are, when they occur as ill-defined images, symbols of former affective experiences. Those which are seen clearly, on the other hand, indicate wounds that are still fresh. . . . The proof of *apatheia* [peacefulness of soul] is had when the spirit begins to see its own light, when it remains in a state of tranquility in the presence of the images it has during sleep and when it maintains its calm as it beholds the affairs of life.

Using naturalistic terms virtually identical to what we have heard from Upanishadic Hindus, Buddhists, Platonists, and others, Evagrius took a firm stance against the dreaming imagination. Nothing good could come from dreams, he asserted, and the only recourse for a true Christian was to strive continuously to break free from such emotionally entangling fantasies in favor of a purity of faith that remained steadfast and divinely illuminated whether awake or asleep. This was the ethos that shaped many of the original Christian monasteries, and anti-dream admonitions became part of the introductory training of novitiates. Antiochus Monachus, a seventh-century-CE official at a monastery near Jerusalem, gave a homily in which he condemned virtually all dream experiences, saying they "are nothing other than things of the imagination and hallucinations of a mind led astray. They are the illusions of evil demons to deceive us and result from their enticements with the attendant purpose of carrying off a man to pleasure."[13] To illustrate his argument, Antiochus told the story of a kind of Jewish counter-conversion mediated by dreaming:

> There was a certain monk, a model solitary, on Mount Sinai who exhibited extraordinary ascetic discipline and for many years remained shut up in his cell. Later he was deceived by diabolical visions and dreams, and he succumbed to Judaism and the circumcision of the flesh. Moreover, the Devil showed him truthful dreams many times, and through them he [the Devil] won over his confused state of mind. Later he showed him the host of martyrs, and the apostles, and all the Christians in the dark and filled completely with shame. As against this, he illuminated with a bright

light Moses, the prophets, and the hateful-to-God Jewish people, and
[showed them] living joyously and full of cheer. Perceiving these things,
the wretched man straightaway rose up and left the Holy Mountain.

Such a bitter tale was clearly intended to foster a skeptical attitude toward all dreams, even those that were vivid, recurrent, and truthful. From
his perspective as a monastic authority and defender of the faith, Antiochus saw dreaming as a threat to the Christian's purity of mind and a
dangerous temptation to stray from the one true God. The unfortunate
irony was that the very monastic practices he was teaching (e.g., praying and sleeping alone on a sacred mountain) were creating the classic
conditions for dream incubation, almost guaranteeing the occurrence of
powerful night visions. We can only wonder how many of his monks experienced such spiritually charged dreams, and never said anything about
them.

Two of the most influential early Christian theologians, Jerome (347–
419 CE) and Augustine (354–430 CE), gave an even stronger stamp to this
emerging church doctrine about the dangers of dreaming, although both
of them paradoxically acknowledged the importance of dreams in their
own spiritual autobiographies. Jerome was born in a Christian family but
educated in Roman and Greek culture, and as a young man he struggled
to reconcile his Christian faith with his love of classical philosophy.[14] One
night, while he was extremely sick, Jerome had a dream in which he was
suddenly "caught up in the spirit" and taken before "the judgment seat of
the Judge." The light was so brilliant that he immediately threw himself to
the ground. The Judge asked Jerome who he was, and he answered, "I am
a Christian." But the Judge replied, 'You lie, you are a follower of Cicero
and not of Christ." Jerome was then lashed and scourged until he finally
swore never again to read the books of pagan authors. With this oath, he
was dismissed by the heavenly tribunal. Then,

> I returned to the upper world, and, to the surprise of all, I opened upon
> them eyes so drenched with tears that my distress served to convince
> even the credulous. And that this was no sleep nor idle dream, such as
> those by which we are often mocked, I call to witness the tribunal be-
> fore which I lay, and the terrible judgment which I feared. . . . I profess
> that my shoulders were black and blue, that I felt the bruises long after I
> awoke from my sleep, and that thenceforth I read the books of God with
> a zeal greater than I had previously given to the books of men.

As in the literary dream visions of Hermas, Jerome was subjected to an arduous test of conscience and spiritual integrity. Previously he considered himself a Christian, but this experience revealed the superficiality of his faith. The strong carryover effects (tears, distress, fear) contributed to the dream's reinvigorating impact on his religious practices, purifying his life of non-Christian influences and intensifying his spiritual ardor. The physical marks on his body sound like post-hoc embellishments, though Jerome anticipated such doubts and insisted on the honesty of his account. In any case, the simple fact that Jerome discussed his dream at all indicated he took dreaming seriously as an authentic source of Christian revelation, indeed as a very useful source at that particular historical moment. Jerome's personal conflict between pagan and Christian cultures was emblematic of a wider clash in the broader Mediterranean world, a clash that accelerated with the crumbling of Roman authority in the late fourth and early fifth centuries CE. His extraordinary dream enabled him to overcome that conflict by breaking his ties with the classical past and surrendering himself entirely to the Christian future.

Whatever its impact on his personal spirituality, the dream did not persuade Jerome to advocate greater popular involvement with dreaming, as he directly warned Christians against the dream incubation practices of pagans who "sit in the graves and the temples of idols where they are accustomed to stretch out on the skins of sacrificial animals in order to know the future by dreams, abominations which are still practiced today in the temples of Asclepius." Furthermore, Jerome's monumental *Vulgate* translation of the Bible from Hebrew and Greek into Latin included two apparently deliberate mistranslations of Leviticus 19:26 and Deuteronomy 18:10, which he rendered thus: "You shall not practice augury nor observe dreams." In this small but decisive way (the Hebrew texts do not specifically mention dreams as a prohibited category), Jerome lumped dream interpretation together with all other forbidden types of pagan divination. For the next thousand years, the Christian Church would find it easy to use this text as an authoritative biblical teaching *against* the religious value of dreaming.

Jerome's more famous contemporary, Augustine, also struggled with a profound split between his Roman education and his desire to become a true Christian, and dreams were an ambivalent factor in his conflict.[15] The appeal of Christianity was personified for Augustine by his mother, Monica, a paragon of spiritual purity who finally persuaded him to convert at the age of thirty-two, after many years of immoral behavior, psychosomatic illness, and pagan philosophizing. Reflecting on his conversion in the *Confessions,* Augustine said his mother knew he would eventually join her in the Christian faith because of a God-sent dream in which a smiling young man showed her that her son was standing on the same wooden rule as she was: "By this dream the joy of this devout woman, to be fulfilled much later, was predicted many years in advance to give consolation at this time in her anxiety." Monica had an uncanny ability to discern true from false dreams: "She used to say that, by a certain smell indescribable in words, she could tell the difference between your [God's] revelation and her own soul dreaming." Augustine's reverence for his mother compelled him to acknowledge her skills as a divine dreamer. But at the same time he emphasized the spiritual dangers of sleep and dreaming, particularly for aspiring Christian ascetics who were trying to renounce their sinful pasts and live a life of pure chastity. Speaking of his own nightmares, he said:

> In my memory . . . there still live images of acts which were fixed there by my sexual habit. These images attack me. While I am awake they have no force, but in sleep they not only arouse pleasure but even elicit consent, and are very like the actual act. The illusory image within the soul has such force upon my flesh that false dreams have an effect on me when asleep, which the reality could not have when I am awake. During this time of sleep surely it is not my true self, Lord my God? Yet how great a difference between myself at the time when I am asleep and myself when I return to the waking state.

Even though he had not been sexually active for years, Augustine still experienced sexually stimulating dreams, and this raised a tough theological question. In what way does the dreaming self relate to the Christian soul? Augustine's answer was to distinguish sharply between the two. He absolved himself of any responsibility for his dreams ("we did not actively do what, to our regret, has somehow been done in us"), and he begged God to help him "extinguish the lascivious impulses of my sleep."

Later in his career, when people from his Christian community in North Africa asked him questions about dreams, Augustine cautiously acknowledged the occurrence and possible spiritual value of visitation dreams, and he once wrote in a letter about a remarkable dream that God sent to a doctor friend named Gennadius.[16] In the dream a young man confronted Gennadius and asked how he was seeing. Confused, Gennadius did not know what to say, and the young man went on:

> As while you are asleep and lying on your bed these eyes of your body are now unemployed and doing nothing, and yet you have eyes with which you behold me, and enjoy this vision, so, after your death, while your bodily eyes shall be wholly inactive, there shall be in you a life by which you shall still live, and a faculty of perception by which you shall still perceive. Beware, therefore, after this of harboring doubts as to whether the life of man shall continue after death.

A self-transcending lucid dream like this was, according to Augustine, a legitimate piece of evidence supporting Christian teachings, and we can readily understand why. The intensity of visual perception and the high-order metacognitive functioning dramatically distinguished Gennadius's experience from ordinary dreaming, enhancing its impact on his waking consciousness. The idea of an autonomous soul that could survive without the body would naturally arise as a result, providing experiential confirmation of the religious doctrine.

Ultimately, however, the main thrust of Augustine's teachings deemphasized dreams. They were difficult to interpret properly and arose from a type of imaginative vision that was limited by the finitude of human mental representations. Augustine placed dreaming below the highest form of religious experience, namely, the intellectual vision of pure mystical ecstasy.

In the later development of Christian history it would be the doubtful voices of Augustine, Jerome, and the desert fathers who most influenced the Church's attitude toward dreaming. Other voices advocating a more appreciative and expansive approach never received as much consideration, perhaps because they echoed too closely the pagan beliefs and practices that Christian authorities were busily trying to stamp out. The theologian Tertullian (155–230 CE?) of Carthage wrote at length about dreams, dividing them into the three categories of *a deo, a daemonio, ab anima* (from God, from the devil, from the soul) and highlighting the universality of dream revelations—"Now, who is such a stranger to human experience as not sometimes to have perceived some truth in dreams?"[17] But Tertullian later broke with the church over his Montanist belief that divine prophecy was a living power which did not end with the apostles but continued into the present day. For this Tertullian was branded a heretic, and his views rejected as contrary to Christian doctrine. The dream reflections of Origen (182–251?), a prominent theologian from Alexandria, made no more of an impact on the Church than did Tertullian's.[18] Origen considered a respect for dreams to be a natural accompaniment to a belief in God: "All who accept the doctrine of providence are obviously agreed in believing that in dreams many people form images in their minds, some of divine things, others being announcements of future events in life, whether clear or mysterious." In fact, Origin saw such dreams as an opportunity to strengthen people's Christian faith and convert skeptical pagans. He said the common experience of divine dreams proved that "there is nothing extraordinary in such things having happened to the prophets when, as the Bible says, they saw certain marvelous visions, or heard utterances of the Lord, or saw the heavens opened." This very strategy was, many centuries later, used with great effectiveness by Christian missionaries in Africa, Oceania, and the Americas, as coming chapters will show. But in the formative years of Christian theology, it was a decidedly minority view.

Surely the most eloquent Christian theologian to affirm the spiritual potential of dreaming was Synesius (373–423 CE), the bishop of Ptolemais in present-day Libya.[19] Like Augustine, Synesius developed his Christian teachings by combining Neoplatonic philosophy with biblical teachings, but his reflections led to a very different view of dreaming. Synesius said, in his *De insomniis* (*Concerning Dreams*):

> We, therefore, have set ourselves to speak of divination through dreams, that men should not despise it, but rather cultivate it, seeing that it fulfills a service to life. . . . [T]he dream is visible to the man who is worth five hundred *medimni*, and equally to the possessor of three hundred, to the teamster no less than to the peasant who tills the boundary land for a livelihood, to the galley slave and the common laborer alike, to the exempted and to the payer of taxes. It makes no difference to the god. . . . And this accessibility to all makes divination very humane; for its simple and artless character is worthy of a philosopher, and its freedom from violence gives it sanctity. . . . Of divination by dreams, each one of us is perforce his own instrument, so much so that it is not possible to desert our oracle there even if we so desired.

The pagan overtones of Synesius's ideas would inevitably conflict with the efforts of the Church to codify a strict monotheism in Christian belief and practice. But setting aside doctrinal politics and looking just at the content of Synesius's text, it is hard to argue with the phenomenological truth of what he was describing. Dreams do indeed come to all people, the highest and lowest among us. They come in "service to life," contributing to mental, physical, and spiritual well-being. Further, the inner processes that generate dreaming are firmly and inextricably rooted in human nature. Synesius was not alone among the Christian faithful in holding these views. A deep veneration for dreaming should be recognized as an authentic element in the piety and religious experience of early Christianity, even if a contrary attitude came to dominate later theological discourse.

Theology contra *Dreaming*

The consolidation of church authority in the fourth and fifth centuries CE coincided with the collapse of Rome, as imperial authority finally caved under the pressure of corruption from within and barbarian invasions from without. The long period of social disintegration that followed the empire's demise provided fertile territory for Christianity's rapid expansion. Church leaders became increasingly adept at providing basic social and economic services in the empire's former territories, enabling the conversion of huge numbers of new people to the faith. The development of Christian dream teachings during these "Middle Ages" was far more eventful than can be summarized here, but a brief consideration of two especially prominent theologians—Thomas Aquinas (1225–1274) and Martin Luther (1483–1546)—provide a sense of how much the leading authorities of medieval Christianity were influenced by the earlier skepticism and hostility of Augustine, Jerome, and the desert fathers.

Aquinas was a leading figure in the Scholastic movement, an effort by medieval theologians to integrate Christian doctrine with the newly translated texts of classical Greece, particularly the philosophy of Aristotle. The *Summa Theologica* was the ultimate compendium of Aquinas's thought, and after his death it became the most authoritative source (other than the Bible) for the core teachings of the Roman Catholic Church. The topics of sleep and dreaming appeared in a few scattered sections of the *Summa*, and Aquinas treated them with the same faith-inspired rationality he applied to every other topic.[20] Closely following Aristotle's psychological theory, Aquinas maintained that the only legitimate source of knowledge for humans was through the concrete impressions of their senses. Because sleep is characterized by a total suspension of the senses, Aquinas concluded that a sleeping mind could not gain true knowledge nor form good judgments. He granted the metacognitive possibility that occasionally "the common sense is partly freed; so that sometimes, while asleep, a man may judge that what he sees is a dream, discerning, as it were, between things and their images." But Aquinas insisted on a fundamental deficiency of reason during sleep that could never be overcome—"if a man syllogizes while asleep, when he wakes up he invariably recognizes a flaw in some respect."

Aquinas also argued for a theologically reasonable understanding of biblical passages describing dream revelations, which he considered a lower but still valid means of divine communication. For example, he cited the dreams of Jesus's father, Joseph, in the first two chapters of Matthew and explained how an angel (or a demon) could act upon the imagination of a sleeping person to compel him to see true (or deceptive) things. Aquinas devoted a whole article of the *Summa* to the question of dream divination, and argued that "there is no unlawful divination in making use of dreams for the foreknowledge of the future, so long as those dreams are due to divine revelation, or to some natural cause inward or outward, and so far as the efficacy of that cause extends." Very much like Aristotle, he allowed for the possibility of dreams providing valuable medical insights about the "internal dispositions" of the body. But going beyond Aristotle, Aquinas affirmed the divine potentiality of dreams according to the causal power of "God, Who reveals certain things to men in their dreams by the ministry of the angels." And in another departure from the elite-minded Aristotle, Aquinas actually considered the popular experience of prophetic dreaming to be a piece of evidence in favor of its authenticity: "It is unreasonable to deny the common experiences of all men. Now it is the experience of all that dreams are significative of the future."

Another article of the *Summa* focused on the question we raised at the beginning of the chapter: How should we regard the sexual images and feelings that arise so often in dreams? It may seem reasonable to suppose that if a person could gain divine favor for his actions in a dream, he could also earn divine *dis*favor for what he does while dreaming, and thus "nocturnal pollution," or wet dreams, would be evidence of mortal sin. But Aquinas rejected this view. Combining Aristotle with Augustine, he explained that people (celibate monks, for example) were not morally responsible for what happened during their dreams. The loss of normal mental functioning during sleep reduced people to a sub-rational status that absolved them of religious culpability: "What a man does while he sleeps and is deprived of reason's judgment is not imputed to him as a sin, as neither are the actions of a maniac or an imbecile." The simplest cases of nocturnal pollution were caused, according to Aquinas, by an "excess of seminal humor in the body" which naturally released itself during sleep to the accompaniment of "phantasms relating to the discharge of those superfluities." Other wet dreams could be attributed to the natural effects of sinful thoughts or past sexual experiences (Augustine being the prime example). The waking thoughts and/or actions might be sinful, but the consequent dreams were not. Still other disturbing sexual dreams were caused "without any fault on man's part, and through the wickedness of the devil alone." Aquinas accepted all these possibilities within the compass of his faith-based, logically structured explanation. Not as hostile as a desert father nor as enthusiastic as a new convert, Aquinas developed a rationally balanced theology of dreams that accepted their occasional physical and spiritual value while clearly defining them as the products of an inferior state of mind that was perennially vulnerable to the temptations of wily demons.

Two hundred years later Martin Luther, an Augustinian monk from Germany, rejected the abstruse theological tomes of Aquinas and the Scholastics.[21] Putting his faith entirely in the Bible, Luther argued for the supreme authority of God's Word over anything taught by the Pope, the Church, or theologians. Luther's absolute commitment to the truth and sufficiency of the Bible colored his attitude toward dreaming, and in the following passage (from his commentary on the story of Joseph and the Pharaoh in Genesis 40) he revealed a brief but fascinating window into his own dream experience and its relationship to his mission as a Christian reformer:

> I have often stated that at the beginning of my cause I always asked the Lord not to send me dreams, visions, or angels. For many fanatical spirits attacked me, one of whom boasted of dreams, another of visions, and another of revelations with which they were striving to instruct me. But I replied that I was not seeking such revelations and that if any were offered, I would put no trust in them. And I prayed ardently to God that He might give me the sure meaning and understanding of Holy Scripture. For if I have the Word, I know that I am proceeding on the right way and cannot easily be deceived or go wrong. . . . With their dreams

the fanatics were trying to drive me, some in one way, others in another. Had I listened to any of them, it would certainly have been necessary to change the character of my doctrine thirty or forty times. But when I rejected them all, they kept crying out that I was stubborn and headstrong, and they let me alone. Therefore I care nothing about visions and dreams. Although they seem to have a meaning, yet I despise them and am content with the sure meaning and trustworthiness of Holy Scripture.

Luther evidently felt comfortable telling people the story of his demonic nightmares, taking it as a badge of spiritual integrity that he had suffered and overcome such temptations. Consistent with his desire to revive the original teachings of Christianity, Luther sounded the tones of a desert father in seeking a pure communion with God, far beyond what any dream or vision could attain. His dream struggles mirrored his waking life struggles with Roman church officials who attacked his beliefs and accused him of selfish obstinacy. Just as Luther refused to yield to the "fanatics" tormenting him in his sleep, he refused to yield in matters of faith to papal authority, and thus his dream story served as a neat parable of the Protestant movement as a whole (with the added bonus of associating his opponents with demons). He went on to grant that divine revelation in sleep was possible, "but the marks of true dreams must be observed," and those marks boiled down to conformity with Holy Scripture—a dream could be accepted as true only if it agreed in all essentials with the Bible. But since Christians already had the Bible, this meant that dreams were in fact superfluous, adding nothing of religious value that was not already available from scripture. Luther denounced the revelation-seeking incubation practices of certain Christian contemplatives ("these monks and nuns were very frequently deceived by delusions of the devil"), and he advocated the exact opposite practice of praying against any dreams at all. Never was the line separating Christian faith from the dreaming imagination more sharply drawn.

Popular Piety

And yet Christians continued to dream. A strong undercurrent of reverence for dreaming survived from the earliest days of the faith all the way through the Middle Ages. This was most easily seen in the transformation of Asclepian temples to Christian churches, where the healing and dream incubation rituals continued more or less intact from one tradition to the next. The cult of Asclepius was one of the last pagan religious practices to succumb to Christianity's ascent, and especially in Greece the Christian Church had to compete vigorously with the Asclepian temples for people's spiritual allegiance. The eventual domination of Christianity depended on a pragmatic willingness to accept popular practices from pre-Christian traditions so long as the ultimate authority of the Church remained unquestioned.

Elsewhere the popular faith found expression in widely circulated stories of fantastic dreams and nocturnal visions. The early Anglo-Saxon Christian literature was filled with such narratives, including dreams of conception and birth, otherworldly journeys, prophecies of death, visitations from saints, nightmarish temptations, and poetic creations.[22] Dream manuals proliferated in which the symbolic equations of Artemidorus were merged with Christian images, themes, and interpretations. Texts known as *Somnialia Danielis* (the "dream keys" of Daniel) circulated widely among Latin Christians, providing interpretations of auspicious or inauspicious dreams relating to health, longevity, finances, emotional well-being, and other ordinary concerns of the general population.[23] At the other end of the literary spectrum, many of the greatest writers of Medieval and Renaissance Christianity included dramatic dream visions and revelations in their stories. The *Divina Commedia* of Dante Alighieri (1265–1321) recounted three dreams he experienced during his three nights in Purgatory, each providing valuable guidance in his journey from Hell to Paradise.[24] As a preface to one of the dreams, Dante offered an explanation that echoed Greek philosophical teachings: in sleep, "the mind, escaped from its submission to flesh and to the chains of waking thought, becomes almost prophetic in its vision."

Geoffrey Chaucer (1343–1400) told a darkly comic dream fable in the "Nun's Priest's Tale."[25] One day a proud rooster named Chauntecleer awoke from a frightening dream of being killed by a fox. But when he described the dream to his wife, Pertelote, he received no comfort; instead, she belittled him for his cowardice. Quoting pagan medical authorities, Pertelote explained that his dream was simply a by-product of bodily distemper. Chauntecleer responded by refering to Macrobius and his category of true dream visions. This amusing intellectual conversation between rooster and hen ended when Pertelote finally persuaded Chauntecleer to ignore the threat-simulating dream, forget his unmanly fears, and go forth with his day. Thus, when the fox arrived at the barnyard later that morning, Chauntecleer was easy prey.

The plays of William Shakespeare (1564–1616) overflow with dreams and dreaming, from the love-drunk fantasies of *A Midsummer Night's Dream* and the politically ominous nightmares of *Richard III* to the wonder-working dream magic of *The Tempest* and the existential soliloquizing of *Hamlet*.[26] A prominent theme in the dark tragedy of *Macbeth* is the intertwining of sleep, dreams, and moral conscience. The famous scene of Lady Macbeth walking and talking in her sleep (V.i) gives the audience a glimpse into her nightmare-plagued inner world, where she suffers horrible visions of guilt over her bloody deeds in helping her husband seize the throne. For Macbeth's part, his violent ambition has caused him to suffer "the affliction of these terrible dreams that shake us nightly" (III. ii.20–21). Macbeth admits that just before he thrust a dagger into the body of the sleeping king, "methought I heard a voice cry 'Sleep no more! Macbeth does murder sleep!'" (II.ii.49–50). Banquo, who was with Macbeth when they first heard the witches' prophecy about becoming king, recognizes the ethical dangers of such unholy wishes, which become especially intense in sleep: "Merciful powers, restrain in me the cursed thoughts that nature gives way to in repose" (II.i.9–11). Although the Christian God is very distant from the bleak Scottish moors where the play is set, Banquo's prayer reflects an essentially Christian belief about dreaming as a moral battleground between good and evil, social order and individual desire.

In *Romeo and Juliet*, Shakespeare approaches the subject of dreaming in a much lighter spirit, though in so doing he moves into deeper philosophical waters. Consider this exchange (I.iv.49–106), when Romeo is expressing reluctance about his friend Mercutio's plan to sneak into the masquerade ball hosted by their rivals, the Capulets:

Romeo: And we mean well in going to this mask;
   But 'tis no wit to go.
Mercutio: Why, may one ask?
Romeo: I dream'd a dream to-night.
Mercutio: And so did I.
Romeo: Well, what was yours?
Mercutio: That dreamers often lie.
Romeo: In bed asleep, while they do dream things true.
Mercutio: Oh, then, I see Queen Mab hath been with you.

She is the fairies' midwife, and she comes
In shape no bigger than an agate-stone
On the fore-finger of an alderman,
Drawn with a team of little atomies
Athwart men's noses as they lie asleep;
Her wagon-spokes made of long spiders' legs,
The cover of the wings of grasshoppers,
The traces of the smallest spider's web,
The collars of the moonshine's watery beams,
Her whip of cricket's bone, the lash of film,
Her wagoner a small grey-coated gnat,
Not so big as a round little worm
Prick'd from the lazy finger of a maid;
Her chariot is an empty hazel-nut
Made by the joiner squirrel or old grub,
Time out o' mind the fairies' coachmakers.
And in this state she gallops night by night
Through lovers' brains, and then they dream of love;
O'er courtiers' knees, that dream on court'sies straight,
O'er lawyers' fingers, who straight dream on fees,
O'er ladies' lips, who straight on kisses dream,
Which oft the angry Mab with blisters plagues,
Because their breaths with sweetmeats tainted are:
Sometime she gallops o'er a courtier's nose,
And then dreams he of smelling out a suit;
And sometime comes she with a tithe-pig's tail
Tickling a parson's nose as a' lies asleep,
Then dreams, he of another benefice:
Sometime she driveth o'er a soldier's neck,
And then dreams he of cutting foreign throats,
Of breaches, ambuscadoes, Spanish blades,
Of healths five-fathom deep; and then anon
Drums in his ear, at which he starts and wakes,
And being thus frighted swears a prayer or two
And sleeps again. This is that very Mab
That plats the manes of horses in the night,
And bakes the elflocks in foul sluttish hairs,
Which once untangled, much misfortune bodes:
This is the hag, when maids lie on their backs,

That presses them and learns them first to bear,
Making them women of good carriage:
This is she—
Romeo: Peace, peace, Mercutio, peace!
Thou talk'st of nothing.
Mercutio: True, I talk of dreams,
Which are the children of an idle brain,
Begot of nothing but vain fantasy,
Which is as thin of substance as the air
And more inconstant than the wind.

The impetuous Mercutio ricochets from one negative assessment of dreams to another—first saying dreams are lies, then attributing them to the mischievous influences of faeries, then becoming consumed with his own dark evocation of sexually violent nightmares, and finally dismissing all dreams as products of "an idle brain." Compared to these wild and self-contradictory rantings, Romeo's simple faith in prophetic dreaming seems the more reasonable approach. The exact nature of Shakespeare's own faith remains uncertain, but in passages like this he acknowledged traditional folk beliefs about dreams that many of his audience members would have shared, "pagan" teachings that very likely predated the arrival of Christianity in England.

Such beliefs could lead to serious trouble, however, and Christian people were undoubtedly cautious about how, when, and with whom they shared their dreams. The *Malleus Maleficarum* (*The Witches' Hammer*) (1487), the manual used by church inquisitors in their hunt for witches and heretics, listed dreams as one of the primary means by which demons attack and seduce people.[27] Anyone who had a reputation as an unusual dreamer could, for that reason alone, fall under suspicion as a witch. Thus a profound split came to characterize the Christian culture of Europe and the Mediterranean. While church officials were doing their best to dampen oneiric enthusiasm and regulate visionary experience, laypeople maintained a strong but cautiously hidden fascination with dreams and their meanings.

Christianity branched out in dramatic fashion from this point, with missionary activities expanding the faith's presence into Africa, Oceania, and the Americas. In the coming chapters we examine the interactions between Christianity and the indigenous religious traditions of these regions, each of which had its own precolonial teachings about dreams.

In many cases we will find that dreaming became a contested arena of spiritual authority between missionaries and natives. The Christian split between official hostility and popular appeal was thereby translated into new settings and dialects, leading to a variety of forced compromises and pragmatic syntheses.

Before that, however, we consider the rise of the third great Abrahamic religion, Islam.

Summary

In Christianity's earliest texts, in the experiences of its martyrs and converts, and in scattered places throughout the tradition's later history, we find clear expressions of the belief that dreams are a legitimate means of communion between humans and God. We also find, especially in later theological writings, warnings against the demon-caused, sexually arousing temptations of dreaming. Most Christian authorities seem to have accepted the supernatural origins of dreams, but as the power of the Church grew these authorities focused more on the dangers of demonic nightmares than on the blessings of heaven-sent visions. In their actual lives and religious practices, ordinary Christian laypeople have looked to their dreams for various purposes, including prophecy, healing, inspiration, guidance, and reassurance in times of fear. Christianity has never developed an official method of dream interpretation, but in practice people have relied heavily on pre-Christian approaches translated from Greek and Roman sources. The popular interest in dreaming has usually been tolerated by Christian leaders, in pragmatic recognition of the fact that other people's dreams cannot be easily controlled or extinguished. But the authorities have almost always insisted on one requirement for Christians trying to interpret their dreams: any message discerned in a dream must conform to the revealed truths of the Bible and the teachings of the Church.

7

Islam

One way to think about the different types of dreams reported so far is to consider them as variations on the theme of *reactions to an existential crisis*. Visitation and pre-death dreams are the most obvious examples, with their vivid evocations of the specter of mortality haunting all human endeavors. The cross-cultural prevalence of threat-simulating nightmares and death-related dream visions is no accident, no mere epiphenomenal product of random neural firings in the brain. The dark forebodings that characterize the most intensified forms of dreams consistently have the effect of stimulating greater existential self-awareness. This should be recognized as a fundamental fact in our knowledge of human dreaming.

Conception dreams arise at the other end of the life cycle, reflecting the wonderful yet frightful moment of a child's entrance into the world. (Anyone who doesn't think of childbirth as an existential crisis has probably never been inside a hospital's labor-and-delivery room.) Other crisis-related examples abound in the world's religious traditions. During times of suffering and illness, before a make-or-break examination, on the eve of a decisive battle—in all these cases, extraordinarily vivid and memorable dreams reflect a natural emergency-response system at work in the dreaming imagination, an innate psychospiritual propensity that every religion considered so far has sought to understand, influence, and cultivate. It would be easy to interpret such dreams as nothing more than wish-fulfillments (e.g., wishing a deceased loved one were still alive, and thus making up a visitation dream about that person). To be sure, humans are wishing and wishful creatures, endlessly seeking satisfaction of their instinctual desires. But we should not underestimate the paradoxical power of the dreaming wish to create new waking realities. As both ancient philosophers and contemporary neuroscientists have taught, the human species is distinguished by tremendous powers of memory, imagination, and forethought. In sleep and dreams these powers have the

potential to expand their functional range in ways that enhance the individual's abilities to meet the challenges of whatever waking-life crisis is at
hand. The dreams that come in such situations may be wish fulfillments,
but they are wish fulfillments in the service of greater confidence, courage, and vitality.

The religious heritage of Islam has drawn deeply from these powers
of the dreaming imagination.[1] Like Buddhism and Christianity, Islam has
grown to become a global faith with more than a billion practicing members, and this chapter highlights only a portion of its rich and sophisticated teachings about the nature and meaning of dreams. As a relatively
young religion (founded in the seventh century CE), Islam has preserved
numerous sources from its founding era that provide excellent insights
into the tradition's reliance upon the crisis-response potentials of oneiric
experience.

The Prophet Muhammad and the Qur'an

The angel Gabriel first came to Muhammad in a cave on Mount Hira
(present-day Saudi Arabia) during the holy month of Ramadan in 610
CE.[2] Muhammad was forty years old at the time, married to a loving wife
named Khadija, and father to several children, stepchildren, and foster
children. In addition to participating in the polytheistic religious rituals of
his city, Muhammad practiced various forms of personal devotion, most
often in the cool, dark caves that dotted the Arabian wilderness. Here he
would pray, think, sleep, and imagine. He began to have dreams, marvelous visions of hope and promise so filled with brilliance that they struck
him "like the dawn of the morning." Then one night, during a month-long
retreat in the caves of Mount Hira, he had an experience that changed
him forever. Muhammad was suddenly awakened by the powerful presence of Gabriel, who appeared beside him and gave him a simple order:
"*Iqra!*" ("Recite!" or "Read!") Terrified, Muhammad initially resisted the
call, but Gabriel's numinous intensity overwhelmed him and compelled
his total assent. He woke up with the angel's words still sharp and vivid in
his memory, "as if they had written a message in my heart." Muhammad
walked outside, and a second time he was struck by the divine: Gabriel
appeared before him as a huge form spanning the whole horizon; wherever Muhammad looked, there was the angel, telling him "You are the
apostle of God."

Over the next twenty-two years Muhammad continued with his devotional practices, and he was rewarded with a number of additional revelations, all of which he reported to his followers. Some of the revelations were visual, involving lights as bright as the breaking dawn. Others were entirely auditory, with distinctly spoken messages and teachings. Still others were bodily perceptions of titanic waves of power, "like the reverberations of a bell, and that is the hardest on me." These experiences strained his physical being to its limit: "Never once did I receive a revelation without thinking that my soul had been torn away from me." Muhammad came to understand himself as a "Warner" sent by Allah to teach people the proper worship of the one God. His writings in the *Qur'an* ("The Recitation") wove together Jewish and Christian scriptures with original theological reflections on the human condition and practical teachings directly responsive to the conditions and crises faced by the Prophet and his followers in their Arabian context. One theme that Muhammad appropriated from the other Abrahamic traditions was a reverence for dreaming. In the *Qur'an*, as in the Jewish *Torah* and the Christian *Novum Testamentum*, dreams served as a medium by which God communicated with His most favored humans. Although Islam, Christianity, and Judaism differ drastically on many other issues, their original scriptures expressed substantial agreement on the core idea that dreaming is a valuable source of religious wisdom and inspiration.

The text of the *Qur'an* contains 114 chapters (*suras*) of varying length and content. Unlike Jewish and Christian scriptures, which were produced by multiple authors from different historical times and cultural backgrounds, the *Qur'an* was the work of a single man, in a single lifetime. The text thus bears a strong stamp of that man's personality—to learn about Islam is inevitably to learn about the Prophet Muhammad. Several passages of the *Qur'an* contain discussions of dreams and dreaming, and because of the absolute centrality of the *Qur'an* to Muslim faith these passages have become fundamental to all later Islamic dream traditions. What follows are brief synopses of five *suras* in which dreams play a significant role.[3]

12: Joseph. In this chapter Muhammad gave a condensed version of the story of Joseph (following the essential outline found in the *Torah*'s Genesis 37–50). Although much of the material from the Genesis version was removed, the three major dream episodes in Joseph's life all remained, and they combined to make a clear point: dreams, and the ability to interpret them, were an important sign of God's favor. Muhammad started *sura* 12 with the young Joseph telling his father that he had a dream in which "eleven stars and the sun and the moon were prostrating themselves before me." Joseph's father warned the boy not to tell the dream to his jealous older brothers, who harbored murderous intentions toward him. Joseph's father prophesized that his youngest son would "be chosen by your Lord. He will teach you to interpret visions." The prophecy was borne out later in the *sura* when Joseph, unjustly imprisoned in Egypt, was asked to interpret the dreams of two fellow prisoners:

> One of them said: "I dreamed that I was pressing grapes." And the other said: "I dreamed that I was carrying a loaf upon my head, and that the birds came and ate of it. Tell us the meaning of these dreams, for we can see you are a man of learning." Joseph replied: "I can interpret them long before they are fulfilled. This knowledge my lord has given me, for I have left the faith of those that disbelieve in Allah and deny the life to come. I follow the faith of my forefathers, Abraham, Isaac, and Jacob."

Joseph told the first man that his dream meant he would be released and serve the king wine, while the second man's dream meant he would be crucified, and the birds would peck at his head. When these predictions came true, Joseph's skill as a dream interpreter reached the attention of Egypt's king, who had been troubled by two dreams of his own, one in which seven fatted cows devoured seven lean ones, and the other in which seven green ears of corn devoured seven dry ones. The king asked his royal advisers to tell him the meaning of these dreams, but they could not do so, saying "It is but an idle dream; nor can we interpret dreams." Joseph, however, was able to interpret the dreams accurately as anticipations of the future welfare of the land and its people, when seven years of plenty would be followed by seven years of famine. The king was pleased with this interpretation, and as a reward made Joseph his personal servant.

Very much like the Genesis version, the *Qur'an* portrayed Joseph as an exemplary man of faith and piety, and one clear sign of his close relationship with God was his ability to see and interpret revelatory dreams.

37. *The Ranks.* Like *sura* 12, this one also retells a story found in Genesis. Here the main subject is Abraham, whose life is recounted in Genesis 12–25. The *Qur'anic* version focused specifically on God's command to Abraham to sacrifice his only son, Isaac (cf. Genesis 22):

[Abraham said] "Grant me a son, Lord, and let him be a righteous man." We [Allah] gave him news of a gentle son. And when he reached the age when he could work with him his father said to him: "My son, I dreamed that I was sacrificing you. Tell me what you think." He replied: "Father, do as you are bidden. Allah willing, you shall find me faithful." And when they had both surrendered themselves to Allah's will, and Abraham had laid down his son prostrate upon his face, We called out to him, saying: "Abraham, you have fulfilled your vision." Thus did We reward the righteous. That was indeed a bitter test.

Several points are worth noting here. First is the explicit reference to a dream as the means by which Abraham received this command; the Genesis version did not emphasize the dream provenance as clearly. Second is the unquestioned assumption by both Abraham and his son that the dream was a command from Allah. The dream as Abraham described it had no special markers of divine origin, yet he and his son immediately agreed that what Abraham has envisioned was ordained by God and must be done. This leads to the third and theologically most important point. The dream and their interpretation of it led Abraham and his son to "surrender themselves to Allah's will." This humble obedience is the very heart of the Muslim faith—the absolute trust in God, even to the point of sacrificing one's most cherished human attachments ("That was indeed a bitter test"). Muhammad's retelling of the story of Abraham and Isaac in many ways encapsulates the whole of the *Qur'an*. Finally, we should note the interesting twist at the end of the story, which differs quite dramatically from the Genesis version. In *sura* 37, Abraham was interrupted in the sacrifice of his son by God's sudden words, "Abraham, you have fulfilled your vision." Abraham was true to his dream *not* by literally enacting it in the physical sacrifice of his son; rather, he fulfills his vision by a *symbolic* demonstration of his absolute obedience to God. This emphasis on the reality of the symbolic opened the way for later Muslim philosophical reflection on the different dimensions of truth that may be discerned via the dreaming imagination.

8: The Spoils. This *sura* described two of Muhammad's own dream experiences. He mentioned them in the context of telling how in the early years of his mission he struggled to lead his followers in battle against their opponents—"some of the faithful were reluctant. They argued with you [Muhammad] about the truth that had been revealed, as though they were being led to certain death." The imminent prospect of dying on a

battlefield is an existential crisis of the first order, and Muhammad said
he prayed to God for help in reviving the confidence of his followers. God
responded as follows:

> You [Muhammad] were overcome by sleep, a token of His [Allah's] pro-
> tection. He sent down water from the sky to cleanse you and to purify
> you of Satan's filth, to strengthen your hearts and to steady your foot-
> steps. Allah revealed His will to the angels, saying: "I shall be with you.
> Give courage to the believers. I shall cast terror into the hearts of the infi-
> dels. Strike off their heads, maim them in every limb!"

Further on, Muhammad described his experience the night before another armed clash, when he and his people were encamped across a valley
from a gathering of hostile warriors:

> Allah made them appear to you in a dream as a small band. Had He
> showed them to you as a great army, your courage would have failed you
> and discord would have triumphed in your ranks. But this Allah spared
> you. He knows your inmost thoughts.

The two dreams reflected the warlike environment in which Muhammad and his followers first established the Muslim faith. Although Muhammad spent much time alone in desert caves praying and meditating,
he was also a charismatic warrior who led his troops through several harrowing battles. The dream experiences reported in this *sura* expressed
Muhammad's faith in God's rousing presence during times of violent
struggle. In this way, the two dreams echoed passages in the *Torah* and
the *Novum Testamentum* where God appeared to His faithful in times of
danger, violence, and despair to offer reassurance and heavenly guidance.
An unusual feature in this *sura* is the frank acknowledgment that God
may use dreams to deceive the faithful for their own good. Muhammad
was grateful that Allah knew his "inmost thoughts," his secret fear that his
army would be defeated, and sent a dream that reassured him. The value
of the dream was clearly not in the accuracy of its representation of physical reality but rather in its inspiring emotional effect on Muhammad—the
dream emboldened him to ignore any "realistic" appraisal of his chances
and to continue fighting in total confidence of ultimate victory.

17: The Night Journey. This *sura* began with the following line: "Glory
be to Him who made His servants go by night from the Sacred Temple [of

Mecca] to the farther temple [the Throne of Allah] whose surroundings we have blessed, that we might show him some of Our signs." The remainder of the chapter described the visions he saw and the teachings he learned, including many of the key ethical, legal, and ritual principles of the Muslim faith. The text did not specifically say whether Muhammad's journey occurred in a waking or dreaming state. The visionary quality of the experience and its allusion to an airborne journey to otherworldly realms, combined with the fact that it happened at night, supports the belief that it was a dream. But later Muslim commentators have argued that it was an actual physical transportation to heaven, not just a product of Muhammad's sleeping mind. Clearly it was no ordinary dream, and to consider *sura* 17 in connection with dreaming is not to deny the transcendent character of Muhammad's night journey but rather to highlight its affinity with other experiences of spectacular night vision and brilliant spiritual insight.

Sura 53: The Star. From the beginning of his prophecy Muhammad faced the hostility of many Meccan people who wanted to know how exactly his teachings about the one God Allah would affect their worship of the other gods traditionally recognized in the city. Many of these deities had been objects of deep veneration for countless centuries, and people were understandably reluctant to accept Muhammad's claim that Allah was ordering them to abruptly abandon these ancient practices. According to one of his earliest biographers, at this tense political moment Muhammad experienced a new revelation in which God said to him, "Have you considered al-Lat and al-Uzza and Manat, the third, the other? These are the exalted birds whose intercession is approved." The three goddesses, known together as "the daughters of Allah" (*banat al-lah*), had long been worshiped at special temples in Mecca and other cities around Arabia. When Muhammad recited these verses, they were enthusiastically welcomed by the Meccans as a sign that he was acknowledging a harmonious continuity between his new religious teachings and traditional Arabian worship practices. Allah was indeed the supreme creator, to be revered as such, and the goddesses al-Lat, al-Uzza, and Manat were acknowledged to be divine intermediaries between God and the human realm and thus deserving of devotion in their own right.

But then Muhammad had another nocturnal revelation, perhaps his most startling one yet. Gabriel spoke to him by night and severely chastised him for reciting words that came not from God but from Satan (*shaitan*). The earlier verses about the three goddesses must be removed from the *Qur'an*, Gabriel commanded, and new verses inserted in their place. These new verses (*sura* 53:23) categorically rejected the goddesses as legitimate deities worthy of any attention, dismissing them as mere projections of human fantasy: "They are naught but names yourselves have named, and your fathers; God has sent down no authority touching them. They follow only surmise and what their whims desire." According to this version of the composition of *sura* 53, Muhammad's fateful decision to reject any worship of the three goddesses was prompted by an angelic night vision that corrected his foolish compromise and reemphasized the incompatibility of Islam's monotheistic purity with the traditional polytheism of Mecca.[4]

The Hadiths

Both during and after Muhammad's death a number of accounts were written of his words and deeds, and these accounts are gathered in the *hadiths* (such as the one just mentioned regarding the "satanic verses" behind *sura* 53). Among the various sayings of the *hadiths* are several detailed discussions of dreams and dreaming.[5] Although secondary in theological importance to the passages from the *Qur'an*, the references to dreaming in the *hadiths* are extremely significant historically, and they have added important conceptual and technical elements to the dream traditions of Islam. In particular, the *hadiths* contain abundant references to the practice of dream interpretation, and many of the interpretive principles enunciated in these passages continue to guide the dream practices of present-day Muslims in countries around the world.

The legitimacy of dream interpretation as a religious activity received strong endorsement from the *hadiths*, most directly in the verses that state: "When the companions of the Messenger of God [Muhammad] saw dreams while he was still alive they would tell him of their dreams and he, for his part, would interpret them as God willed." From this point forward, Muslim dream interpretation could always justify its legitimacy by reference to early authoritative teachings. Many other *hadiths* described Muhammad's interpretations of particular images and symbols in the dreams of his followers, and other verses told of Muhammad's own dreams and his interpretations of them. For example, the *hadiths* reported several dreams in which Muhammad saw his friend 'Umar, who later became one of his successors. The dreams expressed Muhammad's respect and admiration for the power of 'Umar's faith, and this provided 'Umar with a kind of divine sanction for the day when he assumed religious authority following the death of Muhammad. Another *hadith* explained that the origin of the *athan* or "call to prayer" came in a strange state between sleep and wakefulness to two of Muhammad's followers, who then reported their dreams to Muhammad. The Prophet told them to teach the call to the strong-voiced Bilal. Ever since then, the same basic song of gathering has been used in Islam to remind people of the daily times for prayer, focusing the attention of Muhammad's followers on a total devotion to Allah.

According to these texts, Muhammad was sensitive to the practical difficulties encountered by many of his followers who were trying to interpret their own dreams. The first suggestion Muhammad made was to tell the dream to someone else: "A dream rests on the feathers of a bird and will not take effect unless it is related to someone." However, people should be careful not to reveal too much in public: "Tell your dreams only to knowledgeable persons and loved ones," he said, and beware of those who will use your dreams against you (like Joseph's brothers did against him). Muhammad gave a vivid warning to those who were tempted to abuse the practice of dream interpretation: "Whoever claims to have had a dream in which he says he saw something he did not shall be ordered [in Hell] to tie a knot between two barley grains and will not be able to do so." To help people increase their chances of having a good dream, Muhammad offered suggestions about how to approach sleep in a state of religious purity, with the specific instruction to try sleeping on the right side. He affirmed that bad dreams come from Satan, and he instructed people to refrain from talking about such nightmares and to offer a prayer instead and "seek refuge with Allah from [the dream's] evil."

The *hadith* that reads, "Whoever sees me [the Prophet] in dreams will see me in wakefulness [the Hereafter] for Satan cannot take my shape" has long been understood to mean that a dream in which Muhammad appears as a character is unquestionably a true dream. Every other kind of dream *could* be a malevolent deception sent by Satan, but a dream of Muhammad should be accepted with complete confidence as an authentic revelation because Satan does not have the power to assume the shape of God's Prophet. Perhaps the most oft-quoted *hadith* on dreams reads, "The good dream is 1/46th of prophecy." Commentators have long debated the significance of this exact number (perhaps a doubling of the number of years [23] between the beginning of Muhammed's revelation and his death?), but the general sense of the passage seems clear. Dreams are a small but legitimate source of divine knowledge. This basic attitude in the *hadiths*—dreams were not the only source of religious revelation but nevertheless a real and important one available to a wide spectrum of people —was consistent with the positive evaluation of dreams in the *Qur'anic* verses discussed above and gave a more definitive shaping to the beliefs and practices of later Muslims.

The *hadiths* included two particular dreams of Muhammad's that are worth mentioning. In the first, the Prophet explained how he interpreted one of his own dreams:

> I saw in a dream that I waved a sword and it broke in the middle, and behold, that symbolized the casualties the believers suffered on the Day [of the battle] of Uhud. Then I waved the sword again, and it became better than it had ever been before, and behold, that symbolized the Conquest [of Mecca] which Allah brought about and the gathering of the leaders.

The broken sword was a striking emblem of military defeat and social humiliation, a vivid imagistic reference that would be likely to resonate strongly with his battle-tested followers. In that context, the suddenly restored and improved sword symbolized the transcendent power of Muslim faith. What looked impossible could actually be achieved, what appeared lost could be regained, what seemed fractured could be made whole again —all this was possible, if people were willing to give complete trust in the Almighty. Here again, a brief dream memorably expressed one of the pre-eminent themes of Islamic belief and practice.

The second dream to note in the *hadiths* was recounted by A'isha, the woman Muhammad married after the death of his first wife Khadija:

> Allah's Apostle said to me [A'aisha], "You were shown to me twice [in my dream] before I married you. I saw an angel carrying you in a silken piece of cloth, and I said to him, "Uncover [her]," and behold, it was you. I said [to myself], "If this is from Allah, then it must happen." Then you were shown to me, the angel carrying you in a silken piece of cloth, and I said [to him], "Uncover her," and behold, it was you. I said [to myself], "If this is from Allah, then it must happen."

These twin dreams provided Muhammad with divine guidance at a time of major life transition (choosing a new wife), sanctioning his choice of

A'aisha in a manner very much like his dreams legitimating the status of
his successor 'Umar, mentioned above. The repetitive nature of the two
dreams emphasized the clarity of their message, which was that A'aisha
has been presented to Muhammad as a gift from God. Not just in war but
in love as well, dreams revealed the will of Allah.

Classical Typologies and Interpretation Manuals

Inspired by these teachings from the *Qur'an* and *hadiths*, Muslim philosophers and theologians in subsequent years continued the process of
developing new techniques and conceptual frameworks for the practice
of dream interpretation. The most famous of the early dream interpreters
was Ibn Sirin, whose name was reverently attached to dream interpretation manuals for many centuries after his death in 728 CE.[6] One of Ibn
Sirin's key teachings was to pay close attention to the personal characteristics of the dreamer. The following anecdote about his interpretive method
appeared in several texts:

> Two dreamers came to Ibn Sirin within an hour of each other and each
> had dreamed of being the caller to prayer [*muathin*]. The first person was
> told that his dream foretold that he would perform the Muslim pilgrim-
> age to Mecca. The second man, who seemed to be of a baser character,
> was told that he would be accused of a theft. [His] pupils then questioned
> how Ibn Sirin could come up with such radically different interpretations
> for the same dream. His response was that the character of each dreamer
> was evident from his appearance and demeanor. Therefore, the first one's
> dream evoked the *Qur'anic* verse "Proclaim to the people a solemn pil-
> grimage" (20:28) since he was clearly pious. The second man's dream
> evoked the verse "Then a crier called after them, O company of travelers
> [Joseph's brothers], you are surely thieves" (12:70).

Ibn Sirin's reference to specific scriptural passages reflected the fact
that Muslims were, and continue to be, thoroughly steeped from an early
age in the words of the *Qur'an*. In light of the continuity factor between
waking life and dream content, it is quite sensible to ground one's interpretations in a thorough knowledge of the most important religious
scriptures in the dreamer's culture. Memorization of *Qur'anic* verses has
long been a central feature of Muslim education, and Ibn Sirin's inter-

pretive strategy relied heavily on people's intimate familiarity with the language, characters, and themes of the *Qur'an*. He further emphasized that a dream's meaning could not be determined without reference to the personality characteristics of the dreamer. He rejected a "one size fits all" interpretation for dream symbols and taught that their meanings always depended on the personality and life circumstances of the dreamer. This approach corresponded closely to that of Artemidorus in the *Oneirocritica*, which was translated into Arabic in 877 CE and was enthusiastically incorporated into the continuing development of Muslim dream theory and practice.

Here is the point where Muslim traditions begin to expand beyond their Christian and Jewish counterparts. As we discussed in the previous chapter, during its medieval period Christianity effectively repudiated dreaming as a legitimate source of divine revelation by increasingly emphasizing the potential for demonic temptation in dreams. Although spiritually oriented dream traditions continued and in some cases even flourished at the level of popular Christian practice, the attitude of theologians and church officials from Augustine and Jerome to Aquinas and Luther was generally dismissive of dreams and their interpretation. Judaism did not suffer this kind of decline in the religious authority of dreams, and in fact philosophers like Moses Maimonides and the Qabbalistic mystics continued to develop creative new ways of conceptualizing the revelatory power of dreams. But Judaism never achieved anything like the geographic spread of Islam (from the Atlantic to the border of China in just its first hundred years), nor did Judaism ever produce the kind of spectacular efflorescence of scientific and philosophical discovery that occurred in the Classical Era of Islamic history from the ninth to thirteenth centuries CE. The Muslim science of dream interpretation known as *tabir* (literally, "carrying across to the other side of a river") emerged in this period as a dynamic body of knowledge integrating Islamic faith with the classical heritage of the Greeks and Romans.[7] Nothing emerged in Judaism or Christianity to rival the breadth and sophistication of this tradition.

The Muslim teachings of this era revolved around the notion of *Alam al-mithal,* a realm of images between the material and spiritual worlds in which the human soul could journey either in waking visions or nocturnal dreams.[8] Within *Alam al-mithal* the soul could interact with the souls of the deceased, gain prophetic knowledge of the future, and receive divine guidance. The philosopher Ibn Arabi (1164–1240), who devised a grand metaphysical system merging Islamic theology with Greek philosophy, taught that the imaginative powers experienced in *Alam al-mithal* could be actively cultivated and were ultimately capable of creating reality itself (taking the wish-fulfilling process to its ontological extreme).[9] Synthesizing many different oneiric sources, Ibn Arabi constructed a three-part typology of dreaming that established the basic framework used throughout later Muslim history. The first was an "ordinary" dream, produced by the imagination when it took experiences from daily life and magnified them as in a mirror, reflecting in a distorted symbolic fashion people's thoughts and feelings. The second and much more significant type of dream drew its material not from daily life but from the "Universal Soul," a source of knowledge closely associated with the faculty of abstract reasoning. "Universal Soul" dreams revealed fundamental truths about reality, although like the first type of dream they were distorted by the imperfect mirror of the human imagination. Interpretation was therefore required to discover what the symbolic images meant. The third and final type of dream involved a direct revelation of reality, with no distortion or symbolic mediation—a clear vision of divine truth, most likely granted to a person of pure character and steadfast faith.

A further elaboration of this three-part typology appeared in the monumental *Muqaddimah* (An Introduction to History) written by the philosopher Ibn Khaldun (1332–1402).[10] He explained the different types of dreams:

> Real dream vision is an awareness on the part of the rational soul in its spiritual essence, of glimpses of the forms of events. . . . This happens to the soul [by means of] glimpses through the agency of sleep, whereby it gains the knowledge of future events that it desires and regains the perceptions that belong to it. When this process is weak and indistinct, the soul applies to it allegory and imaginary pictures, in order to gain [the desired knowledge]. Such allegory, then, necessitates interpretation. When, on the other hand, this process is strong, it can dispense with allegory. Then, no interpretation is necessary, because the process is free from imaginary pictures. . . . One of the greatest hindrances [to this process] is the external senses. God, therefore, created man in such a way that the veil of the senses could be lifted through sleep, which is a natural function of man. When that veil is lifted, the soul is ready to learn the things it desires to know in the world of Truth. At times, it catches a glimpse of what it seeks. . . . Clear dream visions are from God. Allegorical dream visions,

which call for interpretation, are from the angels. And "confused dreams" are from Satan, because they are altogether futile, as Satan is the source of futility. This is what "dream vision" really is, and how it is caused and encouraged by sleep. It is a particular quality of the human soul common to all mankind. Nobody is free from it. Every human being has, more than once, seen something in his sleep that turned out to be true when he awakened. He knows for certain that the soul must necessarily have supernatural perception in sleep. If this is possible in the realm of sleep, it is not impossible in other conditions, because the perceiving essence is one and its qualities are always present. God guides toward the truth.

Ibn Khaldun refined the philosophical and theological foundations of Ibn Arabi's typology, introducing a physiological notion into the religious discourse. In his view, the state of sleep detached people from their external senses, liberating their rational souls from their bodies and enabling them to gain glimpses of transcendent truth. This same theme ran through Platonic and Neoplatonic thinking about dreams, and it seems likely that Ibn Khaldun was familiar with Graeco-Roman philosophical theories and used them to enrich his own understanding. The distinctive feature in Ibn Khaldun's theory was that God intentionally created sleep as an opportunity for humans to "lift the veil of the senses" and gain access to divine realities and higher forms of knowing. Dreaming appeared in this light as one of God's gifts to humankind, an innate source of spiritual insight potentially available to all people.

The foregoing is only the briefest of surveys of the vast wealth of Islamic dream teachings from the classical era. Although we do not know how many people believed in these mystical ideas or used Ibn Sirin's manuals to interpret actual dreams, the numerous references in both elite and popular literatures certainly suggests a broad Muslim acceptance of dreaming as an integral element in their faith.

Istikhara

At the level of popular practice, pious Muslims had every reason to feel confident in looking to their dreams for divine guidance. Of course, people always had to be cautious regarding the seductive deceptions of demons and *jinn,* but the Islamic tradition provided several trustworthy

means of focusing the dreaming imagination and heightening its receptivity to heavenly influence. One of these means is known as *istikhara,*
which is essentially the Muslim form of dream incubation.[11] Recall the
hadiths in which Muhammad counseled his followers on pre-sleep rituals and prayers to elicit revelatory dreams; the practice of *istikhara* carried those teachings forward, developing them over the centuries into a
widely used method of human-divine communication. The term *istikhara*
comes from the root word *khayr,* which means "beneficence." It refers to
an effort to consult God and ask for the blessing of His knowledge and
guidance. In pre-Islamic Arabia, people regularly practiced divination by
such means as shooting arrows at targets and observing the flight of birds.
These methods were forbidden in the *Qur'an,* and *istikhara* became the
religiously acceptable substitute.[12] It could be used either in waking, in
which case the divine response came in an intuitive "inclination of the
heart," or before sleeping, in which case a positive or negative answer
came in a dream.

The practices of *istikhara* became increasingly elaborate and variable
over time, but the core principles of the ritual have survived throughout Muslim history and into the present day. *Istikhara* may be practiced
anywhere, though many authorities favored spiritually charged locations
like mosques, graves, the tombs of saints, and of course caves. Cleans-
ings, ablutions, and prayers for the forgiveness of sins were performed
beforehand. If these purifying preparations were insufficient, the ritual
would not work; a person whose mind was disturbed and preoccupied by
worldly matters would, according to tradition, be incapable of perceiving
any divine presence in his or her dreams. After these preliminaries, the
individual was instructed to recite the following prayer:

> My God, I entreat You to show me through knowledge that which is
> blessed for me. I entreat You to give me strength; Your strength is enough
> for everything. I entreat You for the grace and favor of showing me which
> way is the blessed way; You are all omnipotent, I am powerless; You are
> omniscient, I am ignorant. You know all the secrets of the unknown. My
> God, if the result of this task (the task is here stated) is of those that are
> beneficial for my religion, my life, and my after life, then make it easy for
> me and destine it. My God, if the result of this task is harmful for my
> religion, life, and after life, then make me turn away from it, distance me
> from it, and do not destine it. Wherever it may be, predestine for me that
> which is beneficial. Then make me satisfied with this benefit.

The individual then lay down on his or her right side, repeating the name of Allah until falling asleep. The dreams that occurred in response to these incubation techniques were interpreted in fairly straightforward ways. For example, a dream of seeing a religious leader or a scene of tranquility or the colors white or green was interpreted as boding well for the issue at hand, whereas a dream of seeing unpleasant people or scenes of ugliness and strife or the colors black, blue, yellow, or red was taken as a bad omen. *Istikhara* was recommended only for spiritually important concerns that were uncertain and anxiety-provoking, such as a marriage choice, an impending journey, a legal decision, or a military conflict. No less an authority than Ibn Khaldun devised an *istikhara* practice that involved reciting what he called "special dream words" while falling asleep to help maintain a degree of conscious awareness of his desire to receive divine wisdom.[13] He said, "With the help of these words, I have myself had remarkable dream visions, through which I learned things about myself I wanted to know."

Sufi Visions

Both Ibn Arabi and Ibn Khaldun were deeply influenced by Sufism, a mystical movement within Islam that promoted an extraordinarily intense personal relationship with the divine.[14] In their ascetic lifestyles and contemplative devotions, the Sufis turned their backs on the cosmopolitan distractions of the Muslim Empire, seeking instead to annihilate their ordinary human selves, purify their souls, and become worthy of a revelation of God's living presence. Sufis were not entirely opposed to the interest in science, rationality, and knowledge seeking that characterized many philosophers and theologians in the Muslim Middle Ages, but they did assert the higher Islamic value of personal religious experience. Sufism branched into many different schools that spread throughout the Muslim world, each drawing its primary inspiration from some aspect of Muhammad's mystical experiences and teachings as recorded in the *Qur'an*. For instance, the ninth-century-CE Sufi visionary al-Tirmidhi interpreted the verses in *sura* 10 about God blessing his faithful with good tidings (*bushra*) as an affirmation of the importance of prophetic dreaming: "The dream of the faithful is God's word spoken to him in his sleep."[15] In his spiritual autobiography, al-Tirmidhi described a number of dreams, visions, and mystical experiences that brought him ever closer to a full communion with the divine. By virtue of his exceptional concentration and ascetic tranquility he was granted clear visions that required no interpretation, such as the following:

> While praying one night, I was overtaken by deep weariness, and as I put my head on the prayer rug, I saw a huge and empty space, a wilderness unfamiliar to me. I saw a huge assembly with an embellished seat and a pitched canopy the clothing and covering of which I cannot describe. And as if it were conveyed to me: "You are taken to your lord." I entered through the veils and saw neither a person nor a form. But as I entered through the veils, awe descended upon my heart. And in my dream I knew with certitude that I was standing in front of Him. After a while I found myself outside the veil. I stood by the opening of the veil, exclaiming: "He has forgiven me!" And I saw that my breath relaxed of the fear.

What seemed at first to be a failure of effort (falling asleep during prayer) turned into a full-blown mystical encounter with God. Unlike the Christian reformer Martin Luther, who could not tell which dreams were from God and which from the devil, al-Tirmidhi was confident in the heavenly origin of this dream because of the traditional Muslim principle that Satan cannot assume the form of the Prophet nor of Allah. Al-Tirmidhi's dreams could thus be explored as an opening to greater spiritual insight, a path complementary with other forms of devotional practice used by Sufis in the waking state. The sense of relief he felt at the end of the dream (during which he had perhaps been holding his breath or physically paralyzed) completed the fulfillment of his wish, the achievement of his ardent spiritual desire—to stand, pure of soul, before God.

Muhammad's "Night Journey" from *sura* 17 naturally attracted great attention in Sufi circles, where it served as a kind of symbolic template for new mystical adventures. Shamsoddin Lahiji, a Persian poet from the fifteenth century CE, wrote of a visionary dream that taught him a surprisingly modern-sounding cosmological truth:

> One night, after prayers were finished and the liturgical recitation prescribed for the nocturnal hours, I continued to meditate. Absorbed in ecstasy, I had a vision. There was a *khanqah* [Sufi lodge], extremely lofty. It was open, and I was inside the *khanqah*. Suddenly I saw that I was outside. I saw the entire universe, in the structure it presents, consists of light. Everything had become one color, and all the atoms of all the

beings proclaimed "I am God" each in the manner proper to its being and with the force particular to each. I was unable to interpret properly what manner of being had made them proclaim this. Having seen these things in my vision, an intoxication and an exaltation, a desire and an extraordinary delectation were born within me. I wanted to fly in the air, but I saw that there was something resembling a piece of wood at my feet which prevented me from taking flight. With violent emotion, I kicked the ground in every possible manner until this piece of wood let go. Like an arrow shooting forth from the bow, but a hundred times stronger, I rose and moved into the distance. When I arrived at the first Heaven, I saw that the moon had split, and I passed through the moon. Then returning from this state and absence, I found myself again present.[16]

The sensation of brilliant light is a familiar one in religiously meaningful dreaming, and in Lahiji's case it generated an insight into the fundamental nature of the universe—*all is light*. God's creation is, in all its multicolored diversity, the ultimate expression of a single pure brilliance. Sufis like Lahiji believed that the human faculty of visual perception was active in both waking and dreaming, and in its highest state could provide visions of pure luminescence, indicating the living presence of God in one's immediate experience.

Many Sufis have used dreams to guide them in the choice of a *pir* who will serve them as spiritual guide and healer. Sufi teachings are traditionally conveyed in the context of a close master-disciple relationship. The Sufi path often begins with a powerful dream in which the disciple sees a venerable but unknown *pir*—after awakening, the disciple must find that same teacher in waking life and pledge total devotion to him. The *pir* then becomes a private counselor who monitors the disciple's spiritual progress, using dreams as a valuable source of information. In some cases, the discipleship may transpire entirely within dreaming, as happens with Muslim women who, having little opportunity for traveling in public, develop instead a relationship with a *pir* in their dreams, following his teachings as seriously as if they came in waking.

Dreams in Contemporary Islam

The basic ideas about dreaming found in the *Qur'an* and the *hadith* are still a living influence in the contemporary Muslim world.[17] In present-day Iran, for example, popular magazines publish columns in which read-ers send in reports of strange dreams along with details about important events around the time of the dream, and Muslim psychiatrists then pro-vide brief interpretations and practical advice. In Jordan, a recent survey of college students found that one in five had personally experienced a dream of the *jinn* or *Shaytan*. Cases of *jinn* possession via bad dreams and nightmares are well known in that country, and ritual specialists are avail-able to exorcise the disturbing spirits. Sufis in contemporary Egypt speak of soul travel via dreaming in terms virtually identical with those used by Ibn Khaldun more than six hundred years before. In Pakistan, Sufis con-tinue to find dreaming a mysterious source of guidance in their quest for a *pir*, no matter that the quest now takes place in a modern technological context—in one case a man had an extremely vivid and realistic dream in which he found himself leafing through a telephone book, looking for the number to ring up his *pir*.

Islam has not been immune to political appropriation of the dreaming imagination. Mollah Omar, leader of the Taliban movement in Afghani-stan, reportedly dreamed in 1994 that Muhammad appeared to him in a dream and instructed him "to take action and save Afghanistan from cor-ruption and foreign powers."[18] Such a case highlights the potential dan-gers of an absolute belief in the truthfulness and authority of dreams of the Prophet. Islamic dream beliefs also appear to have played a significant role among the Al-Qaeda group in Afghanistan who planned and exe-cuted the 9/11 attacks on the U.S. in 2001. In a video released in December of that year, the Al-Qaeda members are shown discussing and interpret-ing one another's dreams in relation to their long-planned attack, seeking favorable omens and encouraging prophecies, although limits were placed on how far their discussion was allowed to go.[19] When a young man de-scribed his dream of a tall building in America, the group's leader, Osama bin Laden, said, "At that point I was worried that maybe the secret would be revealed if everyone starts seeing it in their dreams. So I closed the subject."

Perhaps it would be best if we all closed the subject. A strong argument can be made that religious fanatics of all varieties—Hindu, Christian, Jew-ish, Muslim—are the principal cause of the contemporary world's woeful condition. If dreaming fuels the mad passions and demagogical persua-siveness of such people, then maybe it, too, should be condemned. History has seen far too much violence and bloodshed perpetrated in the name of heavenly visions and prophetic dreams, and humankind may not be able to survive many more of them. Perhaps we should leave the ruminations of our sleeping minds to themselves, and focus our formidable powers of reason exclusively on the real-life concerns of the waking world.

As sensible as that sounds, I cannot agree. The problem with a purely rationalist approach is that it is just not psychologically possible. *Humans are a dreaming species*—history and science join together in confirming this simple fact. If the goal is to develop realistic solutions to urgent global problems, it makes no sense to pretend that so radical a change—a people without dreams!—could ever be achieved, short of a totalitarian regime of mind control. The idea that we could somehow do without the dreaming imagination strikes me as a fundamentally anti-human fantasy, as if the way to save the world was to change people into soulless logic machines. No one who respects the wonderfully chaotic powers of human creativity could make such an implausible proposal. We are better advised to follow those teachers in Islam and other traditions who show us how to integrate rational analysis and skeptical self-criticism with a faithful openness to the consciousness-enhancing impulses of dreaming. Despite the perennial risk of political abuse—and no tradition is innocent of that—dreaming remains an essential faculty of the human psyche, as much now as it ever has been.

Summary

Throughout its history, from its prophetic origins in desert visions to its modern status as the world's second-largest faith, Islam has strongly affirmed the religious power of dreaming. The Prophet Muhammad expressed great interest in the revelatory potential of dreaming, and Muslims ever since have followed his advice to pay close attention to their dreams. Building on the traditions of Judaism and Christianity, and incorporating several elements from Greek and Roman teachings, Islamic dream theory grew into a full-fledged science in the classical era of Muslim scholarship. According to Ibn Khaldun's version of this theory, dreams are formed in one of three ways: by God, by the angels, or by the Devil. The first is a clear dream vision, and it functions to provide true knowledge, guidance, and inspiration. The second is an allegorical dream, and it uses images and symbols from the human mind to express its divine messages. The third is a confused dream that has no meaning and is merely sent to tempt and mislead the dreamer. Only the second type of dream requires interpretation, and through the centuries Muslims have written numerous books to help people analyze the meanings of their allegorical dreams. Most of these books emphasize the importance of contextualizing the dream within the specific life circumstances of the dreamer; associating the dream's images to verses from the *Qur'an*; and sharing the dream only with competent, respectful people whom the dreamer trusts.

8

Religions of Africa

Of all the dream beliefs and practices considered so far, the one that appears strangest to many people is paradoxical interpretation. From a modern perspective, it seems the height of superstitious absurdity to claim that a dream of one thing means that the opposite will happen in waking life. Such an idea flagrantly violates the scientific principle of falsification—nothing can ever disprove it. If a dream can mean one thing *or its opposite,* then there is no check on arbitrary interpretations, no protection against consciously or unconsciously deceitful claims. Ultimately the process becomes nothing but a con game: heads I win, tails you lose. The fact that most religious and cultural traditions make some use of paradoxical dream interpretations is, in this view, an indication that professional interpreters everywhere have been motivated by the same hucksterish desire to protect their authority as the final arbiters of a dream's meaning, even to the extent of creating hermeneutic escape hatches for themselves in case they run into trouble.

All this is true, and yet not entirely so. The evidence in this book indicates that the sharing and interpreting of dreams can be highly charged with micro- and macro-political conflict, but it would be a mistake to think of paradoxical interpretation in those terms alone. Paradoxical interpretations tap into a genuine truth about the dreaming mind, namely, the binary quality of certain images and themes. Few cognitive scientists would dispute that an oppositional logic governs many of the basic metaphorical categories used in waking thought and language. If we follow the continuity principle, it makes sense that much of dream content revolves around the interaction of exactly these kinds of categories. Given that the meaning of any such term depends on the contrast with its opposite ("up" makes no sense except in opposition to "down," "light" is meaningless except in relation to "dark," "death" is the converse of "life"), the potential for each to evoke its conceptual shadow in a dream is real and worth taking into interpretive consideration.

King Shabaka's Paradoxical Interpretation

Nor should we concede the point that paradoxical dream interpretations are always weapons of political abuse. Consider one of the oldest surviving stories of dreaming in African history, that of King Shabaka, the Ethiopian monarch whose vast empire stretched as far north as Egypt in the eighth century BCE.[1] As recorded in the *Histories* of Herodotus, Shabaka decided to voluntarily withdraw his forces from Egypt and return to his Ethiopian home because of an oracle-confirming dream:

> The final deliverance from the Ethiopian came about (they said) as follows: he fled away because he had seen in his sleep a vision, in which it seemed to him that a man came and stood by him and counseled him to gather together all the priests in Egypt and cut them asunder in the midst. Having seen this dream, he said that it seemed to him that the gods were foreshowing him this to furnish an occasion against him, in order that he might do an impious deed with respect to religion, and so receive some evil either from the gods or from men: he would not however do so, but in truth (he said) the time had expired, during which it had been prophesied to him that he should rule Egypt before he departed thence. For when he was in Ethiopia the Oracles which the Ethiopians consult had told him that it was fated for him to rule Egypt fifty years: since then this time was now expiring, and the vision of the dream also disturbed him, Sabacos [Shabaka] departed out of Egypt of his own free will.

Shabaka interpreted the violent images in his dream as a test of faith. The dream itself did not convey a divine message; rather, the religious value of the experience depended on his proper interpretation of it. Shabaka held the dream to a higher standard of morality, and from that perspective he realized the dream's true meaning could only be the opposite of its literal appearance. Instead of executing the local priests (which would have been fairly standard practice for most Mesopotamian kings), Shabaka did the opposite: he gave control of their country back to them and departed for his home, free in spirit and clean of conscience. Paradoxically interpreted, Shabaka's dream gave him a warning *not* to offend the gods and *not* to extend the time of his empire beyond its proper limit. Thus we have at least one report in the history of world religions of a dream turning a ruler *away* from war and the aggressive domination of others. In ancient Ethiopia, perhaps the oldest of all continuous human nations, King Shabaka looked beyond the literal, conventional meaning of his dream to discern an alternative dimension of significance more closely attuned to his religious faith, even if it seemed "paradoxical" from a worldly perspective.

The Dark Continent

This chapter marks a major shift in the book's approach to the comparative study of dreaming and religion. Instead of examining literate, large-scale societies with extensive records of their history, we now survey a scattering of oral, smaller-scale communities that have been colonized and subjugated by more powerful others (primarily Christians and Muslims). Very little can be known with certainty about the earliest religious traditions of these peoples. The lack of written documents and the active suppression of indigenous cultures by the colonizing powers have left us few reliable resources for understanding their pre-contact beliefs about dreaming. A further complication is that some of the best records of those pre-contact beliefs come from the earliest missionaries and colonial government officials who witnessed the local culture in relatively intact form but who were also actively working to persuade or force the indigenous people to give up their old beliefs and adopt new ones. A comparative project such as this must proceed very carefully here, always keeping in mind the biases of the authors and the hostile context in which they gathered their information.

Fortunately, we have developed a few resources of our own that can help navigate through these dangerous methodological shoals. The preceding chapters on Christianity and Islam provide an essential preparation for analyzing the complex and often violent interplay of indigenous and colonial dream traditions throughout the world. Whatever we may or may not be able to say about pre-contact indigenous cultures, we are still in a good position to identify the ways in which Christianity and Islam have themselves been forced to adapt their dream views in the process of trying to convert other people. Furthermore, every chapter in this book has identified pre- and post-dream practices that do not depend on writing or literary culture, giving us several working hypotheses to use in approaching the religious dream practices of Africa, Oceania, and the Americas. Many excellent, highly self-reflective anthropological studies are available that provide trustworthy knowledge on indigenous cultures past and present, and the evidence of contemporary neuroscience can strengthen our confidence in any finding that relates to basic patterns of brain-mind functioning in sleep. All this will help in overcoming the methodological challenges posed by the remaining chapters of the book. It should also be said that challenges like these are opportunities for gaining new knowledge, and I believe the study of dreams can provide a unique perspective on the recent history of indigenous religions. During times of traumatic cultural dislocation, the people of these traditions have repeatedly turned to their dreams for guidance, hope, and consolation. It is in such "contact situations" that we see the crisis-response quality of dreaming developed into a vital source of collective survival and community adaptation.

According to the story of origins told by modern Western evolutionary science, Homo sapiens first appeared in Africa approximately two hundred thousand years ago, branching off from a line of primates (Homo neanderthalensis, Homo erectus, Homo habilis) whose African roots reached back at least two million years. Some religious believers, including a majority of Christians in the contemporary United States, do not accept the evolutionary story of human origins, and that, of course, is their right. But rejecting evolution means rejecting so many basic, commonsense facts about the natural world that it quickly leads to an intellectual dead end. For the study of dreams, evolution is a necessary context in which to analyze and evaluate our findings, even if we also recognize that evolutionary theory is not a perfect or all-embracing conceptual resource and should be supplemented by other perspectives.[2]

To continue the evolutionary story, the line of Homo sapiens who represent our ancestors began migrating out of Africa starting around 50,000 BCE. As they spread, they very likely encountered populations of other Homo species who had left Africa in earlier times and settled in Europe and Asia. The new waves of Homo sapiens may have sexually mingled with their hominid cousins, so that something of their genetic identity continues in us. Whether or not that is true, the older species were soon driven to extinction. By 10,000 BCE, Homo sapiens had spread to, and become the top predator within, every habitable region on the planet. It is important to note that groups of humans were also continuously moving back *into* Africa during this time of rapid geographic expansion. This means that we will never be able to identify a "pure" African tradition of dreams, religion, or anything else. But that is not the goal here. Rather, the aim is to explore African religious traditions as a further source of insight into the fundamental patterns and potentialities of human dreaming. Evolutionary theory gives us good reason to consider Africa to be the earliest ancestral environment of humankind, and it would certainly strengthen our comparative analysis to find dream phenomena in Africa akin to what we have found in other parts of the world.

Diviners and Ancestors

African traditions have long recognized the centrality of vision in the dreaming process, with some groups like the Zulu of South Africa using the same word (*iphupho*) to refer to both sleeping dreams and waking visions. For the Temne of West Africa, dreaming enables the development of extraordinary powers of vision which professional diviners are capable of using for healing and prophecy.[3] According to one Temne diviner, the mystical gift of "four eyes" (*e-for y-anle*) comes from God in dreams:

> Anyone who dreams is a person God [*K-uru*] gives eyes to see. So they're the same. Diviners dream more than most people—they have prophecies that come true. In diviners' dreams, they're in perfect control. But there are ordinary people who sweat after dreaming. There are people who dream and see spirits. If they wake up they have to be helped or they'll die. When someone dreams, what happens to him is just like *no-ru* [the waking world]. If he comes across "bad people" [witches] and they put medicine in his eyes, he'll get four eyes. It's something like when we're near death. I don't have four eyes now, but I do when I sleep. There are other four eyes that people are born with. These people, if God says they'll have a long life, nobody can challenge them. Before people die they dream a lot, and some even dream their death.

The diviner said all this in reply to an anthropologist's question about what kinds of people experience especially powerful dreams. "Four eyes" was his term for an intensification of dreaming vision, something that could be very dangerous if a person was not properly treated and ritually protected in waking life. To gain four eyes involved making a pact with malevolent spirits and moving perilously close to the land of death. If you survived, the dreams gave you the power to communicate with other spirits, heal the sick, and forecast the future.

For the Yansi of Central Africa the word for dreams is *ndoey*, a collective noun that also refers to a beard (the rarely used singular word *londoey* refers to a single hair in a beard).[4] This gives the sense of each individual dream as a part of a larger whole of living dream experience. The Yansi make a basic distinction between dreams that are relatively trivial and insignificant, mere *ndoey mutwe*, "dreams of the head," and those that reveal prophetic visions of the future (*ndoey ndeag*). The latter may be positive or negative in their precognitive anticipations. In the case of nightmares, the Yansi use various rituals to avert the possibly harmful consequences. When they wake up each morning they tell their dreams to their spouses and family members, checking for warning signs about possible threats they might be facing in the coming day and thinking about how to organize their prayers and rituals accordingly.

Swahili-speaking Bantu people of Eastern and Central Africa also distinguish between ordinary and extraordinary types of dreams. According to a leader of the *Jamaa* movement, a contemporary synthesis of Christian and African religious teachings from the Congo River region, the difference lies in the presence of *mawazo*, "spiritual powers":

> Those *mawazo* in dreams: They are, so to speak, the *mawazo* of God as they are present in the soul of man. . . . So, there are dreams that come from man alone, and dreams that come from God to teach man, to make him understand how God loves. . . . Therefore the dream we receive from the *mawazo* of God, the dream that comes from God, we may take as *mawazo*, yes. Because God has thought out and given the dream. . . . But the dream that comes only from us: this is the second case. We have a dream that comes from us, the dream we have at night. One dream we receive as a holy dream, the one we regard as *mawazo* coming from God; that's how we call it, yes, that sort of dream is *mawazo*. Another dream is just a dream, senseless things that come from man alone, yes.[5]

Later in this interview the *Jamaa* leader explained that *mawazo* were seeds of thought and potentialities of future reality, ultimately rooted in the infinite creativity of God. Before humans were created, they were *mawazo* in the mind of God. Thanks to the emergence of *mawazo* in certain extraordinary dream experiences, humans gained the ability of divine communication and enhanced spiritual power. These dreams were considered very different from those "human" dreams with little or no *mawazo* that generated no meaningful action or significant consequences in the waking world.

The African continent is home to thousands of different communities of people who live in complex webs of relationship with one another's languages, cultural traditions, and genetic stock. Dreaming has woven its way into those webs so thoroughly that African religions cannot be understood without an awareness of their dream beliefs and practices. This is especially true regarding ancestral visitation dreams, which for the vast majority of Africans are the most tangible means of interacting with spiritual beings and realities. To dream of a deceased family member is to be reminded of the dead person's ongoing presence in waking life. The dead may be gone in body, but they remain alive in spirit. Dreaming both proves their continued existence and provides a natural conduit for them to communicate with those still living in the physical world. Visitation dreams are a central feature of religious life for most African peoples, a fact that sheds an interesting light on the nature of history in Africa. It would be wrong to say that African peoples do not care about history just because they have relatively few written documents from the past. By all accounts, Africans are keenly aware of how the past influences the present —*their historical awareness emerges in, and is sustained by, their dreaming.* Their dreams of deceased loved ones strongly encourage them to remain conscious of past traditions, ancestral teachings, and spiritual origins, all with an eye toward enhancing future prosperity. Dreams are agents of historically motivated action that inspire people to conduct themselves in their present lives as the bearers of time-honored communal wisdom.

In most African communities, a few particular people develop special skills in spirit communication, healing, and prophecy. "Diviner" is the shorthand term we will use, though "shaman" would also be accurate (but anachronistic). If we described them using contemporary terminology, we would say they combine the abilities of doctor, psychotherapist, minister, legal arbitrator, political pundit, master of ceremonies, and clan historian, with occasional bursts of tricksterish mischief. Their training usually begins with vivid dreams in childhood, sometimes accompanied by physical suffering and emotional distress. Parents may despair at the idea of their child abandoning normal life for the shadowy, dangerous profession of diviner, but the calling cannot be denied. Training is generally provided by an older diviner who instructs the initiate in the potentials of dream knowledge. In rare cases, dreaming itself can be sufficient to launch a diviner's career, as in the following case of a Temne man who practiced river-pebble divination (*an-bere*): "I had no training: I got the knowledge from God. While I slept, I dreamed that a spirit tied me up and said we should do this work together. When I woke up the next morning, I could do it, and gave an egg to the spirit."[6]

Among the Zulu, the calling to divination comes in a dream or a vision, more often to women than men.[7] Their practices center on helping local people diagnose the cause of strange events and misfortunes, ranging from unusual pregnancies and crop failures to marital problems and spirit possession. The Zulu, like many African cultural traditions, also incorporate dreaming into other ritual practices besides those associated with divination. A significant dream marks the beginning of the rite of passage for Zulu males known as the *thomba* ceremony.[8] Each boy is taught to be ready for the night when he first experiences a sexually climactic dream, one producing a nocturnal emission. When such a physically exciting carryover experience from dreaming to waking does occur, the boy is instructed to get up before dawn, open the village cattle pens, and lead the animals to a hiding place, after which he should ritually bathe at a stream and wait for morning. Meanwhile, the villagers will awaken, notice the missing cattle, and realize what has happened. They will immediately begin making preparations for the *thomba* ceremony, which involves strict seclusion from women, secret teachings, dancing and feasting, and a great deal of ritual fighting with sticks. At the end of these ceremonies a fully initiated man emerges, sexually potent and ready to seek (or steal) a bride.

In some African traditions, dreaming serves as a guide for ritual practice in general. For example, the elders of Yansi clans seek ancestor dreams before making any important decision relating to the community's welfare (e.g., whether to leave on a journey or a hunting expedition, how to resolve a property dispute, when to schedule a religious ceremony, etc.).[9] The elders will gather and sleep at night in the open air, awakening in the morning to share and interpret one another's dreams, seeking information and insight regarding the decision at hand. Nor is the dreaming-ritual connection only found among political leaders and the social elite. Many ordinary African people consult diviners for help with recurrent nightmares and frightening sleep experiences.

While virtually everyone recognizes the spiritual potential of dreaming, no African tradition is ignorant of the darker, more malevolent forces also at work, and diviners are the community experts in protecting people from those nightmare powers. Here is an account from a prominent diviner among the Ingessana of East-Central Africa, giving an example of what happens when people are attacked in their dreams by the loathsomely frightening creatures known as *nengk* (singular *nenget*):

> At night a *nenget* will come to you and show you a cow, and before it goes away it will throw sorghum seed around the homestead. Unless you sacrifice a cow, the *nenget,* by the seed it has planted in the homestead, will take the lives of your livestock or even your wife and children and yourself. So you will send for a doctor-diviner and tell him of the dream. That it is a *nenget* will be confirmed by the diviner casting three pieces of tobacco and interpreting how they fall. So the diviner will go around the homestead digging out with his special staff the seed which he is able to see. Sometimes he will also have to pull seeds out of the body of some afflicted person in the homestead. A cow is sacrificed, and then the elders deliver orations addressed to the *nengk* asking them to depart now that they have been given what they demanded.[10]

For the Ingessana, as for many African communities, life involves a constant process of negotiation with spiritual powers that manifest themselves in many types of experience, most reliably in dreaming. The dangers of failing to appease the spirits are believed to be very real, and the diviner takes nightmares like these with the utmost seriousness. The ritual process just described has the effect of bringing the dream into the waking world as fully as possible, first by giving it voice and sharing it with others, then hunting for the seeds, sacrificing the cow, and praying respectfully to the *nengk,* all demonstrating the individual's faith and humility before the spirits. The diviner places him- or herself between the spirits and the suffering individual, mediating their interests and cultivating a pragmatic accommodation of each to the other. With a foot in each reality the diviner bridges the ancestral past and the living present, seeking a new path to a healthier and more prosperous future.

Conversion

The two largest and most powerful religions in the world, Christianity and Islam, have long and troubled histories of missionary activity in Africa. Christian evangelism spread to Egypt within the first few decades after

Jesus's crucifixion, and Muhammad's followers advanced the Muslim faith all the way across North Africa to Morocco in less than a hundred years after his death. In each case it is impossible to separate the religious conversions from the military conquests—Christianity and Islam alike have established themselves in Africa at the point of a sword. Today, the continent's population is about evenly split between the two traditions (approximately 400 million each), as Islam remains the predominant religion in North Africa while Christianity reigns in sub-Saharan Africa. (It must be added that many Africans cannot be exclusively categorized as either Christian or Muslim.) Evaluating the full historical impact of these two monotheistic traditions on the indigenous spiritualities of Africa is a task far beyond the scope of this chapter. We can consider, however, the role of dreaming as a common religious language between Africans and the Christian and Muslim missionaries. Dreams provided the missionaries a means of explaining the tenets of their faith and giving people an experiential source of divine revelation leading to conversion. Dreams also provided indigenous Africans with a vital resource for resisting external missionary coercion and affirming their own independent visionary powers.

Having already discussed the increasingly distrustful view of dreaming in the history of Christian theology, we can appreciate the difficulty some missionaries found in talking to African people about the subject.[11] This theme also recurs in the next two chapters: *dream-doubting Christians meet dream-obsessed natives.* Firsthand reports from missionaries often include a mention of the primitive people's extravagant dream beliefs and inexplicable acceptance of the reality of sleeping experience. Some missionaries tried to dismiss dreams entirely as a source of spiritual guidance. In the words of a twentieth-century Christian from England working in Central Africa, a good response to a dream-obsessed native "is to pooh-pooh his fears and tell him that his dreams are the result of an overwrought imagination, or a little undigested gravy." But this kind of attitude became increasingly difficult once the African people began reading the Bible for themselves and learning about the stories of divine dream revelations in the books of Genesis, Daniel, Matthew, and Acts. For this reason, other missionaries took a more accommodating tone and employed the deeply rooted African interest in dreaming as a means of explaining the superiority of Christian religious understanding. Dream interpretation thus became an active arena of religious persuasion, resistance, and conversion. A nineteenth-century English Christian missionary in North Africa recorded the following dreams:

Today I went back, forgetting what had happened, to a house where the woman had turned me out last week, almost before I had set foot in it, saying she would hear nothing about Jesus. Strangely, I had forgotten it, as we say, when I went in. Her first words were: 'I sent you away last week, I was very wrong. Jesus came to me that night and frightened me. I dared not open my eyes to look at Him. He said: "Why did you not listen? You must listen." His hand was on me. It would have suffocated me if I had not feared and said: "I have had enough, I will listen now." And listen she did.

[An African woman told the same missionary:] "I have had a dream, it was the night after you were here. I saw two *kanouns* [fire pots]. In one was a very little fire, nearly going out; in the other was a bright fire that was increasing. Someone was standing by and he said: "Do you know what these two fires mean?" I said: "No." He went on: "The little fire that is nearly out is the religion of the Arabs, [and] the bright fire is what your friend has told you about Jesus. There is certainty about that. You have to leave the old fire and come to the new." "I believed before," she said, "I believed but now I know. I am one of you now and the sister of the others in the world."[12]

As the latter report suggests, the competition between Christians and Muslims for African converts could be fierce, and dreaming could serve either missionary cause by providing a direct experiential validation of the "true" faith. In some cases, the missionaries found they had an almost magical power to elicit dream conversions by nothing more than their presence. Such is the story of an early twentieth-century Christian evangelist working among the Bantu of South Africa:

Up among the mountains, behind one of my remoter stations, is a steep valley; and up this valley, at the end of everything, is a village. I had never been there, and am still not aware that anyone from there had ever been to see me. Late one afternoon, then, a man came from this village to call me to a "sick" woman of whom, as we went, he related these facts. A month previously the woman's heathen husband had died. A week later she awoke one night screaming, and had said that as she lay asleep she had felt a hand on her shoulder. Awakening—such was her language, but of course she spoke of her dream—she saw her dead husband, in his ordinary clothes and so "real" that she forgot for the moment that he was dead. She gave a cry of joy, and demanded where he had been to return to the hut so late. On that he had said: "Send at once for the priest at — and be washed from your sins." "But why do you come now to tell me that?" she asked. "Lest you die as I have done, unwashed," he replied awfully. And at that she remembered his death, was convulsed with terror, and found herself awake. Her folk had temporized with her, and had not sent for me, none of them being Christian there; but ten days or so later she had dreamed again. This time her husband was angry, had said nothing, had not indeed needed to say anything, for she had known instinctively his anger and the reason for it. From that time she had eaten next to nothing, and had been in a kind of fit all day long, reiterating that I must be sent for. But the night before she had dreamed that a white priest came in, in a white vestment, and, laying hands upon her, had healed her.[13]

When the priest arrived he did as the woman had dreamed, putting his hands upon her and praying for her well-being. She recovered from her illness and went on to become a baptized Christian who converted many other people from her village. So the priest had to do practically nothing —all his work was done by the woman's dreams. Quite a useful missionary tool! Her first dream, a classic visitation complete with hyper-realism and vivid sensation of touch, involved a frightening admonition from her dead husband to convert to Christianity. As someone who had just passed from this world to the next, he would be a credible witness to the conditions of the afterlife, making his message all the more compelling and trustworthy. The woman's kinfolk, trying to maintain village traditions against Christian encroachment, were reluctant to accept her dream at face value. But the wordless urgency of the second dream gave her such inner certainty that she essentially withdrew in body, mind, and soul from the village in order to wait for the priest's arrival.

From a Christian missionary viewpoint, this seems like a perfect illustration of the Holy Spirit as a guiding and liberating force in people's dreams. It may be so. A more socio-psychologically oriented perspective would also want to acknowledge the strategic value of such conversion dreams in relation to the individual's adaptation to a sudden life crisis. A widow in any society faces a grim future, and in such circumstances the fresh promise of a new faith becomes all the more appealing. Considered purely as a matter of survival, it was a reasonable decision for the Bantu woman to follow her dreams and become a Christian. Her chances for physical protection and support were very likely improved as a result (many of the earliest Roman converts to Christianity were widows, the poor, and the sick). Note, too, the priest's mention of all the new converts she then persuaded to join her. This undoubtedly enhanced the woman's prospects even more, as she now rose in social status to an important new position, that of intermediary between her village and the spiritual powers represented by the priest. *A new kind of African diviner had been born,* one who accepted Christianity in order to use it, benefit from it, and then transform it. Where the missionaries saw multitudes of new converts, many Africans themselves saw a new regime of religious and political authority that could, by means of the ancient practices of dreaming, be adapted to their own needs and creative desires.

What has happened to Christianity in Africa has also happened to Islam.[14] At the level of theological doctrine, orthodox Muslim teachings directly contradicted the strong and widespread African belief in the importance of interacting in dreams with a multitude of deceased ancestors who kept the people rooted in traditional religious wisdom. The purest and strictest Muslim faith insists that the only true God is Allah, and no other deities or supernatural beings should be worshiped. In Islam, as in Christianity, the monotheistic imperative could be taken as sufficient cause to doubt any value in dreaming, and thus to forbid indigenous peoples from pursuing and exploring their dreams. The practical realities of African-Muslim relations, however, generated several compromise strategies that allowed people to continue dreaming in the old communal ways, but under the watchful rule of the new Islamic authorities. One of these strategies involved accepting dream visitations from the dead so long as the message of the deceased ancestor compelled the individual to convert to Islam. Much like the Bantu woman just mentioned whose dead husband commanded that she convert to Christianity, many African people adopted Islam because they were inspired by a visitation dream in which a trusted ancestor sanctioned the change in religious worldview. The drawback to this accommodation (from a monotheistic point of view) was that it kept alive the pre-Muslim polytheistic belief in the spiritual potency of dreaming, a belief that fueled the ongoing practice of traditional healing, divination, and other forms of "witchcraft" in African communities long after they had supposedly converted to Islam.[15]

By far the most effective strategy for harmonizing Muslim teachings with traditional African approaches concerned the practice of *istikhara*.[16] Many African cultures had a long history of performing their own dream incubation rituals, making it much easier for the Islamic version of *isti-khara* to be understood and adapted to the African context. This shared practice could then become a useful missionary tool for spreading further information about Islam. Muslim clerics, especially members of the mystically inclined Sufi orders, took on the professional role of public dream guides and interpreters, effectively displacing traditional diviners (and providing themselves with a lucrative source of income). *Istikhara* in Africa could be performed for any of the usual reasons, for example, to diagnose a mysterious illness, seek divine guidance in choosing a marriage partner, gain insight on a particular point of spiritual wisdom, and so on. If the ritual was performed according to basic Muslim requirements (purifying one's body, reciting *Qur'anic* verses, sleeping on the right side with the right hand under one's ear), and if the resultant dream was immediately interpreted by a Muslim cleric, *Istikhara* provided an acceptable arena in which Africans could continue their time-honored communion with dreaming.

At times, the dreaming imagination seemed to be the only power remaining for a subjugated African people, as illustrated by a case from mid-twentieth-century Egypt.[17] The Nubian civilization thrived for thousands of years at the upper reaches of the Nile River, periodically contending for power with the Pharaohs of Egypt down river to the north. In modern times, the Nubians have been largely absorbed into urban Muslim cultures in Egypt and Sudan, and in the 1960s the construction of the High Dam at Aswan resulted in the complete submersion and loss of all their remaining ancestral lands. The Nubian people were relocated to other towns and cities, where they adopted Sufi Islam with a peculiar dream twist. To dream of a Sufi saint was, according to the Islamic authorities, a legitimate religious experience. But the Nubians began reporting saint dreams with messages that led to a very specific goal—the creation of new spiritual homes for their exiled religious community. The ancestral visitation dreams of these displaced Nubians often included a specific request from the saint to build a shrine at a particular location where the people could properly worship God. In just a few years, hundreds of shrines were created in this way. These dream sanctuaries provided a safe and comfortable setting where the devotional ritual of *dhikr* (chanting, singing, and praying to God with total concentration and purity of intent) could be practiced by the Nubian Muslim converts. The dreams of the Nubians gave them the personal motivation and theological justification to build their *own* places of worship, infused with their *own* felt meanings and their *own* sense of religious presence. Completely cut off from their primal homelands and cast adrift in the modern world, the Nubians faced the imminent prospect of their extinction as a community. In that situation of ultimate collective peril they used their dreams as a resource to help reestablish their collective cultural roots both physically and spiritually.

Once again, such cases raise the intriguing question of who exactly is converting whom. Have the Nubians become Muslim, or has Islam (in this specific lived context) become Nubian? Influences are clearly moving in both directions, with dreams providing a crucial bridging experience. According to the evidence we have been discussing, the term "conversion" does not mean a simple act of switching from one religion to another. Rather, the term should denote a mutually transformative process of spiritual identity change in which both religious traditions develop in new directions. In the present case, the question is more historically complex because, as we saw in chapter 7, Islam emerged within the broader context of ancient Fertile Crescent religious traditions, many of which (like the Nubians) venerated the spiritual power of dreaming. The Muslim practice of *istikhara* can therefore be seen as a product of Islam's initial accommodations to earlier religious dream practices that the region's people felt were fundamentally important and worth preserving in the new tradition. This means that the Nubians, by converting to the Muslim faith, were in a sense drawing Islam back to its own spiritual roots.

African Independent Churches

The dire personal and communal circumstances that typically spark religious conversions tell us something important about human nature. When faced with situations of terror, suffering, and death, the human brain-mind system becomes capable of extraordinary creative efforts to make sense of and act effectively in response to those life-threatening conditions. This also tells us something important about dreaming, namely, that we can confidently, if sadly, predict that dreams will become an increasingly important source of personal inspiration and cultural meaning-making in direct proportion to the severity of a crisis situation. In most parts of Africa during the twentieth century the people have struggled through hellish miseries of war, drought, famine, plague, and political oppression. Knowing what we know about dreams, we would expect that the cultural and religious responses of indigenous Africans to these horrors would include a strong reliance on dreaming, and that turns out to be the case.[18] Many of the new religious movements known by the general term "African Independent Churches" proclaimed their spiritual autonomy from both Christianity and ancient African traditions. They offered radically new messages for radically different times, and dreaming was a primary medium for their creative religious responses to the dangers pressing in on all sides.[19]

Dreaming played at least two important roles for the African Independent Churches. First, it provided the initial inspiration for individuals who became charismatic leaders of these new spiritual groups. As usual, we can never be sure if the particular dreams now available for study were accurately reported, and there is always the likelihood that some reports were embellished or made up to enhance a leader's authority. But we can also be sure, based on strong evidence from scientific dream research, that the African people living through these terrifying situations were indeed dreaming about their plight and seeking creative visions to help them survive. A few of these people had dreams in which they envisioned a better future not just for themselves but for their whole community. Thus an individual dream could inspire new hope and vitality for everyone who was suffering through a collective crisis. Examples include the rise of the Kimbangu Church of Congo, born in the militant dreams of Simon Kimbangu (1889–1951), who ended up dying in a colonial prison; the Church of Nazareth Baptists among the Zulu in southern Africa, whose founder Isaiah Shembe (1867–1935) was guided by his early-life dreams to become a healer; and the Aladura movement among the Yoruba in western Africa, in which the faith-healing ministry of founder Joseph Sadare directly relied upon the divine messages of his dreams and visions.[20]

Sadare's movement began during the global influenza pandemic in 1918–19, when millions upon millions of Africans died, and he used dreams to guide his efforts at prayer-based healing (Aladura means "the ones who pray"). Rejecting both Western medicine and traditional African remedies as obviously ineffective in stopping the plague, Sadare and his followers had to look elsewhere for healing power. He and his followers engaged in extensive group discussions about their dreams and visions, which brings us to the second important role of dreaming in the African Independent Churches. The public sharing of dreams became a standard feature of group worship services, and in some churches dream sharing was the central ritual activity. For example, members of the Zulu Zionist churches of southern Africa frequently shared dreams of ancestral visitations, prophetic revelations from the Holy Spirit, and occasionally a demonic temptation in a nightmare.[21] Sharing dreams like this served as a vital source of collective spiritual bonding in these groups, enabling each individual to weave his or her creative visions into a newly emerging whole.

In all African Independent Churches the telling of dreams inevitably became entangled with struggles over social power and religious authority, so the process was hardly a model of utopian harmony. Indeed, one of the most dream-centered groups, the True Church of God among the Igbo people of Nigeria, was exceptionally restrictive and demanding with its members, comparable in many ways to a Christian fundamentalist church in the contemporary United States.[22] Financial donations and frequent attendance at worship were absolutely required; God was repeatedly portrayed by the church leaders as a stern, all-powerful father figure; the Bible was interpreted literally as the only authoritative guide to religious life. From a skeptical perspective, the True Church of God looks like a perfect example of an authoritarian, closed-minded sect. But if we consider the African missionary context in which it emerged, this new religious movement is better understood as an expression of creative spiritual adaptation. The Igbo who joined the church were intentionally separating themselves from both their ancestral heritage *and* the authority of the white European missionaries. They were religious pioneers who pledged themselves to a new and, they hoped, better path, taking the missionaries' most prized source of power—the Bible—and using it to serve their own local needs and purposes. And far from being rigid-thinking automatons, the members of the True Church made open-ended dream sharing a regular feature of their worship services, a practice allowing everyone in the group (children included) to voice their hopes and anxieties, to wonder about the mysterious workings of the divine, and to develop practical strategies for dealing with waking-world problems. Dreams were said to be communications from the Holy Spirit, a belief that added extra incentive for people to remember their sleep experiences and talk about them with others. Many of the Igbo initially joined the church because of dreams that were interpreted as calls to conversion. These dreams then became badges of spiritual status in the group, establishing the authenticity of a person's relationship with God. Church leaders listened to as many dreams as possible to glean information of relevance to the congregation as a whole (and, we may surmise, to monitor nascent heresies and possible deviations from church authority).

The central importance of dreaming for the True Church of God does not mean we should regard the movement as either a "good" or a "bad" religion. Such evaluations are not the concern of this book, and, in any case, are of dubious value. The focus here is on the dynamic interaction of dreaming and religious life, particularly in times of conflict and change. The people of the True Church relied so heavily on their dreams because they were living in a place and time in which they felt an especially urgent need for consolation, hope, and vision. That doesn't make them good or bad, noble or savage, enlightened or ignorant. It just makes them human.

Summary

The history of religions in Africa covers so much territory, so many different peoples, and such a vast stretch of time that any general claims about their dream beliefs and practices must be made with special caution. Based on the evidence in this chapter, it seems fair to say that most African religious traditions have distinguished between dreams originating from human causes (e.g., dreams of a waking preoccupation or physical illness) and divine sources (e.g., an ancestral visitation or a vision from God). At least some African religions have made dreaming a central feature of their worship, indicating a strong desire to enhance the impact of divine dreams in people's waking lives. Along with the now familiar functions of prophecy, healing, and creative inspiration, African religions have shown a special desire to seek the powers of dreaming during times of personal and collective crisis. In some cases, the dream-guided outcome is a conversion to a new faith (Christianity or Islam); in other cases, the dreams prompt a revitalization of traditional religious teachings; and in still other cases, the outgrowth of dreaming is a new synthesis of the old and the new. Regarding interpretation, we know very little about African teachings before the arrival of Christian and Muslim missionaries. The most avid dreamers in Africa today appear to be the members of the Independent African Churches, whose dream interpretation practices involve an elaborate process of public sharing, group discussion, and biblical association.

9

Religions of Oceania

Much of the discussion so far has focused on what people *see* in dreams. Vision is the strongest mode of sense perception in a large majority of the religiously significant dreams that we have considered. Many of the world's cultures have enshrined this perceptual primacy in their definitions of dreaming as a kind of inner seeing. Dreams with strong auditory sensations are less often reported; the most impactful types are those in which a god, spirit, or ancestor delivers a clearly spoken message. Taste and smell are rarely mentioned in dream reports, either historically or in contemporary research. Whatever functions dreams may serve, they apparently do not require the activation of these two sensory modalities. This is a suggestive finding, because taste and smell differ from vision and hearing in the spatial range of their effectiveness. Taste depends on a stimulus directly to the tongue, and smell operates best in an atmospheric zone close to the body, whereas both sight and sound provide detailed information about stimuli located far away from the individual. By means of vision and hearing, humans have developed a dramatically expanded sphere of self-awareness and a greater consciousness of their location in the physical world. Vision and hearing are the best senses for long-distance threat detection and beyond-the-horizon journeying and exploration. These are the senses we bring with us when we dream.

What of the fifth mode of sense perception, touch? If by touch we mean body sensations generally, then it ranks much closer to sight and sound than taste and smell in its importance to dreaming. Besides intensely realistic experiences of direct physical contact with other people (aggressively in a fight, sexually in a romantic tryst), many dreams involve vivid somatic actions such as walking, driving, swimming, running, dancing, playing a sport, and even flying, along with more negative experiences like crying, falling, being paralyzed, losing teeth, being hit, stabbed, or shot. A basic sense of embodiment, personal presence, and physical movement seems to be a standard part of human dreaming, though of course we also find instances of *dis*embodied dreaming experience reported in many traditions. Actually, *all* dreams are disembodied insofar as our bodies remain in bed while we dream of moving in other places. Here is another paradox at the heart of dreaming: it is rooted in, and yet ranges far beyond, the physical location of the sleeping body.

A couple of weeks before writing this particular section of the book, I attended an academic conference in Washington, D.C. My hotel was just a block from the Mall, and each evening after finishing with the conference I strolled around the center of the Capitol, admiring the wartime memorials, laying hands on the Washington Monument, and glaring at the White House. I went to bed at night with my head full of images, feelings, and ideas from lively conversations at the conference and from my ambivalent musings on the sacred grounds of the Union. But my dreams made no explicit reference to any of that; instead, they continuously brought me back to my home, three thousand miles away. Their content revolved around emotionally laden images of being with my family, passing through neighborhood streets, shopping at the market, driving the family car, with nothing directly relating either to the conference or the governmental surroundings. Though my waking self was in Washington, my dreaming self was transported back to the familiar haunts of home. No expert interpretation was needed to explain this—I missed my family and worried about their well-being. My dreams were continuous not with my physical location but with my emotional concerns, specifically a longing for home. This is one small illustration of how dreams can be both highly realistic *and* unrealistic at the same time. Readers may want to consider how often their own dreams bring them back to places (houses, neighborhoods, schools, dorms, camps) that are distant from their current physical locations but close to the deepest realities of their present-day emotional lives.

Indeed, the evidence gathered in this book supports the idea of a dynamic relationship between waking and dreaming movement. How people move in the waking world can impact their dreams, and how they move in dreaming can influence their actions while awake. In the religions of Oceania, these mind-body processes of dreaming and waking movement have been developed into mutually supportive cultural systems with origins stretching far into the ancestral past. Like humans everywhere, the people of these Pacific Island communities have dreamed of fantastic visions and clear verbal messages. But more than most, the peoples of

Oceania have *journeyed* in their dreams, moving in spirit as energetically as they moved physically during the original era of human settlement in their part of the world.[1]

Age of Exploration

Around the same time that bands of Homo sapiens in southern Europe were "creatively exploding" in their beautifully decorated, ritually consecrated caves, other groups were taking advantage of relatively low sea levels to travel across land bridges to what we now call Australia (from Latin, "to the south"). What they found was a temperate, ecologically abundant country that had never known the presence of humans. Short sailing trips from Australia and various parts of southern Asia led to the discovery of other biologically plentiful islands where humans could settle in prosperity and comfort. These voyages in quest of new islands became increasingly skillful and daring, covering hundreds and then thousands of miles of open ocean. Naturally no records remain of the many explorers who perished in the uncharted seas. But those who survived their journeys and succeeded in finding land were rewarded with the opportunity to wield unrivaled power in bountiful new environments. In time, every habitable island in the western Pacific was settled, generating rapid bursts of cultural creativity as the people of each new community took control of the virgin lands and prepared themselves for new expeditions.

The nineteenth-century French term "Oceania," as imperfect as any other expression used in this book, is a collective noun denoting the kindred cultures of Australia, New Guinea, the Malay Archipelago, New Zealand, and the hundreds of western Pacific islands stretching as far north as Hawaii and as far east as Easter Island. What binds these widely dispersed cultures and peoples together is a historically unfolding web of genetics, language, social structure, and ceremonial customs. Information about their earliest religious beliefs and practices exists only in the form of scattered rock paintings, artifacts, and fragments of myth and legend. Similar to the situation in Africa, the most detailed records of Oceanic cultures come from the very people (European colonizers) who were actively working to replace the indigenous spiritual traditions with a new regime of Christian control over thought and deed. Once again, our historical vision is drastically limited by the elusiveness of reliable evidence.

Without ignoring all the specialized research on the incredible diversity of cultural groups in this region (New Guinea alone is home to roughly one thousand different languages),[2] this chapter takes a broader comparative approach, with the aim of outlining the shared dream teachings of Oceania. Wherever these adventurous seafaring folk traveled, they brought with them traditions of dreaming that helped them remain connected to their ancestral lands while inspiring them to embark on new journeys into the unknown.

Tjukurrpa, *or Dreamtime*

The arrival of humans in Australia was, from the perspective of the other creatures living there, a cataclysmic event. The same climate changes that allowed humans to reach Australia probably put additional stress on some of the native species, but even taking that into account it is clear that human activities greatly contributed to the mass extinctions that swept over the land soon after they appeared. The combination of improved weaponry and strategic use of brush-clearing fires enabled the first settlers to hunt and kill at will, essentially remaking the face of the continent. For the next forty thousand years the descendents of these Neolithic pioneers prospered in small bands of nomadic wanderers. Agriculture never developed in any large-scale form, and their social groupings remained fairly small, though, as mentioned, their linguistic and cultural dynamism was impressive. Their religious beliefs and practices revolved around an ancient myth that explained the creation of the world and the proper place of humans within it. This myth was the ultimate source of meaning and spiritual guidance in aboriginal life, and its roots reached as far into the past as anyone could remember. It was a myth of primordial, autochthonous dreaming.

The local terms used for this myth, *Tjukurrpa, Alchera,* and *Alcheringa,* have been translated by anthropologists as "The Dreaming" or "Dreamtime."[3] This is only partly accurate. "Ancestral Order" is another possible translation, though even that phrase obscures the restless stirring of creative potency that is part of it, too. *Tjukurrpa* is a realm outside ordinary physical time and space, yet vibrantly present in every feature of the world —land and sea, plants and animals, sun and stars. It is the beginning of all that is, the creative labor of the ancestors striding the land and singing its nature into being. The ancestors still live in *Tjukurrpa*, and humans have the ability to connect with them through their personal dreaming. *Tjukurrpa* is not synonymous with individual dreams experienced during sleep (called *kapukurri*), but the Australian aborigines recognized a strong and vital relationship between the two. Personal dreaming was a means of entering into *Tjukurrpa*, allowing each person his or her own access to the powers of the ancestors. The aborigines affirmed the democratic accessibility of dreaming as much as any culture in history, and they made a point of teaching their children about dreaming from early in life so they would be prepared for the opportunities and dangers that arose in their sleep experiences. In fact, the aborigines believed each child was born into this world through a dream experienced by the mother or other close relative (whether or not they remembered having the dream). In this dream the spirit-child began the process of moving from the *Tjukurrpa* into human form. Death for the aborigines was a movement in the other direction, from physical embodiment back into *Tjukurrpa*.[4]

We do not know how far back in history the aboriginal teachings about *Tjukurrpa* can be traced. Prior to contact with Western missionaries and colonizers, we have no clear view of the changes and continuities in Australian aboriginal cultures. Maybe the mythic concept of *Tjukurrpa* is a recent development with no connection to past cultural teachings. Maybe it is a foreign idea imported by visitors to Australia long after the era of original settlement. *But maybe it is what the aborigines say it is,* namely, a true history of the creation of their land. Any argument here is speculative; I believe, however, that the *Tjukurrpa* myth, more likely than not, represents a forty-thousand-year-old spiritual insight about the creative powers of dreaming. The first human settlers in Australia *really did* create the land their descendents inherited from them, discovering it after long and perilous travels and violently transforming its biosystem according to their needs and desires. This isn't just superstitious fancy, it is an accurate representation of what actually happened. The unprecedented creative feats of those heroic people would naturally echo in later aboriginal dreams, reinforced by rituals, stories, and "walk-abouts" along the ancestral song lines criss-crossing the continent. The Dreaming was a never-ending song of the birth of aboriginal life in a mythic realm woven of history, geography, and psychophysiological experience, where living people can roam freely in the company of their extended spiritual family.

Soul Journeys

Implicit in this myth is a fairly straightforward explanation of what happens in a dream. When a person goes to sleep, his or her dream-spirit (*partunjarri*) is released from the physical body and is able to fly in the realm of the Dreaming. We have encountered different versions of this folk theory many times before, and more instances are still to come. The notion of dreams as the experiences of the liberated soul is so widespread in cross-cultural history that it should be considered *the* commonsensical human view, the cognitive default position for Homo sapiens reasoning about dreams. It is certainly the easiest way to explain the obvious phenomenon that everyone knows from personal experience, namely, the disjunction between an unconscious, physically motionless sleeping body and a conscious, active, and mobile dream-self. (Hence the corollary folk warning, found in Australia and elsewhere, that one should never awaken a sleeping person too suddenly, lest the dream-self not have enough time to return to the body.) The key religious consequence of this idea is that it validates the special ontological status of dreaming, establishing it as a type of reality proper to the qualities of the liberated spirit or soul. Dreaming provides prima facie evidence for the authenticity of religious teachings, and anyone who doubts that evidence can test its truthfulness in their own dream experiences.

The aboriginal Australians took the reality of dreaming so seriously that they developed methods of collective action in dreams, in which whole groups would join together to journey in the Dreaming. These journeys were led by divination and healing experts known as *maparn*. The *maparn* led the participants in pre-sleep ritual preparations, after which everyone joined in a shared dream in which the *maparn* piloted them in a flying convoy aboard a sacred object or spiritually charged creature like a snake. Particularly in recent times, when the aborigines have been compelled by modernization to live far from their home territories, dream-spirit journeys have taken on special significance as a means of remaining connected to ancestral lands. To Western ears the experience of shared dreaming may sound silly, but in aboriginal practice it was often associated with feelings of danger and vulnerability. The *maparn*-guided dream convoys provided people with a safety-in-numbers kind of protection against the malevolent forces and beings that their dream-spirits were likely to encounter in their travels. The release of the soul from the sleeping body was a double-edged sword, making it equally possible to meet helpful ancestors or fall prey to hostile spirits. As a result, the aboriginal Australians did not undertake dream journeys for light entertainment or whimsical diversion. These were deadly serious religious practices aimed at rejuvenating the fundamental life energy of the community. Despite repeated criticism from disapproving Christian missionaries, many aborigines have continued to practice the dream-journeying tradition, seeking in personal dreaming a true connection to their ancestral lands in *Tjukurrpa*.

Many other cultural groups in Oceania also shared this notion of dreaming as a soul journey, and at this point we can widen our discussion to include the hundreds of different human communities living in New Guinea. The world's second-largest island lying just to the north of Australia, New Guinea was until five thousand years ago connected to the Australian continent by a land bridge. People had been living, fighting, and developing the land there for tens of thousands of years before that, hence the close relationship between the indigenous cultures of New Guinea and Australia (though more recent migrations of human populations from Asia have also had a strong cultural impact). Most interesting, from our perspective, is the strong continuity of dream traditions across these different cultures. Through all the long ages of changing climates and fluctuating sea levels, while the people spread far and settled in separate regions where they developed distinctive linguistic identities, virtually every culture continued to rely on dreaming as a valuable source of spiritual insight and community guidance.

Among the Mekeo people, who live in small villages carved out of the bush in a humid river valley in central New Guinea, a dream (*nipi*) takes place when a person's body sleeps and his or her dream-self (*lalauga*) leaves to see and do various things.[5] The *lalauga* is real but has no material substance, and people may perceive it in waking life as an apparition or ghost. The separation of *lalauga* and the body creates an existentially threatening condition in which a person can easily fall sick, become injured, even die. Nevertheless, dreaming experiences are highly prized as means of gaining spiritual power, and so the risks are considered worth taking. The Mekeo recognize that some dreams are relatively trivial reflections of daily life, with little or no significance, whereas other dreams offer opportunities for soul travel to otherworldly realms, including the land of the dead, magical European cities, and the deep aquatic abodes of *faifai* water spirits. The Mekeo regard most of their dreams as *palopole*, metaphorical riddles whose meanings must be searched for and discovered by the waking mind. Interpretation depends on both the personal situation of the dreamer and the social context in which he or she experienced the dream. Many Mekeo dreams are interpreted as omens of waking-life danger, particularly the possible death of a relative or friend. This is not an unreasonable concern for people living in a region with constant threats from disease, storms, earthquakes, volcanoes, and attacks from warring neighbors. Dreams of sexual encounters are widely experienced but carefully guarded and kept secret. The Mekeo belief in the reality of the *lalauga*'s travels during sleep implies that an erotic dream with another person should be taken as an urgent warning, especially for women who may realize from these dreams that they are the targets of the love rituals of unknown men. Dreaming of sex with a water spirit or a dead person is never good and foreshadows illness and destruction. Whether the content of their dreams is good or bad, the Mekeo cherish the capacity of the *lalauga* to discover hidden knowledge and perceive hidden truths. Religious rituals may enhance and focus this capacity, but its basic functioning is innate in all people.

For the Mekeo and other New Guinea peoples, the metaphorical dimensions of dreaming require looking past the literal imagery to recognize and appreciate a dream's most important meaning. A good example of this principle comes from the Mae Enga, a rough community of warriors and farmers in New Guinea.[6] One of the Mae Enga elders, a man named Anggauwane who was well known for his moral integrity, mentioned to an anthropologist a dream in which he was walking along an unknown path through the tall cane grass when he suddenly found himself face to face with an attractive woman from a rival village. Anggauwane immediately proceeded to seduce the woman, and they began to make love right there on the path. One of the woman's male relatives appeared and threatened Anggauwane with an axe, but the clan leader merely glared at the man, who fled in fear. After reaching a satisfying conclusion, the dream ended. To the anthropologist's surprise, when Anggauwane reported the dream he evinced none of the shame or embarrassment that would normally accompany a story that violated so many basic sexual taboos. Instead, he interpreted the dream in a nonsexual way, as a metaphor for his current land dispute with the people of the woman's village. Anggauwane said it predicted that his clan would triumph as easily as he had ravished the dream woman, and subsequent events in the waking world confirmed his prophecy. We might suspect that at another level the dream relates to unconscious sexual desires that Anggauwane did not want to recognize in himself, but we can hardly argue with his view that the dream metaphorically portrayed a favorable solution to an important problem in his current waking life.

For the Melpa of the New Guinea western highlands it is the *min* or life-spirit that travels beyond the body in dreaming.[7] The Melpa differentiate between *ur kumb*, a positive "sleep dream" and *mi kumb*, a negative "taboo dream." When they speak of dreaming they say *ur kumb etepa koni*, meaning to "make a sleep-likeness and see something." Likewise, the Ngaing people of the mountainous regions to the north use the visually oriented phrase *amang enatemang*, meaning "I have seen a dream," and they regard dreams, illness, death, and divination practice as kindred experiences in which a person's *asabeiyang* or spirit-being detaches from the body, allowing access to secret knowledge but inevitably rendering a person vulnerable to spirit attack.[8] Many Oceanic cultures include dreaming in their initiation rituals, such as the Sambia of New Guinea's central highlands whose shamanic specialists (*kwooluku*) are originally called to their profession by vivid dreams and nightmares in childhood.[9] These dreams indicate that ghosts and spirits are interested in the child, and further dreams lead to the discovery of the special *numilyu* or ancestral familiar who will teach the shaman powerful songs and guide him or her in future rituals, healing practices, and prophetic visions. Because of their special skills in the realm of dreaming, the Sambian *kwooluku* serve as spiritual sentinels for the whole community, watching carefully for the first inklings of a surprise attack such as an epidemic or a raid by hostile neighbors. The same is true for the *manang* shamans of the Iban people from Borneo, east of New Guinea, whose dream-spirits (*semengat*) are trained to find other people's dream-spirits if they become lost in dreaming.[10] The *manang* also have the responsibility of protecting Iban infants from the malevolent demons who threaten to steal these newly born, highly vulnerable dream-spirits.

Christianization

The arrival of European Christian missionaries in Oceania prompted massive numbers of people to adopt the new faith, though not always with the ideological purity that might be expected of a complete religious conversion. Like their counterparts in Africa, the missionaries in Oceania made effective use of the indigenous people's interest in dreaming, reinterpreting their night visions in Christian terms while denying the validity of traditional spiritual beliefs. This process of dream-mediated religious change can be observed among the Asabano, a small group of semi-nomadic pig herders in central New Guinea who were first contacted by colonial authorities in 1963 and who were converted to a charismatic form of Christianity in 1977 by a Baptist pastor named Diyos.[11] Diyos organized a series of emotionally arousing revival meetings in which dreams (*aluma*), visions, and experiences of the Holy Spirit were shared, interpreted, and religiously validated. The movement spread rapidly throughout the Asabano community, and as part of their new faith the people destroyed their sacred houses and ancestral relics, pledging themselves to the superior spiritual power of Christianity. Dreams were frequently the catalyst for conversion, as in the case of an older Asabano woman named Wosono:

> God's talk is true. I am a woman who likes to chew betelnut and smoke, but when Diyos preached I started spirit work and I left all these old ways. Diyos and Wani [his wife] talked, and my spirit also talked. The Holy Spirit told me, "Whatever custom your father taught you, it was a lie. You must follow God's word." He showed me in a dream—it was his thoughts, not mine. I was asleep and I saw fire, and heard it said, "If you are stubborn you will go to the fire." I saw the ocean, and he said, "On the last day the ocean will come and cover everyone. If you believe you will turn into birds and fly to heaven." I was afraid and so I left my old customs. I saw this after the revival. Then a second time I dreamed the earth was changing, and I wanted to run away, but I turned into a butterfly and flew up. Then I was happy and clapped my hands. I thought it was real, but then I woke up. After this I just wanted to think about the new things and the Bible all the time.

Wosono's remarkable reveries combine the frightening divine judgment of St. Jerome's conversion nightmare with the spiritual metamorphosis and existential freedom of Lao Tzu's butterfly dream. In a culture where people strongly believed in the reality of dreaming, Wosono's experiences could not help but appear as convincing empirical proof of the truth of Christianity. At the same time, dreams like this testified to the difficulty of giving up ancestral traditions, generating a psychospiritual conflict between longing for the old ways and feeling attracted to the new. A young Asabano man who was attending a missionary school in the nearby town of Telefomin had the following dream:

In the dream I was holding a magic piece of ginger to attract girls—you put it in your pocket. I was standing with a man in the Telefomin hospital. Then I saw a fairly old light-skinned woman [*Semodu,* a mythic Old Woman who created the Asabano's land] come in. She came to fight with us two men. She asked us, "Do you belong to me or to Jesus?" We answered that we belonged to Jesus, and she was mad and took a swipe at me. I avoided her blow. We kept fighting, and eventually I told her, "I don't belong to you, I belong to Jesus" repeatedly. I was holding up my thumb [a symbol of defiance]. Then I woke up.

Immediately after awakening the young man went to his schoolteacher to relate the dream, and the teacher interpreted it as a heavenly sign that the young man should throw away the magic piece of ginger and pray more fervently to the Christian God. The young man accepted this interpretation and acted accordingly. From a Christian perspective, this was a missionary success story. From a modern skeptic's perspective, it might look like a not very subtle form of brainwashing, a forced reattribution of religious meaning and social authority. But both readings fail to credit the young man with any agency or personal power in his spiritual conflict. They both treat him as a passive recipient of external influence, either beneficially in the Christian view or oppressively in the skeptical view. An alternative approach, more in keeping with the dreamer-centered perspective of this book, views dreams like that of the young Asabano man as expressions of a free creative energy latent within the dreaming imagination, an energy that enables the dreamer to innovate and adapt effectively to changing circumstances in the waking world. The young man, the older Asabano woman, and the Asabano people as a whole were struggling to reorient themselves amid seismic shifts in everything from their family structures and food production technologies to religious beliefs about creation and the afterlife. They had suffered a profound sense of cultural dislocation, but they had not yet lost all connection to their ancestral wisdom. *They were still dreaming.* The content of their dreams may have changed, in keeping with the sociopolitically accurate observation that the Christian deity was more powerful than the Asabano spirits and ghosts. Now they dreamed more of Jesus and angels than the magical *wobuno* nature spirits of before. But what continued was their traditional reliance on dreaming for religious insight and guidance. Like their forebearers, the Asabano were still looking to their dreams for spiritual insight in times of difficulty, uncertainty, and collective danger.

The creative process develops in unique ways for each individual, and much more research needs to be done on the interpersonal dynamics of meaning-making via dreams in "Christianized" cultures like that of the Asabano. But current research is sufficient to establish the fact that the communities of Oceania have maintained a remarkable consistency in their traditional dreaming beliefs and practices. Even though their world has been turned upside down in the space of just a few years, the spiritual potency of dreaming remains a central feature of their lives. Another young Asabano man named Obai related the following to an anthropologist:

> I have strange dreams. At night I dream women come and take me away; or evil spirits come to kill me and I can fly, I don't turn into a bird; I just fly. I think in dreams the spirit goes and the body stays. So the things we dream really happen. When I'm totally asleep, and I want to go to the bush, and stone and tree spirits want to kill me, I just fly. In dreams it's safe; I move about well.[12]

Cargo Cults

The most decisive moment in Oceania's encounter with modernity came during World War II (1941–1945) when American and Japanese armies fought each other all across the Pacific. The sudden appearance of mechanized warfare made a profound impact on the indigenous people's imaginations. Staring in wonder at the noisily droning airplanes flying high overhead, witnessing spectacular battles between unknown enemies using fantastically destructive weapons, meeting people with white skin who possessed an incredible abundance of food and material goods—the closest analogy for the readers of this book would probably be an alien invasion from outer space. The abrupt confrontation with powers far beyond their own prompted a collective crisis throughout Oceania, raising several urgent questions. Where did these white people come from? Where did they get all their wealth? How did their machines work? What were their intentions? The need to find answers to these questions became all the more pressing once government officials and Christian missionaries began seizing control of various aspects of the indigenous people's lives, including land, natural resources, legal decision making, and religious practice.

What anthropologists called "cargo cults" represented an initial type of response to the profoundly disorienting encounter with white civilization.[13] Cargo cults focused people's minds on a practical question: How could they gain access to the sources of power controlled by the whites? Drawing on the traditional belief that power is rooted in secret places, they searched the spirit world in dreams, visions, and emotionally arousing rituals, asking the ancestors for help and guidance. In multiple communities in and around New Guinea there arose certain individuals who prophesized the imminent arrival of magical vehicles that would bring a bounty of material goods (cargo) for all the people. The popular excitement and air of expectation generated by these visions was tremendous, despite the scorn of white officials who regarded them as further proof of the natives' pathetic ignorance. But that kind of self-serving interpretation failed to recognize the deeper processes of meaning-making at work in the cargo cults. The wildfire appeal of these groups lay in their inspiring examples of daring, defiant creativity from the charismatic leaders who sought access for *everyone* to the mysterious powers that produced cargo. At a fundamental level, the cults were generating a kind of collective dream force, trying to bend a frighteningly turbulent waking world to the indigenous people's spiritual will. Individual dreams were important, but more important was the community's united dreaming intentionality. Together they would prepare themselves for a new and better reality, still rooted in ancestral wisdom yet creatively embracing the possibilities of the future.

Ultimately, the cargo never arrived. The power disparity was too great, the secret sources of white power too well hidden. So the dreams and visions led nowhere? Perhaps. Better, I think, to say they led where so many of the earliest seafaring explorers of Oceania went. Out of this world entirely.

The Changing Pacific

Cargo cults were not the only type of spiritual reaction to the arrival of white civilization in Oceania. Over time, the indigenous peoples developed various means of accommodating, adapting to, and in some cases appropriating the powers of the Christian authorities. While the cargo cults followed a millennialist impulse that led them beyond the manifest limits of colonial reality, other new religious movements worked to transform that reality from within. Much like the African communities whose apparent conversions to Christianity and Islam masked a deeper process of struggle and negotiation between traditional spiritualities and missionary imperatives, many in Oceania became Christian only insofar as they could usefully incorporate the new teachings into their time-honored religious beliefs and practices. God, Jesus, angels, Satan, demons, all were absorbed into people's imaginations but then creatively reworked and reinterpreted according to local traditions and needs. Some of the missionaries considered this a threat to their authority, whereas others saw it as a positive sign of missionary success. This tension is well illustrated in a report from a Baptist missionary who worked with the Enga people in the mid-twentieth century.[14] He described a "graveyard cult" initiated by a man named Pyanjuwa, a prominent member of the Enga community who was a leader in the missionary church. One morning Pyanjuwa had a vision of Christ appearing to him in brilliant white clothing and commanding him to clear the brush from the old village graveyard. Pyanjuwa immediately obeyed, and subsequent dreams and visions inspired him to convene dawn services at the freshly landscaped graveyard which were attended by crowds of increasingly enthusiastic people. At this point the missionary authorities became involved:

> Graveyards for many miles around were cleaned up and shrubs planted, and it seemed likely that the movement would spread. A meeting of the Church District Executive was convened to discuss the new movement. Many of the pastors saw it as an exciting new possibility for renewal in the churches, but others saw the dangers of incorporating beliefs from the old religion, especially in regard to ancestor spirits. It was decided not to encourage the spread of the cult until the church leaders had time to observe its fruits. The pastors agreed that to try and ban the cult would send it underground, whereas for the present it was operating in the open and could easily be observed.

Dramas like this unfolded everywhere the missionaries went. No further information is available about the subsequent development of Pyanjuwa's movement, nor the church's official evaluation of its "fruits," but the nature of the dilemma itself is worth highlighting. The pastors were understandably torn in their feelings toward Pyanjuwa. An inspiring dream of Jesus would seem to promote the Christian cause, but the graveyard ceremonies could only help to revive the ancestor worship that the missionaries were trying to stamp out. Their "wait-and-see" attitude signaled a pragmatic willingness to allow at least some space for traditional dreaming experience, combined with a realistic appraisal of the likely results if the pastors tried to impose a heavy-handed prohibition. Nevertheless their anxious uncertainty remained, and the determination to maintain constant surveillance over Pyanjuwa and his followers suggested that the missionaries would show little patience with dreams or visions that strayed too far from Christian orthodoxy.

Still the dreaming continued, and continues to this day. In fact, the cargo themes and ancestral teachings have woven themselves so deeply into the modern Christian symbolic universe that it would be nearly impossible at this point to identify most people in Oceania as completely Christian or completely *not* Christian. Consider these two dreams, from native Samoans who spoke with an anthropologist in the 1980s:

[Fia, a young woman:] I had an unforgettable dream last night. . . . A handsome prince from out of space came to my village and was on earth for the first time. His name was unknown and even the language he speaks was not understandable by most people. . . . He dressed all [in] white and . . . [no] one knew where he came from, except that he travels around in his UFO. . . . He was kind. . . . He never showed any hard face but he greets everyone with a big, friendly smile. He visits every family of my village and writes things down on his small writing pad. When he was done, he waved good-bye and was gone on this unidentified flying object. Two days later . . . the people of my village were no longer sad but just happy. They were no longer poor, but rich. Everyone had their free will to do anything they wished.

[Malaga, a young man:] "I was running up these stairs. I was running faster and faster. I got to the top. A man dressed in white was waiting for me. He asked me, "Are you Malaga?" I said yes. "Well, sit down. Buckle up your safety belt." Now we were in this spaceship . . . going to heaven. When we got to heaven, there he was my great-grandfather Manga, the Paramount Chief. Then I seen him sign a piece of paper with this navy white guy. The paper was the treaty between Samoa and the United States. My grandfather told me to go to Samoa and get ready for a big hurricane that was about to come."[15]

246 Religions of Oceania

Both these dreams made direct allusions to Christian imagery (the magical, benevolent men dressed in white) and modern technology (the amazing flying machines), but neither followed an orthodox Christian path nor succumbed to the dictates of modernization. Fia's dream concluded with a classic cargo cult vision of abundance for all, and Malaga's dream reunited him with a powerful ancestor who provided a valuable prophetic message. Despite the devastating changes imposed on them in the waking world, these Samoan people continued to dream according to their traditional beliefs and expectations. Their dreams accurately reflected the hurricane-like impact of white civilization on their culture, yet the dreaming itself testified to the continuing survival of at least some aspects of their ancestral spirituality. More detailed information than this would be difficult to gather, but the available evidence indicates that dreaming has remained a vital resource for the peoples of Oceania in their ongoing efforts to reorient themselves and their communities in the midst of all the cultural chaos and forced changes brought on by white colonization.

The most common solution to the challenge was to adopt Christianity as a public faith but to continue practicing the traditional customs in private. This kind of secretive compromise was not easy to maintain, and the psychospiritual tension frequently played itself out in people's dreaming. A senior ritual elder named Pa Rarovi from Tikopia, a small island southeast of New Guinea, reported a series of dreams (*miti*) to an anthropologist that illustrated his divided condition.[16] Before he became a Christian Pa Rarovi was besieged by dreams in which evil female spirits tried to bewitch and seduce him. He used to pray to his Tikopian ancestors to protect him, but once he joined the church he started praying to the Christian God, and then he slept much better. One of his dreams seemed to confirm the wisdom of his choice. It started as a nightmare, with a crowd of men threatening to shoot arrows at him; he ran away, and when he got to the beach he looked back at the hills and saw that they had divided in two, creating a middle path. Down the path came two whites, one with a staff, who beckoned him to join them. Pa Rarovi did so, and he felt safe and protected. Such a dream could serve as an allegory of the frightening process of conversion itself, a vividly rendered experience of struggle, danger, and ultimate salvation. Still, even after joining the church Pa Rarovi felt guilty about neglecting the spirits who had guarded him his whole life. He had always believed that maintaining friendly and respectful relations with the ancestors was absolutely essential to the well-being of his community, and he worried that becoming a Christian was disrupting those important relationships. One night after his conversion Pa Rarovi had another frightening dream:

> The spirit came to scold me! He said, "You rejected my rites; for what reason did you go away?" Thereupon I woke up and was all limp. I spoke to him in a respectful manner. "Oh, I have gone to Church but I have not rejected you. When I bring in coconuts from the heart of the woods and pierce them [to drink] I do not raise them first to my lips; first I pour a libation to you."

This was exactly the kind of nightmare that Tikopian tradition taught was caused by a failure to show due respect and veneration for the ancestors. The feeling of limpness in his body upon awakening added a frightening physiological carryover dimension, reminding Pa Rarovi of his existential vulnerability every time he entered the realm of dreaming. Such a warning could not be ignored, and yet he could not risk the opposite danger of rejecting the missionary authorities. So Pa Rarovi tried to negotiate, seeking a pragmatic accommodation between the two sides of his divided spiritual identity, trying to satisfy the basic needs of both without overly angering either, creatively maneuvering his way through the challenges of each day, and each night. The tension between Christianity and traditional spirituality could only be held together by constant improvisation, vigilance, and careful preservation of the public/private boundaries.

In some communities the tension was too great to be borne. When the people of Fulaga, a tiny island near Fiji, converted to Methodism they totally rejected any further worship of their ancestors, who were now considered to be devils trying to drag people back into their sinful past.[17] Unfortunately, the Fulagans still accepted the reality of their dream-spirit experiences during sleep, and thus every time they saw a dream (*tadra*) of encountering an ancestor, a dead person, or any other being of pre-Christian spiritual power (animals, plants, natural forces) they believed they were truly under demonic attack. Such a large percentage of their dreams fell into this proscribed category that the Fulagans began praying to the Christian God to give them nothing but dreamless sleep. According to private reports gathered by an anthropologist, virtually everyone on the island still remembered his or her dreams every night, but no one talked about them openly, and the proper, socially expected response to the normal morning greeting "Did you have a dream last night?" became "No, I did not."

Summary

The religious communities of Oceania (Australia, New Zealand, New Guinea, and the other island cultures of the south Pacific) have traditionally focused their attention on the psychospiritual process of dreaming rather than on the analysis of individual dreams. The emphasis in these traditions is very much on the dreamer actively moving into the dreaming world rather than passively receiving an image or visitation. The origin of ordinary dreams is believed to be the human mind, but some dreams enable the soul to leave the body and journey to the realm of the ancestors. The power of connecting with the ancestors underlies all the dream functions reported in Oceania, functions virtually identical to those discussed in the preceding chapters: prophetic knowledge, healing energy, guidance in times of crisis, and creative inspiration. The most unique feature of Oceania's dream teaching is the relative lack of specialized systems for dream interpretation. For these peoples, dreams are treated as real experiences that in most cases do not require special analysis or decoding. They try as much as possible to *live* the meanings of their dreams in action, ritual, and movement. The more constricted their waking lives become in a white-dominated world, the more dreaming becomes a valued means of remaining in communion with the revitalizing power of the ancestors.

10

Religions of the Americas

The comparative study of dreaming makes its claims most persuasively when it focuses on identifying patterns that are clear, simple, and widely distributed. A good example of this is dreaming about animals. Counting animal characters in dream reports is a relatively easy analytic task, and multiple studies using both quantitative and qualitative methods have provided a great deal of data regarding the frequency with which animals appear in dreams.[1] Two findings stand out. First, adults in modern, large-scale industrial societies (the United States, Western Europe, Japan) rarely dream about animals, whereas children in those societies and adults from smaller, preindustrial societies (Australia, the Americas) dream about animals much more frequently. Second, the most common form of interaction in these animal dreams is a nightmare scenario in which the animals are threatening or attacking the dreamer. By this point in the book, readers are apt to recognize the most likely explanation for these two findings: the frequency of animals in dreaming is continuous with the waking-life circumstances, experiences, and concerns of the dreamer.

Children in modern societies tend to have more frequent, intense, and complex relationships with animals than adults do. This includes daily interactions with family and neighborhood pets; awareness of bugs, birds, and other creatures in the local environment; strong attachments to stuffed animals; repeated stories about animals in books, movies, and television shows; and studies of wildlife in school and field trips to farms and zoos. Many children grow up with family dogs that are physically bigger than they are; few adults have the experience of living with a nonhuman creature larger than themselves. It does no disservice to children's mental abilities to conclude that, compared to adults, they are more aware of and interested in the animal world. Considering this waking-life preoccupation in light of the continuity principle, it follows that children will report a higher frequency of animals in their dreams.

For adults in small-scale societies who often dream of animals, the continuity principle also applies. The waking lives of tribal peoples depend on constant interactions with animals both domesticated and wild, far more so than for people in modern industrial societies. In many small-scale societies people are constantly vulnerable to life-threatening attack by aggressive animals. To survive, the group's members must devote considerable attention to defending against such dangers. In such circumstances it is almost inevitable that waking-life concerns will find their way into the people's dreams. More speculatively, that children in modern societies still dream so frequently of animal attacks may reflect an inherent imaginal predisposition to remain vigilant against the waking-world threats that pervaded the earliest ancestral environments of human evolution. A standard strategy of mammalian predators the world over is to attack the youngest and weakest members of a group, and we may assume that human children have always recognized their vulnerability in this regard and done whatever possible to protect themselves. Even in twenty-first-century urban settings, children's dreams and nightmares still echo with the primal growls and gnashing teeth of stalking beasts.

All this is prelude to a consideration of dreaming in the multiple cultures and religious traditions of the Americas. When the first bands of Homo sapiens crossed the land bridges from eastern Siberia into present-day Alaska sometime during the Upper Paleolithic period (40,000–10,000 BCE), they encountered a unique environmental opportunity: two vast, ecologically rich land masses filled with an abundance of life forms that had flourished for millions of years without any human contact or interaction.[2] Even more than the people who first discovered the tropical islands of Oceania, the adventuresome humans who survived the epic trek across the Bering Straits were rewarded with a glorious bounty of virgin land, and they soon established prosperous settlements throughout the length and breadth of the two continents. In the course of this rapid territorial expansion, the human immigrants were forced by survival needs to develop fast, accurate knowledge regarding the various indigenous creatures whom they were encountering for the very first time—learning to recognize their forms and behaviors, accurately identifying them as potential dangers or potential nourishment, and comprehending their complex relations with other creatures and with the land. No wonder, then, that we find people's dreaming experiences to be consistent with these waking concerns, serving them as valuable resources in their efforts at better understanding the local flora and fauna. As this chapter will show, the many different religious traditions of the Americas have long shared a fundamental awareness of dreaming as a means of enhancing knowledge of, and control over, the creatures that had dwelt in this part of the world for countless millennia before the arrival of Homo sapiens.

Missionary Encounters

There never has been a single, unitary religion to which all Native Americans have pledged their faith. On the contrary, the diverse peoples who journeyed to the Americas spread out both geographically *and* religiously, developing a wide variety of different languages, philosophical concepts, artistic expressions, and spiritual practices. Hundreds of distinct cultural groups have survived into the present, and archeological evidence suggests that hundreds and perhaps thousands of other cultures rose and fell during the long era of human occupation prior to modern European contact. The challenges involved in studying the religious beliefs and practices of the earliest Americans are just as formidable as those we found in the study of Africa and Oceania. In addition to their seemingly endless cultural diversity these traditions did not (with a few exceptions) develop literacy as a means of recording their experiences. They lived as semi-nomadic hunters who moved in small, lightly equipped groups, rarely engaging in the kinds of giant monument making or socially stratified city building found among other ancient peoples. As a result, very little physical or textual evidence remains about their past activities. Complicating matters even further, the best sources of information available to contemporary scholars are, once again, precisely those gathered by the original agents of colonial conquest—the missionaries, government officials, and ethnographers who recorded their observations in the course of aiding the forced resettlement process imposed on the local communities. For all these reasons, any investigation into the dream traditions of the earliest Americans is severely constrained in terms of the depth of its access to primary data and the range of its explanatory insights.

However, if there is a single theme that recurs throughout these religious traditions, a single spiritual principle shared by virtually every cultural group in the Americas, it would have to be a profound respect for the powers of dreaming. This, at any rate, was one of the strongest impressions reported by colonizing Europeans when they found themselves face to face with the peoples of the New World. Consider the following passage, from a letter sent by a Jesuit missionary in 1688 to his superiors regarding the progress of his evangelical activities among the Iroquois of the Great Lakes region in North America:

> The Iroquois have, properly speaking, only a single Divinity—the Dream. To it they render their submission, and follow all its orders with the utmost exactness. Tsonnontouens [Seneca] are more attached to this superstition than any of the others; their Religion in this respect becomes even a matter of scruple; whatever it be, whatever it is that they think they have done in their dreams, they believe themselves absolutely obliged to execute at the earliest moment. The other nations content themselves with observing those of their dreams which are the most important; but this people, which has the reputation of living more religiously than its neighbors, would think itself guilty of a great crime if it failed in its observance of a single dream. The people think only of that, they talk about nothing else, and all their cabins are filled with their dreams. They spare no pains, no industry, to show their attachment thereto, and their folly in this particular goes to such an excess as would be hard to imagine. He who has dreamed during the night that he was bathing runs immediately, as soon as he rises, all naked, to several cabins, in each of which he has a kettleful of water thrown over his body, however cold the weather may be. Another who has dreamed that he was taken prisoner and burned alive, has found himself bound and burned like a captive on the next day, being persuaded that by thus satisfying his dream, this fidelity will avert from him the pain and infamy of captivity and death. . . . Some have been known to go as far as Quebec, traveling a hundred and fifty leagues, for the sake of getting a dog that they had dreamed of buying there.[3]

The Jesuit father's letter revealed at least as much about his own religious tradition as about the local people he was trying to describe. Given what we learned in chapter 6 about developments in medieval Christian theology that increasingly associated dreaming with devil worship and witchcraft, the missionary encounter with a dream-saturated culture like that of the Iroquois was bound to be shocking, alienating, and frightening. The battle lines were immediately drawn: the God of the Christians versus the Dreaming Divinity of the Iroquois. What most baffled the Jesuit father was the intensity of the native people's efforts to properly respond in waking life to something seen in a dream. The father attributed this partly

to the excessive religious zeal of the Iroquois (this from a Jesuit missionary!) and partly to the widespread veneration for dreaming among all the
indigenous peoples he had contacted. We cannot know if his examples
were representative of broader practices among the Iroquois, but it seems
fairly clear that he was correct in identifying a basic religious difference.
In stark contrast to European Christianity, the sacred traditions of the
Americas were openly and enthusiastically influenced by their dreaming.
In both personal behavior and collective decision making, dreams shaped
the daily lives of these peoples in ways that were impossible for the first
European colonists to perceive as anything other than demonic heresies
that must be eliminated.[4]

The religious battle for control of dreaming could also be found thousands of miles to the south, among the Quechua people of the Andes in
present-day Peru. The Quechua were colonized in the sixteenth and seventeenth centuries by Spanish Catholics who worked energetically to destroy the local cultures and replace them with Christian teachings.[5] Idolatry was strictly forbidden, meaning that any kind of religious practice,
belief, or experience relating to traditional spirituality was prohibited.
Dream practices were natural targets for this kind of attack. The missionaries directly challenged the Quechua people's beliefs about dreaming and
rejected the authority of the traditional leaders of dream divination, as
expressed in this missionary's blunt instruction to turn away from past
practices: "Don't be keeping dreams: 'I dreamed this or that, why did I
dream it?' Don't ask: dreams are just worthless and not to be kept."

The strategy here was not exclusively Christian, though Christian missionaries made frequent use of it. In any struggle for political control, an
effective means of weakening the cognitive resistance of one's opponents
and disrupting their cultural integrity is to shut off the free flow of imaginal energy between dreaming and waking. Break that dynamic spiritual
connection, and no culture can long survive the determined onslaught of
another.

Some of the missionaries felt an extra degree of urgency to finish the
battle as soon as possible. The Jesuit father who visited the Iroquois realized that the local people's extreme fidelity to their dreams had sinister
potential for his own well-being: "What peril we are in every day among
people who will murder us in cold blood if they have dreamed of doing
so; and how slight needs to be an offense that a Barbarian has received
from someone, to enable his heated imagination to represent to him in

a dream that he takes revenge on the offender." Most amazing, perhaps, is how few missionaries were in fact murdered in this way, despite giving the indigenous peoples ample cause to feel homicidal anger.

Cultures of Dreaming

Perhaps there simply wasn't enough time for their dreams to generate a more aggressive defense of their traditions. The impact of colonization was swift and devastating, with European infectious diseases wiping out whole communities and conquering armies finishing off the survivors. The genocidal effect of European settlement in the Americas darkens anything we try to learn about the indigenous peoples' precolonization dream beliefs and practices. Simply put, the native people had every reason to mistrust the European colonists, to lie about their dream traditions, and to keep secret their most vital teachings. Every source of information about early American dreaming is haunted by the bloody historical clash between the Old World and the New.

That said, a large body of evidence is still available regarding at least some of the most widespread and important roles of dreaming in traditional, pre-colonial lives. This evidence is broadly consistent with the shamanistic dream practices of Neolithic cultures in Europe and Asia, reflecting what is apparently a long-term process of cultural diffusion that shaped and influenced virtually every human community that took root in the Americas. Wherever these people went—plains, mountains, lakes, jungles, or coasts—they brought with them a tradition of dreaming, a time-honored respect for night visions as sources of spiritual knowledge and communal guidance.

As noted, these were primarily groups of hunters who lived in constant interaction with other animals, both as predators and prey. Dreaming served them most directly and practically as a means of enhancing their power in relation to the animals. For example, among the Cree people of modern-day Quebec each adult male formed a special relationship with the *powatakan,* the animal spirits who appeared in dreams to guide hunters toward success in waking life.[6] The Cree hunters reciprocated for the assistance of the *powatakan* by performing rituals, sacrifices, and prayers of gratitude. Everyone knew of the *powatakan* and discussed them in general terms, but each hunter was careful to keep the exact nature of his own dreams a secret from everyone else, lest the spirit-given power be misused or lost. In the 1930s an elderly Cree man was willing to tell ethnographers about his *powatakan* dreams because he no longer needed them:

> I can't hunt anymore because though I dream I can't remember them when I get up in the morning. . . . Every animal I killed I dreamed about. I first dreamed about *Memekwesiw* [Bear, his personal animal spirit] before I was married when I was yet living with my father. In my dream I thought I went to *Memekwesiw*'s place and I thought the door was of stone. He had a hairy face and hair hanging down all over. He came and got hold of my hand. There were lots of trees standing in a bunch and he said to me, "That is where my little pup is." . . . I didn't tell my dream but the next day I put on my new mittens and went out hunting. At the place I had been shown I found a bear and killed it. I took a branch that the bear had broken off and went back to camp. I didn't say a word, just as though I hadn't killed anything. I gave the branch to my father who knew right away it was *Memekwesiw*'s little dog that had broken the branch. He went for the bear and brought it back to the tent. He laid him on his back and placed tobacco on his chest. Then we made a currant cake in the oven and put the cake on his chest because he likes blueberries. The women skinned the bear and then I cut it up myself. Then at one side in the tent I spread a cloth and all the men sat on one side of it and the women on the other side of it. The children sat together in another place. That first time I killed a bear I put some meat in the fire and said, "Be pleased, *Memekwesiw*, so you will let go your pup soon again."

Memekwesiw, the great Spirit of the Bears, willingly gave this Cree hunter the information he needed to find and kill a bear, and the Cree hunter willingly gave thanks in return to *Memekwesiw* by means of an elaborate communal ceremony. Dreaming, hunting, celebrating, praying— these practices formed a self-sustaining circuit of spiritual knowledge that embraced all forms of experience within a framework of sacred meaning. The reciprocal relationship between humans, animals, and dream-spirits was central to the worldview of the Cree and many other early American cultures. The people needed to hunt for their survival, but they knew that taking an animal's life tore a piece out of the densely interwoven spiritual fabric of the land. Dreaming offered a mediating experience by which humans bowed to the superior power of Nature's elemental life forces, in exchange for which they were granted the hunting success they needed to live and prosper.

To some extent, this could be considered a religious version of the contemporary scientific idea that dreaming sometimes enables the mind to find creative solutions to problems in waking life that are difficult, pressing, and not entirely in human control (like trying to find enough wild game to support a nomadic community). What the Cree called *Pow-atakan* could in this view be understood as the personification of unconscious thought processes that continued working on such problems while the conscious mind slept. This suggests a degree of directionality to the dreaming-waking relationship: that which is most vividly represented in dreaming tends to revolve around, and seek creative resolution of, highly salient waking-life problems and challenges. The process should not be regarded as permanent or automatic, however. Just as prayers and rituals could enhance it, deteriorating cultural circumstances could diminish it. The Cree man's experience of no longer remembering his dreams and thus not being able to hunt reflected the sudden disruption of his community's traditions and the people's near-total reliance now on white civilization.

Farther to the south and west, the Mohave people of the present-day Colorado River basin referred to their special power-inducing night visions as "dreams lucky" (*sumach ahot*), which they distinguished from "ordinary dreams" (*sumach*).[7] In their *sumach ahot* the Mohave gained hunting guidance, methods of healing, bravery for a coming battle, new songs and prayers, and other forms of practical wisdom. They talked each day among their families and friends about their dreams from the previous night, particularly any bad dreams whose ill effects could be prevented by the right kinds of ritual practice. An especially good dream like a *sumach ahot,* however, was often kept secret to preserve its power. Still farther southward, the Quiche people of the Central Guatemalan highlands used the transitive verb *wachic'aj* ("to dream of"), with the connotation that dreaming was an active process of the dreamer relating to something or someone else.[8] This sense of personal agency in dreaming inspired the Quiche to travel in free-soul form (*uwach uk'ij* or *nawal*) through their dreams to seek out the free souls of animals and other people. They regularly shared their dreams in public settings, and they taught their children to try to remember their dreams every single night. The most powerful dreams were those in which the dreamer received a visitation from an ancestor or god; in such dreams the Quiche believed the individual's lightning soul (*coyopa*) should wrestle with the spirit being until it granted the dreamer a divine message. Sometimes, however, the Quiche were afflicted with *c'ulwachic,* horrible dreams that Western psychology would diagnose as night terrors: "When one is in bed, not yet really sleeping but in the white sleep (*sak waram,* analogous to hypnogogia?), then comes the apparition; it is represented. A person comes right up to touch one, one feels they are coming to touch one directly, but one can neither move nor cry out."[9]

This underscores the wariness most early Americans felt toward personal dream experiences. Going to sleep meant surrendering to a realm of harrowing existential vulnerability, leaving the individual defenseless against external attack and exposed to internal threats from mysterious spirit enemies. A good example of this cultural circumspection toward dreaming comes from the Makiritare people of the mountainous river valleys of present-day Venezuela, who conceived of dreams as voyages of the *adekato,* the spirit double that lies within each person.[10] The Makiritare believed these nocturnal travels were always dangerous because the lone *adekato* could at any moment be assaulted, abducted, or afflicted with a fatal illness. Dreams brought a person precariously close to death, and, as a result, the Makiritare approached dreaming with profound caution. In the *Watunna,* the oral composition of Makiritare myth and sacred history, these dangers were illustrated by a story about a woman whose brother tricked her into being bitten by a snake:

> Now she began dreaming. Her *adekato* went traveling outside her body. It went dreaming to Nomo's house, to the mistress of that poison. Now dreaming the woman said, "I'm thirsty. Give me something to drink." Now Nomo came out with a gourd in her hand: "Here, drink this *iukuta*. It'll make you better." The woman took the gourd. It wasn't *iukuta*. It was a trick. When she drank it, she forgot her empty body there on earth. She stayed there dreaming, dreaming forever as a spirit in Nomo's house. She's still a prisoner there because of the drink Nomo gave her, when she told her: "Here, take this *iukuta*." She never returned to her body. That's how she died. Now she's like a spirit in the Snake House. Because of that poison. Because of the wickedness of her brother.

Another passage of the *Watunna* carried this theme of dreaming danger all the way back to the creation of the world by the culture-hero Wanadi, child of the Sun, who first brought humans into existence. One time during his process of creation, Wanadi came into direct conflict with Odo'sha, the master of the dark forces of the earth:

> Wanadi sat down, silent, calm, not eating, not doing anything. He put his elbows on his knees, his head in his hands. He was just thinking, dreaming. Dreaming. That's the way Wanadi did everything. "This is what I dream," he would say. "I'm dreaming there's lots of food." No food came. Odo'sha was right in front of him. Odo'sha didn't want that. He started dreaming evil. He answered Wanadi with evil. "I dreamed: we have cassava," said Wanadi, dreaming. "This is my dream," answered Odo'sha. "Lots of hunger." He was answering with evil. [Wanadi said,] "I'm dreaming there are conucos. There's yucca everywhere. I'm cutting down the yucca. There's a great harvest." "Here's how I dreamed it first," answered Odo'sha. "Many sick people."

The primordial forces of creation and destruction eternally battled each other in the Makiritare notion of dreaming. The final outcome of this mythic conflict was unknown, leaving humans to face a dangerous and uncertain future. In such conditions the best the Makiritare could do was remain vigilant for all possible threats and deceptions, guarding their most important cultural traditions and developing whatever new powers they could to promote their personal and communal survival. Keeping close watch on their dreams was a vital part of this effort. Every morning the men of the Makiritare villages gathered to discuss the coming day's activities, and dreams from the previous night were included as relevant information in making group decisions.

For the Makiritare and other small communities in the Amazon River basin, the geographic remoteness of their living areas shielded them from contact with European colonists and their descendents until much more recently, with less damaging cultural effects. In many cases, the native peoples have been governmentally protected to enable them to continue with their traditional practices, and their material lives today remain largely the same as before. But of course their knowledge of white civilization has profoundly impacted their view of reality, a process that can be clearly tracked within their dreaming.

The Mehinaku people of central Brazil provide a good illustration of this. Like most other indigenous traditions throughout the Americas, the Mehinaku dreamed of aggressive interactions with animals far more often than occurs with people living in modern urban societies.[11] The rain forest environment of the Mehinaku was, in fact, filled with dangerous wild animals like jaguars, wild pigs, snakes, and poisonous insects, providing fertile grounds for nightmarish anticipations of actual waking-world threats. Also consistent with what we have found in other traditions, the Mehinaku made a basic distinction between dreams of greater and lesser significance. *Jepuni he te* were "mere dreams" reflecting ordinary events of daily life, and *jupuni yaja* were "true dreams" providing valuable information about the future. Occasionally a person's *jupani yaja* were strong enough to mark the dreamer as a possible initiate for training by local shamans. The Mehinaku believed that the process of dreaming involved the nightly wanderings of a shadow soul (*iyeweku*) residing in each person's eyes. What was seen in a dream was accepted as a real experience of the eye soul, with potentially (though not automatically) meaningful significance for waking life. During the night and each morning the Mehinaku shared their dreams with one another, sifting through the images for symbolic omens of the future. Of those dream portents they agreed to describe to ethnographers, many revolved around themes of sexuality and reproduction, including dreams of explicit sexual behavior and dreams the Mehinaku interpreted as sexually meaningful even though there was no direct sexual imagery in the dream itself. Animal aggression dreams were very frequent, as noted above, as were dreams relating to disease, death, and loss of personal integrity.

Not surprisingly, the most dangerous characters in Mehinaku dreams were white people. The Brazilian government established a small air force base near their village, and although the official policy was to leave the Mehinaku to their own affairs, the intimidating presence of the whites was enough to prompt a continuous stream of nightmarish warnings. Some examples:

> At the post a plane landed. Many, many passengers got off. It seemed as if there was a village in the plane. I was very frightened of them and the things they carried. I was afraid they would bring a disease to the village, the white man's "witchcraft."

> We were at the air force base, and a soldier wanted to have sex with my sister. He took her arm and tried to pull her away. We shouted at the soldier and at my sister. My aunt and I tried to pull her back. But the soldier

was too strong for us. He was very strong. He said, "If you don't let me have sex with Mehinaku women I will shoot you." I got a gun and shot at him, many times. But he was hidden and I couldn't see him.

A guard pointed a gun at me. He told me to go through a door. I did. The room was filled with a beautiful light. The guard gave me a watch and told me I could come out at a certain time. He locked the door. I looked at the watch, and I realized I did not know how to tell time. There was a wind and a strange smell.

In waking life the interactions between the Mehinaku and the whites were infrequent and fairly benign. But in the Mehinaku people's dreams the Brazilian characters were almost always figures of extreme hostility, unpredictability, and lethality. The dreams were expressing not what was happening at the moment, but what *might* happen in the immediate future. Although discontinuous with actual waking-life events, the dreams were continuous with the well-justified Mehinaku anxiety that *any* contact with the Brazilian officials was potentially dangerous. A powerful new predator had entered the Mehinaku cosmos, and the people's dreams were telling them to beware.[12]

The anthropological data we have considered so far represents only a tiny fraction of the countless number of different cultural groups that have peopled the Americas over the past ten thousand to twenty thousand years. But even this brief survey of a few traditions—the Cree, Mohave, Quiche, Makiritare, and Mehinaku—suggests a deeply ingrained culture of dreaming shared widely among the earliest Americans, spreading across both continents and taking root in many different kinds of environments. The dream traditions seem to have been especially influential in smaller-scale communities, and there is some evidence that interest in dreaming diminished in larger societies that adopted an agricultural system of food production.[13] For example, in one text from the Aztec civilization (fourteenth to sixteenth centuries CE) dreaming is mentioned in passing as an inferior form of knowing and being: "Therefore, the ancients said that when they died, men did not perish, but began to live again almost as if awakened from a dream and that they became spirits or gods."[14] Insufficient information remains from the Mesoamerican civilizations of the Olmecs, Mayans, and Aztecs to determine if a lessening of dream interest with the shift from small-scale hunting to large-scale agricultural societies is genuine and not just an artifact of limited research data. If true, it would provide an intriguing counterpoint to the dream traditions of early agricultural civilizations in India, China, and Mesopotamia.

Vision Quest

The two dozen or so cultural groups who lived in the expansive prairies, valleys, and forests of central North America, practiced what appears to be the most sophisticated ritual technique of dream incubation found in the Americas. Variously known as the vision quest, the dream fast, or crying for a vision, it involved a series of ritual preparations aimed at eliciting power-bestowing visionary experiences, either in waking or dreaming.[15] For adolescents, the vision quest served as an all-important rite of passage, transforming them into spiritually powerful individuals capable of assuming adult responsibilities in their families and bands. This association with the life cycle transition of adolescence meant that the dream-seeking rituals were being practiced at a time when the young people were in the midst of a rapid and tumultuous phase of psychophysiological growth with fundamental shifts in brain-mind functioning. If one's goal is to generate a dream vision of maximum power and long-lasting impact, adolescence would be an exceptionally fertile time to make the attempt.

The vision quest process was usually initiated by a parent or grandparent who told the child it was time—based on what precise signs or indicators, we do not know. A period of fasting would begin, with sharp restrictions on the intake of food and water. The child (usually a boy, but girls were occasionally allowed to participate) was brought to a sacred place far removed from ordinary village life. In high places like hills and buttes, in the dark foliage of primeval forests, in caves and rock formations decorated with ancient paintings and pictograms, the child was left alone to pray for a vision from the animal spirits. Having grown up hearing stories about other people's vision quests, the youth would probably have formed some expectations of what was to come and would feel a degree of safety knowing that other people had survived the ordeal. Nevertheless, the ritual was deliberately designed to place the child in a condition of extreme physical pain and emotional distress—socially isolated, deprived of food and water, exposed to the elements, and vulnerable to attack by wild animals. Judged by contemporary American legal standards, these practices would probably be considered child abuse. But in the religious context of the Great Plains traditions, the vision quest was a highly effective means of stimulating, training, and focusing the personal powers most valued in their culture. If the quest was successful (and not all were), it emblazoned a lifelong religious stamp on the individual's personality. By pushing a child's bodily endurance to its very limits, the ritual sparked the emergence of an extraordinary vision that became the living touchstone for his or her future adult identity. For those seekers who were able to overcome their natural fears and maintain a respectful intentionality, the visions provided an opportunity for unique spiritual insights and discoveries.

Consider the following from an Ojibwa man named Agabegijik who described his dream fast to an ethnographer in the early nineteenth century.[16] When he was a "half-grown lad" Agabegijik's grandfather took him to the forest to seek a dream, but the boy broke the fast by drinking water from a nearby stream. As a result, his grandfather had to take him back home in failure. The next spring Agabegijik resolved to do better, and he went by himself to a small island in the middle of an ice-covered lake. There he built an elevated bed in the branches of a red pine tree and lay down to wait for a dream.

> In the first nights nothing appeared to me; all was quiet. But on the eighth night I heard a rustling and waving in the branches. It was like a heavy bear or elk breaking through the shrubs and forest. I was greatly afraid. I thought there were too many of them, and I made preparations for flight. But the man who approached me, whoever he may be, read my thoughts and saw my fear at a distance; so he came towards me more and more gently, and rested, quite noiselessly, on the branches over my head. Then he began to speak to me, and asked me, "Are you afraid, my son?"
> "No," I replied; "I no longer fear."
> "Why are you here in this tree?"
> "To fast."
> "Why do you fast?"
> "To gain strength, and know my life."
> "That is good."

From there Agabegijik described flying into the sky with the spirit-being, meeting a group of four men sitting around a large white stone, ascending a ladder to receive precious medicines and animal lore, then returning to his bed in the red pines with a final admonition from the four men — "Forget nothing of all that has been said to you. And all who sit round here will remember you, and pray for you as your guardian spirits." When he awoke, Agabegijik did as he was told, and for the rest of his life he regarded this dream as the foundational experience for his career as a healer.

After making the transition from childhood to adulthood, people of the Great Plains continued to practice the vision quest whenever they felt the need for additional guidance, knowledge, and power. Whether motivated by a desire for hunting information, healing methods, courage in battle, or insights into the future, the basic ritual of the dream fast remained a culturally approved means of maintaining a living connection with the spirit realm. As already noted, the earliest Americans were very cautious in telling other people about their highly significant dream-visions. Such experiences were considered precious gifts of power, not to be carelessly squandered in idle talk. Only in special ceremonies among a trusted audience would a person share the specific results of his or her quest. But spoken words *about* dreams were not nearly as important to the Great Plains people as actions *inspired by* dreams. The proper response to a powerful dream was to actualize it, to carry its energy, imagery, and intentionality into the waking world. In practical terms, this could take the form of creating a new design for a weapon or piece of clothing, retelling a traditional myth with new images from the dream, testing the medicinal uses of a particular herb, or organizing a group ceremony of spiritual renewal. The people of the Great Plains were avid explorers of dreaming consciousness who freely experimented with the potentials of their visionary capacities. Few human societies have ever been as fluid and flexible in allowing individual dreams to shape the behavioral contours of daily life.

Of course, being human, even *they* were prone to false steps and misinterpretations. Such is the case with the dream vision of a Blackfoot man:

The male hawk came and put me to sleep right where I was. This hawk immediately turned into a man, wearing a buffalo robe who addressed me, "My son, leave the children alone. I will give you my body that you may live long. Look at me. I am never sick. So you will never have any sickness. I will give you power to fly. You see that ridge (about a mile away), well, I will give you power to fly there." On awakening . . . I took off my clothes, and with a buffalo robe went back some distance from the edge of the river. Then I took a run and springing from the edge of the cliff, spread out my arms with the blanket for wings. I seemed to be going all right for a moment, but soon lost control and fell. I was stunned by the fall and was drawn under a rock by the [river] current where I went round and round, striking my head. . . . This is one time in which I was fooled in my dreams.[17]

Dreamer Religions

We do not know how far back in time the peoples of the Great Plains practiced vision quest rituals. But once the European settlers began arriving and pushing their sphere of control farther and farther westward, the indigenous peoples increasingly turned to dreams and visions for help in defending their lands and cultural traditions. Like the Independent Churches of Africa and the cargo cults of Oceania, numerous movements of spiritual renewal sprang up in the Americas (North America especially) aiming at the creation of new syntheses of past religious traditions with the white-dominated reality of the present. The leaders of these movements (e.g., Handsome Lake of the Iroquois, Smohalla of the Wanapum) were inspired by vibrant dream visions to teach their people a better path to the future, calling for greater devotion to core religious practices and deeper reliance on traditional spiritual powers. Scornfully referred to as "Dreamer Religions" by U.S. government officials in the nineteenth century, the movements had strong appeal for the disoriented and dispirited survivors of white expansionism.[18] Considering these Dreamer Religions from a comparative historical perspective, what looked to the U.S. officials like the stubborn superstitions of a primitive race is better understood as a reasonable (if desperate) attempt by an oppressed group to preserve its cultural integrity and powers of imagination. When all else is lost, dreaming offers a kind of spiritual life-preserver that keeps people afloat in times of crisis, rejuvenating their hopes and illuminating possible remedies for their sufferings in waking life.

Two final examples underscore the continuing influence of dreaming on cultural adaptation in post-white contact times. The first comes from the Algonquian-speaking Menomini people of present-day Wisconsin, where a small, mystically inclined society of dreamers (*nemowuk*, "dancing men") practiced ritual drumming, tobacco smoking, and ceremonial dream singing.[19] The founding myth of this group (as recounted to an early twentieth-century ethnographer) originated in an unintentional vision quest by a refugee girl:

Many years ago, during a war between the Indians and the whites, the natives were driven out of their country. A young girl became separated from the rest of her party and secreted herself in the bushes until dark, when she made her way to a river and hid under an overhanging bank. There she remained for eight days. All that time she had nothing to eat and saw no one. As she fasted with a downcast heart, a spirit came to her in her hiding place, and called to her in her own language: "Poor little girl. Come out and eat. It is time for you to break your fast. Do not be afraid, I am going to give you happiness because your people have been expelled from their country, and because of your suffering you have won my pity. Now your troubles are at an end. Go and join the enemy, but say nothing. Go to their table, help yourself, and no one shall see that you are not one of them. Then come away and you shall find your friends. You shall travel through the thick forests and over open plains, even among the white people, but fear nothing. Look straight ahead and not backwards or downwards. Even though the white people pass so closely in front of you as almost to touch you, do not fear, for they shall not see you."

After teaching her this magical power of moving invisibly through white civilization, the spirit went on to instruct the girl in the proper construction of a drum called "grandfather," which could be used any time she and her people needed help. When the girl finally reunited with her people they were amazed and inspired by her vision, and an elite group of "dancing men" decided to commit themselves to carrying out the spirit's teachings. In addition to making exquisitely crafted drums and percussion instruments, the members of the dreamer society devoted considerable time to decorating staffs, fans, pipes, and headdresses. The rituals themselves were held in open dancing grounds or inside log cabins, and could last as long as four days. The secrecy surrounding the Menomini ceremonies meant that outsiders would never know the full nature of the dreams they shared or the knowledge they developed. What was fairly clear, however, was that by dreaming, drumming, and dancing together the participants renewed their feelings of cultural coherence and reoriented themselves toward the future. As leading members of Menomini society whose decisions directly impacted the survival prospects of the group as a whole, the "dancing men" sought the strongest possible guidance from the spirits of dream and vision.

The final tradition to consider, the Onondaga people of present-day

New York, continued practicing well into the twentieth century a midwinter ceremony that revolved around a collective game of dream-
guessing.[20] Conducted over three days and three long, dark nights near
the time of the winter solstice, the game was played by a whole village
divided into two moieties (clan groups) that gathered in different public
meeting houses. Individuals from one house walked to the other people's
house and told them a dream in riddle form. The people in that house
tried to guess what the dream was from the clues given, and once they
discovered the correct answer they gave to the individual from the other
house the object about which he or she had dreamed. For example, "it
whistles in the wind" might refer to a dream of a corn husk spirit, and "it
has holes, yet it catches" could indicate a dream of a lacrosse stick. The
two clan groups competed in their skillfulness as interpreters and their
generosity as fulfillers of dream wishes. A sense of light-hearted playfulness characterized the whole process, and when a difficult dream riddle
was finally guessed the people burst out with laughter and applause. The
ceremony ended at the close of the third night when the number of accurately guessed dreams was added up and publicly announced along with
the names of the dreamers.

Such a ritual could not help but enhance and strengthen people's feelings of creative bonding with the group. By establishing a relaxed and
good-natured atmosphere in which to share their dreams, the Onondaga encouraged each person to contribute a bit of his or her personal
dream energy to the collective ritual. The people teased and joked with
each other at that tense interpersonal border between secrecy and disclo-
sure, revealing their deepest desires only to those who truly knew and
respected them. The material objects given to the dreamers were markers
in the physical world for the spiritual powers disclosed in their dreams,
and thus the group validated each member's potential to be an authentic
voice of religious truth. All in all, the dream-guessing rite served as a vital
cultural resource for this small, embattled group of people who were con-
fined to a reservation designated for them by the U.S. government.

As testimony to the long-term power of this ritual, Jesuit missionaries
described a virtually identical midwinter ceremony among the Onondaga
more than three hundred years previously, in the late 1600s:

> There are two divisions of that tribe [the Onondaga], one that is called
> the Wolf Tribe and the other the Bear Tribe and they have two coun-
> cil houses; they separate, one gathering at the small council house and

holding services there, and the other at the large council house at the same time; every little while a message will be sent from one council house to the other. . . . A woman came in with a mat, which she spread out and arranged as if she wished to catch some fish. She thus indicated that some must be given to her to satisfy her dream. . . . It would be cruelty, nay murder, not to give a man the subject of his dream; for such a refusal might cause his death.

The continuity of this ritual over so many centuries, despite the radical changes forced upon the Onondaga by white civilization, reflects a remarkable durability in the core spiritual traditions of their culture.

Manifest Dreaming

The Europeans who moved into the Americas in the sixteenth and seventeenth centuries were driven by a kind of shared dream of the "New World," which they envisioned as a place of boundless possibility, a God-given paradise for their personal enjoyment. For conquistadores and other military explorers, it was a place where their weapons were invincible and they could defeat huge armies with magical ease. For Catholic missionaries, it offered a vast new population of potential converts to the faith. For Protestants, the North American colonies represented a religious sanctuary where they could worship in isolated purity. For the rising commercial classes of the early industrial age, the Americas presented an incredible bounty of natural resources just waiting to be seized, exploited, and sold on the growing global marketplace. For political radicals frustrated with European monarchies, the New World gave them opportunities to experiment with representative democracy and utopian social arrangements. For the captive Africans shipped across the Atlantic as slaves, the Americas were a nightmare of cruelty and humiliation; in response they created their own "Dreamer Religions," adaptively developing new visions and spiritual teachings that combined the lost traditions of their African homelands with the Christian world of their enslaved present.[21]

In this way the human presence in North America was radically transformed by the influx of millions of new people from a multitude of different cultures, all of whom brought with them the dreaming (or anti-dreaming) traditions of their ancestors. In economic practice, the European immigrants were typical of most ruling powers in human history in that they generated their wealth by seizing the lands of weaker groups and exploiting the labor of slaves. Yet, in political theory, many of the Euro-Americas were inspired to try and create a new kind of social organization that gave ultimate power to the citizens (originally restricted to white men), a system that protected religious freedom and put its trust in the common sense, good judgment, and moral imagination of ordinary people. The Declaration of Independence in 1776 and the ratification of the U.S. Constitution in 1788 and Bill of Rights in 1791 made manifest a narrow but powerful vision of innate human dignity in which the purpose of government was to create, sustain, and defend a sphere within which its citizens were free to dream.

But that is another historical tale.

Summary

Throughout the religious traditions of the Americas, dreams have played a central role in giving meaning and purpose to people's lives. Dream experiences have enabled them to interact with animal spirits and other mythic beings who have directly influenced their waking-life activities. Most of these cultures have been aware of physical and psychological factors in dreaming, but their primary interest has been trying to strengthen people's ability to form mutually beneficial alliances with powerful forces in the spirit world. An individual's dreams are a portal to that world, and their highest function is to enable a free flow of experience and energy between the waking and dreaming realms. Because of their emphasis on respect for the spirits, the people of the Americas have been very cautious about revealing their methods of dream interpretation. In many of their cultures a kind of communal dream-sharing has prevailed in which families, friends, and village elders talk each morning about their previous night's dreams and what they might mean. When practiced over a long period of time, we can imagine that these dream conversations would have the potential to generate an unusually deep and well-integrated sense of collective self-awareness and spiritual creativity. In such cases, the epithet "Dreamer Religions" might be taken as a badge of pride.

Conclusion

The stories that I have told, analyzed, and compared in the ten chapters of this book provide a basic historical context for understanding the major patterns and themes of human dreaming. They provide a necessary resource for the comparative study of religion and for scientific investigations into the evolving dynamics of the brain-mind system. Any general theory in dream research, religious studies, or the science of consciousness that fails to take this historical material into account should, in my view, be considered inadequate. Dreams and dreaming have been a widely recognized and highly valued part of human life—particularly in relation to people's religious beliefs and practices—in virtually every cultural community known to have populated the planet. Although we should always acknowledge the methodological limitations in how much we can understand of dream reports from people in different places and time, the extensive multidisciplinary research presented in this book makes the case for a new appreciation of dreaming as an integral element of healthy human functioning and development. The best way, in my view, to summarize all this information and illuminate its ultimate significance is to see dreaming as a primal wellspring of religious experience. This means that dreams, by virtue of their natural emergence out of the immensely complex, internally generated activities of the mammalian brain during sleep, offer all human beings a potential source of visionary insight, creative inspiration, and expanded self-awareness. The abundant evidence of cross-cultural history proves that we are indeed a dreaming species. Through dreams humans have discovered the deepest realms of their psyches and grown in awareness of the powerful relational bonds that connect them to their families, communities, natural environments, religious traditions, and ultimately the cosmos itself. What comes through the historical record with unmistakable clarity is the powerful impact of dreaming as an experiential agent of psychological growth and spiritual enlightenment.

Comparing Religious and Scientific Evidence on Dreaming

In the introduction we considered several key findings of contemporary scientific research on sleep and dreaming. Now, at the conclusion, let us revisit the scientific findings described at the outset and evaluate them in light of the cumulative findings of research on the world's religious traditions.

Sleep. An alternating cycle of waking and sleeping has been reported in all human populations in all periods of history. Consistent with current scientific research, sleep has been generally recognized in the world's cultures and religions as an absolute necessity for biological health. More than that, sleep is usually considered a pleasurable blessing that brings rest, recuperation, and relief from the toils and cares of waking life. At the same time, people in many different cultures have also expressed considerable fear about the dangers that come with sleep. They have understood that while sleeping we relax our physical guard and withdraw perceptual attention from the waking world, leaving our bodies vulnerable to attack from wild animals or antagonistic humans. Many religious traditions have further taught that during sleep people are also vulnerable to attack from malevolent spiritual beings like ghosts, witches, and demons. Although belief in such beings might seem impossible to reconcile with contemporary cognitive science, I have argued that significant scholarly progress can be made without getting bogged down in debates over natural vs. supernatural causation. The focus in this book has been on a different kind of question, namely, how best to understand the felt qualities and experiential patterns of the most intensified types of dreaming as reported in multiple places and times. A pragmatic approach like mine sets aside metaphysical controversies and concentrates instead on providing an empirically based phenomenology of the recurrent forms, functions, and personal meanings of human dream experience.

Following this approach, we can see that the sleeping incidents of spirit attack so frequently described in the literature of religious history correspond very closely to contemporary psychological research on nightmares and night terrors.[1] The extreme fear, the dreadful feelings of paralysis and constriction, the shockingly realistic imagery, the haunting specter of death—in all these details the nocturnal spirit attacks reported in many different religious traditions closely match the primary features of nightmares and night terrors as observed by modern science. The first lesson to draw from this correspondence is a methodological one: dream reports from different religious and cultural traditions should be accepted as accurate sources of information about actual human dream experiences. Whatever doubts one may have about the authenticity of particular dream episodes, the deeper drumbeat of prototypical dreaming experiences cannot be ignored. Religious history may fare poorly as a source of episodic memory about specific dreams, but it serves as an excellent repository of information on the human species' semantic memory regarding the full range and potentiality of dreaming.

The second lesson goes to a more substantive point about the impact of nightmares and night terrors on the individuals who suffer them. In cultures worldwide and throughout history, these kinds of dreams have provoked urgent conscious reflections on dark existential questions of evil, suffering, death, and finitude. People's interpretations have naturally gravitated toward religious and spiritual ideas, since the dreams themselves are so clearly felt to be encounters with, or possessions by, overwhelmingly powerful nonhuman entities. Following a pragmatic approach, I set aside the metaphysical concepts used in different religions and focus instead on the pan-human process by which nightmarish experiences in sleep provoke greater existential self-awareness in waking life. Contemporary scientists should acknowledge that nightmares and night terrors regularly have this kind of psychospiritual impact on people. Particularly at a time when mental health professionals are seeking improved methods of treating people suffering from post-traumatic stress disorder (PTSD), the value of recognizing and actively working with the dimensions of existential fear and religious transformation in dreaming can be tremendous if the therapeutic goal is to heal the whole person (as opposed to simply eliminating his or her behavioral symptoms).

All in all, the world's religious traditions and modern science strongly agree that sleep is an overall benefit and necessity for healthy human existence, even though people are perennially vulnerable to vivid, emotionally upsetting sleep experiences at various times in their lives.

Prototypical dreams. In the folk psychology of many religious traditions the sleeping condition of the body is believed to enable the liberation of a spiritual essence within the individual, freeing it to journey in otherworldly realms and encounter nonhuman forces and intelligences. This inner spirit or soul varies in strength and mobility, and religions have devised various methods for cultivating its power so that people can fight off bad dreams and enhance good ones. Considered purely in descriptive terms, the dreams most often reported by people in these religious

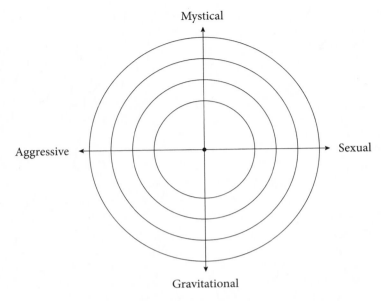

Fig. 1. Protoypical Dreaming

traditions are identical to the types of dreams found by contemporary researchers to recur with special intensity and memorability in present-day populations. We do not have enough data to say anything definitive about individual rates of dream recall in past times, nor can we be sure about the exact frequency of particular dream characteristics. But we have more than enough evidence to recognize the recurrence of a broad range of prototypical dreams across all human groups.

I find it most useful, and most empirically grounded, to think of four different directions of intensified dreaming, oriented along two axes as illustrated in Figure 1. These four directions represent prototypes of dreaming, meaning the deepest innate oneiric capacities of our species, the primal templates of this hard-wired modality of human brain-mind functioning. In the terms of chaos theory, the prototypes are basins of attraction for the self-organizing emergence of spontaneous psychological order. In spiritual terms, they are manifestations of the divine and the demonic in human life.

The concentric circles indicate the extent of a dream's intensity, memorability, and impact on the individual. At the center are dreams that possess insufficient strength to cross the memory threshold, that is, dreams never rising to the level of waking awareness. Most of what passes through the mind during each night's sleep is forgotten in this sense. Close to the center are "little dreams" relating to the ordinary, mundane concerns of daily life. Such dreams do little more than reflect the current physical and emotional conditions of the individual. Preoccupied with ordinary daily concerns, they have no deeper significance and are usually forgotten soon after waking.

The wider the circle in the diagram, the greater the dream's intensity and the more likely it will be remembered upon awakening. Farther from the center of the diagram are dreams that, though less frequent, are extremely memorable and impactful when they do occur. With physically arousing surges of raw emotion (both positive and negative), amazing visual imagery, feelings of intense realism, or striking interactions with powerful beings, these "big dreams" have the tangible effect of expanding the individual's range of imaginative understanding and religious sensitivity.[2] The widest circle of the diagram stands for the boundaries of sleep itself, which some dreams overleap in the form of psychophysiological carryover effects into waking awareness.

The horizontal line represents the *relational axis,* expressing the quality and feeling tone of the dreamer's relationship with other characters. On the left end of the relational axis are *aggressive dreams,* including dreams of being chased, attacked, or threatened by another character (e.g., another person, an animal, a spiritual being). Sometimes the dreamer is acting aggressively toward other characters, but the most intense manifestations of this prototype are generally nightmares of being on the receiving end of aggression, with painful feelings of helplessness in the face of extreme danger from malevolent antagonists. I believe such dreams reflect the deep biological imperative in all species to *stay alive,* to protect oneself against attack and avoid becoming some other creature's prey.

At the other end of the relational axis, *sexual dreams* reflect an equally urgent biological imperative, to reproduce and spread our progeny as far and wide as possible. The dreams that develop in this direction include not only experiences of vivid and physically arousing sexual encounters but also powerful dreams relating to pregnancy, birth, and the care of children. The widespread prevalence of these kinds of dreams suggests that they, too, are hard-wired into us as a way of priming the human reproductive system, stimulating our positive relational desires, and guiding us in the process of creating new life.

The vertical line represents the *elemental axis,* showing the extent to which a dream is characterized by increasing complexity and structure (low entropy) or fragmentation and decay (high entropy). At the bottom of the axis, *gravitational dreams* encompass a host of extremely memorable and almost always unpleasant experiences such as falling, being paralyzed, being unable to speak, losing one's teeth or other body parts, watching things fall apart, crashing, becoming lost in a void, being swept away by a wave, and so on. Religious versions include images of apocalypse and cosmic cataclysm. The common theme in these different manifestations of the prototype is the weakness and impotence of the dreamer against gravity and other elemental powers. The individual is threatened not by another aggressive character but by the inescapable forces of physics. I believe this accurately reflects a fundamental reality of all animate life on earth, namely, that our bodies have developed in response to the planet's gravitational field. Life on earth is a kind of existential defiance against gravity, an emergence of self-directed matter rising up to take form and act with intention. When we die we surrender to gravity as our bodies decay, their elements dispersing and scattering to the winds. Dreaming is naturally predisposed to express our cellular awareness of these entropic truths.

At the upper end of the elemental axis are *mystical dreams*. Mystical dreams express the human capacity to envision a transcendental freedom from the oppressive limitations of gravity, entropy, and death. These include flying dreams, which give the dreamer a vivid physiological experience of being liberated from the shackles of earthly existence; visitation dreams, in which the dreamer encounters deceased loved ones whose living presence defies the finality of physical death; and healing dreams, which bring tangible relief from mental or physical suffering. Also included here are ecstatic dreams of brilliant light and divine union, along with aesthetically creative dreams of astonishing beauty and cosmic harmony.

To recognize and accept the recurrent phenomenon of mystical dreams does not mean abandoning science or pledging faith to some religious creed or dogma. Rather, it means acknowledging the reality of an autonomous visionary capacity within the human brain-mind system, a capacity driven by an unconscious intelligence deeply rooted in our biological nature yet continuously striving for transcendent understanding and insight.

My hope is that the benefits of this provisional mapping outweigh the inevitable drawbacks of any system of dream categorization. Many dreams combine two or more prototypes (e.g., sexual dreams leading to mystical ecstasy or nightmares including aggressive attacks and gravitational misfortunes), and this means that we always have to pay attention to such conceptual blendings and their distinctive dynamics of significance. I have emphasized the visionary aspects of dreaming, but some dreams are clearly characterized by intensified sensations of sound, touch, or movement, and a few include powerful smells and tastes. The manifestations of each prototype vary greatly in terms of their realism or bizarreness. Some dreams are quite realistic and literal in terms of portraying familiar places, people, and situations, and others are filled with strange images and otherworldly realms that deviate radically from the ordinary conditions of waking life. Metacognitive awareness can emerge in any of the prototypes, though it is too soon to tell whether this represents a separate developmental axis of dreaming. My impression at this point is that many different kinds of metacognitive awareness have the potential to emerge in dreams. A more pluralistic approach is required in the exploration of their developmental possibilities.

A major reason why I believe that this fourfold mapping of prototypical dreams makes good sense is that each of the prototypes is clearly associated with a distinct kind of carryover effect of dreaming experience into the waking state. With sexual dreams the carry-over is a physical orgasm, of both the male and female varieties. With aggressive dreams it is the hyperactivation of the fight/flight response—extreme fear, racing heart, rapid breathing, and full-body sweat. With gravitational dreams it is the horribly realistic sensation of falling and waking up with a sudden gasping start. With mystical dreams it is the blissful, ultra-realistic sensation of flying or the profound joy of being reunited with a deceased loved one. These kinds of direct emotional and bodily continuations of the dreaming experience into the person's waking life are perhaps the strongest and most easily observed instances of the deeply rooted interplay of dreaming and waking consciousness.

Waking impact. The strong carryover effects associated with prototypical dreams are clues to the specific processes by which dreaming contributes to healthy brain-mind functioning. Aggressive dreams reflect an adaptive concern with identifying and responding to threats in the waking world. Although emotionally disturbing, such nightmares have the beneficial effect (in survival terms) of stimulating greater vigilance toward similar threats in the waking world. The evolutionary logic is simple: the more often and more intensely one dreams of various kinds of threatening situations, the better prepared one is to react effectively to those situations if and when they occur in waking life. Likewise with gravitational dreams, which accurately reflect and simulate the existential dangers of entropic destruction. The intense fear and horror generated by these dreams activates the fundamental instincts of self-preservation that must always be ready to respond immediately should a comparable danger arise in waking life, whether it is falling from a great height, being involved in a car crash, or losing physical mobility. Sexual dreams prompt the reproductive system and envision possible ways of satisfying its desires. Their stimulating and taboo-defying effect on the erotic imagination is, I suspect, self-evident to most readers. The impact of mystical dreams is less directly tied to evolutionary biology, and more to the emerging spirit of human creativity. Dreams of the mystical prototype have the effect of enlarging people's sense of life's possibilities, expanding their awareness from a narrow fixation on what *is* to a broader consideration of what *might be*. Such dreams stretch the mind by pushing it to become more conscious of its own powers and the realities that extend beyond what is immediately present in normal perceptions of the waking world.

Another kind of significant waking-world impact can be discerned in an unlikely place: rationalist skepticism. Voices of critical questioning and naturalistic analysis have arisen wherever and whenever humans have explored their dreams. It might be a surprise to those who assume that modern scientists were the first to explain dreaming as the mental by-products of sleep, but many ancient traditions recognized exactly the same psychophysiological dynamics at work in people's dreams. The skeptical perspective did not come after the religious perspective, nor even before it. Historically the two approaches are not mutually exclusive. *They have coexisted from the start.* The prototypical experiences of dreaming have provoked not only religious and spiritual experience but also a deeply human capacity for rational thought and critical reflection. Dreams have stimulated the power of reason to become increasingly aware of deceptive appearances, hidden connections, subtle perceptions, and cognitively impactful emotions. The biography of Rene Descartes, the seventeenth-century French sage whose writings sparked the rationalizing explosion of the European Enlightenment, offers a good example of this dream-inspired process of philosophical discovery.[3]

The healing impact of dreaming has been noted in many different religious traditions, closely associated with spiritual experience but also occurring independently in the context of local medical practices. In this regard the modern West is unusual in the way it excludes dreams from its mainstream healing systems. Present-day medical doctors have virtually no interest in dreaming as a potential source of diagnostic insight or curative power, and a surprisingly small number of contemporary psychiatrists make the effort to look into their clients' dreams for help or guidance. This is especially disappointing from professionals whose symbol is the *caduceus,* a serpent-entwined staff honored by its association with Asclepius. It is my hope that future researchers will revive the long-neglected process of exploring, and learning from, the complex interaction of illness, dreaming, and healing. The simplest way to start this research is by looking at the diagnostic potentials of dreaming as an internally directed form of anticipatory threat simulation. Further clues to a deeper understanding of the healing impact of dreams include the curative power of intensified personal bonding, the natural activation of the immune system during sleep, and the healing forces of belief that are too quickly dismissed as "placebo effects." None of this requires a religious or spiritual worldview to appreciate. Indeed, rationalist skeptics themselves emphasize this very point, that dreams are the psychological manifestations of underlying physiological conditions in the body of the sleeping individual. If that is indeed true, then Western scientists have only just begun the process of exploring their medical significance.

Interpretations. Three different approaches to the interpretation of dreams have been practiced in most religious traditions: literal, metaphorical, and paradoxical. The *literal approach* takes a dream as a direct portrayal of something that is actually happening, or will happen, in the dreamer's waking life. The meaning of the dream is self-evident to the individual and requires no additional interpretation. The *metaphorical approach* is more expansive, and more elusive. It considers a dream as an indirect expression of valuable meanings that can be interpreted and understood through the intuitive analysis of signs, symbols, analogies, and allegories. The same metaphor-making powers of cognition that produce language, culture, and artistic creativity in waking life are also active in sleep and dreaming, and the challenge for the interpreter (whether the dreamer or someone else) is to discover the strongest and most useful metaphorical connections between the dream and the individual's waking life. Traditions using the metaphorical approach have generally recognized that interpretation always depends on the personal circumstances of the dreamer. The same dream can mean different things for different people, and every symbol has multiple dimensions of significance. A metaphorical interpretation is tested and judged by its coherence, plausibility, gut-level intuitive response (the "aha" experience), and pragmatic fruits in waking life.

Paradoxical interpretations involve a direct reversal of the dream's imagery, so that a dream of one event means that the opposite will occur in waking life. This is the most suspicious type of interpretation from a skeptic's perspective, and the preceding chapters have illustrated the all-too-human temptation to manipulate the interpretation of other people's dreams in order to control those people more effectively and promote one's own personal power. That said, I do not rule out the possibility of a genuinely paradoxical dimension of dreaming, given that binary processes are central to many brain-mind functions, and binary symbols and themes are pervasive throughout the world's religious and mythological systems.

Dream incubation is the general term for all the various kinds of pre-sleep rituals and prayers whose aim is to create a heightened context for the reception of clear, vivid, meaningful dreams. Each religious tradition's version of dream incubation is oriented toward its own most powerful spiritual figures, and the different practices (e.g., special places to sleep, clothes to wear, furs to lie on, foods to eat or not eat, bodily postures to use, words to pray while drifting off, etc.) have the cumulative effect of separating people from the ordinary realities of their waking lives and bringing them closer to whatever it is they consider sacred or divine. The purposes of dream incubation have ranged widely, from healing and prophecy to romance and hunting. A few traditions have taught that people can achieve so much self-awareness and control within sleep that they transcend dreaming entirely and dwell within a pure state of empty consciousness. In actual practice, most religions have looked to dream incubation for assistance with urgent problems in daily life. The pre-sleep rituals and prayers are motivated by a need for new energy and creative insight to help people transform their waking realities.

Along with efforts to incubate positive dreams, most traditions have also employed various methods of fending off negative dreams such as nightmares and night terrors. These practices reflect the vulnerability humans have always felt when sleeping and their desire for as much protection as possible from spiritual danger and demonic attack. In a few cases, religious and political authorities have declared that all dreams are dangerous and have ordered people to ignore them. This has been an effective means of one group establishing dominance over another, since it directly breaks the weaker people's experiential connection to their spiritual traditions, rendering them more pliant subjects for the ideological control of the stronger group.

The rise of modern industrial civilization, with its mechanized timekeeping devices, darkness-banishing electric lights, and increasingly dense urban populations, has produced dramatic changes in the waking and sleeping patterns of the human race. For the past century, people in modern industrial societies have been sleeping less than in the past, with greater variations in their hours of wakefulness and more abrupt arousals out of sleep (i.e., by the ring of an alarm clock). The impact of mass media such as films, television, music, and video games on the modern experience of sleeping and dreaming has also been considerable. Environmental problems such as climate change, toxic pollution, deforestation, and species extinction may also shape certain trends in people's dreaming today insofar as such factors reflect troubling changes in the natural world that pose potentially catastrophic dangers to human survival.

The question of what is distinctive and new in the dreaming experiences of humans living today, in the early years of the twenty-first century, is a story that begins where this book ends.

Dream Books

An impulse to write about dreams has arisen in the earliest eras of most literate civilizations. We have encountered numerous examples of the dream book genre in a variety of religious traditions, from the Hindu *Atharva Veda* to Artemidorus's *Oneirocritica*, from the Egyptian Ramesside Dream Book to Zhang Fengyi's *Meng-chan lei-k'so*. Although appearing in quite different cultural contexts, these books share several basic insights about the prototypical forms of human dream experience. The authors are frequently motivated to write by their own dreams, and their works aim to provide a systematic overview of their civilization's current knowledge of dreams. Of course, many of the interpretive subtleties of these books are lost in the translation to modern English. The meanings are so closely related to the particular details of the individual's waking life that we today will never be able to fully grasp the metaphorical connections identified in the ancient books. But certain aspects of the dreaming experience survive the passage through history and across language, aspects that we recognize in the findings of contemporary scientific research and in our own dreams. Many of the books make their final appeal to the reader's personal sleep and dream experiences as the only reliable way to evaluate the author's claims. And that, too, is how this dream book will close.

Notes

NOTES TO THE INTRODUCTION

1. For general discussions on the comparative study of religion, see Serinity Young, *Encyclopedia of Women and Religion* (1999); John Bowker, *The Oxford Dictionary of World Religions* (1997); David Wulff, *Psychology of Religion: Classic and Contemporary* (1997); Wendy Doniger O'Flaherty, *Other People's Myths* (1988); Lee Irwin, *Visionary Worlds: The Making and Unmaking of Reality* (1996); Kimberley C. Patton and Benjamin C. Ray, *A Magic Still Dwells: Comparative Religion in the Postmodern Age* (2000); Huston Smith, *The World's Religions* (1991); Jeffrey J. Kripal, *The Serpent's Gift: Gnostic Reflections on the Study of Religion* (2007); Harvey Whitehouse, *Modes of Religiosity: A Cognitive Theory of Religious Transmission* (2004).

2. Historical migration patterns of *Homo sapiens*: Jared Diamond, *Guns, Germs, and Steel: The Fates of Human Societies* (1997). Not all researchers agree on the nature of the "early ancestral environment" of human beings nor on how much influence that environment had on human cognitive abilities.

3. Ongoing nature of evolution: Jonathan Weiner, *The Beak of the Finch: A Story of Evolution in Our Time* (1995); and Michael Balter, "Are Human Brains Still Evolving? Brain Genes Show Signs of Selection" (2005).

4. Neurophysiology of sleep: Meir H. Kryger, Thomas Roth, and William C. Dement, *Principles and Practices of Sleep Medicine* (2005); Mary A. Carskadon, *Encyclopedia of Sleep and Dreaming* (1993); Edward F. Pace-Schott, Mark Solms, and Mark Blagrove, *Sleep and Dreaming: Scientific Advances and Reconsiderations* (2005); Deirdre Barrett and Patrick McNamara, *The New Science of Dreaming* (2007); A. R. Braun et al., "Dissociated Pattern of Activity in Visual Cortices and Their Projections during Human Rapid-Eye-Movement Sleep" (1998); Pierre Maquet et al., "Functional Neuroanatomy of Human Rapid-Eye-Movement Sleep and Dreaming" (1996); E. A. Nofzinger et al., "Forebrain Activation in REM Sleep: An FDG PET Study" (1997); Mark Solms, *The Neuropsychology of Dreaming* (1997); and David Kahn, "From Chaos to Self-Organization: The Brain, Dreaming, and Religious Experience" (2005). Regarding the extreme limits of sleep deprivation, William Dement (*The Problem of Sleep* [1999]) reports a case of a young man staying awake nearly eleven days (260 hours) and then sleeping normally

afterward and suffering no apparent mental or physical damage. Future research may show that this kind of elasticity in sleep patterns is more widespread, but the basic need for sleep in healthy human functioning remains true. It is worth noting that, despite an intense search for more than half a century, no one has been able to explain scientifically *why,* exactly, sleep is so necessary.

5. Interactive dualism: see James W. Jones, "Brain, Mind, and Spirit—A Clinician's Perspective, or Why I Am Not Afraid of Dualism" (2005).

6. Dream recall: Eugene Aserinsky and Nathaniel Kleitman, "Regularly Occurring Periods of Eye Motility, and Concomitant Phenomena, during Sleep" (1953), and idem, "Two Types of Ocular Motility in Sleep" (1955); David Foulkes, "Dream Reports from Different States of Sleep" (1962); Kathryn Belicki, "Recalling Dreams: An Examination of Daily Variation and Individual Difference" (1986); Ernest Hartmann, *Dreams and Nightmares: The New Theory on the Origin and Meaning of Dreams* (1998); Michael Schredl, "Dream Recall: Research, Clinical Implications, and Future Directions" (1999); Tracey L. Kahan, "The 'Problem' of Dreaming in NREM Sleep Continues to Challenge Reductionist (2-Gen) Models of Dream Generation" (2000); James Pagel, "Non-Dreamers" (2003); Tore Nielsen, "Cognition in REM and NREM Sleep: A Review and Possible Reconciliation of Two Models of Sleep Mentation" (2000).

7. Contra animals dreaming: David Foulkes, *Children's Dreaming and the Development of Consciousness* (1999); G. William Domhoff, *The Scientific Study of Sleep* (2003). Arguments and evidence in favor of animals dreaming: Michel Jouvet, *The Paradox of Sleep: The Story of Dreaming* (1999); Katje Valli et al., "The Threat Simulation Theory of the Evolutionary Function of Dreaming: Evidence from Dreams of Traumatized Children" (2005); M. A. Wilson and B. L. McNaughton, "Reactivation of Hippocampal Ensemble Memories during Sleep" (1994); K. Louie and M. A. Wilson, "Temporally Structured Replay of Awake Hippocampal Ensemble Activity during Rapid Eye Movement Sleep" (2001).

8. Improving dream recall: Schredl, "Dream Recall."

9. Experimentally influencing dream content: for a review of early research, see David Koulack, *To Catch a Dream: Explorations in Dreaming* (1991).

10. Continuity in dream content: G. William Domhoff, *Finding Meaning in Dreams: A Quantitative Approach* (1996); Inge Strauch and B. Meier, *In Search of Dreams: Results from Experimental Dream Research* (1996).

11. Blind analysis: Kelly Bulkeley, "Religious Dimensions of a Dream Series," presentation at the annual conference of the Association for the Study of Dreams, June 2003, Berkeley, California.

12. Dreaming as emotional thermostat: Milton Kramer, *The Dream Experience: A Systematic Exploration* (2007).

13. Bizarreness: J. Allan Hobson, *The Dreaming Brain: How the Brain Creates Both the Sense and the Nonsense of Dreams* (1988); and idem, *Dreaming and*

Delirium: How the Brain Goes Out of Its Mind (1999). Hobson is the main proponent of what I call the mainstream view; see his "Dreaming and the Brain: Towards a Cognitive Neuroscience of Conscious States" (2000).

14. Lucid dreaming: Jayne Gackenbach and Stephen LaBerge, *Conscious Mind, Sleeping Brain* (1988).

15. Type dreams: C. G. Seligman, "Type Dreams: A Request" (1923); big dreams: C. G. Jung, "General Aspects of Dream Psychology" (1974); culture pattern dreams: J. S. Lincoln, *The Dream in Primitive Cultures* (1935); intensified dreams: Harry Hunt, *The Multiplicity of Dreams: Memory, Imagination, and Consciousness* (1989); impactful dreams: Don Kuiken and Shelley Sikora, "The Impact of Dreams on Waking Thoughts and Feelings" (1993); highly significant dreams: Roger Knudson, "The Significant Dream as Emblem of Uniqueness: The Fertilizer Does Not Explain the Flower" (2003); extraordinary dreams: Stanley Krippner, Fariba Bogzaran, and Andre Percia de Carvalho, *Extraordinary Dreams and How to Work with Them* (2002); apex dreaming: Nielsen, "Cognition in REM and NREM Sleep"; prototypes: Eleanor Rosch, "Natural Categories" (1973).

NOTES TO CHAPTER 1

1. Cognitive development and children's dream concepts: Jean Piaget, *Play, Dreams, and Imitation in Childhood* (1962); Richard Shweder and R. A. Levine, "Dream Concepts of Hausa Children: A Critique of the 'Doctrine of Invariant Sequence'" (1975); Foulkes, *Children's Dreaming.*

2. *Rig Veda* 10.162, 7.55, 7.86, 10.164, and 2.28, translated by Wendy Doniger O'Flaherty (1981), pp. 291–292, 288, 214, 287–288, and 218.

3. *Atharva Veda* 6.46, translated by Maurice Bloomfield (1897). See also Wendy Doniger O'Flaherty, *Dreams, Illusion, and Other Realities* (1984); and Alex Wayman, "Significance of Dreams in India and Tibet" (1967).

4. *Kalpa Sutra*, translated by Hermann Jacobi (1884), pp. 218–247.

5. *Chandogya Upanishad* 5.2.4–9, translated by Patrick Olivelle (1996), pp. 139–140.

6. *Kausitaki Upanishad* 2.5: Olivelle, p. 208.

7. *Brhadaranyaka Upanishad* 2.1, 4.3: Olivelle, pp. 25ff., 59ff.

8. Analysis of the word *srj*: O'Flaherty, *Dreams, Illusion, and Other Realities*, p. 16.

9. Western psychology on negative dream experience: Ernest Hartmann, *The Nightmare: the Psychology and Biology of Terrifying Dreams* (1984).

10. *Mandukya Upanishad*: Olivelle, p. 289.

11. *Mahabharata*: O'Flaherty, *Dreams, Illusion, and Other Realities*, pp. 31–32.

12. *Ramayana*: translated by H. P. Shastri, *The Ramayana of Valmiki* (1953), pp. 331–332.

13. *Yogavasistha*: O'Flaherty, *Dreams, Illusion, and Other Realities*, pp. 127ff.

14. Ramakrishna: Sri Ramakrishna, *The Gospel of Sri Ramakrishna* (1942), pp. 3–4, 13, 17–18; Wayman, "Significance of Dreams in India and Tibet," p. 9.

15. Debendranath Tagore: Whalen Lai, "Debendranath Tagore's Dream: The Soul and the Mother" (1982), p. 30.

16. Aurobindo: Sri Aurobindo, *The Integral Yoga: Sri Aurobindo's Teaching and Method of Practice* (1993), pp. 6, 312–313, 198.

17. The Mother on dreams: Sri Aurobindo and The Mother, *The Yoga of Sleep and Dreams: The Night School of Sadhana* (2004), p. xx.

18. I first used these three questions as explanatory tools in *An Introduction to the Psychology of Dreaming* (Westport: Praeger, 1997).

NOTES TO CHAPTER 2

1. Exam dream: Robert Knox Dentan and Laura J. McClusky, "Pity the Bones by Wandering River Which Still in Lovers' Dreams Appear as Men" (1993), p. 522. In light of this, it is noteworthy that the anti-Confucian Tai-ping Rebellion led by a visionary Chinese-Christian named Hong Xiuquan (1814–1864) was inspired by a dream he experienced *after* failing several times to pass the civil service exams.

2. Prevalence of school anxiety in dreams: see Tore Nielsen et al., "Typical Dreams of Canadian University Students" (2003).

3. Shamanic practices: see David Lewis-Williams, *The Mind in the Cave* (2002); Barbara Tedlock, *The Woman in the Shaman's Body: Reclaiming the Feminine in Religion and Medicine* (2005); Graham Harvey, *Shamanism: A Reader* (2003); Brian Hayden, *Shamans, Sorcerers, and Saints: A Prehistory of Religion* (2003); Mircea Eliade, *Shamanism: Archaic Techniques of Ecstasy* (1964).

4. *Tai Pu*: Fang Jing Pei and Zhang Juwen, *The Interpretation of Dreams in Chinese Culture* (2000), p. 12.

5. *Wu* shamans: Dentan and McClusky, "Pity the Bones," p. 515; Eliade, *Shamanism*, p. 452.

6. *Shu-jing* stories of Kings Wu and Wu-Ting: Roberto Ong, *The Interpretation of Dreams in Ancient China* (1985), pp. 12–13.

7. Duke of Zhou: Patricia Buckley Ebry, *The Cambridge Illustrated History of China* (1996), p. 32.

8. *Shi-jing* dream symbols: Richard J. Smith, *Fortune-Tellers and Philosophers: Divination in Traditional Chinese Society* (1991), p. 247.

9. *Zuo-zhuan* pre-battle dreams: Wai-yee Li, "Dreams of Interpretation in Early Chinese Historical and Philosophical Writings" (1999), pp. 18, 26; dream of the Duke of Jin, pp. 22–23. Paradoxical interpretation in Chinese tradition: Smith, *Fortune-Tellers and Philosophers*, p. 252; Pei and Juwen, *The Interpretation of Dreams in Chinese Culture*, p. 35.

10. Confucian dreams: Ong, *The Interpretation of Dreams in Ancient China*, pp. 60–61, 15–16.

11. Zhuang-zi: Chuang Tzu, *The Inner Chapters* (1998), pp. 18, 32, 34 (emphasis in original). Zhuang-zi and Chuang Tzu are two different transliterations of the same name.

12. *Lie-zi*: Ong, *The Interpretation of Dreams in Ancient China*, pp. 85–86.

13. Yellow millet dream: Ong, *The Interpretation of Dreams in Ancient China*, pp. 110–111.

14. Matteo Ricci: Ebry, *History of China*, p. 201.

15. Dream books: Ong, *The Interpretation of Dreams in Ancient China*, pp. 3–9; Smith, *Fortune-Tellers and Philosophers*, pp. 250ff.

16. Ong, The Interpretation of Dreams in Ancient China, pp. 128–129.

17. *Hun* and *Po* souls: Dentan and McClusky, "Pity the Bones," pp. 498ff.

18. Dream typologies: Pei and Juwen, *The Interpretation of Dreams in Chinese Culture*, pp. 22–28; Smith, *Fortune-Tellers and Philosophers*, p. 247.

19. Wang Chong: Ong, *The Interpretation of Dreams in Ancient China*, pp. 67, 69–70.

20. Incubation: Berthold Laufer, "Inspirational Dreams in East Asia" (1931), pp. 210–211; Ong, *The Interpretation of Dreams in Ancient China*, pp. 37–41; Smith, *Fortune-Tellers and Philosophers*, pp. 245, 256; Pei and Juwen, *The Interpretation of Dreams in Chinese Culture*, pp. 39–40.

21. Xiang-shu: Smith, *Fortune-Tellers and Philosophers*, p. 250.

22. Theater and dreams: Ebry, *History of China*, p. 202.

23. *Dream of the Red Chamber*: Ebry, *History of China*, pp. 231–233. Quotes are from the translation of Tsao Hsueh-chin (1958), pp. 5–8, 91–92, and 40–47.

24. Chen Shiyuan's ancestor dream: Ong, *The Interpretation of Dreams in Ancient China*, p. 35.

25. Contemporary Chinese dreaming: Dentan and McClusky, "Pity the Bones"; Smith, *Fortune-Tellers and Philosophers*, pp. 245, 256; Ong, *The Interpretation of Dreams in Ancient China*, p. 128. A few years ago a Chinese-American woman who was a reporter for a radio news program told me of a radiant, life-altering dream she had experienced of Kwan Yin, the Chinese goddess of compassion, who had helped the woman reconnect with her ancestral traditions.

NOTES TO CHAPTER 3

1. Metacognition: Tracey Kahan, "Consciousness in Dreaming: A Metacognitive Approach" (2001); Sheila Purcell, Alan Moffitt, and Robert Hoffman, "Waking, Dreaming, and Self-Regulation" (1993).

2. Deficiency theories: Sigmund Freud, *The Interpretation of Dreams* (1965); A. Rechtschaffen, "The Single-Mindedness and Isolation of Dreams" (1978); Fran-

cis Crick and Graeme Mitchison, "The Function of Dream Sleep" (1983); Hobson, *The Dreaming Brain*; John Antrobus, "Dreaming: Could We Do Without It?" (1993); Owen Flanagan, *Dreaming Souls: Sleep, Dreams, and the Evolution of the Conscious Mind* (2000).

3. Queen Maya's dream: Serinity Young, *Dreaming in the Lotus: Buddhist Dream Narrative, Imagery, and Practice* (1999), p. 22. See also Jagdish Sharma and Lee Siegel, *Dream-Symbolism in the Sramanic Tradition: Two Psychoanalytical Studies in Jinist and Buddhist Dream Legends* (1980). For information on the tradition of birth dreams in Korea, see Hyesung Kang, *Taemong: Korean Birth Dreams* (2003).

4. Gopa's dream: Young, *Dreaming in the Lotus*, pp. 35ff.

5. Buddha's dreams: Young, *Dreaming in the Lotus*, pp. 25ff. Other texts describe additional dreams, but these five are the most widely attested in early Buddhist literature.

6. "The Questions of King Milinda," translated by T.W. Rhys Davids (1894), pp. 157–162.

7. Wang Chiu-lien's dream: Ong, *The Interpretation of Dreams in Ancient China*, pp. 93–94.

8. Arhat paintings: Laufer, "Inspirational Dreams in East Asia," p. 213.

9. Buddha and the three women dreams: Ong, *The Interpretation of Dreams in Ancient China*, pp. 99–100.

10. Japanese dreams: Michio Araki, "Dream and Japanese Buddhism" (1992).

11. Lady Sarashina's dream: *As I Crossed a Bridge of Dreams*, translated by Ivan Morris (1971), p. 107.

12. Myoe: George J. Tanabe Jr., *Myoe the Dreamkeeper: Fantasy and Knowledge in Early Kamakura Buddhism* (1992), p. 174.

13. Naropa's dream teachings: *The Practice of the Six Yogas of Naropa*, translated by Glenn H. Mullin (2006); George Gillespie, "Lucid Dreaming in Tibetan Buddhism" (1988).

14. Milarepa: *The Life of Milarepa*, translated by Lobsang P. Lhalungpa (1985), pp. 43–44, 80, 82–86, 89, 110, 112, 129.

15. Dalai Lama on dreaming: *Sleeping, Dreaming, and Dying* (1997), pp. 38–39, 42, 124.

16. Dalai Lama ritual: Young, *Dreaming in the Lotus*, pp. 133–134. Another good source on dreaming in Tibetan Buddhism is Angela Sumegi, *The Third Place: Tension and Resolution in the Dream Worlds of Shamanism and Tibetan Buddhism* (2008).

NOTES TO CHAPTER 4

1. For more discussion of dream phenomena like precognition, telepathy, and clairvoyance, see Krippner, Bogzaran, and de Carvalho, *Extraordinary*

Dreams; Robert Van de Castle, *Our Dreaming Mind* (1994); Mongague Ullman, Stanley Krippner, and Alan Vaughan, *Dream Telepathy: Experiments in Nocturnal ESP* (1989).

2. Stele of Vultures: Scott Noegel, "Dreams and Dream Interpreters in Mesopotamia and in the Hebrew Bible (Old Testament)" (2001), p. 46.

3. Gudea's dream: A. Leo Oppenheim, "The Interpretation of Dreams in the Ancient Near East with a Translation of an Assyrian Dream Book" (1956), pp. 245–246. Oppenheim's work includes translations of several other royal dreams of Gyges, Ashburnipal, and many other Mesopotamian rulers.

4. Dumuzi's dream: Oppenheim, "The Interpretation of Dreams in the Ancient Near East," p. 246. For more on the Sumerian term *bur* and the Akkadian *pasaru,* see pp. 213, 217ff.

5. Lugulbanda's dream: Noegel, "Dreams and Dream Interpreters," p. 47.

6. Dreams in *Gilgamesh* I.ii, I.v, I.vi, V.i, V.iii, V.iv, VII.i, VII.iv, VII.ii, IX.i, XI.iv: translated by John Gardner and John Maier (1984), pp. 67, 81, 86, 134, 138, 139, 140, 167, 177–178, 169, 196, 250.

7. Addu-duri's dreams: Jack M. Sasson, "Mari Dreams" (1983), pp. 286, 289. For more on the Mari, see Wolfgang Heimpel, *Letters to the King of Mari: A New Translation, with Historical Introduction, Notes, and Commentary* (2003).

8. Babylonian and Assyrian dream books: Oppenheim, "The Interpretation of Dreams in the Ancient Near East"; Noegel, "Dreams and Dream Interpreters," esp. pp. 51–52. The list of dream book themes is adapted from Noegel, p. 51.

9. *Namburbu* rituals: Noegel, "Dreams and Dream Interpreters," p. 53; Oppenheim, "The Interpretation of Dreams in the Ancient Near East," pp. 346–347.

10. Egyptian Letters to the Dead: Kasia Szpakowska, *Behind Closed Eyes: Dreams and Nightmares in Ancient Egypt* (2003), p. 186.

11. Amenhotep II's dream: Szpakowska, *Behind Closed Eyes,* p. 188.

12. Merneptah's dream: ibid., p. 196.

13. Thutmose IV's dream: Oppenheim, "The Interpretation of Dreams in the Ancient Near East," p. 251, with some additions for clarity from Szpakowska, *Behind Closed Eyes,* p. 189.

14. Ipuy's dream: Szpakowska, *Behind Closed Eyes,* p. 194.

15. Ramesside Dream Book (also known as the Chester Beatty Papyrus): Szpakowska, *Behind Closed Eyes,* pp. 34, 72, 102, 86, 83, 80, 84, 88, 109.

16. Isis: Kasia Szpakowska, "Playing with Fire: Initial Observations on the Religious Uses of Clay Cobras from Amarna" (2003), p. 120. Further studies of Egyptian dreaming would include Pharaoh Tanutamani's symbolic dream of the two snakes, which priests interpreted as foretelling the reunification of Egypt (even though he ended up being the last Pharaoh of the last autonomous Egyptian dynasty); the role of the dream god Bes, who became in later Egyptian history an important figure in dream incubation and anti-nightmare rituals; the so-called Demotic Dream Book, written in the Late Period with influences from

other Fertile Crescent and Mediterranean cultures; the many fascinating dream spells and magical sleep practices outlined in later Egyptian texts; and the alleged dream of the Old Kingdom Pharaoh Djozer, most likely written much later in the Greek period as a means of establishing ancestral support for the current rulers.

17. Abram's visions and dreams: Genesis 15:8, 12, 17–18 (All Genesis quotes are from Roger Alter's translation (1996); all other quotes are from the Revised Standard Version of the Bible). The Hebrew word for dream is *halom,* with etymological connections to good health, egg yolks, and seminal emission.

18. Jacob's dream: Genesis 28:11–17. For more on *ziggurats,* see Alter, *Genesis,* p. 149. Jacob also benefits from a God-sent dream in his goat dealings with Laban (Genesis 31); he wrestles with a magical being until daybreak (Genesis 32); and he experiences pre-death "visions of the night [*mahazeh*]" telling him not to be afraid to lead his family to Egypt, where he will finally die.

19. Joseph's dreams: Genesis 37.

20. The story of Joseph, the Butler, the Baker, and the Pharaoh: Genesis 40–41.

21. Moses and "dark speech": Numbers 12:6–8.

22. Daniel and Nebuchadnezzar: Daniel 2, 4.

23. Joel's prophecy: Joel 2:28–29.

24. Jeremiah's skepticism: Jeremiah 23:25–28. See also Jeremiah 27 and 29, and the apocryphal Book of Sirach 34:1–8

25. For a Jewish version of the pre-battle dream theme, see the apocryphal 2 Maccabees 15:12–16.

26. Dreams in the Talmudic text *Berachot*: Monford Harris, *Studies in Jewish Dream Interpretation* (1994); Sandor Lorand, "Dream Interpretation in the Talmud (Babylonian and Graeco-Roman Period)" (1957); John F. Priest, "Myth and Dream in Hebrew Scripture" (1970); Noegel, "Dreams and Dream Interpretation."

27. Other Jewish dream teachings: Robert Gnuse, "Dream Reports in the Writings of Flavius Josephus" (1989); Philo, *On Dreams* (1988); Alan Brill, "The Phenomenology of True Dreams in Maimonides" (2000); Joel Covitz, *Visions of the Night: A Study of Jewish Dream Interpretation* (1990); Edward Hoffman, *The Way of Splendor: Jewish Mysticism and Modern Psychology* (1981); Howard Schwartz, *Lilith's Cave: Jewish Tales of the Supernatural* (1988).

NOTES TO CHAPTER 5

1. For more on dream incubation, see Kimberley C. Patton, "'A Great and Strange Correction': Intentionality, Locality, and Epiphany in the Category of Dream Incubation" (2004); C. A. Meier, *Ancient Incubation and Modern Psychotherapy* (1967).

2. Neolithic caves and the "Creative Explosion": Lewis-Williams, *The Mind in the Cave*; Diamond, *Guns, Germs, and Steel*; Steven Mithen, *The Prehistory of*

the Mind: The Cognitive Origins of Art and Science (1996); John E. Pfeiffer, *The Creative Explosion: An Inquiry into the Origins of Art and Religion* (1982).

3. This discussion of dreams in Homer draws in several places on an earlier essay of mine, "Penelope as Dreamer: The Perils of Interpretation" (2001).

4. All *Iliad* quotes are translated by Richmond Lattimore (1951). Regarding the terms for the Greeks and Achaeans: Agamemnon was king of Achaea and leader of the military expedition against Troy, hence the warriors from Greece are collectively known as Achaeans. Agamemnon's dream: *Iliad*, 2.1–83. Achilles chasing Hektor: *Iliad*, 22.199–201. Achilles' dream of Patroklos: *Iliad*, 23.54–107. Priam's dream: *Iliad*, 24.677–691.

5. All *Odyssey* quotes are translated by Robert Fagles (1996). Penelope's dream of her sister: *Odyssey*, 4.884–946. Nausicaa's marriage dream: *Odyssey*, 6.15–79. Penelope's dream and the two gates: *Odyssey*, 19.603–640; see Anne Amory, "The Gates of Horn and Ivory" (1966). The land of dreams: *Odyssey*, 24.1–14.

6. *Theogony*, vv. 108, 134, 211–212, translated by Dorothea Wender (1973).

7. Heraclitus, fragment 89, translated by T. M. Robinson (1987).

8. Parmenides: Peter Kingsley, *In the Dark Places of Wisdom* (1999). For comments on Pythagoras as another early Greek philosopher who practiced dream incubation, see pp. 102–103.

9. Socrates' dream: *Crito*, 44, translated by Hugh Tredennick (1961).

10. Dreaming and wonder: *Theaetetus*, 155 and 150, translated by F. M. Cornford (1961).

11. Socrates' recurrent dream in *Phaedo*, 60, translated by Hugh Tredennick (1961).

12. For more on the debate about Socrates, Plato, and the Dialogues, see E. R. Dodds, *The Greeks and the Irrational* (1951); Gregory Vlastos, *The Philosophy of Socrates: A Collection of Critical Essays* (1971); and Richard Kraut, *The Cambridge Companion to Plato* (1992). In this context, mention should also be made of Xenophon, another of Socrates' students, who wrote a concise statement of the common thread in the Greek philosophy of dreaming: "It is in sleep that the soul (*psyche*) best shows its divine nature; it is in sleep that it enjoys a certain insight into the future; and this is, apparently, because it is freest in sleep" (quoted in Dodds, *The Greeks and the Irrational*, p. 135).

13. Condemning Homer: *Republic*, 382a, translated by Paul Shorey (1961).

14. Savage instincts released in dreaming: *Republic* IX, 571c.

15. The most evil type of man: *Republic* IX, 576b.

16. Clear self-consciousness in dreaming: *Republic* IX, 571d–572b. The final passage is similar to the brief discussion of the physiological dynamics underlying predictive dreams in *Timaeus*, 71d.

17. Also worth noting are (1) the "Myth of Er" narrated at the very end of the *Republic* (IX, 614–621), a decidedly nonrational visionary dream of the afterlife (and predecessor to Cicero's account of the dream of Scipio in the sixth book of

De re publica (*On the Republic*); and (2) the reference to the "nocturnal council of magistrates" at the very end of the *Laws* (968a), a group of ultra-executive political authorities who provide shadowy but ultimately trustworthy guidance for the community.

18. All Aristotle quotes are translated by Richard MacKeon (1941). Emotion and deceptive perceptions: *De Insomniis*, 460b. Skepticism toward prophetic dreams: *De Divinatione per Somnum*, 462b. Explaining precognitive dreams: *De Divinatione per Somnum*, 462b–463b. Prognostic perceptions of the beginnings of movements during sleep: *De Divinatione per Somnum*, 463a. (Similar views were held by Pindar and Xenophon; see Dodds, *The Greeks and the Irrational*; Angelo Brelich, "The Place of Dreams in the Religious World Concept of the Greeks" [1965].) Dream interpretation and observing resemblances: *De Divinatione per Somnum*, 464b.

19. Sophocles, *Oedipus Rex*, 980–983, translated by David Grene (1942).

20. Euripides, *Hecuba*, 69–76, translated by William Arrowsmith (1992).

21. Euripides, *Iphigenia in Tauris*, 1263–1267, translated by Witter Bynner (1956).

22. Aeschylus, *The Libation Bearers*, 540–549, translated by David Grene and Wendy Doniger O'Flaherty (1989). For more on dreams in Greek drama, see George Devereux, *Dreams in Greek Tragedy: An Ethno-Psycho-Analytical Study* (1976).

23. Pindar, *Olympian*, 13:65ff. See also *Fragment* 131, about which Brelich has said: "Pindar . . . viewed the dream as the very symbol of all that is meaningless—we, men, are the dream of a shadow—but he does not hesitate to say that the soul (*eidolon*), which is divine and sleeps while we are awake, makes its correct judgments known in dreams while we are asleep" ("The Place of Dreams," p. 294).

24. Herodotus's report of the incestuous dream of Hippias, *Histories*, 6.106–108, quoted in Cristiano Grottanelli, "On the Mantic Meaning of Incestuous Dreams" (1999), pp. 148–149. Xerxes, 7.12–18; Astyages, 1.107–108.

25. Hippocrates on dreams: Dodds, *The Greeks and the Irrational*, p. 119.

26. Galen on Asclepius and dreams: Miller, *Dreams in Late Antiquity*, p. 108; Steven M. Oberhelman, "Galen, *On Diagnosis by Dreams*" (1983). For more on the Greek medical view of dreams, see Wilhelm H. Roscher and James Hillman, *Pan and Nightmare* (1979).

27. Worship at the Asclepian temples: Aelius Aristides, *The Collected Works* (1981); Ludwig and Emma Edelstein, *Asclepius: A Collection and Interpretation of the Testimonies* (1975); Andre-Jean Festugiere, *Personal Religion among the Greeks* (1984); Howard C. Kee, "Self-Definition in the Asclepius Cult" (1982); Peter Brown, *The Making of Late Antiquity* (1978); Charles Stewart, "Ritual Dreams and Historical Orders: Incubation between Paganism and Christianity" (2003); C. A.

Meier, *Ancient Incubation and Modern Psychotherapy*; Dodds, *The Greeks and the Irrational*. I disagree with Dodds in his overly harsh dismissal of Aslepian cures (p. 116).

28. Placebo effect: Anne Harrington, *The Placebo Effect: An Interdisciplinary Exploration* (1997).

29. Sources on dreams in Roman civilization: Hubert Cancik, *"Idolum and Imago*: Roman Dreams and Dream Theories" (1999); Brown, *The Making of Late Antiquity*; Miller, *Dreams in Late Antiquity*. Primary texts meriting further study include Ovid's *Metamorphoses*, Cicero's *On Divination*, Apuleius's *The Golden Ass*, Plutarch's *Lives*, and Lucretius's *On the Nature of Things*. A particularly influential late Roman dream text came from an unlikely source: Macrobius's commentary on the "Dream of Scipio" in Cicero's *Republic*. Macrobius described and briefly analyzed five types of dreams (enigmatic, prophetic, oracular, nightmares, and apparitions), and his categorization was regularly cited in Christian texts throughout the medieval era. For more on Greek–Egyptian–Roman dream magic, see Hans Dieter Betz, *The Greek Magical Papyri in Translation* (1992).

30. Tree of Dreams: *Aeneid*, 6.373ff., translated by Allen Mandelbaum (1971).

31. Two gates: *Aeneid*, 6.1191ff.

32. Artemidorus's *Oneirocritica*, translated by Robert J. White (1975), pp. 13, 14, 15, 20–21, 22, 188, 137. For more on Artemidorus, see Christine Walde, "Dream Interpretation in a Prosperous Age? Artemidorus, the Greek Interpreter of Dreams" (1999); Luther Martin, "Artemidorus: Dream Theory in Late Antiquity" (1991); Michel Foucault, *The History of Sexuality* (1988); Arthur S. Osley, "Notes on Artemidorus' *Oneirocritica*" (1963).

33. Greek dream beliefs and practices in modern times: Charles Stewart, "Fields in Dreams: Anxiety, Experience, and the Limits of Social Constructionism in Modern Greek Dream Narratives" (1997); Dimitris Xygalatas, "Firewalking in the Balkans: High Arousal Rituals and Memory" (2006); Patton, "A Great and Strange Connection."

NOTES TO CHAPTER 6

1. For current research on sleep, dreaming, and sexuality, see Carskadon, *Encyclopedia of Sleep and Dreaming*; Kryger, Roth, and Dement, *Principles and Practices of Sleep Medicine*.

2. All *Novum Testamentum* quotes are from the Revised Standard Version of the Bible. Joseph's dreams: Matthew 1–2. See Robert Gnuse, "Dream Genre in the Matthean Infancy Narratives" (1990).

3. Jesus in the wilderness: Mark 1:12–13.

4. Transfiguration of Jesus: Mark 9:2–8.

5. The interaction of early Christianity with its surrounding cultures is

an enormously complex subject. For further discussion, see David Stroumsa, "Dreams and Visions in Early Christian Discourse" (1999); Morton Kelsey, *God, Dreams, and Revelation: A Christian Interpretation of Dreams* (1991); E. R. Dodds, *Pagan and Christian in an Age of Anxiety* (1965).

6. Pilate's Wife's dream: Matthew 27:19.

7. Paul's dreams: Acts 16:9, 18:9–11, 23:11, 27:23–25.

8. Joel 2:28–32 quotation in Acts 2:17–21. For more on dreams in the Christian apocrypha, see Kelsey, *God, Dreams, and Revelation,* p. 101ff.; and Stroumsa, "Dreams and Visions," pp. 194–195.

9. Shepherd of Hermas: quoted in Miller, *Dreams in Late Antiquity,* p. 136.

10. Perpetua's dreams: quoted in Peter Dronke, *Women Writers of the Middle Ages: A Critical Study of Texts from Perpetua to Margeurite Porete* (1984), pp. 2–4. For more on Perpetua's dreams, see Joyce Salisbury, *Perpetua's Passion: The Death and Memory of a Young Roman Woman* (1994); Patricia M. Davis, "The Weaning of Perpetua: Female Embodiment and Spiritual Growth Metaphor in the Dream of an Early Christian Martyr" (2005); Mary R. Lefkowitz, "The Motivations of St. Perpetua's Martyrdom" (1976).

11. Constantine's conversion dream: Kelsey, *God, Dreams, and Revelation,* pp. 115–119.

12. Evagrius Ponticus: quoted in Stroumsa, "Dreams and Visions," pp. 199–202.

13. Antiochus Monachus: quoted in Philip Mayerson, "Antiochus Monachus' Homily on Dreams: An Historical Note" (1984), pp. 51–52.

14. Jerome's dream: quoted in Kelsey, *God, Dreams, and Revelation,* pp. 136–137. For more on Jerome, see J. J. Theirry, "The Date of the Dream of Jerome" (1963).

15. Prophetic dream of Augustine's mother, Monica: *Confessions* 3:20, translated by Henry Chadwick (1991). Monica's discernment of divine dreams: *Confessions* 6:13. Augustine on the moral dangers of sleep: *Confessions* 10:30.

16. Augustine on Gennadius's dream: "Letter to Evodius," in *The Works of Aurelius Augustine,* Vol. 13: *The Letters of Saint Augustine,* translated by J. G. Cunningham (1870).

17. Tertullian, *De anima,* 44–49, quoted in Stroumsa, "Dreams and Visions," p. 196. See also Kelsey, *God, Dreams, and Revelation,* pp. 217–222.

18. Origin, *Against Celsus,* I.48, quoted in Stroumsa, "Dreams and Visions," p. 194. See also Kelsey, *God, Dreams, and Revelation,* pp. 223–225.

19. Synesius, *Concerning Dreams,* quoted in Kelsey, *God, Dreams, and Revelation,* p. 247.

20. Aquinas discussions of sleep and dreams: *Summa Theologica,* II–II.171–174; I.84.8, reply to objection 2; I.111.3; II–II.95.6; II–II.154.5. Translated by the Fathers of the English Dominican Province (1920).

21. Luther's disregard for dreaming: *Collected Works,* vol. 7, p. 120, translated

by Jaroslav Pelikan (1945). Luther against monks and nuns incubating dreams: "Commentary on Genesis 19:14" in *Collected Works,* vol. 3, p. 275.

22. Anglo-Saxon dream practices: Patricia M. Davis, "Dreams and Visions in the Anglo-Saxon Conversion to Christianity" (2005); Jesse Keskiaho, "The Handling and Interpretation of Dreams and Visions in Late Sixth- to Eighth-Century Gallic and Anglo-Latin Hagiography and Histories" (2005).

23. *Somnialia Danielis:* Jean-Claude Schmitt, "The Liminality and Centrality of Dreams in the Medieval West" (1999), pp. 275–276.

24. Dante quote: *Purgatorio* IX.16–18, translated by John Ciardi (1980). For more on Dante and dreams, see Carol Schreier Rupprechet, "Dreams and Dismemberment: Transformations of the Female Body in Dante's *Purgatorio*" (1992).

25. Chaucer on dreams: Walter Clyde Curry, *Chaucer and the Medieval Sciences* (1960).

26. For more on Shakespearean dreaming, see Marjorie Garber, *Dream in Shakespeare: From Metaphor to Metamorphosis* (1974); and Carol Schreier Rupprecht, "The Drama of History and Prophecy: Shakespeare's use of Dream in *2 Henry VI*" (1993). For more on dreams in literary history, see Roger Callois, *The Dream Adventure: A Literary Anthology* (1963); and Rupprecht, "Dream, Language, Literature" (2007).

27. Dreams as signs of witchcraft: Heinrich Kramer and James Sprenger, *Malleus Maleficarum* (1971), part 1, question 3. See also Carlo Ginzburg, *The Night Battles: Witchcraft and Agrarian Cults in the Sixteenth and Seventeenth Centuries* (1992). Other influential dream-related texts in the Renaissance and in early modern Christianity include John Milton's *Paradise Lost,* the astrological works of Girolamo Cardano, and the dream diary of Emmanuel Swedenborg, which prompted one of Immanuel Kant's earliest writings, *Dreams of a Spirit-Seer.* For information on Eastern Orthodox Christianity approaches to dreams, particularly the medieval text *Oneirocriticon* by Achmet, see the translations of Steven M. Oberhelman (1991) and Maria Mavroudi (2001).

NOTES TO CHAPTER 7

1. General sources on Islam and dreaming: Marcia Hermansen, "Dreams and Dreaming in Islam" (2001); G. E. Von Grunebaum and Roger Callois, *The Dream and Human Societies* (1966); John C. Lamoreaux, *The Early Muslim Tradition of Dream Interpretation* (2002); Sara Sviri, "Dreaming Analyzed and Recorded: Dreams in the World of Medieval Islam (1999); Mohsen Ashtiany, *Dreaming across Boundaries: The Interpretation of Dreams in Islamic Lands* (2007); Kelly Bulkeley, Kate Adams, and Patricia M. Davis, *Dreaming in Christianity and Islam: Culture, Conflict, Creativity* (2009).

2. Muhammad's life and call to Prophecy: Martin Lings, *Muhammad: His Life Based on the Earliest Sources* (1983); Hajjah Amina Adil, *Muhammad: The Mes-*

L

senger of Islam: His Life and Prophecy (2002); Tor Andrae, *Mohammed: The Man and His Faith* (1960); Karen Armstrong, *Muhammad: A Biography of the Prophet* (1992). Commentators on Islam continue to debate the question of whether Muhammad experienced one or the other or both of the revelatory events described in the caves of Mount Hira.

3. All *Qur'an* quotes are from the translation of N. J. Dawood (1974).

4. Many Muslim scholars do not believe that the "Satanic Verses" incident ever occurred.

5. All *hadiths* are from Hermansen, "Dreams and Dreaming in Islam," pp. 74–76.

6. Ibn Sirin: Hermansen, "Dreams and Dreaming in Islam," p. 78.

7. Interpretive practices: Lamoreaux, *The Early Muslim Tradition of Dream Interpretation;* Jean LeCerf, "The Dream in Popular Culture: Arab and Islamic" (1966); M. Hidayet Hosain, "A Treatise on the Interpretation of Dreams" (1932); Nathaniel Bland, "On the Muhammedan Science of *Tabir,* or Interpretation of Dreams" (1856).

8. *Tabir* and *Alam al-mithal*: Fazlur Rahman, "Dream, Imagination, and *Alam al-mithal*" (1966).

9. Ibn Arabi: Rom Landau, "The Philosophy of Ibn Arabi" (1967).

10. Ibn Khaldun: *The Muqaddimah* (1967).

11. *Istikhara*: Hidayet Aydar, "*Istikhara* and Dreams" (2009); LeCerf, "The Dream in Popular Culture"; Hermansen, "Dreams and Dreaming in Islam"; J. Spencer Trimmingham, *Islam in West Africa* (1956).

12. Pre-Islamic Arabian divination practices forbidden: *Qur'an* 5:90.

13. Ibn Khaldun on dream words: *Muqaddimah,* p. 84.

14. Sufism and dreams: Jonathan G. Katz, "An Egyptian Sufi Interprets His Dreams: 'Abd al-Wahhab al-Sha'rani 1493–1565" (1997); Marcia Hermansen, "Visions as 'Good to Think': A Cognitive Approach to Visionary Experience in Islamic Sufi Thought" (1997); Lewellyn Vaughan-Lee, *Catching the Thread: Sufism, Dreamwork, and Jungian Psychology* (1998); Patricia M. Davis and Lewis Rambo, "Dreams in Conversion to Islam and Initiation to Sufism" (forthcoming). For a scholarly voice of criticism against Sufism, see Fazlur Rahman, *Islam* (1979), p. 153.

15. Al-Tirmidhi: Sviri, "Dreaming Analyzed and Recorded," pp. 260–262.

16. Lahiji: Henri Corbin, "The Visionary Dream in Islamic Spirituality" (1966), pp. 396–397.

17. Contemporary Muslim dream practices: in Iran, Parisa Rahman, "Dreams in Iran Today" (2009); in Jordan, Lana Nasser, "Dreaming and *Jinn* possession in Jordan" (2009); in Egypt, Valerie J. Hoffman, "The Role of Visions in Contemporary Egyptian Religious Life" (1997); in Pakistan, Katherine P. Ewing, "The Dream of Spiritual Initiation and the Organization of Self-Representations among Pakistani Sufis" (1989).

18. Mollah Omar: Iain Edgar, "The Dream Will Tell: Militant Muslim Dreaming in the Context of Traditional and Contemporary Islamic Dream Theory" (2004), p. 22.

19. Osama bin Laden videotape released by the U.S. government on December 14, 2001.

NOTES TO CHAPTER 8

1. Shabaka's dream: Herodotus, *Histories* 2.139. See Stephanie West, "And It Came to Pass that Pharaoh Dreamed: Notes on Herodotus 2.139, 141" (1987).

2. The science of evolution: E. O. Wilson, *Sociobiology: The New Synthesis* (2000).

3. Temne "four eyes": Rosalind Shaw, "Dreaming as Accomplishment: Power, the Individual, and Temne Divination" (1993), p. 42.

4. Yansi: Mubuy Mubay Mpier, "Dreams among the Yansi" (1993), pp. 100–110.

5. *Jamaa* movement and *mawazo*: Johannes Fabian, "Dream and Charisma: 'Theories of Dreams' in the Jamaa-Movement (Congo)" (1966).

6. Temne river-pebble divination: Shaw, "Dreaming as Accomplishment," p. 48.

7. Zulu calling dreams: E. Thomas Lawson, "Religions of Africa: Traditions in Transformation" (1993), p. 35.

8. Zulu *thomba* ceremony: Lawson, "Religions of Africa," pp. 47–48.

9. Yansi incubation: Mpier, "Dreams among the Yansi," pp. 106–107.

10. Ingessana bad dream ritual: M. C. Jedrej, "Ingessana Dreaming" (1993), p. 114.

11. Christian missionary on dreaming: Floyd W. Taber, "How Real Are Dreams?" (1972), p. 109. For more, see Aylward Shorter, "Dreams in Africa" (1978), pp. 281–287.

12. Lilias Trotter's dream reports: C. E. Padwick, "Dream and Vision: Some Notes from a Diary" (1939), pp. 208, 211.

13. Robert Keable, "A People of Dreams" (1921), p. 525.

14. Conversion dreams in Islam: Humphrey J. Fisher, "Dreams and Conversion in Black Africa" (1979); M. C. Jedrej and Rosalind Shaw, *Dreaming, Religion, and Society in Africa* (1993).

15. Witchcraft and dreams: E. E. Evans-Pritchard, "Witchcraft, Oracles, and Magic among the Azande" (1976); Fisher, "Dreams and Conversion in Black Africa."

16. *Istikhara* and Muslim clerics: J. Spencer Trimingham, *Islam in West Africa* (1959); Victor Crapanzano, "Saints, Jnun, and Dreams: An Essay in Moroccan Ethnopsychology" (1975); Fisher, "Dreams and Conversion in Black Africa."

17. Nubian dream shrines: John G. Kennedy and Hussein Fahim, "Nubian

Dhikr Rituals and Cultural Change" (1974). For more on dream shrines, see Crapanzano, "Saints, Jnun, and Dreams."

18. For more on African dream traditions as related to healing, see Gordon Chavunduka, "Dreams and Traditional Healing in Africa with Special Reference to Zimbabwe" (2004).

19. African Independent Churches: Simon Charsley, "Dreams in an Independent African Church" (1973); and idem, "Dreams and Purposes: An Analysis of Dream Narratives in an Independent African Church" (1987).

20. Kimbangu Church: John S. Mbiti, "God, Dreams, and African Militancy" (1976). Isaiah Shembe: Donald M'Timkulu, "Some Aspects of Zulu Religion" (1977). Joseph Sadare: Lawson, "Religions of Africa"; Fisher, "Dreams and Conversion in Black Africa."

21. Zulu Zionist: J. P. Kiernan, "The Social Stuff of Revelation: Pattern and Purpose in Zionist Dreams and Visions" (1985).

22. True Church of God: Richard T. Curley, "Dreams of Power: Social Process in a West African Religious Movement" (1983); "Private Dreams and Public Knowledge in a Camerounian Independent Church" (1992).

NOTES TO CHAPTER 9

1. The best overall summaries of the literature on dreaming and religion in Oceania are Michele Stephen, "Dreams of Change: The Innovative Role of Altered States of Consciousness in Traditional Melanesian Religion" (1979); and idem, *A'aisa's Gifts: A Study of Magic and the Self* (1995); G. W. Trompf, *Melanesian Religion* (1990); Roger Ivar Lohmann, *Dream Travelers: Sleep Experiences and Culture in the Western Pacific* (2003), especially Lohmann's introduction and Waud Kracke's afterword; and Jeannette Marie Mageo, "Race, Postcoloniality, and Identity in Samoan Dreams" (2003). The present chapter does not directly refer to the Senoi people of Malaysia because the main goals of this book can be achieved without reliance on the controversial and problematic evidence regarding their dream theories and practices. The literature on the Senoi stands as a cautionary tale of the methodological challenges facing the cross-cultural study of dreaming. See Kilton Stewart, "Dream Theory in Malaya" (1951); G. William Domhoff, *The Mystique of Dreams: A Search for Utopia Through Senoi Dream Theory* (1985); Marina Roseman, *Healing Sounds from the Malaysian Rainforest: Temniar Music and Medicine* (1991); Jeremy Taylor and G. William Domhoff, "Debate on the Legacy of the Senoi" (1995).

2. New Guinea languages: Diamond, *Guns, Germs, and Steel*, p. 27.

3. Australian aboriginal dream beliefs: Sylvia Poirier, " 'This is Good Country. We Are Good Dreamers": Dreams and Dreaming in the Australian Western Desert" (2003).

4. Soul journeys among aboriginal Australians: The terms used are from the

Mardu people, as recounted in Robert Tonkinson, "Ambrymese Dreams and the Mardu Dreaming" (2003), pp. 92–93. See also Tonkinson, "Aboriginal Dream-Spirit Beliefs in a Contact Situation: Jigalong, Western Australia" (1970). In the former article, Tonkinson points out the unusual disinterest of the Ambrymese in dreaming; it is difficult to distinguish disinterest in dreams from unwillingness to talk about one's dreams with other people.

5. The Mekeo: Stephen, *A'aisa's Gifts,* esp. pp. 111–176.

6. The Mae Enga: M. J. Meggitt, "Dream Interpretation among the Mae Enga of New Guinea" (1962).

7. The Melpa: Pamela J. Stewart and Andrew J. Strathern, "Dreaming and Ghosts among the Hagen and Duna of the Southern Highlands, Papua New Guinea" (2003).

8. The Ngaing: Wolfgang Kempf and Elfriede Hermann, "Dreamscapes: Transcending the Local in Initiation Rites among the Ngaing of Papua New Guinea" (2003).

9. The Sambia: Gilbert H. Herdt, "The Shaman's 'Calling' among the Sambia of New Guinea" (1977).

10. The Iban: Derek Freeman, "Shaman and Incubus" (1967).

11. The Asabano and Wobono: Roger Ivar Lohmann, "The Role of Dreams in Religious Enculturation among the Asabono of Papua New Guinea" (1999), p. 123. Young Asabano man: Roger Ivar Lohmann, "Supernatural Encounters of the Asabano in Two Traditions and Three States of Consciousness" (2003), p. 197.

12. The Asabano, Obai: Lohmann, "Supernatural Encounters of the Asabano," p. 192.

13. Cargo Cults: G. W. Trompf, "Cargo Cults" (2004); Kenelm Burridge, *Mambu: A Melanesian Millennium* (1960); Stephen, "Dreams of Change."

14. Enga graveyard cults: Kenneth B. Osborne, "A Christian Graveyard Cult in the New Guinea Highlands" (1970), pp. 11–12.

15. Samoan dreams: Mageo, "Samoan Dreams" (2003), pp. 79, 83.

16. Tikopian dreams: Raymond Firth, "The Meaning of Dreams in Tikopia" (1934); and idem, "Tikopia Dreams: Personal Images of Social Reality" (2001), p. 21.

17. Fulagan nightmares: Barbara Herr, "The Expressive Character of Fijian Dream and Nightmare Experiences" (1981). Tainyandawari flying and falling dreams: Trompf, *Melanesian Religion,* pp. 116–117.

NOTES TO CHAPTER 10

1. Frequency of animals as characters in dreams: Domhoff, *Finding Meaning in Dreams,* pp. 89–95, 99–129. See also David Foulkes, *Children's Dreams: Longitudinal Studies* (1982), and idem, *Children's Dreaming and the Development of Consciousness* (1999); Strauch and Meier, *In Search of Dreams.*

2. Spread of Homo sapiens into the Americas: Diamond, *Guns, Germs, and Steel.* It is possible that explorers from Oceania reached the west coast of South America sometime before the circumpolar peoples got there.

3. Jesuit missionary: quoted in Anthony F. C. Wallace, "Dreams and the Wishes of the Soul: A Type of Psychoanalytic Theory among the Seventeenth Century Iroquois" (1958), p. 235.

4. Early missionary disregard for indigenous dream beliefs: Ake Hultkrantz, "Native Religions of North America: The Power of Visions and Fertility" (1993), p. 278.

5. Andean missionary: quoted in Bruce Mannheim, "A Semiotic of Andean Dreams" (1987), p. 137. Mannheim made the intriguing discovery that over a 350 year time span there has been a "near-total replacement of the lexicon of dream signs" among the Quechua.

6. Cree: Regina Flannery and Elizabeth Chambers, "Each Man Has His Own Friends: The Role of Dream Visitors in Traditional East Cree Belief and Practice" (1985), pp. 4–5.

7. Mohave: W. J. Wallace, "The Dream in Mohave Life" (1947).

8. Quiche: Barbara Tedlock, "Zuni and Quiche Dream Sharing and Interpreting" (1987), pp. 115–116.

9. For more on sleep paralysis, see the literature on the "Old Hag" phenomenon in the folk culture of English and Irish immigrants in Newfoundland: David J. Hufford, "A New Approach to the 'Old Hag': The Nightmare Tradition Revisited" (1976); Robert C. Ness, "The Old Hag Phenomenon as Sleep Paralysis: A Biocultural Interpretation" (1978); and Melvin Firestone, "The 'Old Hag': Sleep Paralysis in Newfoundland" (1985).

10. Makiritare *Watunna*: David M. Guss, "Steering for Dream: Dream Concepts of the Makiritare" (1980), pp. 304–305, 310.

11. Mehinaku: Thomas Gregor, "Dark Dreams about the White Man" (1983), pp. 10, 12–13; idem, "'Far, far away my shadow wandered . . .': The Dream Symbolism and Dream Theories of the Mehinaku Indians of Brazil" (1981); and idem, "A Content Analysis of Mehinaku Dreams" (1981). In the latter article Gregor makes an encouraging point: "The special value of dream research . . . is that it takes us beyond the impact of waking experiences on personality to reach conclusions we could only guess at from a knowledge of everyday life. . . . Attention to dreams thereby systematically enriches the account of Mehinaku culture provided by descriptive social anthropology" (p. 389).

12. For other good sources on dreams among indigenous peoples of the Amazon region, see Howard Reid, "Dreams and Their Interpretation among the Hupdu Maku Indians of Brazil" (1978); Waud Kracke, "Kagwahiv Mourning: Dreams of a Bereaved Father" (2001); Phillipe Descola, *The Spears of Twilight: Life and Death in the Amazon Jungle* (1993).

13. Interest in dreaming diminishes with agriculture: Hultkrantz, "Native Religions of North America."

14. Aztec text: David Carrasco, "Religions of Mesoamerica: Cosmovision and Ceremonial Centers" (1993), p. 172.

15. Vision quests in the Great Plains: Lee Irwin, *The Dream Seekers: Native American Visionary Traditions of the Great Plains* (1994), and idem, "Sending a Voice, Seeking a Place: Visionary Traditions among Native Women of the Plains" (2001); Hultkrantz, "Native Religions of North America"; Paul Radin, "Ojibwa and Ottawa Puberty Dreams" (1936); J. S. Lincoln, *The Dream in Primitive Cultures* (1935); Ruth Fulton Benedict, "The Vision in Plains Culture" (1922).

16. Ojibwa man Agabegijik's dream fast: quoted in Radin, "Ojibwa and Ottawa Puberty Dreams," pp. 237–241.

17. Blackfoot man's flying dream: Irwin, *The Dream Seekers*, p. 133.

18. Dreamer Religions: Clifford E. Trafzer and Margery Ann Beach, "Smohalla, the Washini, and Religion as a Factor in Northwestern Indian History" (1985); Anthony F. C. Wallace, *The Death and Rebirth of the Seneca* (1969).

19. Menomini society of dreamers myth: Alanson Skinner, "Associations and Ceremonies of the Menomini Indians" (1915), p. 175. See also Skinner, "Social Life and Ceremonial Bundles of the Menomini Indians" (1913).

20. Onondaga dream-guessing rite: Harold Blau, "Dream Guessing: A Comparative Analysis" (1963), pp. 234, 240, 246.

21. Dreaming among European immigrants and African slaves: Mechal Sobel, *Teach Me Dreams: The Search for Self in the Revolutionary Era* (2000); dreaming among European and American Quakers: Carla Gerona, *Night Journeys: The Power of Dreams in Transatlantic Quaker Culture* (2004); dreaming among the early leaders of the Church of Latter Day Saints: Lucy Smith, *Biographical Sketches of Joseph Smith the Prophet and His Progenitors for Many Generations* (2006), Joseph Smith, *An American Prophet's Record: The Diaries and Journals of Joseph Smith* (1987), and Francis M. Gibbons, *Joseph F. Smith: Patriarch and Preacher, Prophet of God* (1984); dreaming in the mass media, popular culture, and religious expressions of nineteenth-century U.S. citizens: Hendrika Vande Kemp, "The Dream In Periodical Literature: 1860–1910" (1981), idem, "Psycho-Spiritual Dreams in the Nineteenth Century, Part I: Dreams of Death" (1994), and idem, "Psycho-Spiritual Dreams in the Nineteenth Century, Part II: Metaphysics and Immortality" (1994); dreaming among contemporary African Americans: Anthony Shafton, *Dream-Singers: The African American Way with Dreams* (2002).

NOTES TO THE CONCLUSION

1. Contemporary research on nightmares: Hartmann, *The Nightmare*; Kryger, Roth, and Dement, *Principles and Practices of Sleep Medicine*; Levin and Nielsen,

"Disturbed Dreaming, Posttraumatic Stress Disorder, and Affect Distress: A Review and Neurocognitive Model."

2. The terms *little dreams* and *big dreams* were coined by Jung, *On the Nature of Dreams* (1974), p. 76. He never specifically detailed their characteristics or illustrated their various types, so my usage includes more than was originally stated in Jung's texts.

3. Biography of Rene Descartes: John Cole, *The Olympian Dreams and Youthful Rebellion of Rene Descartes* (1992); Kelly Bulkeley, *The Wondering Brain: Thinking about Religion with and beyond Cognitive Neuroscience* (2005).

Bibliography

Achmet. 1991. *Oneirocriticon*. Translated by S. M. Oberhelman. Lubbock: Texas Tech University Press.

Adil, Hajjah Amina. 2002. *Muhammad: The Messenger of Islam: His Life and Prophecy*. Washington, D.C.: Islamic Supreme Council of America.

Aeschylus. 1989. *The Oresteia*. Translated by D. Grene and W. D. O'Flaherty. Chicago: University of Chicago Press.

Alter, Robert. 1996. *Genesis: Translation and Commentary*. New York: W. W. Norton.

Amory, Anne. 1966. The Gates of Horn and Ivory. *Yale Classical Studies* 20:1–57.

Andrae, Tor. 1960. *Mohammed: The Man and His Faith*. Translated by T. Menzel. New York: Harper Torchbooks. Original edition, 1936.

Anon. 1971. *As I Crossed a Bridge of Dreams: Recollections of a Woman in 11th-Century Japan*. Translated by I. Morris. London: Penguin Books.

Antrobus, John. 1993. Dreaming: Could We Do Without It? In *The Functions of Dreaming*, edited by A. Moffitt, M. Kramer, and R. Hoffman. Albany: State University of New York Press.

Araki, Michio. 1992. Dreams and Japanese Buddhism. Paper read at The Numata Lecture, 2 June, at University of Chicago Divinity School.

Aristides, Aelius. 1981. *The Complete Works*. Translated by C. A. Behr. Leiden: E. J. Brill.

Aristotle. 1941. On Dreams. In *The Collected Works of Aristotle*, edited by R. McKeon. New York: Random House.

———. 1941. On Prophesying by Dreams. In *The Collected Works of Aristotle*, edited by R. McKeon. New York: Random House.

Armstrong, Karen. 1992. *Muhammad: A Biography of the Prophet*. New York: HarperCollins.

Artemidorus. 1975. *The Interpretation of Dreams*. Translated by R. J. White. Park Ridge, N.J.: Noyes.

Aserinsky, Eugene, and Nathaniel Kleitman. 1953. Regularly Occurring Periods of Eye Motility, and Concomitant Phenomena, during Sleep. *Science* 118:273–274.

———. 1955. Two Types of Ocular Motility Occurring in Sleep. *Journal of Applied Physiology* 8:1–10.

Augustine. 1870. *The Works of Aurelius Augustine, Volume XIII: The Letters of Saint Augustine*. Translated by J. G. Cunningham. Edinburgh: T & T Clark.

———. 1991. *Confessions*. Translated by H. Chadwick. Oxford: Oxford University Press.

Aurobindo, Sri. 1993. *The Integral Yoga: Sri Aurobindo's Teaching and Method of Practice*. Twin Lakes, Wis.: Lotus.

Aurobindo, Sri, and The Mother. 2004. *The Yoga of Sleep and Dreams: The Night School of Sadhana*. Twin Lakes, Wis.: Lotus.

Aydar, Hidayet. 2009. *Istikhara* and Dreams. In *Dreaming in Christianity and Islam: Culture, Conflict, Creativity*, edited by K. Bulkeley, K. Adams, and P. M. Davis. New Brunswick, N.J.: Rutgers University Press.

Balter, Michael. 2005. Are Human Brains Still Evolving? Brain Genes Show Signs of Selection. *Science* 309 (5741): 1662–1663.

Belicki, Kathryn. 1986. Recalling Dreams: An Examination of Daily Variation and Individual Difference. In *Sleep and Dreams: A Sourcebook*, edited by J. Gackenbach. New York: Garland.

Benedict, Ruth Fulton. 1922. The Vision in Plains Culture. *American Anthropologist* 24 (1): 1–23.

Betz, Hans Dieter, ed. 1992. *The Greek Magical Papyri in Translation*. 2nd ed. Chicago: University of Chicago Press.

Bland, Nathaniel. 1856. On the Muhammedan Science of *Tabir*; or, Interpretation of Dreams. *Journal of the Royal Asiatic Society of Great Britain and Ireland* 16:118–171.

Blau, Harold. 1963. Dream-Guessing: A Comparative Analysis. *Ethnohistory* 10 (3): 233–249.

Bloomfield, Maurice. *Hymns of the Atharva-Veda* 1897 (cited February 2, 2007). Available at www.sacred-texts.com.

Bowker, John, ed. 1997. *The Oxford Dictionary of World Religions*. Oxford: Oxford University Press.

Braun, A. R., T. J. Balkin, N. J. Wesensten, F. Gwadry, R. E. Carson, M. Varga, P. Baldwin, G. Belenky, and P. Herscovitch. 1998. Dissociated Pattern of Activity in Visual Cortices and Their Projections during Human Rapid Eye-Movement Sleep. *Science* 279:91–95.

Brelich, Angelo. 1965. The Place of Dreams in the Religious World Concept of the Greeks. In *The Dream and Human Societies*, edited by G. E. Von Grunebaum and R. Callois. Berkeley: University of California Press.

Brill, Alan. 2000. The Phenomenology of True Dreams in Maimonides. *Dreaming* 10 (1):43–54.

Bulkeley, Kelly. 2001. Penelope as Dreamer: The Perils of Interpretation. In *Dreams: A Reader on the Religious, Cultural, and Psychological Dimensions of Dreaming*, edited by K. Bulkeley. New York: Palgrave.

———. 2003. "Religious Dimensions of a Dream Series," presentation at the annual conference of the Association for the Study of Dreams, June, Berkeley, California.

———. 2005. *The Wondering Brain: Thinking about Religion with and beyond Cognitive Neuroscience.* New York: Routledge.

Bulkeley, Kelly, Kate Adams, and Patricia M. Davis, eds. 2009. *Dreaming in Christianity and Islam: Culture, Conflict, Creativity.* New Brunswick, N.J.: Rutgers University Press.

Burridge, Kenelm. 1960. *Mambu: A Melanesian Millenium.* London: Methuen.

Callois, Roger. 1963. *The Dream Adventure: A Literary Anthology.* New York: Orion.

Cancik, Hubert. 1999. *Idolum and Imago*: Roman Dreams and Dream Theories. In *Dream Cultures: Explorations in the Comparative History of Dreaming,* edited by D. Shulman and G. G. Stroumsa. New York: Oxford University Press.

Carrasco, David. 1993. Religions of Mesoamerica: Cosmovision and Ceremonial Centers. In *Religious Traditions of the World,* edited by H. B. Earhart. San Francisco: HarperCollins.

Carskadon, Mary A., ed. 1993. *Encyclopedia of Sleep and Dreaming.* New York: Macmillan.

Charsley, S. R. 1973. Dreams in an Independent African Church. *Africa: Journal of the International African Institute* 43 (3): 244–257.

———. 1987. Dreams and Purposes: An Analysis of Dream Narratives in an Independent African Church. *Africa: Journal of the International African Institute* 57 (3):281–296.

Cole, John R. 1992. *The Olympian Dreams and Youthful Rebellion of Rene Descartes.* Urbana: University of Illinois Press.

Corbin, Henry. 1966. The Visionary Dream in Islamic Spirituality. In *The Dream and Human Societies,* edited by G. E. Von Grunebaum and R. Callois. Berkeley: University of California Press.

Covitz, Joel. 1990. *Visions of the Night: A Study of Jewish Dream Interpretation.* Boston: Shambhala.

Crapanzano, Victor. 1975. Saints, Jnun, and Demons: An Essay in Moroccan Ethnopsychology. *Psychiatry* 38:145–159.

Crick, Francis, and Graeme Mitchison. 1983. The Function of Dream Sleep. *Nature* 304:111–114.

Curley, R. T. 1992. Private Dreams and Public Knowledge in a Camerounian Independent Church. In *Dreaming, Religion, and Society in Africa,* edited by M. C. Jedrej and R. Shaw. Leiden: E. J. Brill.

Curley, Richard T. 1983. Dreams of Power: Social Process in a West African Religious Movement. *Africa: Journal of the International African Institute* 53 (3): 20–37.

Curry, Walter Clyde. 1960. *Chaucer and the Medieval Sciences.* New York: Barnes and Noble.

Dante. 1957. *The Purgatorio.* Translated by J. Ciardi. New York: Mentor.

Davis, Patricia M. 2005. Dreams and Visions in the Anglo-Saxon Conversion to Christianity. *Dreaming* 15 (2):75–88.

———. 2005. The Weaning of Perpetua: Female Embodiment and Spiritual Growth Metaphor in the Dream of an Early Christian Martyr. *Dreaming* 15 (4): 261–270.

Dement, William C., and Christopher Vaughn. 1999. *The Promise of Sleep.* New York: Dell.

Dentan, Robert Knox, and Laura J. McClusky. 1993. "Pity the Bones by Wandering River Which Still in Lovers' Dreams Appear as Men." In *The Functions of Dreaming,* edited by A. Moffitt, M. Kramer, and R. Hoffman. Albany: State University of New York Press.

Descola, Phillipe. 1993. *The Spears of Twilight: Life and Death in the Amazon Jungle.* New York: New Press.

Devereux, George. 1976. *Dreams in Greek Tragedy: An Ethno-Psycho-Analytical Study.* Berkeley: University of California Press.

Diamond, Jared. 1997. *Guns, Germs, and Steel: The Fates of Human Societies.* New York: W. W. Norton.

Dodds, E. R. 1951. *The Greeks and the Irrational.* Berkeley: University of California Press.

———. 1970. *Pagan and Christian in an Age of Anxiety.* New York: W. W. Norton.

Domhoff, G. William. 1985. *The Mystique of Dreams: A Search for Utopia Through Senoi Dream Theory.* Berkeley: University of California Press.

———. 1996. *Finding Meaning in Dreams: A Quantitative Approach.* New York: Plenum.

———. 2003. *The Scientific Study of Dreams: Neural Networks, Cognitive Development, and Content Analysis.* Washington, D.C.: American Psychological Association.

Dronke, Peter. 1984. *Women Writers of the Middle Ages: A Critical Study of Texts from Perpetua to Margeurite Porete.* Cambridge: Cambridge University Press.

Ebry, Patricia Buckley. 1996. *The Cambridge Illustrated History of China.* Cambridge: Cambridge University Press.

Edelstein, Ludwig, and Emma Edelstein. 1975. *Asclepius: A Collection and Interpretation of the Testimonies.* New York: Arno.

Edgar, Iain R. 2004. The Dream Will Tell: Militant Muslim Dreaming in the Context of Traditional and Contemporary Islamic Dream Theory and Practice. *Dreaming* 14 (1): 21–29.

Eliade, Mircea. 1964. *Shamanism: Archaic Techniques of Ecstasy.* Translated by W. R. Trask. Princeton, N.J.: Princeton University Press.

Euripides. 1956. Iphigenia in Tauris. In *Greek Tragedies,* edited by D. Grene and R. Lattimore. Chicago: University of Chicago Press.

———. 1992. Hecuba. In *The Complete Greek Tragedies,* edited by D. Grene and R. Lattimore. Chicago: University of Chicago Press.

Evans-Pritchard, E. E. 1976. *Witchcraft, Oracles, and Magic among the Azande.* Oxford, U.K.: Clarendon.

Ewing, Katherine. 1989. The Dream of Spiritual Initiation and the Organization of Self Representations among Pakistani Sufis. *American Ethnologist* 16:56–74.

Fabian, Johannes. 1966. Dreams and Charisma: "Theories of Dreams" in the Jamaa-Movement (Congo). *Anthropos* 61:544–560.

Festugiere, Andre-Jean. 1984. *Personal Religion among the Greeks.* Westport, Conn.: Greenwood.

Firestone, Melvin. 1985. The "Old Hag": Sleep Paralysis in Newfoundland. *Journal of Psychoanalytic Anthropology* 8 (1): 47–66.

Firth, Raymond. 1934. The Meaning of Dreams in Tikopia. In *Essays Presented to C. G. Seligman,* edited by E. E. Evans-Pritchard. London: Kegan Paul.

———. 2001. Tikopia Dreams: Personal Images of Social Reality. *Journal of the Polynesian Society* 110 (1): 7–29.

Fisher, Humphrey J. 1979. Dreams and Conversion in Black Africa. In *Conversion to Islam,* edited by N. Levtzion. New York: Holmes and Meier.

Flanagan, Owen. 2000. *Dreaming Souls: Sleep, Dreams, and the Evolution of the Conscious Mind.* Oxford: Oxford University Press.

Flannery, Regina, and Mary Elizabeth Chambers. 1985. Each Man Has His Own Friends: The Role of Dream Visitors in Traditional East Cree Belief and Practice. *Arctic Anthropology* 22 (1): 1–22.

Foucault, Michel. 1988. *The History of Sexuality.* Translated by R. Hurley. 3 vols. New York: Vintage Books.

Foulkes, David. 1962. Dream Reports from Different States of Sleep. *Journal of Abnormal and Social Psychology* 65:14–25.

———. 1982. *Children's Dreams: Longitudinal Studies.* New York: Wiley.

———. 1999. *Children's Dreaming and the Development of Consciousness.* Cambridge, Mass.: Harvard University Press.

Freeman, Derek. 1967. Shaman and Incubus. *The Psychoanalytic Study of Society* 4:315–343.

Freud, Sigmund. 1965. *The Interpretation of Dreams.* Translated by J. Strachey. New York: Avon Books.

Gackenbach, Jayne, and Stephen LaBerge, eds. 1988. *Conscious Mind, Sleeping Brain: Perspectives on Lucid Dreaming.* New York: Plenum.

Garber, Marjorie B. 1974. *Dream in Shakespeare: From Metaphor to Metamorphosis.* New Haven, Conn.: Yale University Press.

Gerona, Carla. 2004. *Night Journeys: The Power of Dreams in Transatlantic Quaker Culture.* Charlottesville: University of Virginia Press.

Gibbons, Francis M. 1984. *Joseph F. Smith: Patriarch and Preacher, Prophet of God.* Salt Lake City: Deseret Books.

Gilgamesh. 1984. Translated by J. Gardner and J. Maier. New York: Vintage.

Gillespie, George. 1988. Lucid Dreams in Tibetan Buddhism. In *Conscious Mind, Sleeping Brain: Perspectives on Lucid Dreaming,* edited by J. Gackenbach and S. LaBerge. New York: Plenum.

Ginzburg, Carlo. 1992. *The Night Battles: Witchcraft and Agrarian Cults in the Sixteenth and Seventeenth Centuries.* Translated by J. Tedeschi and A. Tedeschi. Baltimore, Md.: Johns Hopkins University Press.

Gnuse, Robert. 1989. Dream Reports in the Writings of Flavius Josephus. *Revue Biblique* 24 (3): 358–390.

———. 1990. Dream Genre in the Matthean Infancy Narratives. *Novum Testamentum* 32:97–120.

Gregor, Thomas. 1981. "Far, Far Away My Shadow Wandered . . .": The Dream Symbolism and Dream Theories of the Mehinaku Indians of Brazil. *American Ethnologist* 8 (4): 709–729.

———. 1983. Dark Dreams about the White Man. *Natural History* 92 (1): 8–14.

———. 2001. A Content Analysis of Mehinaku Dreams. In *Dreams: A Reader on the Religious, Cultural, and Psychological Dimensions of Dreaming,* edited by K. Bulkeley. New York: Palgrave.

Grottanelli, Cristiano. 1999. On the Mantic Meaning of Incestuous Dreams. In *Dream Cultures: Explorations in the Comparative History of Dreaming,* edited by D. Shulman and G. G. Stroumsa. New York: Oxford University Press.

Guss, David M. 1980. Steering for Dream: Dream Concepts of the Makiritare. *Journal of Latin American Lore* 6 (2): 297–312.

Harrington, Anne, ed. 1997. *The Placebo Effect: An Interdisciplinary Exploration.* Cambridge, Mass.: Harvard University Press.

Harris, Monford. 1994. *Studies in Jewish Dream Interpretation.* Northvale, N.J.: Jason Aronson.

Hartmann, Ernest. 1984. *The Nightmare: The Psychology and Biology of Terrifying Dreams.* New York: Basic Books.

———. 1998. *Dreams and Nightmares: The New Theory on the Origin and Meaning of Dreams.* New York: Plenum.

Harvey, Graham, ed. 2003. *Shamanism: A Reader.* London: Routledge.

Hayden, Brian. 2003. *Shamans, Sorcerers, and Saints: A Prehistory of Religion.* Washington, D.C.: Smithsonian Books.

Heimpel, Wolfgang. 2003. *Letters to the King of Mari: A New Translation, with Historical Introduction, Notes, and Commentary.* Winona Lake, Ind.: Eisenbrauns.

Heraclitus. 1987. *Fragments.* Translated by T. M. Robinson. Toronto: University of Toronto Press.

Herdt, Gilbert. 1977. The Shaman's "Calling" among the Sambia of New Guinea. *Journal de la Societe des Oceanistes* 33:153–167.

Hermansen, Marcia. 1997. Visions as "Good to Think": A Cognitive Approach to Visionary Experience in Islamic Sufi Thought. *Religion* 27 (1): 25–44.

————. 2001. Dreams and Dreaming in Islam. In *Dreams: A Reader on the Religious, Cultural, and Psychological Dimensions of Dreaming*, edited by K. Bulkeley. New York: Palgrave.

Herr, Barbara. 1981. The Expressive Character of Fijian Dream and Nightmare Experiences. *Ethos* 9 (4): 331–352.

Hesiod. 1973. *Theogony*. Translated by D. Wender. New York: Penguin Books.

Hobson, J. Allan. 1988. *The Dreaming Brain*. New York: Basic Books.

————. 1999. *Dreaming as Delirium: How the Brain Goes Out of Its Mind*. Cambridge, Mass.: MIT Press.

Hobson, J. Allan, Edward Pace-Schott, and Robert Stickgold. 2000. Dreaming and the Brain: Towards a Cognitive Neuroscience of Conscious States. *Behavioral and Brain Sciences* 23 (6): 793–842.

Hoffman, Edward. 1981. *The Way of Splendor: Jewish Mysticism and Modern Psychology*. Boulder, Colo.: Shambhala.

Hoffman, Valerie. 1997. The Role of Visions in Contemporary Egyptian Religious Life. *Religion* 27 (1): 45–64.

Homer. 1951. *The Iliad*. Translated by R. Lattimore. Chicago: University of Chicago Press.

Hosain, M. Hidayet. 1932. A Treatise on the Interpretation of Dreams. *Islamic Culture* 6 (4): 568–585.

Hsueh-Chin, Tsao. 1958. *Dream of the Red Chamber*. Translated by C.-C. Wang. New York: Anchor.

Hufford, David J. 1976. A New Approach to the "Old Hag": The Nightmare Tradition Revisited. In *American Folk Medicine: A Symposium*, edited by W. D. Hand. Berkeley: University of California Press.

Hultkrantz, Ake. 1993. Native Religions of North America: The Power of Visions and Fertility. In *Religious Traditions of the World*, edited by H. B. Earhart. San Francisco: HarperCollins.

Hunt, Harry. 1989. *The Multiplicity of Dreams: Memory, Imagination, and Consciousness*. New Haven, Conn.: Yale University Press.

Irwin, Lee. 1994. *The Dream Seekers: Native American Visionary Traditions of the Great Plains*. Norman: University of Oklahoma Press.

————. 1996. *Visionary Worlds: The Making and Unmaking of Reality*. Albany: State University of New York Press.

————. 2001. Sending a Voice, Seeking a Place: Visionary Traditions among Native Women of the Plains. In *Dreams: A Reader on the Religious, Cultural, and Psychological Dimensions of Dreaming*, edited by K. Bulkeley. New York: Palgrave.

Jedrej, M.C. 1992. Ingessana Dreaming. In *Dreaming, Religion, and Society in Africa*, edited by M. C. Jedrej and R. Shaw. Leiden: E. J. Brill.

Jedrej, M. C. , and Rosalind Shaw, eds. 1992. *Dreaming, Religion, and Society in Africa*. Leiden: E. J. Brill.

Jones, James W. 2005. Brain, Mind, and Spirit—A Clinician's Perspective, or Why

I Am Not Afraid of Dualism. In *Soul, Psyche, Brain: New Directions in the Study of Religion and Brain-Mind Science,* edited by K. Bulkeley. New York: Palgrave Macmillan.

Jouvet, Michel. 1999. *The Paradox of Sleep: The Story of Dreaming.* Translated by L. Garey. Cambridge, Mass.: MIT Press.

Jung, C. G. 1974. General Aspects of Dream Psychology. In *Dreams.* Princeton, N.J.: Princeton University Press.

———. 1974. On the Nature of Dreams. In *Dreams.* Princeton, N.J.: Princeton University Press. Original edition, 1948.

Kahan, Tracey L. 2000. The "Problem" of Dreaming in NREM Sleep Continues to Challenge Reductionist (2-Gen) Models of Dream Generation (Commentary). *Behavioral and Brain Sciences* 23 (6): 956–958.

———. 2001. Consciousness in Dreaming: A Metacognitive Approach. In *Dreams: A Reader on the Religious, Cultural, and Psychological Dimensions of Dreaming,* edited by K. Bulkeley. New York: Palgrave.

Kahn, David. 2005. From Chaos to Self-Organization: The Brain, Dreaming, and Religious Experience. In *Soul, Psyche, Brain: New Directions in the Study of Religion and Brain-Mind Science,* edited by K. Bulkeley. New York: Palgrave Macmillan.

Kalpa Sutra. 1884. In *The Sacred Books of the East,* edited by F. M. Muller. Oxford, U.K.: Clarendon.

Kang, Hyesung. 2003. Taemong: Korean Birth Dreams. Master's thesis, The Graduate Theological Union, University of California, Berkeley.

Katz, Jonathan G. 1997. An Egyptian Sufi Interprets His Dreams: 'Abd al-Wahhab al-Sha'rani 1493–1565. *Religion* 27 (1): 7–24.

Keable, Robert. 1921. A People of Dreams. *The Hibbert Journal* 19:522–531.

Kee, Howard C. 1982. Self-Definition in the Asclepius Cult. In *Jewish and Christian Self Definition,* edited by B. F. Meyer and E. P. Sanders. Philadelphia: Fortress.

Kelsey, Morton. 1991. *God, Dreams, and Revelation: A Christian Interpretation of Dreams.* Minneapolis: Augsburg.

Kempf, Wolfgang, and Elfriede Hermann. 2003. Dreamscapes: Transcending the Local in Initiation Rites among the Ngaing of Papua New Guinea. In *Dream Travelers: Sleep Experiences and Culture in the South Pacific,* edited by R. Lohmann. New York: Palgrave Macmillan.

Kennedy, John G., and Hussein Fahim. 1974. Nubian Dihkr Rituals and Cultural Change. *The Muslim World* 64:205–219.

Keskiaho, Jesse. 2005. The Handling and Interpretation of Dreams and Visions in Late Sixth- to Eighth-Century Gallic and Anglo-Latin Hagiography and Histories. *Early Medieval Europe* 13 (3): 227–248.

Khaldun, Ibn. 1967. *The Muqaddimah.* Translated by F. Rosenthal. Princeton, N.J.: Princeton University Press.

Kiernan, J. P. 1985. The Social Stuff of Revelation: Pattern and Purpose in Zionist Dreams and Visions. *Africa: Journal of the International African Institute* 55 (3): 304–317.

Kingsley, Peter. 1999. *In the Dark Places of Wisdom.* Inverness, Calif.: Golden Sufi Center.

Knudson, Roger. 2003. The Significant Dream as Emblem of Uniqueness: The Fertilizer Does Not Explain the Flower. *Dreaming* 13 (3): 121–134.

The Koran. 1974. Translated by N. J. Dawood. London: Penguin Books.

Koulack, David. 1993. *To Catch a Dream: Explorations in Dreaming.* Albany: State University of New York Press.

Kracke, Waud. 2001. Kagwahiv Mourning: Dreams of a Bereaved Father. In *Dreams: A Reader on the Religious, Cultural, and Psychological Dimensions of Dreaming,* edited by K. Bulkeley. New York: Palgrave.

Kramer, Heinrich, and James Sprenger. 1971. *The Malleus Maleficarum.* Translated by M. Summers. New York: Dover.

Kramer, Milton. 2007. *The Dream Experience: A Systematic Exploration.* New York: Routledge.

Kraut, Richard, ed. 1992. *The Cambridge Companion to Plato.* Cambridge: Cambridge University Press.

Kripal, Jeffrey J. 2007. *The Serpent's Gift: Gnostic Reflections on the Study of Religion.* Chicago: University of Chicago Press.

Krippner, Stanley, Fariba Bogzaran, and Andre Percia de Carvalho. 2002. *Extraordinary Dreams and How to Work with Them.* Albany: State University of New York Press.

Kryger, Meir H., Thomas Roth, and William C. Dement, eds. 2005. *Principles and Practices of Sleep Medicine.* 4th ed. Philadelphia: Elsevier Saunders.

Kuiken, Don, and Shelley Sikora. 1993. The Impact of Dreams on Waking Thoughts and Feelings. In *The Functions of Dreaming,* edited by A. Moffitt, M. Kramer, and R. Hoffmann. Albany: State University of New York Press.

Lai, Whalen W. 1982. Debendranath Tagore's Dream: The Soul and the Mother. *Anima* 9 (1): 29–32.

Lamoreaux, John C. 2002. *The Early Muslim Tradition of Dream Interpretation.* Albany: State University of New York Press.

Landau, Rom. 1967. The Philosophy of Ibn Arabi. *The Muslim World* 47:46–61.

Laufer, Bertold. 1931. Inspirational Dreams in East Asia. *Journal of American Folk-Lore* 44:208–216.

Lawson, E. Thomas. 1993. Religions of Africa: Traditions in Transformation. In *Religious Traditions of the World,* edited by H. B. Earhart. San Francisco: HarperSanFrancisco.

LeCerf, Jean. 1966. The Dream in Popular Culture: Arab and Islamic. In *The Dream and Human Societies,* edited by G. E. Von Grunebaum and R. Callois. Berkeley: University of California Press.

Lefkowitz, Mary R. 1976. The Motivations for St. Perpetua's Martyrdom. *Journal of the American Academy of Religion* 44 (3): 417–421.

Levin, Ross, and Tore A. Nielsen. 2007. Disturbed Dreaming, Posttraumatic Stress Disorder, and Affect Distress: A Review and Neurocognitive Model. *Psychological Bulletin* 133 (3): 482–528.

Lewis-Williams, David. 2002. *The Mind in the Cave.* London: Thames and Hudson.

Li, Wai-yee. 1999. Dreams of Interpretation in Early Chinese Historical and Philosophical Writings. In *Dream Cultures: Explorations in the Comparative History of Dreaming,* edited by D. Shulman and D. Stroumsa. New York: Oxford University Press.

The Life of Milarepa. 1985. Translated by L. P. Lhalungpa. Boston: Shambhala.

Lincoln, Jackson Stewart. 1935. *The Dream in Primitive Cultures.* London: University of London Press.

Lings, Martin. 1983. *Muhammad: His Life Based on the Earliest Sources.* Rochester, Vt.: Inner Traditions International.

Lohmann, Roger. 2003. Supernatural Encounters of the Asabano in Two Traditions and Three States of Consciousness. In *Dream Travelers: Sleep Experiences and Culture in the South Pacific,* edited by R. Lohmann. New York: Palgrave Macmillan.

———, ed. 2003. *Dream Travelers: Sleep Experiences and Culture in the South Pacific.* New York: Palgrave Macmillan.

Lorand, Sandor. 1957. Dream Interpretation in the Talmud (Babylonian and Graeco-Roman Period). *International Journal of Psychoanalysis* 38:92–97.

Louie, K., and M. A. Wilson. 2001. Temporally Structured Replay of Awake Hippocampal Ensemble Activity during Rapid Eye Movement Sleep. *Neuron* 29: 145–156.

Luther, Martin. 1945. *Luther's Works.* Translated by J. Pelikan. St. Louis: Concordia.

Mageo, Jeannette Marie. 2003. Samoan Dreams. In *Dreaming and the Self: New Perspectives on Subjectivity, Identity, and Emotion,* edited by J. M. Mageo. Albany: State University of New York Press.

———, ed. 2003. *Dreaming and the Self: New Perspectives on Subjectivity, Identity, and Emotion.* Albany: State University of New York Press.

Mannheim, Bruce. 1987. A Semiotic of Andean Dreams. In *Dreaming: Anthropological and Psychological Interpretations,* edited by B. Tedlock. New York: Cambridge University Press.

Maquet, P., J. M. Peteres, J. Aerts, G. Delfiore, C. Degueldre, A. Luxen, and G. Franck. 1996. Functional Neuroanatomy of Human Rapid-Eye-Movement Sleep and Dreaming. *Nature* 383:163.

Martin, Luther. 1991. Artemidorus: Dream Theory in Late Antiquity. *The Second Century: A Journal of Early Christian Studies* 8 (2): 97–108.

Mavroudi, Maria. 2001. *A Byzantine Book on Dream Interpretation: The Oneiro-criticon of Achmet and Its Arabic Sources.* Leiden: E. J. Brill.

Mayerson, Philip. 1984. Antiochus Monachus' Homily on Dreams: An Historical Note. *Journal of Jewish Studies* 35 (1): 51–56.

Mbiti, John S. 1976. God, Dreams, and African Militancy. In *Religion in a Pluralistic Society,* edited by J. S. Pobee. Leiden: E. J. Brill.

Meggitt, M. J. 1962. Dream Interpretation among the Mae Enga of New Guinea. *Southwestern Journal of Anthropology* 18:216–229.

Meier, C.A. 1967. *Ancient Incubation and Modern Psychotherapy.* Translated by M. Curtis. Evanston, Ill.: Northwestern University Press.

Mithen, Steven. 1996. *The Prehistory of the Mind: The Cognitive Origins of Art and Science.* London: Thames and Hudson.

Mohsen, Ashtiany, ed. 2007. *Dreaming across Boundaries: The Interpretation of Dreams in Islamic Lands.* Cambridge, Mass.: Harvard University Press.

Mpier, Mubuy Mubay. 1992. Dreams among the Yansi. In *Dreaming, Religion, and Society in Africa,* edited by M. C. Jedrej and R. Shaw. Leiden: E. J. Brill.

M'Timkulu, Donald. 1977. Some Aspects of Zulu Religion. In *African Religions: A Symposium,* edited by J. Newell S. Booth. New York: NOK.

Ness, Robert C. 1978. The Old Hag Phenomenon as Sleep Paralysis: A Biocultural Interpretation. *Culture, Medicine, and Psychiatry* 2:15–39.

Nielsen, Tore. 2000. Cognition in REM and NREM Sleep: A Review and Possible Reconciliation of Two Models of Sleep Mentation." *Behavioral and Brain Sciences* 23 (6): 851–866.

Nielsen, Tore, Anthony Zadra, Valerie Simard, Sebastian Saucier, Philippe Stenstrom, Carlyle Smith, and Don Kuiken. 2003. The Typical Dreams of Canadian University Students. *Dreaming* 13 (4): 211–235.

Noegel, Scott. 2001. Dreams and Dream Interpreters in Mesopotamia and in the Hebrew Bible (Old Testament). In *Dreams: A Reader on the Religious, Cultural, and Psychological Dimensions of Dreaming,* edited by K. Bulkeley. New York: Palgrave.

Nofzinger, E. A., M. A. Mintun, M. B. Wiseman, D. J. Kupfer, and R. Y. Moore. 1997. Forebrain Activation in REM Sleep: An FDG PET Study. *Brain Research* 770:192–201.

Oberhelman, Steven M. 1983. Galen, On Diagnosis from Dreams. *Journal of the History of Medicine and Allied Sciences* 38:36–47.

O'Flaherty, Wendy Doniger. 1984. *Dreams, Illusion, and Other Realities.* Chicago: University of Chicago Press.

———. 1988. *Other People's Myths.* New York: Macmillan.

Ong, Roberto K. 1985. *The Interpretation of Dreams in Ancient China.* Bochum: Studienverlag Brockmeyer.

Oppenheim, A. Leo. 1956. The Interpretation of Dreams in the Ancient Near East with a Translation of an Assyrian Dream-Book. *Transactions of the American Philosophical Society* 46 (3): 179–343.

Osborne, Kenneth E. 1970. A Christian Graveyard Cult in the New Guinea Highlands. *Practical Anthropologist* 46 (3): 10–15.

Osley, Arthur S. 1963. Notes on Artemidorus' *Oneirocritica. Classical Journal* 59 (2): 65–70.

Pace-Schott, Ed, Mark Solms, Mark Blagrove, and Stevan Harnad, eds. 2003. *Sleep and Dreaming: Scientific Advances and Reconsiderations.* Cambridge: Cambridge University Press.

Padwick, C. E. 1939. Dream and Vision: Some Notes from a Diary. *International Review of Missions* 28:205–216.

Pagel, James F. 2003. Non-dreamers. *Sleep Medicine* 4:235–241.

Patton, Kimberley. 2004. "A Great and Strange Correction": Intentionality, Locality, and Epiphany in the Category of Dream Incubation. *History of Religions* 43 (3): 194–223.

Patton, Kimberley C., and Benjamin C. Ray, eds. 2000. *A Magic Still Dwells: Comparative Religion in the Postmodern Age.* Berkeley: University of California Press.

Pei, Fang Jing, and Zhang Juwen. 2000. *The Interpretation of Dreams in Chinese Culture.* Trumbull, Conn.: Weatherhill.

Pfeiffer, John E. 1982. *The Creative Explosion: An Inquiry into the Origins of Art and Religion.* New York: Harper and Row.

Philo. 1988. *On Dreams, Loeb Classical Library.* Cambridge, Mass.: Harvard University Press.

Piaget, Jean. 1962. *Play, Dreams, and Imitation in Childhood.* Translated by C. Gattegno and F. M. Hodgson. New York: W. W. Norton.

Plato. 1961. Crito. In *Plato: Collected Dialogues,* edited by E. Hamilton and H. Cairns. Princeton, N.J.: Princeton University Press.

———. 1961. Laws. In *The Collected Dialogues of Plato,* edited by E. Hamilton and H. Cairns. Princeton, N.J.: Princeton University Press.

———. 1961. Phaedo. In *Plato: Collected Dialogues,* edited by E. Hamilton and H. Cairns. Princeton, N.J.: Princeton University Press.

———. 1961. The Republic. In *Plato: Collected Dialogues,* edited by E. Hamilton and H. Cairns. Princeton, N.J.: Princeton University Press.

———. 1961. Theaetetus. In *Plato: Collected Dialogues,* edited by E. Hamilton and H. Cairns. Princeton, N.J.: Princeton University Press.

Poirer, Sylvia. 2003. "This is Good Country. We Are Good Dreamers": Dreams and Dreaming in the Australian Western Desert. In *Dream Travelers: Sleep Experiences and Culture in the South Pacific,* edited by R. Lohmann. New York: Palgrave Macmillan.

The Practice of the Six Yogas of Naropa. 2006. Translated by G. H. Mullin. Ithaca, N.Y.: Snow Lion.

Priest, John F. 1970. Myth and Dream in Hebrew Scripture. In *Myth, Dreams, and Religion,* edited by J. Campbell. New York: Dutton.

Purcell, Sheila, Alan Moffitt, and Robert Hoffman. 1993. Waking, Dreaming, and Self-Regulation. In *The Functions of Dreaming,* edited by A. Moffitt, M. Kramer, and R. Hoffman. Albany: State University of New York Press.

Questions of King Milinda. 1894. In *The Sacred Books of the East,* edited by F. M. Muller. Oxford, U.K.: Clarendon.

Radin, Paul. 1936. Ojibwa and Ottawa Puberty Dreams. In *Essays in Anthropology Presented to A.L. Kroeber.* Berkeley: University of California Press.

Rahman, Fazlur. 1966. Dream, Imagination, and *Alam al-mithal.* In *The Dream and Human Societies,* edited by G. E. Von Grunebaum and R. Callois. Berkeley: University of California Press.

———. 1979. *Islam.* 2nd ed. Chicago: University of Chicago Press.

Ramakrishna, Sri. 1942. *The Gospel of Sri Ramakrishna.* Translated by S. Nikhilananda. New York: Ramakrishna-Vivekananda Center.

Ramayana of Valmiki. 1953. Translated by H. P. Shastri. London: Shyantisdan.

Rechtschaffen, A. 1978. The Single-Mindedness and Isolation of Dreams. *Sleep* 1 (1): 97–109.

Reid, Howard. 1978. Dreams and Their Interpretation among the Hupdu Maku Indians of Brazil. *Cambridge Anthropology* 4 (3): 2–29.

Rig Veda. 1981. Translated by W. D. O'Flaherty. London: Penguin Books.

Rosch, Eleanor H. 1973. Natural Categories. *Cognitive Psychology* 4:328–350.

Roscher, Wilhelm H., and James Hillman. 1979. *Pan and the Nightmare.* Dallas: Spring.

Roseman, Marina. 1991. *Healing Sounds from the Malaysian Rainforest: Temniar Music and Medicine.* Berkeley: University of California Press.

Rupprecht, Carol Schreier. 1992. Dreams and Dismemberment: Transformations of the Female Body in Dante's *Purgatorio. Quadrant* 25 (2).

———. 1993. The Drama of History and Prophecy: Shakespeare's Use of Dream in *2 Henry VI. Dreaming* 3 (3): 211–227.

———. 2007. Dream, Language, Literature. In *The New Science of Dreaming,* edited by D. Barrett and P. McNamara. Westport, Conn.: Praeger.

Salisbury, Joyce E. 1997. *Perpetua's Passion: The Death and Memory of a Young Roman Woman.* New York: Routledge.

Sasson, Jack M. 1983. Mari Dreams. *Journal of the American Oriental Society* 103 (1): 283–293.

Schmitt, Jean-Claude. 1999. The Liminality and Centrality of Dreams in the Medieval West. In *Dream Cultures: Explorations in the Comparative History of Dreaming,* edited by D. Shulman and D. Stroumsa. New York: Oxford University Press.

Schredl, Michael. 1999. Dream Recall: Research, Clinical Implications, and Future Directions. *Sleep and Hypnosis* 1:99–108.

Schwartz, Howard, ed. 1988. *Lilith's Cave: Jewish Tales of the Supernatural*. New York: Oxford University Press.

Seligman, C. G. 1923. Type Dreams: A Request. *Folk-Lore: Transactions of the Folk-Lore Society* 34 (4): 376–378.

Shafton, Anthony. 2002. *Dream-Singers: The African American Way with Dreams*. New York: Wiley.

Sharma, Jagdish, and Lee Siegel. 1980. *Dream Symbolism in the Sramanic Tradition: Two Psychoanalytical Studies in Jinist and Buddhist Dream Legends*. Calcutta: Firma KLM.

Shaw, Rosalind. 1992. Dreaming as Accomplishment: Power, the Individual, and Temne Divination. In *Religion, Dreaming, and Society in Africa*, edited by M. C. Jedrej and R. Shaw. Leiden: E. J. Brill.

Shorter, Aylward. 1978. Dreams in Africa. *African Ecclesial Review* 20 (1): 281–287.

Shweder, Richard, and R.A. Levine. 1975. Dream Concepts of Hausa Children: A Critique of the "Doctrine of Invariant Sequence." *Ethos* 3:209–230.

Skinner, Alanson. 1913. Social Life and Ceremonial Bundles of the Menomini Indians. *Anthropological Papers of the American Museum of Natural History* 13 (1): 1–159.

———. 1915. Associations and Ceremonies of the Menomini Indians. *Anthropological Papers of the American Museum of Natural History* 13 (2): 171–214.

Smith, Huston. 1991. *The World's Religions*. San Francisco: HarperSanFrancisco.

Smith, Joseph. 1987. *An American Prophet's Record: The Diaries and Journals of Joseph Smith*. Edited by S. H. Faulring. Salt Lake City: Signature Books.

Smith, Lucy. 2006. *Biographical Sketches of Joseph Smith the Prophet and His Progenitors for Many Generations*. Kila, Mont.: Kessinger.

Smith, Richard J. 1991. *Fortune-Tellers and Philosophers: Divination in Traditional Chinese Society*. Boulder, Colo.: Westview.

Sobel, Mechal. 2000. *Teach Me Dreams: The Search for Self in the Revolutionary Era*. Princeton, N.J.: Princeton University Press.

Solms, Mark. 1997. *The Neuropsychology of Dreams: A Clinico-Anatomical Study*. Mahway, N.J.: Lawrence Erlbaum.

Sophocles. 1942. Oedipus the King. In *Greek Tragedies*, edited by D. Grene and R. Lattimore. Chicago: University of Chicago Press.

Stephen, Michelle. 1979. Dreams of Change: The Innovative Role of Altered States of Consciousness in Traditional Melanesian Religion. *Oceania* 50 (1): 3–22.

———. 1995. *A'Aisa's Gifts: A Study of Magic and the Self*. Berkeley: University of California Press.

Stewart, Charles. 1997. Fields in Dreams: Anxiety, Experience, and the Limits of Social Constructionism in Modern Greek Dream Narratives. *American Ethnologist* 24 (4): 877–894.

———. 2003. Ritual Dreams and Historical Orders: Incubation between Paganism and Christianity. In *Ritual Poetics in Greek Culture*, edited by P. Roilos and Yatromanolakis. Cambridge, Mass.: Harvard University Press.

Stewart, Kilton. 1951. Dream Theory in Malaya. *Complex* 6:21–33.

Stewart, Pamela J., and Andrew J. Strathern. 2003. Dreaming and Ghosts among the Hagen and Duna of the Southern Highlands, Papua New Guinea. In *Dream Travelers: Sleep Experiences and Culture in the South Pacific*, edited by R. Lohmann. New York: Palgrave Macmillan.

Strauch, Inge, and B. Meier. 1996. *In Search of Dreams: Results of Experimental Dream Research*. Albany: State University of New York Press.

Stroumsa, David. 1999. Dreams and Visions in Early Christian Discourse. In *Dream Cultures: Explorations in the Comparative History of Dreaming*, edited by D. Shulman and D. Stroumsa. New York: Oxford University Press.

Sviri, Sara. 1999. Dreaming Analyzed and Recorded: Dreams in the World of Medieval Islam. In *Dream Cultures: Explorations in the Comparative History of Dreaming*, edited by D. Stroumsa and D. Shulman. New York: Oxford University Press.

Szpakowska, Kasia. 2003. *Behind Closed Eyes: Dreams and Nightmares in Ancient Egypt*. Swansea: Classical Press of Wales.

———. 2003. Playing with Fire: Initial Observations on the Religious Uses of Clay Cobras from Amarna. *Journal of the American Research Center in Egypt* 40: 113–122.

Taber, Floyd W. 1972. How Real Are Dreams? *Practical Anthropology* 19:108–109.

Tanabe, George J., Jr. 1992. *Myoe the Dreamkeeper: Fantasy and Knowledge in Early Kamakura Buddhism*. Cambridge, Mass.: Harvard University Press.

Taylor, Jeremy, and G. William Domhoff. 1995. Debate on the Legacy of the Senoi. *Dream Time: Newsletter of the Association for the Study of Dreams* 12 (2): 30–34.

Tedlock, Barbara. 1987. Zuni and Quiche Dream Sharing and Interpreting. In *Dreaming: Anthropological and Psychological Interpretations*, edited by B. Tedlock. New York: Cambridge University Press.

———. 2005. *The Woman in the Shaman's Body: Reclaiming the Feminine in Religion and Medicine*. New York: Bantam.

Thierry, J. J. 1963. The Date of the Dream of Jerome. *Vigiliae Christiannae* 17:28–40.

Tonkinson, Robert. 1970. Aboriginal Dream-Spirit Beliefs in a Contact Situation: Jigalong, Western Australia. In *Australian Aboriginal Anthropology*, edited by R. M. Berndt. Perth: University of Western Australia Press.

———. 2003. Ambrymese Dreams and the Mardu Dreaming. In *Dream Travelers: Sleep Experiences and Culture in the South Pacific*, edited by R. Lohmann. New York: Palgrave Macmillan.

Trafzer, Clifford E., and Margery A. Beach. 1985. Smohalla, the Washani, and Religion as a Factor in Northwestern Indian History. *American Indian Quarterly* 9 (3): 309–324.

Trimingham, Spencer. 1959. *Islam in West Africa*. Oxford, U.K.: Clarendon.

Trompf, G. W. 1990. *Melanesian Religion*. Cambridge: Cambridge University Press.

———. 2004. Cargo Cults. In *New Religions: A Guide*, edited by C. Partridge. Oxford: Oxford University Press.

Tzu, Chuang. 1997. *The Inner Chapters*. Translated by D. Hinton. New York: Counterpoint.

Ullman, Montague, Stanley Krippner, and Alan Vaughan. 1989. *Dream Telepathy: Experiments in Nocturnal ESP*. 2nd ed. Jefferson, N.C.: McFarland.

Upanisads. 1996. Translated by P. Olivelle. Oxford: Oxford University Press.

Valli, Katja, Antti Revonsuo, Outi Palkas, Kamaran Hassan Ismail, Karzan Jallal Ali, and Raija-Leena Punamaki. 2005. The Threat Simulation Theory of the Evolutionary Function of Dreaming: Evidence from Dreams of Traumatized Children. *Consciousness and Cognition* 14:188–218.

Van de Castle, Robert. 1994. *Our Dreaming Mind*. New York: Ballantine Books.

Vande Kemp, Hendrika. 1981. The Dream in Periodical Literature: 1860–1910. *Journal of the History of the Behavioral Sciences* 17:88–113.

———. 1994. Psycho-Spiritual Dreams in the Nineteenth Century, Part I: Dreams of Death. *Journal of Psychology and Theology* 22 (2): 97–108.

———. 1994. Psycho-Spiritual Dreams in the Nineteenth Century, Part II: Metaphysics and Immortality. *Journal of Psychology and Theology* 22 (2): 109–119.

Vaughan-Lee, Llewellyn. 1998. *Catching the Thread: Sufism, Dreamwork, & Jungian Psychology*. Inverness, Calif.: Golden Sufi Center.

Virgil. 1971. *The Aeneid*. Translated by A. Mandelbaum. New York: Bantam.

Vlastos, Gregory, ed. 1971. *The Philosophy of Socrates: A Collection of Critical Essays*. Notre Dame, Ind.: University of Notre Dame Press.

Von Grunebaum, G. E., and Roger Callois, eds. 1966. *The Dream and Human Societies*. Berkeley: University of California Press.

Walde, Christine. 1999. Dream Interpretation in a Prosperous Age? Artemidorus, the Greek Interpreter of Dreams. In *Dream Cultures: Explorations in the Comparative History of Dreaming*, edited by D. Shulman and G. G. Stroumsa. New York: Oxford University Press.

Wallace, Anthony F. C. 1958. Dreams and Wishes of the Soul: A Type of Psychoanalytic Theory among the Seventeenth Century Iroquois. *American Anthropologist* 60:234–248.

———. 1969. *The Death and Rebirth of the Seneca*. New York: Vintage Books.

Wallace, W. J. 1947. The Dream in Mohave Life. *Journal of American Folk-Lore* 60: 252–258.

Wayman, Alex. 1967. Significance of Dreams in India and Tibet. *History of Religions* 7:1–12.

Weiner, Jonathan. 1995. *The Beak of the Finch: A Story of Evolution in Our Time.* New York: Vintage.

West, Stephanie. 1987. And It Came to Pass That Pharaoh Dreamed: Notes on Herodotus 2.139, 141. *Classical Quarterly* 37 (2): 262–271.

Whitehouse, Harvey. 2004. *Modes of Religiosity: A Cognitive Theory of Religious Transmission.* Walnut Creek, Calif.: Altamira Press.

Wilson, Edward O. 2000. *Sociobiology: The New Synthesis.* 25th ed. Cambridge, Mass.: Belknap.

Wilson, M. A., and B. L. McNaughton. 1994. Reactivation of Hippocampal Ensemble Memories during Sleep. *Science* 265:676–679.

Wulff, David. 1997. *Psychology of Religion: Classic and Contemporary.* New York: Wiley.

Xygalatas, Dimitris. 2006. Firewalking in the Balkans: High Arousal Rituals and Memory. Paper read at Workshop on Religion and Cognitive Science, at Groningen.

Young, Serinity. 1999. *Dreaming in the Lotus: Buddhist Dream Narrative, Imagery, and Practice.* Boston: Wisdom.

———, ed. 1999. *Encyclopedia of Women and World Religion.* New York: Macmillan Reference.

Index

aborigines, Australian, 234–236

Abraham: dream of Canaan (Genesis), 128–129; symbolic sacrifice of Isaac (*Qur'an*), 196

Achilles, 141–142

Addu-duri, 120–121

adolescence, vision quests in, 261–264

Aeneas, 160

aesthetics and dreaming, 33–34, 68, 93–94, 256, 274

African Independent Churches, 227–230

African religions, 7, 213 (Ch. 8), 215–217, 227–230; historical awareness through dreaming in, 219; religious movements of colonized Africans, 218. *See also by culture, e.g.,* Zulu

Agabegijik's dream, 262–263

Agamemnon, 141–142, 150

aggression, dreams of, 19, 35, 249–250, 273

Agni, prayer to, 22–23

agriculture, 112

A'isha, 201–202

Ajatashatru, 32–33

Akkadians, 119

Al Qaeda, 210

Aladura movement, 228

Allah, 195; appearing in dreams, 195, 196, 197–198

al-Lat, al-Uzza and Manat, 198–199

allegory in dreaming, 163, 204–205

al-mithal (metaphysics), 203–204

altered modes of consciousness, 53

al-Tirmidhi, 207–208

Amenho, Pharaoh, 125

Amithaba Buddha (Boundless Light), 92

ancestral environment(s), 7, 250, 254, 281n.2. *See also* evolution; prehistory

ancestral visitations, 56, 58–60, 64, 93, 127; conveying wisdom, 5, 51, 70; giving warnings, 70, 160; making demands, 74; missionaries discouraging in colonized peoples, 226–227, 240, 244–245, 252–254; rituals to encourage, 124; in African religions, 219; in Native American religions, 256–257; in Oceanic religions, 226, 244–248

ancient peoples, 111, 167

angels, 172, 193–194, 198–199

Anggauwane's dream, 238–239

animal spirits and divinities, 252–253, 254–257, 263–264

animals appearing in dreams, 14–15, 57, 85, 249; attacking or chasing dreamers, 35, 249–250; bears, 255; elephants, 81, 82; hawks, 263–264; humans transformed to animals, 121–122; killed or dead, 128–129, 143–144, 179; in Native American cultures, 250–251, 254–261; serpents, 174, 257, 276, 287n.16

animals dreaming, 187–188

anti-dream admonitions, 177–178. *See also* missionaries

Antiochus Monachus, 177–178

anxious dreams, 72

apatheia (peacefulness of soul), 177

Aquinas, Thomas, *Summa Theologica*, 183–185

Arabi, Ibn, 203–204

Aristotle: *De Insomniis*, 152–153; *De Divinatione per Somnum*, 152, 153–154; naturalistic approach to dreams, 153–154, 167

Artemidorus of Daldis, *Oneirocritica* (*Interpretation of Dreams*), 162–165, 187, 279

aruru (sleep), 25–26

Asclepius, 139, 157–158, 166, 277; temples of, 158–160, 187

Asebano people, 240–241

Assyrians, 119

236, 252–259, 262–264; Yahweh, 198–199, 128–130. *See also* malevolent forces in dreams
spiritual authority, 190–191
spirituality in dream experience: in ancient Egypt, 124–125; in the Buddhist tradition, 85–87, 90–91, 103; 106–109; in Christian religions, 173, 180–182, 184; in Islam, 193, 196, 197–198; as insight or inspiration (Greek), 147, 151–152; in the Jewish religion, 129–130; in Oceania, 242. *See also* divine inspiration or guidance; mysticism
Sri Lanka, 91
Star, The (*sura 53*), 198–199
"Stele of Vultures," 113
subha (auspicious dreams), 27
Sufism, 207–209
Sumerian script, 112, 113
Sumerians, dream theory of, 112–116
svapna (place of the dream), 33
symbolic expression, 140
symbolism, 196
Synesius, *De insomniis* (*Concerning Dreams*), 182–183
tahir (dream interpretation), 195, 199–200, 203–205
Tai Pu (dream interpreter), 18, 54–55, 57
Talmud, 135
Tanakh, 128, 133, 135
Tang Xianzu: (*The Dream of Han Tan*), 74; (*Peony Pavilion*), 74–75
Tantrayana path of Buddhism, 99–108
Tantric Buddhism, 100–106; "special dream body," 107–108
Taoism. *See* Daoism
Telemachus, 143
Temne people, 217
temples of Asclepius, 139, 187; dream incubation at, 158–160; priest healers at, 157–158
temporal dimensions of dreams, 110
temptations: dreams as, 133, 134–135; devil-sent dreams, 168, 176–178, 186, 190, 191, 198–199
Tertullian, 181–182
theophanies. *See* dream theophanies
theorematic dreams (Artemidorus), 163
Theravada ("The Way of the Elders"), 91
Theravada school of Buddhism, 81, 108
thomba (rite of passage), 220

Thutmose IV, Pharaoh, 125–126
Tibet, 91. *See also* Tantric Buddhism
Tikopian people, 246–247
Tjurrpa (dreamtime), Australian, 234–235
Tongas people, 52
Torah, 133, 194; *Book of Daniel*, 133–134; *Book of Ecclesiastes*, 134; *Book of Joel*, 134, 171; *Book of Judges*, 133; *Book of Samuel*, 133; *Book of Zechariah*, 134–135
transcendance. *See* liberation/ transcendance in dreaming
transference of consciousness, 101, 103
Tree of Dreams, 161
True Church of God, 229
turia (self-realization), 36, 48

Umar, 199–200
"Universal Soul" dreams, 204
Upanishads, 31–36, 49, 177; modes of self-awareness in, 32–33, 111

Vajrayana (Tantric Buddhism), 99–108
Vedas, 21–22, 36l; *Atharva Veda*, 25–27, 279; dreaming as a condition of danger in, 31, 32. *See also Rig Veda*
Vietnam, 91
Virgil, *The Aeneid*, 160–162
vision quest, Native American, 261–264
vision, sense of, 231

Wanadi, 257–258
Wang Chong, 73, 111, 167
warfare, 112
"watchful" dreaming, 90, 91
Watunna, 257–258
Wei Xiang-shu, 74
wet dreams. *See under* sexual dreams
Wu (shamanic healer), 54–55, 68
Wu Ting, King, 55
Wu-Ding's dream, 61
Wu-meng (transient-state dreams), 71

Xenophon, 289n.12
Xerxes of Persia, 157
Xiang-meng (symbolic dreams), 72
Xian-men-tong (Cave of the Immortals' Gate), 74
Xi-meng (happy dreams), 71
Xing-meng (affective dreams), 72

About the Author

Kelly Bulkeley, Ph.D., is Visiting Scholar at the Graduate Theological Union and teaches in the Dream Studies Program at John F. Kennedy University, both in the San Francisco Bay Area. He earned his doctorate in Religion and Psychological Studies from the University of Chicago Divinity School, and is a former president of the International Association for the Study of Dreams. He has written and edited several books, including *The Wilderness of Dreams: Exploring the Religious Meanings of Dreams in Modern Western Culture, An Introduction to the Psychology of Dreaming, Visions of the Night: Dreams, Religion, and Psychology, The Wondering Brain: Thinking about Religion with and beyond Cognitive Neuroscience, Dreaming beyond Death: A Guide to Pre-Death Dreams and Visions,* and *Soul, Psyche, Brain: New Directions in the Study of Religion and Brain-Mind Science.*